a 3
D1142163

THE HISTORY OF UNILEVER

VOLUME I

THE HISTORY OF
UNILEVER
A STUDY IN ECONOMIC GROWTH AND SOCIAL CHANGE

BY

CHARLES WILSON

Fellow of Jesus College
Cambridge

IN TWO VOLUMES · VOLUME I

CASSELL & COMPANY LTD
LONDON

CASSELL & CO LTD
37/38 St. Andrew's Hill, Queen Victoria Street, London, E.C.4
and at
31/34 George IV Bridge, Edinburgh
210 Queen Street, Melbourne
26/30 Clarence Street, Sydney
Haddon Hall, City Road, Auckland, N.Z.
1068 Broadview Avenue, Toronto 6
420 West 45th Street, New York 36
Avenida 9 de Julho 1138, São Paulo
Galeria Güemes, Escritorio 518/520
Florida 165, Buenos Aires
Haroon Chambers, South Napier Road, Karachi
15 Graham Road, Ballard Estate, Bombay 1
17 Central Avenue P.O. Dharamtala, Calcutta
P.O. Box 275, Cape Town
P.O. Box 1386, Salisbury, S. Rhodesia
P.O. Box 959, Accra, Gold Coast
25 rue Henri Barbusse, Paris 5e
Islands Brygge 5, Copenhagen

First published 1954

PRINTED IN ENGLAND AT THE CURWEN PRESS

F. 953

AUTHOR'S PREFACE

THIS HISTORY represents an attempt to fill one of the many gaps in our knowledge of the nature of the world of business. That there has been much confusion about the problems of business, its management, its organization, and its place in the social framework, can hardly be doubted. This is in part a legacy from the days of economic liberalism, when business was regarded as the concern of the business man: what he did was his affair. It is surely anachronistic in an age which, rejecting *laissez-faire*, continually acts on the assumption that it is right and proper for government to intervene in business affairs on behalf of the electorate, which is accordingly required at intervals to make up its mind about economic issues: many of these issues demand—or should demand—a knowledge of what business is and how it works. This in turn demands some knowledge of its historical evolution.

Considerations such as these suggested to the directors of Unilever that it would be useful to have an objective history showing how their particular business came to be what it is today. Besides serving as a reference work for the Company itself, such an account might (they felt) contribute towards a better understanding of the nature of industry in the academic world and elsewhere. For business history has as yet been but little studied in Britain and the inquiring reader still has to choose between what are virtually two sorts of propaganda: an heroic mythology on the one hand and a kind of economic Crime Club on the other. In 1947, therefore, the directors asked the advice of the then Regius Professor of History in the University of Cambridge (Professor G. N. Clark) regarding the writing of a history which would aim to give a balanced view of the evolution of a large-scale business. At his suggestion, I was brought into the discussions and eventually accepted an invitation to undertake the task. It was agreed that it should be a comprehensive and critical study, founded on a full and free investigation of all the material which the author might consider relevant.

For my own part, the task offered an opportunity to extend our knowledge of Anglo-Dutch economic relationships. Further, I was interested to see how far the study of an individual business, and that a business closely connected with a vast demand for products in common use, might illuminate those processes of economic and social change which have been largely studied in national and general terms: in particular, to find out whether it might throw even a ray of light on the central problem of economic life—the mystery of economic growth. Social injustice has often been the dominant theme of economic history: and while the inequalities of wealth which are the alleged result of industrial revolution have received their full share of attention, the process of total economic growth has been much less studied.

Looking at the economic development of states or regions, or considering whole industries or groups of industries, historians have often written as if growth and material progress were a natural and inevitable process needing no propulsion from human enterprise. This was partly a natural revolt against early Victorian faith in individual initiative, and it is symptomatic that of recent years such writers as Samuel Smiles have been a subject for mild derision. Yet for all the limitations of Smiles's *The Lives of the Engineers* there remains more merit in the biographical method than has sometimes been allowed. 'It is men who make history,' wrote Professor Butterfield recently. Economic historians have not always been as ready to recognize that this is as true of economic history as it is of other branches of history. In economic history as elsewhere a man is limited by circumstances: yet at the heart of the economic process there is human intelligence, human character, ingenuity, and enterprise. The inventor is still allowed (though doubtfully) to edge his way into the books. Kay, Watt, Stephenson, Bessemer, Gilchrist, Thomas, and the rest are there: but of the men who organized the great industries, who studied the application of inventions on a large scale, raised the capital, followed or created the markets and—above all—shouldered the risks, we hear little. One has to search long and hard for the book which thinks it worth while to give more than passing mention to John Horrocks of Preston, William Armstrong of Newcastle, the Henrys of Manchester and Bradford, the Crossleys of Halifax, the Kitsons of Leeds. In their anxiety to diagnose the nature of social ills and prescribe remedies, the politico-economic practitioners have neglected the particular for the general; men have been sacrificed to trends; the concrete to the abstract. If much that has been written about the earlier phases of industrialism seems unsatisfactory to the historian, it is because it has so often defied the rules of historical perspective. The actions and policies of yesterday, severed from their true context, have been judged summarily by the standards of today. Conversely, contemporary problems and future possibilities have often been surveyed through a mist of inherited prejudices. Sometimes such judgements have arisen from ignorance, sometimes from doctrine. Whatever else changed, it seemed, 'capitalism' and 'capitalists' did not. Yet if the only purpose of the study of business history were the negative one of refuting such a proposition, of showing—as Professor Tawney wrote recently—that 'capitalism, not less than the other works of man is the creature of time or place', one might well doubt whether it was justified. There are, however, in a world once again less certain of an abundance or even of an adequacy of the necessities of life, more positive reasons for such inquiries. The close study of the history of private business provides a salutary warning against the temptation to reduce enterprise too easily to a formula.

Even in the modern world, where the problems of size and complexity have deprived business of some of its excitement, some of its opportunities and some of its risks, where the heroic age is perhaps over, business seems to me to retain more of the characteristics of a game or a battle than of a scientific process. There is no trick or sequence of tricks that can be learnt to be repeated successfully: too many factors are changing too much of the time. In the real life of business, the task remains to calculate, by a curious mixture of rational judgement and developed intuition, the nature of those risks which lie somewhere between the two fixed points of inertia and plain gambling. Hence perhaps the fondness of the business man (to which this history bears frequent witness) for the metaphor drawn from the cricket pitch and the battlefield.

No historian can approach a task like this with a mind entirely open or entirely closed; for the one has always been a fiction, and however strong initial prejudices may be it is improbable that the investigator will not be influenced by what he finds in the course of his inquiries. The reader is nevertheless entitled to know something of the general attitude of his author. Briefly, it is that capitalism, like any other economic or social system, must be judged on its merits; likewise the capitalist, being inherently neither better nor worse than other men but only having greater power than some for good or evil. Such an approach requires that we should re-examine some of the assumptions of our history books.

'It is', wrote Alfred Marshall in his *Principles of Economics*, 'to the activity and resource of the leading minds in this class (the middle class) that most of the inventions and improvements are due, which enable the working man of today to have comforts and luxuries that were rare or unknown among the richest of a few generations ago: and without which indeed England could not supply her present population with a sufficiency of common food. And it is a vast and wholly unmixed gain when the children of any class press within the relatively small charmed circle of those who create new ideas, and who embody those new ideas in solid constructions. Their profits are sometimes large: but taking one with another they have probably earned for the world a hundred times or more as much as they have earned for themselves.' Marshall was talking of England but, with due adjustment, his conclusions are equally applicable to other countries. Such views have not been fashionable in recent years. Some of the most popular and influential textbooks used in universities and schools have created the impression that the industrial revolution brought prosperity only for a privileged few, while for the great majority it portended misery, oppression, and degrading poverty. It is no part of the purpose of this study to underrate the social problems of the industrial age, nor to suggest that whatever was was necessarily right. Misery and poverty there was in plenty in the industrial age: it could hardly be otherwise while the population was increasing so rapidly. Yet, when the problems which faced the new society are clearly understood, it is difficult to see how anyone can dissent from Marshall's opinion. Indeed, the striking fact is not the failure of the industrial society to conquer all its problems but its success in conquering so many. Malthus, whose gloomy prophecies shocked his generation at the beginning of the nineteenth century, would have been astonished if he could have witnessed the relative abundance enjoyed a century later by a population some two and a half times that of 1801. It is my hope that this study of a few of the great *entrepreneurs* whose genius helped to provide that abundance may lead to other similar studies and that these will do something to redress the balance of our history and focus attention on the processes by which wealth was created as well as on those by which it was shared out.

A word must be said as to the methods and sources used. Like all stories this one could be told in many different ways. Business histories vary from the austerely statistical to the richly romantic and dramatic. Both extremes have been rejected here. A purely quantitative study would not have touched the problem of 'why' in the story of growth. Figures may illuminate, but they themselves stand in need of explanation in terms of real life. But if there is more to a business than figures, it is equally true that business life is not continuously romantic or dramatic, though there may well be moments when it is both. The circumstances seemed to me to demand, therefore, that a history of this kind should be both narrative and analytical, though the attempt to combine the two added seriously to the difficulties of a task already complex enough by the very nature of the business itself. H. A. L. Fisher once remarked that 'great history was not made from laundry bills . . . ': the rebuke was that of a political historian tilting at social history. There is a measure of truth in it; it is not necessary to claim that business history is history of the highest calibre. But it has at least one merit: it brings the historian to close grips with a problem fundamental to the philosophy of history—the essential relationship of the individual and society. Thus, the business historian must sometimes feel that he is a biographer writing primarily biography conceived in terms of a particular kind of concrete achievement—the business itself. Then, with only a slight shift of emphasis his function changes, and he becomes the analyst of—what I conceive to be—a socially valuable process initiated, guided, and developed by human agency. The reader should therefore be warned that as well as the occasionally exciting event and the illuminating economic trend, he will have to tolerate a certain amount of the ordinary humdrum stuff of which business life often consists. My yardstick in measuring the evidence has been—did this event or that person contribute something indispensable to the growing business? Such contributions may be negative as well as positive: a failure may determine the future course of growth as much as a success.

The sources I have used are set out in the Bibliography. So far as possible I have avoided footnotes, and references have been mainly limited to cross references: for the primary sources used are not available to the public, and while a private record of all references has been kept, I felt that to print it could serve no useful purpose. Early on, my collaborators and I stumbled on the whole of William Lever's business correspondence—in all some thirty thousand files each containing up to a hundred letters. Here indeed was *embarras de richesse*. Yet, somehow, the mass was sifted, providing, I think, invaluable commentary on the working of a business mind of genius: for Lever loved writing down his thoughts on everything, and in his way was a writer of unusual quality. Nothing comparable turned up in the Dutch archives; alas, few of the daily letters that passed between the Van den Berghs in Rotterdam and London for some fifty or more years survived, and such as did were destroyed or lost in the Second World War. Yet if the Dutch firms were poorer in narrative material, they were in some ways richer in the statistical material which made closer analysis possible. There is, therefore, an unavoidable difference of emphasis between Book I and Book II, the first tending more to narrative, the second more to analysis. Yet documents are not all. One lesson the task of writing recent history teaches the historian: the inadequacy of documents as the sole source of history. True, there is no better single source for history, but where there is opportunity—as there is here—for the historian to take personal testimony not from one but from many actors in the play itself, where recollections can be checked and counter-checked, one becomes acutely aware of the complexity of human motive, the fugitive nature of historical 'truth', the gaps in the evidence, the sometimes tenuous relationship of word and deed. Documents by themselves can be as misleading as human memory—and even the most clear and honest memory is often at fault: interpretation becomes a task without end or certainty. It is a sobering and gruelling discipline but one which has its moral for the day when the apprentice turns back to those centuries whose witnesses have long since ceased to be available for cross-examination.

It need hardly be said that the task of collecting, sifting, and using a mass of material relating to some six hundred firms, some of them dating back as far as the seventeenth century and scattered over the whole world, was one which I could not do by myself. My first task was to prepare the plan of work: secondly to choose my team. It was my good fortune to find helpers whose enthusiasm, energy, and patience have never flagged. Much depended on our keeping the plan flexible so that each of them had the maximum freedom to develop his inquiries within very broad limits. For the final narrative and conclusions I must take sole responsibility; but my contribution was sometimes as much that of editor as of author. For Book I, I had the help of Mr. William J. Reader, and the volume owes much to his imaginative insight: I am especially indebted to him for those sections dealing with the African enterprises. In Book II, I was assisted by Mr. Hans de Roos, without whose shrewd analysis much of the significance of the Dutch evidence would have escaped me. Mr. de Roos was joined by Mr. Gijs de Haan, whose knowledge of the business structure has been invaluable. Finally, Miss Karla Oosterveen has helped in a variety of ways to bring the work to fruition. Raw materials were her especial field of research, and she shared with Mr. de Haan the responsibility for the primary research on Book III and for the work on graphs and charts. Mr. Reader and Miss Oosterveen had their headquarters in London: Mr. de Roos and Mr. de Haan in Rotterdam. Members of the team met at intervals to exchange views and visited factories in Scandinavia, Holland, Belgium, Germany, France, Switzerland, and the United Kingdom. No tribute I can pay to them all can seem anything but inadequate: this is their book as much as mine.

Finally, I must try to thank all those who in different ways have helped to make it possible to write this history. I have tried to compile a list which is printed in the Bibliography and I hasten to offer apologies to any—and there must be some—who may accidentally have been omitted.

I must mention here one or two whose help has been of special significance. From the outset I had the good fortune to have the constant help and guidance of Mr. L. V. Fildes, the former secretary of the English parent company. Mr. Fildes has presided over a small committee[1] set up to help the historian and his team to obtain the evidence and assistance necessary to their work. With a conviction of the importance of the historian's independence certainly not less than that of the historian himself, Mr. Fildes has smoothed my way on all occasions, preserved me from error on many, and never failed to give advice, friendly and frank, deriving from some thirty years of experience in the business. With him I must bracket the late Mr. Joost de Blank. For many years Mr. de Blank played an important part in the Dutch concern. He combined in a remarkable way a profound knowledge of economic affairs with a rare quality of scholarship. It is sad that he did not live to see the publication of a work in which he had from the outset taken the keenest interest. Sir Geoffrey Heyworth, Dr. Paul Rijkens, Sir Herbert Davis, and the late Lord Leverhulme have all put valuable time at my disposal and given me the kind of assistance which could come from no one else. Mr. Hugh Saunders in London and Mr. E. A. Hofman in Rotterdam have given much practical assistance to my team and myself. I must also thank Sir Henry Clay, Sir Keith Hancock, and Professor van Dillen for reading the manuscript and for giving helpful advice. To all these and to many others—directors, managers, and staff of every grade—I am deeply grateful: all the more because, though help has been given without stint, it has never infringed that independence which from the start was agreed to be an indispensable condition of the writing of the history.

I remember once reading a novel dedicated—if my memory serves me aright—to a friendship that survived a collaboration. If this work had a dedication it might well be to those friendships that have grown out of a collaboration.

[1] L. V. Fildes (Chairman); E. A. Hofman; Professor P. Kuin; R. J. Maunsell; Professor D. Mitrany; P. M. Rees; H. Saunders.

CONTENTS OF VOLUME I

PART III

BUSINESS IN WARTIME, 1914–18

PART IV

CRISIS AND RECONSTRUCTION, 1919–29

LIST OF ILLUSTRATIONS

PROLOGUE

ON THE 2nd of September 1929 an agreement was signed which was to create what the *Economist* described as '. . . one of the biggest industrial amalgamations in European history'. This was the fusion between the group of companies of Dutch origin known as the Margarine Union in Great Britain and the Margarine Unie in Holland, and the group of companies controlled by the British firm of Lever Brothers. Union and Unie supplied a large part of the edible fats market in Europe and Great Britain: Lever Brothers had a large share of the soap market in Britain and the Empire, as well as a sizable share of the soap trade elsewhere. Both groups, as will be shown later, had many other associated industrial and commercial interests. The corporate structure which emerged from the transaction of 1929 was legally a dualism: there were two 'parent' companies—Unilever Limited in Great Britain and Unilever N.V. (*Naamlooze Vennootschap* or limited liability company) in Holland. This dual structure had to be accepted. If the new amalgamation had taken the form of the single company it would have been taxed twice over: once in England and again in Holland. But since the purpose of the fusion was single, not divided, direction of policy, nothing was left undone to diminish the effects of dualism in practice. The membership of the boards of the two companies was identical, their interests were linked and largely identified by an agreement providing for an equal dividend to be paid by each, and equal distribution on liquidation, while the Chairman of each company became automatically the Vice-Chairman of the other. And so terse and convenient was the name coined for the new companies—Unilever—that it survived subsequent changes in the corporate structure and passed into general use as a means of denoting the entire complex of the two parent companies together with their hundreds of subsidiary companies.

The parent companies which went under the name Unilever in 1929 were not themselves manufacturing or trading companies. Their function was to hold the shares in, and therefore to supervise the operations of, a number of other companies most of which did carry on either manufacture or trade. By 1949, Unilever, through this dual system, owned and directed more than five hundred companies spread all over the world. It held a majority of shares in another fifty-five companies, and a minority of shares in several more. The value of the manufacture and trade of these businesses was £603,633,000, plus the turnover of certain businesses in Central and Eastern Europe and China which could not be estimated. The manufacturing activities of Unilever fell into four main groups: detergents and toilet preparations; margarine and edible fats; food products; oil milling with its ancillary industries. Of the value of total produce, soap, margarine, and oil milling accounted for eighty-seven per cent. Now soap and margarine are both made from oils and fats, and both depend on the same ancillary industries—oil milling, refining, and fat hardening. Herein lies one reason why the six hundred odd firms controlled by Unilever have come to share this common destiny: they were mostly firms which used the same raw and refined materials: the oils of the coconut, palm, palm kernel, cottonseed, groundnut, and soya bean, together with whale oil and animal fats.

The merger of 1929 was only the climax of a long series of amalgamations between businesses which had a stake in all of the several phases of manufacture and trade in oils and fats—tropical plantations, Antarctic whaling companies, oil mills, refineries, hardening plants, soap and margarine factories, and retail stores. Between the eighteen-seventies and the late nineteen-twenties, they had passed through every variety of relationship which separates unrestricted competition from final fusion and identity of interests. The most bitter rivalry had alternated with—sometimes accompanied—trade associations, price agreements, selling quotas, raw material buying pools, profit pooling agreements, and so on. By 1920 most of the firms destined to become part of Unilever in 1929 had been gathered into four main groups. By 1927 these were reduced to three, in 1928 to two, and in 1929 were finally unified. What ultimately emerged was a concern which bought and processed more than a third of the whole tonnage of oils and fats which find their way into world commerce, which traded in more places and in more products than any other concern in the world, which employed nearly a quarter of a million people, represented capital supplied by about 300,000 investors, and counted its customers not in thousands but in millions. Clearly the story of how all this came about must be not only an important chapter in industrial history but a significant phase in social evolution.

Such a history might have been written in a number of different ways. Probably none would have been wholly satisfactory, for inevitably this is not the history of one business but of a congeries of businesses, each of which has its own story—some of them reaching back as far as the seventeenth century. The method eventually followed was chosen because it seemed to correspond most closely to the organic process by which the concern had grown together and to offer the best chance of success in illuminating that process. The history has been divided into three Books. Book I deals with the history of Lever Brothers, one of the two parent groups which survived as a separate entity on the eve of the merger in 1929. The story is one of expansion accompanied by the acquisition of a large number of existing businesses. Book II deals mainly with the history of the two largest components of the other parent group, Jurgens' and Van den Bergh's. From 1870 to 1907 they were sufficiently separate to demand separate histories. But from 1907 their fortunes began to be so entwined that their stories can conveniently be combined. Then from about 1920, these two Dutch firms were increasingly linked with a third group: this was the firm of Schicht, of Aussig in Bohemia, which controlled a large part of the Central and Eastern European markets in oils and fats. Book II concludes with an account of the period from 1927 to 1929 when these three parent companies, Jurgens', Van den Bergh's, and Schicht's together with another Dutch concern, Hartog's of Oss, joined together in the Margarine Union and Margarine Unie. Although the method of treatment in Book II is similar to that employed in Book I, the story itself is different in one important respect. For the story of Lever Brothers is the story of the formation of one relatively self-contained group. Book II is the story of a series of relationships always complicated and often difficult to define precisely, between at least three main industrial groups. Book III deals with the period since 1929, when all five principals, together with their hundreds of subsidiaries, have formed the Unilever concern. And because the structure of these combines is a complex matter, it has been thought useful to set it out diagrammatically from time to time, at what seemed to be key points in the story—1906—1927—1929—1937.

To describe the process by which the constituent firms of Unilever were brought together in groups of increasing size until they finally coalesced into one, and to illuminate the forces and motives behind the process—this, rather than a collection of detailed histories of individual firms, is what is attempted here. It follows that the amount of space devoted to any particular firm must depend on several variable factors—on the volume and nature of such of its records as have survived, on the importance of the firm judged by such *criteria* as capital, profits, and output, but most of all on the *quality* of the contribution it seems to have made to the character and fortunes of the concern. In so far as technology has played a large part in the growth of large-scale organization, there must necessarily be some examination of the principal technological advances in the oils and fats industries: and because the businesses with which we are concerned are mostly ones which sell goods for immediate consumption to millions of ordinary people, their history cannot be understood without constant reference to levels of income and standards of living.

Finally, because I am not able to regard these developments as inevitable and because I believe that the principal reason why some firms survive, prosper, and expand while others dwindle, perish, or sell out must be sought in the personalities of the men who managed them, I have tried throughout to give the reader some idea of the leading actors in the play. In the history of business, as in other kinds of history, biography is a powerful element.

WILLIAM HESKETH LEVER
FIRST VISCOUNT LEVERHULME
1851–1925

BOOK I

LEVER BROTHERS

PART I

AN AGE OF NEW CUSTOMERS 1851–1906

CHAPTER I

THE SOCIAL SETTING

'The Legislature, even as it now is, could order all dingy manufacturing Towns to cease from their soot and darkness: to let in the blessed sunlight, the blue of Heaven, and become clear and clean. . . . Every toiling Manchester, its smoke and soot all burnt, ought it not amongst so many world-wide conquests to have a hundred acres or so of free green fields, with trees on it, conquered, for its little children to disport in; for its conquering workers to take a breath of twilight air in?'

Thomas Carlyle, Past and Present, 1843

Of the early eighties:
'. . . this was a time of great and many-sided advance in the nation's general standard of living.'

R. C. K. Ensor, England 1870–1914

THE soap industry of the nineteenth century was the product of an industrial society. It grew in response to the demands of an expanding population, an increasing proportion of which was being gathered into the great industrial towns. There, the smoke and grime of urban industrial life made soap a necessity where previously it had been almost a luxury: and as the standard of living of the town workers rose from 1860 onwards, vast potential markets for soap were created. Hence it is that the pedigree of the modern soap industry is a short one. Some of its component businesses go back into the eighteenth century; most are products of the Victorian age.

That is not to say there was no soap industry at all in the older agrarian England which gave way to modern industrial society in the nineteenth century. The bigger cities, London, Bristol, and Norwich especially, had for centuries had their soap boilers. In the early seventeenth century, they were amongst the first industrialists to use coal as an industrial fuel. Good soap was usually made from olive oil and tallow 'boiled for many hours together' and then mixed with potash 'first slacked with lime'.[1] Soap boilers were amongst the best customers of the Muscovy, Greenland, and Levant Companies for oil. Demand for soap in London was large enough to attract the attention of the early

[1] J. U. Nef, *Rise of the British Coal Industry*, Vol. I, p. 212.

Stuart Kings, searching for additional sources of revenue. In 1631, Charles I sold a charter to the so-called London Society of Soap Boilers and thus began a long series of disputes with the existing manufacturers which lasted up to the Civil War and which may well have contributed to the increasing tension between King and Parliament in these years. Soap monopolists were amongst the objects of attack from the Long Parliament: like the 'frogs of Egypt' they were to be found 'in the wash-bowl and powdering tub'. Government favourites—'Knights, Esquires and Gentlemen, never bred up to the Trade'—were unpopular with the established manufacturers, who suffered both in pocket and pride for infringing the upstarts' privileges. 'Their Pannes', they complained, were 'broken and destroyed, their houses of a great yearly value made unuseful: their families dispersed and necessitated and their estates almost ruined.' All this is evidence of the existence of an industry and of some substantial industrialists by seventeenth-century standards. But it was all on a tiny scale. The truth was that countrymen—and the greater part of the population consisted of country dwellers—made their own soap, just as they often made their own beer and their own clothes. In seventeenth- and eighteenth-century England, soap making was a domestic affair, as it still is in parts of Europe and America and even more so in Asia and Africa. None of the conditions favouring the growth of a substantial industry was present. Even in 1800, some two-thirds of the population still lived in conditions which might be called rural—on farms or in villages or small market towns. The squalor of Georgian England was a human squalor to which Englishmen had become accustomed by centuries of close acquaintance. By any statistical computation, living standards were low and the customers for such refinements as soap few. Even those who could afford desirable luxuries were not yet convinced that soap was necessarily among them. A Royal Duke remarked that it was sweat that kept a man clean.

The essential alterations in the structure of this society were taking place during the first half of the nineteenth century. By 1850, a population which had almost doubled in size was concentrating increasingly in towns. In those towns, factories were rapidly replacing the older forms of household industry. In the factories, power-driven machinery was replacing hand tools.

Everywhere craftsmen survived, but they were beginning to be outnumbered by factory workers. More and more families were coming to be clustered round the cotton mills of Lancashire, the woollen mills of Yorkshire, and the potteries, foundries, and engineering shops of the Midlands. The factory chimney towered over a society that was moving out of the age of the plough into the age of the steam engine, and it was the rapidly increasing industrial and domestic use of coal which undoubtedly was an important factor in converting soap from an article of luxury into an article of necessity. In 1790 the total production of coal in Britain was ten million tons; by 1900 it was nearly 242 million tons. At both dates a high proportion of the coal produced was consumed in Britain itself. Coal was the foundation of Britain's industrial wealth, but it was also the cause of the smoky pall which lay over most of the large industrial towns, descending as a relentless deposit of dirt on the face of Britain. Remorselessly, in the course of the nineteenth century, the old London of Canaletto, with its clear skies and glistening white stonework, was blotted out. The ships, towers, domes, theatres and temples which Wordsworth had beheld in wonder upon Westminster Bridge were no longer all bright and glittering in the smokeless air half a century later. With the generation of Ruskin and Morris came a new outlook; the sooty civilization that had seemed symbolic of the conquest of poverty to the age of the inventors now became a source of disgust and indignation. William Morris in *The Earthly Paradise* (1868–70) was nostalgic for the age of the plough:

> Forget six counties overhung with smoke,
> Forget the snorting steam and piston stroke,
> Forget the spreading of the hideous town;
> Think rather of the pack-horse on the down,
> And dream of London, small and white and clean,
> The clear Thames bordered by its gardens green . . .

Yet, as G. M. Trevelyan has remarked, except in imagination there was no going back to the past.[1] The people of Lancashire or the Potteries might dream, like Morris, of cities of the past that were 'small and white and clean' but they had to live in the intractably dirty present and make the best of it. The problem

[1] G. M. Trevelyan, *English Social History*, p. 579.

of keeping clean in a world growing ever dirtier was common to all classes, and with the advance in education and general prosperity in the second half of the century, all classes came to share to a greater or lesser degree in the desire to solve the problem.

It was the Duke of Wellington who probably did most to spread the fashion for the daily bath among the upper and middle classes, against the not inconsiderable opposition of those who alleged that daily bathing would expose the foolhardy to rheumatic fever, lung trouble, and other kindred diseases. By the sixties, a daily bath was usual among those who could afford the coal for heating the water and the labour to carry the great jugs from which the hot water was poured into the movable tub. A little lower in the social scale, the bath was a weekly ritual but washing took place daily, and everywhere the wash-hand stand, with its basin, jug, and soap dish, was making its appearance in the Victorian bedroom. Among the working classes, a spreading system of elementary education was inculcating ideals of respectability and cleanliness throughout the second half of the century, and educational influences were powerfully supplemented by the ethics of a popular Nonconformity which put cleanliness very close indeed to Godliness. Consumption of soap rose significantly between the year of Waterloo and the year of the Great Exhibition. Yet it was kept back by lack of water and lack of money. Lack of water was a hardship which bore grievously on the poor. In the London slums, water was often turned on for about an hour a day and turned off entirely at weekends. If the pump was too far away, water would have to be bought from the water-carrier's cart. In Lancashire some workpeople were having to pay as much as two shillings a week for carted water. The free water supplies of the later years of the century removed one obstacle to the achievement of reasonable cleanliness. But it was increasing wages and falling prices that did most to create the vast and spreading demand for the means of cleanliness in the last quarter of the century.

Until the third quarter of the nineteenth century, the new industrial system was hard put to it to keep pace with the increase of population. Between the middle of the eighteenth and the middle of the nineteenth century the population of Britain more than trebled and in the first half of the nineteenth century was increasing at the rate of more than a million every ten years. At this distance in time it seems remarkable that the transition from the old England to the new was accomplished with relatively little dislocation and violence: for the problem of feeding, clothing, housing, and employing the new masses was one which might have puzzled and defeated far better organized societies than the England of Victoria. Yet to contemporaries it seemed that social conditions gave the lie to statisticians who talked of increasing wealth. The new England seemed to them to be divided into Disraeli's Two Nations, the rich and the poor. Wealth had in fact increased in the aggregate, but so had numbers, and it was not until after the middle of the century that there was widespread and well-attested evidence that the real wages of the workers in general were beginning to rise. The industrial towns of the North, where the industrial revolution was most advanced, shared in the change to the full, and late in the century a shrewd observer remarked that the visitor who went there expecting to find 'a race of men half of whom are pre-occupied with the anxieties of opulence, while the other half are consumed with the cares of poverty' was to discover his error.[1] Everywhere wage rates moved upwards in the fifties and sixties. Then from the seventies to the nineties, falling prices also worked to the advantage of the working classes. Taken in conjunction with a moderate rise in money wages, falling prices probably increased the value of the wages of a skilled worker by from thirty-five to forty per cent in this period. Many unskilled workers shared to a greater or lesser extent in the general improvement in conditions. Sidney Webb, giving evidence before the Royal Commission on Labour in 1892, attributed the improvement to the 'growing increase of collectivism'. Whether he was right or not, there was no doubt of the facts, though of course there remained a mass of depressed poor (many of them Irish) living on the minimum standards of existence in towns like Glasgow, Liverpool, and London, whose plight was revealed by Victorian investigators. Generally, however, the condition of the working classes was showing a steady improvement, and nowhere more than in Lancashire, where an observer noted that 'the working classes are a much more visible power than in London'. At Manchester, high wages were said to have given

[1] T. H. Escott, *Social Transformations of the Victorian Age* (1897), pp. 33–43.

the mill hands 'exceptional means'. Improvidence and extravagance were 'comparatively rare'. Poor relief payments were on the decrease; deposits in the Savings Banks on the up-grade. 'Articles of necessity', said the same writer, 'not more than of luxury never before known in industrial households, are today common beneath the workman's roof. With comfort, sobriety and thrift (which are indeed the parents of comfort) have increased too.'[1]

Thanks, then, to a combination of factors, economic, political, social, and religious, the whole structure and outlook of English society had undergone a radical transformation in the fifty years that preceded the eighteen-eighties. Nowhere was the pace of industrial change more rapid, nowhere was the pall of industrialism blacker, nowhere was the working man more self-respecting, nowhere was the power of dissent and all the moral forces for which it stood stronger, than in the industrial North. The increased consumption of soap is a yardstick by which both the material and mental transformation can be measured. It was certainly no accident that the largest nucleus of soap manufacturers was gathered in Lancashire and the West Riding.

[1] Escott, op. cit., pp. 44–6.

CHAPTER II

THE BRITISH SOAP INDUSTRY BEFORE THE RISE OF LEVER

'Personal knowledge of each other is a great factor in the cohesion of the soap trade.'

Edward Simpson of Hodgson & Simpson, 1904

THE growing demand for soap, first among the middle, then the working classes, had called into being a prosperous and widespread industry. National consumption, estimated at 24,106 tons in 1801, rose steadily until the thirties: between 1831 and 1841 there was a sharp increase from 47,768 tons to 75,893 tons. Until 1853, excise was levied at the rate of 3d. a pound. Soap was made in bond and excise officers locked the pans at night. When Mr. Gladstone repealed the tax in 1853, he gave a fillip, no doubt, to production, and by 1861 England was probably producing rather more than 100,000 tons of soap a year; the figures show however that the repeal was, if not exactly the fly on the chariot wheel, of less importance than has sometimes been supposed to the progress of the industry. The consumption per head of the population was increasing as standards of life and the value of real wages rose—3·6 lb. per annum in 1801, 8·0 lb. in 1861. The sixties and seventies saw a further spectacular expansion—production was over 150,000 tons by 1871, well over 200,000 tons by 1881, and nearly 260,000 tons by 1891. Thereafter, the rate of growth was slower, and by the early years of the twentieth century there is plenty of evidence that the period of expansion, if not entirely over, was moving to a close. But between 1861 and 1891 the consumption per head of the population had nearly doubled—from 8 to 15·4 lb.

With the increase in production went changes in the process of making soap; these, along with advances in sea and land transport, helped to determine the location of the industry. The simple facts of soap making had, of course, been known for centuries, and as early as the beginning of the thirteenth century Marseilles had a flourishing industry based on olive oil. For long, however, the process was thought to be simply a mechanical mixing of fats and alkali, and it was not until the nineteenth century that the researches of the French chemist, Chevreul, showed that the formation was in fact a chemical process in accordance with well-defined reactions. Chevreul showed that the oils and fats from animals were actually glycerides, i.e. compounds of fatty acids with glycerine, and that in the process of 'saponification' the fatty acids combined with the alkali during boiling, leaving the glycerine free.[1] Until the end of the eighteenth century, shortage of alkali supplies may well have been a brake on soap production; the only sources had been the ashes from seaweed and limited natural deposits. But in 1793 Leblanc had shown that alkali could be obtained from common salt, and from 1814 his process was worked continuously in England.

The discoveries of Leblanc and Chevreul revolutionized the industry in the first half of the nineteenth century. But a glance back at the materials used in soap-making formulae indicates that the enormous growth of soap making in England could not have taken place without the revolution in transport which gave her access to the markets of Asia and the New World. The principal type of fat was tallow; apart from limited home supplies, mutton tallow came chiefly from Australia, beef tallow mainly from North and South America. As vegetable oil soaps grew more popular the demand for these oils rose sharply. Tropical West Africa was the home of the oil palm, and from the flesh of the palm fruits came a bright red substance, something like butter in consistency and smelling like violets. It had the disadvantage that it was apt to contain fibres which caused soap to go rancid on the outside. But the nut of the palm fruit also gave a kernel fat, pale primrose in colour, and smelling not unlike coconut fat. From the South Sea Islands (later from Ceylon, also Malabar) came copra, the dried flesh of the coconut; and from the copra was pressed coconut fat, a pure white substance excellent for soap making. From the southern states of the U.S.A. came cottonseed oil, obtained by crushing the seed of the cotton plant. Cottonseed oil resembled a yellow olive oil. A small proportion of resin was also desirable in soap in order

[1] See also Appendix 1, Diagram of the Soap-making Process.

to make it more soluble and cause it to lather freely. The main source of this was the yellow pine of Virginia and California.

This brief survey of the fats and oils used in soap helps to explain why the industry tended to centre round ports—round Merseyside, Bristol, London, and Newcastle. Further inland transport of cargoes of raw material only added to production costs. Finally there was the alkali, caustic soda, and perhaps the proximity of the salt deposits of Cheshire helps to explain why the largest aggregation of soap firms grew up in Lancashire. Certainly there was a close connection between the growth of the soap and the chemical industries.

Time, rationalization, and paper drives have dealt hardly with the records of the individual firms but enough has survived to enable us to gain some idea of the size and qualities of the main firms. The biggest groups of soap-making firms were to be found in the North, the West and London, with a smaller group in Norwich. To take the Northern makers first, William Gossage & Sons of Widnes, the biggest, had strong affinities with the chemical industry. William Gossage, who founded the firm in 1855, was a chemist by training—almost by birth. From retail pharmacy he had gone into manufacturing, as a maker of Leamington salts, and thence to the manufacture of bleaching agents and alkalis. It was the high price of tallow in 1854, caused by the Crimean War, which led Gossage to turn his attention to soap making. After much experimenting he succeeded in producing a good cheap soap from palm oil and silicate of soda. The works at Widnes were partly on the Mersey but the larger frontage lay alongside the St. Helens Canal. Gossage's had their own fleet of lighters which sailed down the river laden with soap and silicate of soda. The cargoes for export were then transferred direct to ocean-going steamers sailing from Liverpool and Birkenhead. On the return journey the lighters would bring back raw material—tallow, oil, resin, and perhaps timber for use in making boxes. The export trade was Gossage's speciality: they were famous for a 'mottled' soap which sold particularly well in Africa, India, and China. At one time, they were reputed to control between two-thirds and three-quarters of the export trade: statistics are not available but in the late nineteenth century that probably meant an annual export by Gossage's of between 15,000 and 20,000 tons a year.

Amongst Gossage's customers was a firm of an entirely different type. The business of R. S. Hudson had been founded in 1837 at West Bromwich. Its beginnings were small—not more than a handful of female workers—and it remained small until the fifties. When Hudson's began to produce the speciality for which they became famous—Hudson's Dry Soap Powder—is not clear, but by 1875 it was a substantial business, with an export trade to Australia and New Zealand and, on a small scale, to the Continent. Transport facilities for the export trade were no doubt in Hudson's mind when, in that year, he opened a new works at Bank Hall, Liverpool. Nearby docks, sidings, and a canal all combined to make for easy distribution. Hudson did not himself manufacture soap—the chief ingredient of his powder—but bought what he needed from Gossage's. The connection was to have a curious sequel.[1]

The story of Joseph Crosfield, of Warrington, is in some ways strikingly similar to that of Gossage's. The founder was born in 1792, the son of a Warrington manufacturer—'to the great joy of us all' as his father recorded. 'We mean to call him Joseph.' Joseph Crosfield, like William Gossage, was apprenticed to a chemist and druggist at Newcastle, but by 1815 he was installed in his first soapery on the present Warrington site. Conscious forethought obviously played some part in determining the site, but unto this were added the windfalls of one of the first railways (between Liverpool and Manchester) and later the Manchester Ship Canal. Joseph had seen his opportunities clearly: soap was increasingly in demand, and chemical discoveries and increased supplies of raw materials favoured its manufacture. At his death, in 1844, he left a flourishing business to his brother, George, and his three sons. But even in 1851, the business was still small—two offices, two soap pans, and a laboratory 'little bigger than a double bed'. Cottages covered the rest of the space later occupied by the factory. Factory extensions followed fairly rapidly: in the sixties, Crosfield's were making their own caustic soda and had put up a plant for making silicate of soda on the lines of Gossage's process. The silicate was added to the oils and fats in the manufacture of a cheap household soap—the kind known as a 'filled' soap. Plant for the recovery of glycerine followed later. By the eighties, while still a family partnership,

[1] See Chapter VIII.

Crosfield's had established a formidable reputation for their export trade and their prowess in industrial chemistry. That reputation was to be maintained and extended into the twentieth century.

The soap factory of Joseph Watson & Sons at Leeds had grown out of a hide and skin business established in the eighteen-twenties, and the hide and skin business itself was an offshoot of Yorkshire sheep rearing. From tanning hides, the original Joseph, a substantial merchant who travelled every week by stage coach to the Liverpool markets, turned to the manufacture of fat and tallow, now much in demand as a lubricant for the new machines of the industrial age. From tallow, it was a short step to tallow candles, and tallow soap, in long bars, followed naturally. By the eighties the firm employed eleven clerks and about sixty workpeople, and in 1885 Watson's succeeded for the first time in making and delivering a hundred tons of soap in one week. Nor were they behind on the chemical side. Julius Lewkowitsch, an able German chemist, joined them as chief chemist and technical manager to deal with the new glycerine department in 1887. There was plenty of Yorkshire shrewdness in the management too. Joseph's two sons, Charles and George, inherited their father's ability; his grandson, Joseph, still at Rugby in the eighties, was to prove Lever's biggest rival.

The other two Northern firms were Hazlehurst of Runcorn and Hodgson & Simpson of Wakefield. Thomas Hazlehurst had started business in 1816 as a manufacturer of resin. His sons developed the chemical side of the business, and did a large trade in carbonate of soda with America. As with Gossage's and Crosfield's, this in turn led to an export trade in a 'filled' soap in the seventies and eighties. Hodgson & Simpson of Wakefield were a typically comfortable family business, begun, like Hazlehurst's, in the early years of the century. Their site, at the junction of the river Calder and the local canal, was in contact with Liverpool and Hull, while cheap fuel could be brought direct from the pit head at Barnsley.

Widely as they differed in size and perhaps in efficiency these Northern firms had one thing in common: they were all, with the exception of Hazlehurst's, who had been bought up by the United Alkali Company, family partnerships; and several of them had substantial foreign connections. There was also a strong technical and chemical bias to the Lancashire firms. The founders of Gossage's, Crosfield's, and Hazlehurst's were all, in a sense, inventors.

In the West Country group, comprising Christr. Thomas & Bros. of Bristol, Lawsons of Bristol, the Victoria Soap Company and a good many others, Christr. Thomas's were the leaders. Christr. Thomas's could trace their ancestry back through various changes of name and ownership to a firm established in 1743. Even in the eighteenth century it had had far more than local trade. By the eighteen-eighties its soaps had penetrated into Gloucestershire and Wiltshire, into South and West Wales and even into Scotland. The business remained a private partnership but the principal interest had long since passed into the hands of the Thomas's, a family of Welsh Unitarians from Llangadock in Carmarthenshire, who had emigrated to Bristol in the eighteen-twenties and rooted themselves firmly in the public life of the city. Probably their principal market still lay in Bristol itself—in 1878 they sold more than one thousand tons in the city alone—but their household soaps and candles were reaching more distant markets. They were to the West Country industry what Gossage's were to the North and what John Knight was to the London group. In particular, they were able to claim that 'we were the first soap makers to produce glycerine from spent lyes in the United Kingdom or elsewhere'—fruit no doubt of the employment of 'a general and analytical chemist' who had been engaged as early as 1872. Thomas's continued to develop their invention and were soon in close relationship with Nobel's, their chief customers for glycerine: so close that in 1888 they were refusing to disturb them by joining an association of glycerine producers which was formed to combat the price policy of the explosives combine. Glycerine was no doubt a large factor in the prosperity of Thomas's in the early eighties. They were well enough to the fore in technical development to face with confidence the competition of their big rivals from London and the North. So long as no revolutionary development took place in the soap trade, Christr. Thomas's could feel confident: of their kind their products were good, and a century and a half of goodwill in the West Country was worth a lot.

It was more than could be said of some other West Country firms—of the small Victoria Soap Company Ltd., of Plymouth, for example, whose main interest lies in its claim to be the first limited liability company in the soap trade, and which was founded by a group of Plymouth business men in 1858 under the terms of the Joint Stock Companies Act of 1856. It was never a large concern; it started with an authorized capital of £10,000 of which £4,695 was issued. In its early days, it seems to have concentrated fairly successfully on the production of a type of yellow bar household soap; in 1866 an attack on the London market was even contemplated. But throughout the seventies its board of ageing directors were faced with falling profits, and in the eighties they were trading at a loss. The future might lie with the limited liability company, but not with this one.

London soap makers comprised a group by themselves—John Knight, Pears, Edward Cook and dozens of smaller firms—but there was no doubt who were the leaders. In the Knight business, a strong family tradition was combined with a long continuity of efficiency. Old John Knight, who founded the firm in 1817, is one of the few pioneers of soap making who conforms to what some historians consider to be the orthodox lineage of the industrial revolutionaries. He was a yeoman, the son of a Hertfordshire farmer. In the thirties his factory in Old Gravel Lane, Wapping, was still small, employing three copper pans, eight candle-machines and a handful of workpeople. John Knight, described by one of his descendants as 'an old tyrant', died in the mid-sixties. His sons had already been constrained to rebel against the old man in order to secure the fair share of control due to them as partners, but towards employees and customers alike, the firm's attitude was always just and courtly. Silk hats and frock coats long remained standard office dress, office employees were addressed as 'gentlemen', and the quest for new orders in the West End was made in a brougham. Until 1902, John Knight's remained a private partnership in the hands of the founder's direct descendants unto the third and fourth generations. In the fifties it was a sizeable business employing a hundred and fifty people and producing between two thousand and three thousand tons of soap a year. In the sixties the four partners were sharing a comfortable income from £15,000 to £17,000. When it was decided, in 1880, to move the business to Silvertown, they explained that 'one of the reasons of our making the change was the desire to be able to conduct our increasing business with more ease and comfort to our work-people'. Both supplies and sales centred on London. In the early days most of Knight's supplies had come from London butchers —'our butchers'—to whom on occasion the firm was willing to lend money. The trade was not elegant and local authorities relegated the carting of tallow, along with sewage, to the hours of darkness. Breaches of these regulations led to several prosecutions. In cool weather tallow supplies were obtained from dealers in provincial cities; when the weather was hot Knight's prudently released them from their obligations and allowed them to sell locally. Supplies of caustic were another difficulty: there was none near at hand and this fact, together with the increasing proportion of oils and fats coming from abroad, no doubt influenced Knight's in their decision to move nearer the London Docks. Resin had for long come from America—one partner was there on a buying expedition in 1870—but in the eighties Knight's were branching out into new lines which made transport of the first importance. 'In 1883', recorded the partners at the end of the year, 'we added to our business that of oil seed crushing—first cotton seed and afterwards linseed; we also commenced the recovery of glycerine from spent lyes.' During 1884, the capacity of the crushing plant was increased by two-thirds, and experiments with glycerine continued.

Knight's reputation rested on a soap called 'Royal Primrose'. As early as 1844 advertisements of Knight's 'Primrose' were appearing in *The Times* and in the Great Exhibition of 1851 Knight's took the Prize Medal. 'Royal Primrose' was made in many varieties: it was a good household and laundry soap and the partners watched over its quality with jealous care. Knight's were always against what they called 'aggressive advertising' as contrary to their established custom and liable to offend the very customers whom they wished to attract. These are defined as 'high-class family grocers and substantial professional men . . . and ladies scheduled in the Ladies' Court Book'. Knight's were traditionalists. They never ceased to insist on high quality, but their belief that quality alone would sell their goods was to give them trouble in the new world of 'aggressive advertising'. Their costs were often high, their management and accounting of doubtful efficiency, and things were not made any easier by the wrangling between the six partners (representing three different generations) who were responsible for the business in the latter years of the century.

Pears', Knight's biggest rivals in the toilet trade, were another old family firm. Andrew Pears was a Cornish yeoman who opened a barber's shop in Soho in 1789. The needs of his customers led him into manufacturing soap at a factory just off Oxford Street—'squares at 1s. each, large squares perfumed with Otto of Roses at 2s. 6d., Gentlemen's Shaving Sticks at 2s. 6d.' In 1862, Pears' built their factory at Isleworth and round about the same time there came into the business a young man of twenty-four 'who had met the eldest daughter of Francis Pears at an Academy of Dancing and Deportment in the West End'. Miss Pears became Mrs. Thomas J. Barratt, and her husband became London Manager for his father-in-law. Barratt was above all things a salesman, with startling and ingenious ideas on advertising. In 1886 he purchased from the *Illustrated London News* the painting of 'Bubbles' by Millais and used it as advertising material—an achievement which set the world of artists by the ears and goaded Marie Corelli into making one of the characters in *The Sorrows of Satan* remark: 'I am one of those who think the fame of Millais as an artist was marred when he degraded himself to the level of painting the little green boy blowing bubbles of Pears' Soap.' (After exchange of letters the misunderstanding was eventually cleared up: the novelist admitted that Millais had had 'nothing to do in the soap business'.) This 'blatant advertisement' might be regrettable to sensitive souls. Barratt merely went on from strength to strength, coining one slogan after another. 'Good-morning,' said a famous one, 'have you used Pears' Soap?' And another announced (under Harry Furniss's well-known drawing of a ragged tramp) in terms which were to become familiar, 'Two years ago I used your soap, since when I have used no other'. Barratt certainly shared none of the Knight family's scruples about 'aggressive advertisement'. Another of his devices—'French pennies' (ten-centime pieces) stamped with the name 'Pears' and put into circulation—had to be stopped by Act of Parliament. For all his flamboyance, Barratt had made his mark. Pears' famous 'Transparent Soap' became known all over the civilized world. 'The great firm of Pears in those days', wrote H. G. Wells, 'had already thrust an individuality upon soap. Pears' soap marks an epoch: I hope history will not neglect it.'

None of the other London makers—Edward Cook, Wilkie & Soames, Richard Wheen & Sons—could really challenge the old-established supremacy of Knight's, which a leading figure in the industry later described, a trifle unkindly, as 'the old-fogey-dom which rules at Silvertown'. Cook's were one of the most vigorous of the secondary firms. By the eighties their factory was at Bow though the Cooks themselves were no Cockneys. In the late eighteenth century Edward Cook was making soap at Norwich and Lynn: something of an experimenter in fine soaps, he had been amongst the first to appreciate the importance of Leblanc's discovery. Soon he was supplying soap to the Royal Household and in 1820 moved his works to London. In the sixties and seventies Cook's Primrose Soap was amongst the most popular brands of household soap: British and foreign Royalty, the War Office and the Admiralty, and municipal authorities all bought from Cook's.

Scotland had a number of prosperous soap firms; Ogston & Sons of Aberdeen and Isdaile & McCallum of Paisley were well known both inside and outside Scottish borders; Ogston's had been making soft soap (black soap it was called locally) since 1802. Linseed and cottonseed oil were obtainable in Aberdeen at the crushing mills; potash came from Germany; while Aberdeen slaughter houses provided a tallow supply that was later supplemented from Australia and the Argentine.

Bar soap of the tallow variety in four-pound bars succeeded soft soap as standards of living rose, and Ogston's dealt with the grocery trade all over Scotland as well as with areas of England served by Newcastle, Hull, Liverpool, and London. Scotland's industry had to meet a certain amount of competition from a number of small makers in Ireland. The biggest of them in the eighties was John Barrington & Sons of Dublin. Sir John Barrington, Lord Mayor of Dublin, was great-grandson of the original John, a philanthropic Quaker tallow chandler who moved into soap making about 1775. Barrington's production was never large by English standards, and even in 1911 it was only of the order of some thirty tons a week. In the eighties their output was confined to bar soaps of a good quality which sold in both town and country markets.

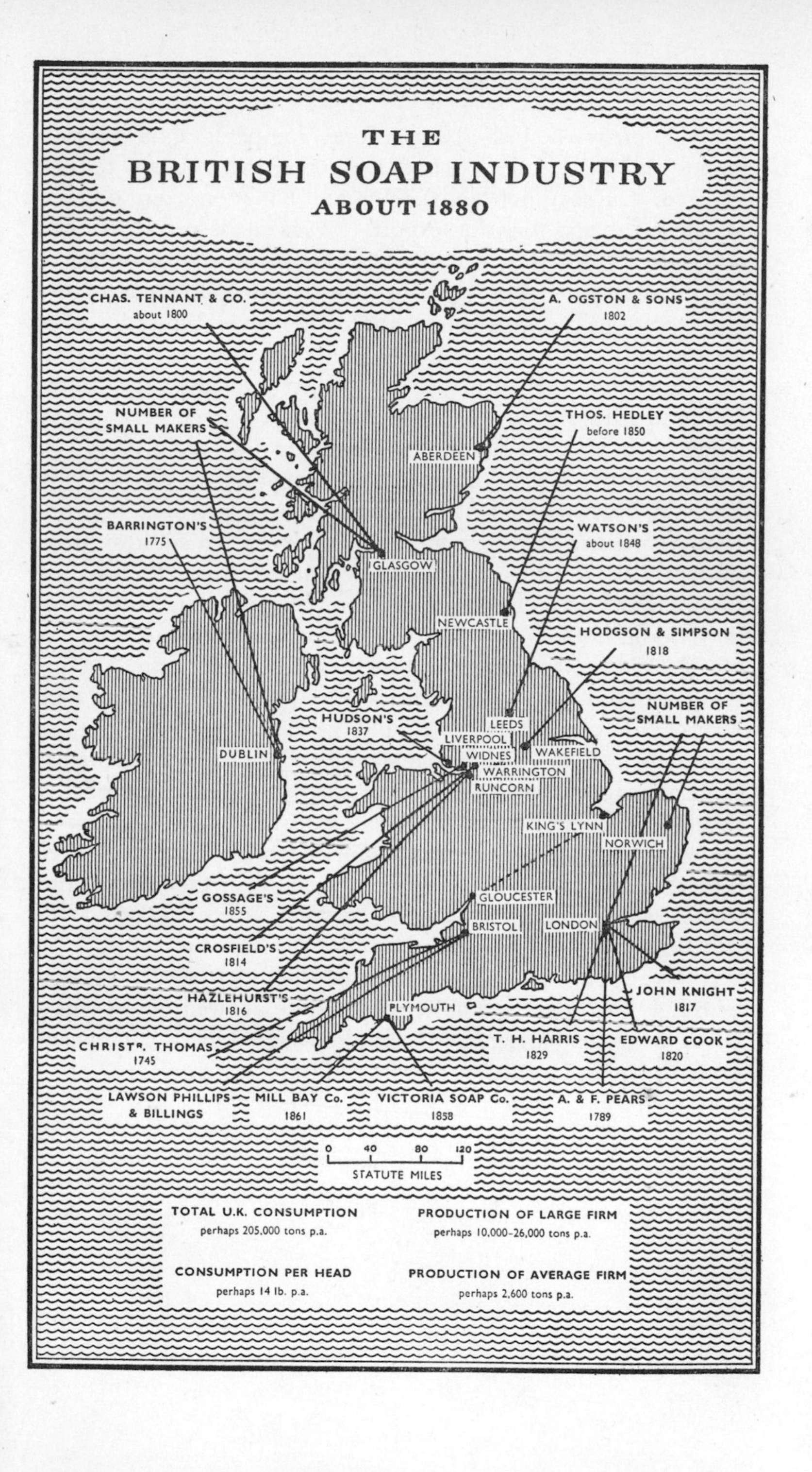
THE
BRITISH SOAP INDUSTRY
ABOUT 1880
CHAS. TENNANT & CO.
about 1800
A. OGSTON & SONS
1802
NUMBER OF
SMALL MAKERS
THOS. HEDLEY
before 1850
ABERDEEN
BARRINGTON'S
1775
WATSON'S
about 1848
GLASGOW
NEWCASTLE
HODGSON & SIMPSON
1818
NUMBER OF
SMALL MAKERS
HUDSON'S
1837
LEEDS
LIVERPOOL
WIDNES
WAKEFIELD
DUBLIN
WARRINGTON
RUNCORN
KING'S LYNN
NORWICH
GOSSAGE'S
1855
GLOUCESTER
BRISTOL
LONDON
CROSFIELD'S
1814
HAZLEHURST'S
1816
JOHN KNIGHT
1817
PLYMOUTH
CHRISTR. THOMAS
1745
T. H. HARRIS
1829
EDWARD COOK
1820
LAWSON PHILLIPS
& BILLINGS
MILL BAY Co.
1861
VICTORIA SOAP Co.
1858
A. & F. PEARS
1789
0
40
80
120
STATUTE MILES
TOTAL U.K. CONSUMPTION
perhaps 205,000 tons p.a.
PRODUCTION OF LARGE FIRM
perhaps 10,000-26,000 tons p.a.
CONSUMPTION PER HEAD
perhaps 14 lb. p.a.
PRODUCTION OF AVERAGE FIRM
perhaps 2,600 tons p.a.

The industry described in the foregoing paragraphs was producing, in the eighties, between 200,000 and 250,000 tons of soap for consumption in the United Kingdom and perhaps 20,000 to 25,000 tons for export. It was made up of firms of every size—from those producing a few tons a week and employing a handful of employees, to those making upwards of five hundred tons a week and employing several hundreds of workpeople.

The outstanding feature of the industry was the very limited and local nature of the markets. A series of conventions, almost medieval in their parochialism, maintained a system of zones, so that Northern soap makers held the markets in the North of England, Norwich makers held the East Anglian markets, while London makers held London and the South. In addition there were private treaties such as that by which Christr. Thomas's of Bristol obtained an undertaking from Gossage's of Widnes that they would not come South of a line drawn from Birmingham, North of Bristol, to the Severn in the West, and to the Wash in the East. This zone system rested on the assumption that a local manufacturer could always supply the local trade more cheaply than makers who lived at a distance and who therefore had to make a bigger charge for the cost of carriage. The old-established manufacturers prided themselves not a little on the 'personal knowledge' and 'good fellowship' which pervaded their industry. In general there was much truth in their contention that it was 'a happy industry'. Preserves were respected and poaching was kept to a minimum. This was the comfortable world, gentlemanly and harmonious, the quiet of which was to be rudely shattered by a newcomer whose avowed object was to break down the barriers between these agreed local markets and to make and sell an article recognized universally.

CHAPTER III

MR. SMILES'S DISCIPLE

'The ordinary methods of the pill and patent medicine man in his pamphlet do have a way of attracting attention and impressing the reader. In fact after reading one of his pamphlets, like Jerome K. Jerome, in *Three Men in a Boat*, one is inclined to think that one had every complaint under the sun except Housemaid's Knee and that is threatening. We want to have this hypnotic effect with soap. . . . The whole object of advertising is to build a halo round the article. No doubt we shall gradually get to it.'

W. H. Lever to John Cheshire, 13 *June* 1909

'The factory housewife is saving, cleanly, loquacious, and very often extremely shrewd.'

T. H. S. Escott, England, Its People, Polity and Pursuits, 1885, *p.* 80

WILLIAM HESKETH LEVER was born on the 19th of September 1851 at a house in Wood Street, Bolton. In the seventeenth century Bolton had been ' . . . a fair, well-built town with broad streets. . . . ' Seen against the background of the forest of Horwich with its streams and valleys, cottages and spreading orchards, Bolton before the days of the steam engine and the factory chimney must have been one of the most picturesque of Lancashire towns. By 1851 it had undergone a melancholy transformation. Here, at the heart of the new factory industry, Friedrich Engels, in 1844, described Bolton as the worst of the Lancashire industrial towns after Preston and Oldham. It had only one main street, the older part of the town was ruinous and miserable, while a dirty brook, or string of puddles, added to the pollution of the air. Nowhere was distress worse than at Bolton in the forties. The Borough Members 'never witnessed scenes in which wretchedness so deplorable was depicted'. In many streets the houses were without furniture, hundreds of families slept on the ground without bed or bedding, were without bread and had never known the luxury of meat. Pestilence spread from the cellars where Irish immigrants herded together in conditions of indescribable filth. With the Irish came typhus, and what were baldly described as 'large fever sheds' had to be hastily erected in 1846 to house hundreds of patients.

Yet even Bolton was not wholly a place of squalor and poverty. William Lever was to grow up well acquainted with both, but there was little of either in Wood Street itself. Wood Street was one of those pleasantly undistinguished streets of Georgian houses which still survive here and there in the industrial towns of England; an island of middle-class comfort set in a sea of poverty and drabness. For Lever belonged to that class which often escaped the notice of the publicists, the class of those who were neither plutocrats nor paupers but which, like the plutocracy and the poor, was also a-growing. This class, the lower middle class, was much in evidence in mid-Victorian Lancashire. Its ideals were decent respectability, business probity, the gospel of work and an untheological brand of piety, mostly of the Dissenting kind. Such were the Levers. James Lever, the father, was a Bolton man; apprenticed to a Bolton grocer at the age of fourteen, he had lived the hard life of a bound apprentice 'living in' under the strict tutelage of his employer. As a young man he had gone to Manchester to take charge of a new branch grocery shop. The Manchester period had brought with it marriage and the strong influence of urban Nonconformity. James Lever became a Congregationalist: thereafter the Lever household knew not alcohol, though cards were tolerated and theatres and dancing just missed prohibition. After ten years in Manchester James Lever accepted a proposal from a former fellow apprentice to go into partnership in a retail grocery at Bolton. In February 1842 the shop was opened. Since many of the potential customers were still illiterate, shop signs were common; the figure of a blackamoor was placed in the window and as 'The Lower Blackamoor' the new venture was known. It continued successfully until 1864 when James Lever gave up the retail business in favour of a wholesale business which he acquired from his former partners.

This, then, was the thriving family business which William Lever, at the age of sixteen, entered. The year was 1867; under the strict supervision of his father, the new apprentice received 'a thorough, detailed, strict, and disciplined grounding in every business operation'.[1] At seven in the morning he was taking

[1] *Viscount Leverhulme by His Son*, p. 19.

down the shutters, tidying up and preparing for the business of the day, and there was much to learn, first in the warehouse, later in the office. The Victorian apprentice to business needed a good training. He could not, like his descendants, trust the label; for branded goods were still rare, most goods were sold in bulk and taste and smell had to be trained as aids to knowledge and skill. Amongst the first jobs which Lever had to learn was the cutting and wrapping of soap, which in those days came to the wholesale grocer in long three-pound bars from the maker and was then cut into lengths and weights, to suit the retailer's customer. Likewise the technicalities of sugar, flour, cheese, and a score of other commodities were in turn mastered. From the warehouse he passed to the office to study the accountancy side of the business and it was not long before he was introducing reforms and refinements into his father's book-keeping system. Three years of work indoors was sufficient to give him a sound working knowledge of the business and more than enough to make him chafe for a more active way of life. In 1870, a vacancy occurred on the travelling staff: William pointed out to his father that a new clerk (at thirty shillings a week) would be cheaper than a new traveller—travellers at four pounds a week were amongst the aristocrats of business employees in Victorian England. The argument prevailed and for the next few years the daily round consisted of an early breakfast followed by journeys, usually in a one-horse gig, to the retail grocers in the neighbourhood of Bolton. About five o'clock he would turn for home, make up his order book, hand in the new orders and the day's cash settlements of accounts. No further comment on the value of Lever's services to the business is required than to note that in 1872, the prudent James took his son into partnership at a salary of £800 a year—for a young man who had just attained his majority, a very considerable income. It was, however, already clear that William Lever was no ordinary young man. True, his school career had not been spectacular, but the breadth of his interests even at the schoolboy age was remarkable; more remarkable still, they continued to develop after he left school. Not the least of Lever's weapons in later life was a gift of fluent and compelling speech. Clearly this derived in part from the voracious reading of his boyhood and youth. From the daily reading of the family circle he knew his Bible intimately. At home too he formed a book-reading circle with several school friends—among them were Jonathan Simpson and Alfred Robinson, of whom more later—when Shakespeare shared the honours with Dickens, Fenimore Cooper, Artemus Ward, and W. S. Gilbert (*The Bab Ballads*). Jonathan Simpson, now articled to an architect, was also his companion on visits to Manchester—sometimes to see Mr. and Mrs. Calvert's productions of Shakespeare, at others to hear a reading by Charles Dickens or a lecture by Bradlaugh, or to listen to Harry Clifton singing 'Paddle Your Own Canoe'. It was a healthy and catholic course of self-education that he was following: many a University provides a worse; and it was perfectly in accord with the principles of a book that Lever was given on his sixteenth birthday, Samuel Smiles's *Self Help* that had first appeared in 1859. It elaborated, with a wealth of historical allusion and example, a formula for success in business, and its influence was immediate and enormous. Twenty thousand copies were sold in the first year and throughout the sixties and seventies it continued to be a best seller. Abroad it was translated into seventeen languages. Lever shared to the full the robust individualism which characterized the third quarter of the nineteenth century and Smiles's homespun philosophy fitted in admirably with his times and his temperament, confirming him in his natural energy, ambition, and optimism. 'I know', he wrote much later, 'that people nowadays are inclined to scoff at Smiles and his gospel of Self Help, but my advice to the young man of the present generation is to act on the principles taught in Smiles's philosophy. He will go further than his competitor who does not.' So convinced was he of the powerful influence Smiles had on his own career that he made a practice in later life of giving a copy of *Self Help* to any boy of an impressionable age in whom he was interested. Under the guidance of this philosophy of work and ambition, the waking hours became too short to contain the tasks to be done, the things to be learnt and seen. The hours, almost the minutes, of the day were reckoned out and planned to the best advantage: the habit never left him. Reading by himself or in the book-circle would be varied with interludes of carpentry: country rambles provided material for hours with the microscope: private lessons in French competed with the gymnasium and the Bolton swimming-baths for the spare half hour.

Life as the junior partner continued much as before. He kept up his travelling but already his restless energies were looking for a wider sphere of operations for the business. A trip to Ince, a village lying beyond the normal confines of the business, led to an expedition to Wigan. The new trade with Wigan throve and it became clear that it was absurd to bring goods from Liverpool to Bolton and then send them back to Wigan. The answer was obviously a branch in Wigan and it was not long before William Lever was installed as manager of this new venture. By 1881, the original premises at Wigan had become too small and a new warehouse and office, designed by Jonathan Simpson, were opened in Market Street.

By this time, the Bolton and Wigan businesses were expanding in such a way as to offer a more satisfactory outlet for Lever's energies. There was a large trade in soap, potted meat, mustard, starch, blacklead, and dairy produce. It was above all in the consumption of imported butter and eggs that the spreading benefits of Victorian prosperity were to be seen. Even before Lever was born, farmers in Lancashire and Cheshire were grumbling about the competition of Irish butter brought over on the new steamboats. The Englishman of 1881 was eating about six times as much in the way of imported foods as his parents had done in 1840. Smiles's disciple was quick to seize the opportunity. He saw that to buy supplies from middlemen meant unnecessary expense and a delay of at least twenty-four hours in delivery. Already in 1874 he had been searching for supplies of butter in Brittany. In 1879 he was in Ireland, appointing his own agents to attend the markets. These buyers had their own stands, and would meet the farmers on their way to market and so get the first and freshest butter and eggs. Packing and despatch depots were set up and William Lever, jointly with his brother, James Darcy, patented a special packing case for eggs. But already, at this early stage, Lever grasped firmly a principle that he was to follow throughout his career. Standards of living and individual incomes might be rising, but it was not enough to wait for a market to develop. The market could be created and expanded. Accordingly he began an intensive campaign of advertising Irish butter in the Press: a great trade in 'Ulster Fresh Lumps' grew up, mainly with Lancashire customers, and Lever & Co. became the largest wholesale grocers between Manchester and Liverpool. In 1886 Lever was in Holland looking for more butter. There he had some dealings with a Dutch merchant and manufacturer called Anton Jurgens—he was to become more familiar with the name later. In the same year he was buying dairy produce from Copenhagen. In all these operations he tried to carry out the sound principle—enunciated by writers on business methods since the seventeenth century but seemingly an eternal novelty —of buying from the original producer, selling to the final customer and eliminating middlemen's profits. His methods did not go unchallenged. There was energetic opposition from the merchants who suffered by it and Lever gladly seized upon the opportunity for publicity offered by a controversy in the local Press.

To Lever, however, the Press was not enough to provide a link between a business and its customers, and a desire for some more intimate connection combined naturally with his own flair for journalism to produce the *Lancashire Grocer* in 1885. This was a monthly private trade publication which printed price lists, advertisements of leading brands of commodities, items of current interest to the trade, technical articles, and moral anecdotes designed to drive home the virtues of high probity in business dealings. The *Lancashire Grocer* did not run for very long but it provides a valuable link between two distinct phases in Lever's career. For in 1884, Lever had come to the conclusion that he had exploited the potentialities of the grocery business to the full. Indeed, the idea of retirement had crossed his mind, and while on holiday in the Orkneys he confessed to Jonathan Simpson that he never felt more disinclined to return to business in his life, and was toying with the idea of turning his business into a limited liability company and buying a small island in the Orkneys. But time was to prove that this kind of mood was invariably the prelude to a new burst of activity. His thoughts turned back to soap—wrapping of soap had been his first occupation when he entered the grocery business: if the rising standard of living enabled people to buy more butter and eggs, why should it not enable them to buy more soap? Since 1874, the grocery business had been selling a soap made especially for Lever, called 'Lever's Pure Honey'. But in 1875 the Trade Marks Act had come into operation: there was no goodwill in the name: many grocers were selling soaps described as 'Pure Honey'. It is clear that already Lever, though not technically expert in soap making, had the firm intention of establishing a soap of distinctive quality. The more successful it was, the greater the risk that others would try to copy his trade-mark. A distinctive trade-mark was as important as a distinctive soap. On his return from his Hebridean holiday his first business was to call on the best trade-mark and patent agent in Liverpool, W. P. Thompson, to ask for a suitable trade-mark—one which could be upheld in the law courts if an imitation came along. Thompson wrote down half a dozen names on half a sheet of notepaper. 'But really,' said Lever later, 'at first blush, none of those names appealed to me. I had big ideas of some sort of name—I did not know what—but it was going to be such a marvel, and when I saw it written down in cold ink—the names that were possible—names that you could register and fight for, names that did not describe the article, that were neither geographical nor descriptive, did not refer to quality, and got over all the obstacles that the Trade Marks Law has very properly put in front of us—none of them appealed to me. I put the list in my pocket and went away feeling disappointed.' All the same he kept the list before him. Three or four days later it flashed across him that on the list was the name he was looking for. The name was 'Sunlight'. 'When that occurred to me I had to go straight off to Liverpool and ask Thompson to register it at once: I was all in a tremble to have it registered, for fear somebody else had got it.' Lever's intuition did not mislead him. He had stumbled on a name that could not only be registered in England but in every country in the world.

As the pages of the *Lancashire Grocer* show, the soap that later came to be known as 'Sunlight' did not, in these early days, occupy the whole of the picture. The name was used to cover a range of bar soaps of the traditional character—pale, mottled, and so on—which Lever had made for him as 'own name' soaps, i.e. soaps made for Lever to sell and have stamped with his brand name instead of the maker's. The system was described in a contemporary advertisement in the *Lancashire Grocer*:

> NO SINGLE MANUFACTURER is equally successful in the boiling of every soap he makes: some being noted as the best makers for Pale soap, others, again, as the best for Mottled and so on through each variety.
>
> BY SELECTING ONLY THE BEST SOAPS from each maker, we present a uniformity of quality, under 'Sunlight' Brand, obtainable from no individual maker in the United Kingdom.

All the soaps then were branded 'Sunlight'. And they were made for Lever by a number of manufacturers—Hazlehurst's of Runcorn, noted for their brown bar soaps, Gossage's of Widnes, whose 'blue mottled' was famous outside England as well as at home, and Joseph Watson's of Leeds, a growing firm of tallow soap makers. And Lever was probably satisfied by the ordinary soaps they made for him. There was, however, one soap made from oils rather than tallow. It was described in the same advertisement:

> BESIDES THE ORDINARY CLASSES OF SOAPS, we have had manufactured expressly for 'Sunlight' Brand and from our own instructions, 'special' soaps, such as 'SELF-WASHER' (Registered) 'HARD WATER', in the making of which great attention has been given to quality and the requirements of the district.

When or where Lever obtained the formula for this soap is not clear but it was from the first his favourite child. Describing it late in life, he wrote, 'I liked this soap very much. I made a speciality of it, and called it "Sunlight Self-Washer", for I claimed that it could wash of itself.' The new soap was widely advertised around Wigan and Bolton. A contract was fixed up with the London and North-Western and the Lancashire and Yorkshire Railway Companies: plates were to be exhibited on the stations. Shakespeare came in handy:

SUNLIGHT SELF-WASHER SOAP
'SEE HOW THIS BECOMES THE HOUSE'

But there were difficulties: the manufacture of the new soap was not properly understood by the makers. It sweated drops of oil, and made the fingers oily; in time it went rancid and smelt badly; and the defects outweighed its good lathering qualities. Customers sent the soap back and Lever remonstrated with the makers. The makers tried again but still the same thing happened, and Lever was getting disheartened. Then an incident happened which made him think that he was right after all, in spite of the makers' opposition. 'One day', wrote Lever, 'a customer walked into our warehouse at Wigan—I remember her quite well: it is funny how I still remember the names of those old customers—and said *I want some more of that stinking soap*. Her customers, although the soap stank, came back for it because, of course, it was only rancid on the outside; you had just got to use the soap for a few times in your hands and this outer skin which had gone rancid was all washed away, and the soap underneath was as good and sweet and fresh as soap could possibly be. It was not rancid right through: it was only the effect of the oxygen in the air, which oxygenized the oil and made it rancid; the inside, if you cut a bar in two, was always perfect soap.'

Lever had not only produced a new type of soap: he had evolved a new way of presenting it to the public. For the anonymous bulk of the existing bar soaps he substituted tablet soap wrapped in imitation parchment which preserved both appearance and scent and kept his name before the buyer. The idea was of American origin, unlike the next development, which was entirely his own. 'In the spring of 1886 I was going from Liverpool and I noticed in a grocer's shop window he had put our tablets of soap, which were wrapped in parchment papers, close up against the glass which interfered with the good appearance of the soap. I had to consider how I could remedy this and decided to put the soap in cartons. I had never heard of a laundry soap to that time, in any part of the world, being put in cartons.'

The makers, however, continued to dislike the new soap; more serious, having secured Lever as a regular customer, they were showing signs of putting up their prices. Lever surveyed the situation as a whole: if the incompetence and ill-will of the manufacturers encouraged him to contemplate manufacturing for himself, there were other factors pointing in the same direction. The onset of the Great Depression of the mid-eighties might spell gloom for the basic industries; for the soap industry it promised cheap raw materials and bigger profits, for falling prices meant that money would buy more consumer goods, and reduced employment in the textile industries made available ample labour for soap making. A big London soap manufacturer could report: 'The year 1885 was again a prosperous one, showing a considerable increase in the sale of soap . . . prices of Soap, Tallow and Oils were lower this year than we had ever previously known. . . .' And the following year: 'Prices of Tallow, Soap Tallow and Oils show no advance on last year, in fact we have never known them so low.'

Such were the economic conditions which encouraged Lever to consider manufacture. James Lever did not agree: once a grocer, always a grocer, was his motto, and he flatly refused to lend capital for the venture. His opposition crumbled, however, in face of William's determination, and a loan was arranged to enable William to start a soap factory as a branch of the wholesale grocery business. Lever already had his eye on a works at Warrington, Winser & Company, run by a chemical firm which had made good soap but lost money every year. 'A few tons a week' was how Lever described their output; his conviction was that nobody could make a profit unless he sold at least a hundred tons a week. He approached Winser's, and agreed to take their works on a six years' lease at a rental, including the plant and machinery, with an option of purchasing the plant and machinery at any time during the six years. Although the Warrington business was tiny by later Lever standards, small even by comparison with neighbours like Gossage's or Crosfield's, its beginnings were not unambitious. The original capital was £27,000 raised partly by withdrawals from the grocery business, and partly by loans within the family. The works might be small, but Lever had made his plans and they would need capital. Lever never failed to give himself plenty of financial elbow-room.

Along with the works, Lever took over two men who were to make a substantial contribution to his success—Percy J. Winser, the works manager, and Edward Wainwright, the soap boiler. Winser was a trained chemist, and evidently a better technician than business man. Lever had great confidence in Winser; he was at once admitted to the management of the new business and continued to hold a responsible and confidential position until his health failed. Probably he was at his best as second-in-command with the real decisions and responsibilities resting on a more robust personality. He in turn trusted his chief and was, for the most part, content to accept his lead. In Edward Wainwright, Lever was fortunate to inherit a practical soap boiler of great resource and experience—the founder, moreover, of a dynasty of soap boilers, for Edward had a brother and three sons; between them they pretty well monopolized the knowledge of practical soap making of Lever Brothers. So long as Edward could deal directly with Mr. Lever and Mr. Winser he was content. He did not aspire to the board. Edward's value was revealed when he took offence over a staff appointment and threatened to remove himself, his family and his secrets elsewhere. Winser wrote to Lever: 'There is no one in his Dept. (except his *son* and his *brother*) who has *any idea* of soap making, and a change would be very awkward.' Lever himself smoothed the matter over. The Wainwrights were too good to lose.

The factory at Warrington was taken over by William Lever and his brother in August 1885, and the first experimental boil of soap took place on October 27th. The original formula contained a very high proportion of vegetable oil—Palm Kernel oil 46 per cent, Cottonseed oil 44 per cent, Tallow 3 per cent, and Resin 7 per cent—and it was not entirely satisfactory. 'Nut oil', Winser explained, created 'an irritating effect on the skins of many persons', and the soap when dry 'was like a stone'. Cotton oil, he added, made soap unfit for laundry use. Yet in proper proportion the two ingredients made an excellent soap. The amount of cotton oil eventually had to be reduced because the soap proved wasteful in hot water and the smell lingered in the clothes; so cottonseed oil was partly replaced by tallow. Eventually, after a series of trials and errors, the ideal formula was settled on: it was:

	%
Copra Oil or Kernel Oil	41·9
Tallow	24·8
Cotton Oil	23·8
Resin	9·5

and until the twentieth century it varied but little. Unlike the majority of its competitors, Lever's soap was a 'pure' soap which contained no 'filling' of silicate of soda.

By January 1886, the works were turning out twenty tons a week. 'That', remarked Lever, 'was the utmost capacity of the works.' Having perfected his quality, however, Lever turned his mind to the question of quantity; and if output be the criterion of industrial progress, he achieved, within a short time and with the aid of nothing more technical than common sense and ingenuity, a minor industrial revolution. Together with Winser and Wainwright he studied the problems of quantity production. 'I had first to resort', he explained, 'to putting rings round the soap pans—that is, carved iron rings which increased the depth of the pan by two or three feet, and gave greater boiling capacity that in our case increased the capacity by about fifty per cent. Then I had to get more pans, and had struggles with the makers to get the pans down in a hurry.' For although he had as yet only one agent (H. Whitehead who had been manager of a Co-operative Society) orders were pouring in. The warehouseman was seen every day to ensure that orders were despatched without delay and, confident that somehow or other the soap would be forthcoming, Lever went on advertising. 'We ourselves chose the positions for our advertising plates on the railways, and the advantages of right hand or left hand side of a booking office were matters that received personal and weighty consideration.' By the end of 1886 the new pans were installed and a new wooden building was run up to house them. By December 1887, the works had a capacity of 450 tons a week—more than twenty-two times the original production. In addition to soap, a valuable side-line was developed in glycerine. Since 1880, leading soap makers had been working on the production of this valuable by-product of soap manufacture. Lever saw its tremendous possibilities from the start, and by the end of 1886 a glycerine plant was working. Lever found his market for soap locally in Bolton and Wigan. The subsequent growth of sales is best described in his own vigorous language: 'When I got it established there and making money, I ventured forth to Liverpool and Manchester. Established there and making money I ventured as far north as Newcastle and as far south as Plymouth with the intervening country more or less opened up. Established there and making money I opened up in London, Scotland and elsewhere and covered the United Kingdom. The following year I opened up overseas, in Holland, Belgium, Sydney, South Africa, Canada, etc., and so I let it grow in this way.'

To some men, progress of these dimensions would have been satisfying enough. It merely whetted Lever's appetite. In 1887 he was negotiating with his landlord for a further building lease. The landlord proved unhelpful. There was trouble about the construction of sidings and quays; and the new rent for a small piece of land was bigger than the rent for the whole of the original site. In the end Lever began to build without waiting for the completion of the lease. 'I had to do so. To think of all those orders pouring in and having no soap! I was going to keep the customers supplied, and I built the new works without a lease.' But it was already clear that the Warrington site was unsatisfactory: it was hedged in by the London and North Western Railway on two sides, the Mersey on the third side, and a pumping station and reservoirs on the fourth. With his thoughts running in terms of thousands of tons a week, this was not good enough: moreover, the landlord had annoyed him. He began to look for fresh fields.

Meantime, though Warrington was run on economical enough lines so far as staff was concerned—Lever used to say that he was advertising manager, cashier, and sales manager all rolled into one—the financing of the new plant and building, and larger stocks of raw materials created serious problems. The Warrington bankers were not particularly forthcoming: Warrington was also the home of the second biggest firm of soap manufacturers in England, Joseph Crosfield & Sons, and the bankers may well have doubted the capacity of the newcomer to stand up to their competition. Lever therefore found a different way of meeting the needs of his new project: he realized his share in the wholesale grocery business. His faith, thus demonstrated, was justified, for a year later he was able to claim that the sales of the new brand of 'Sunlight' were larger than those of any other single brand of soap in the United Kingdom. But the incident left its mark. He never lost his impatience with the timidity of what he used to call 'the banker's mind'.

Lever had no intention of remaining at Warrington, at a landlord's mercy, a moment longer than necessary. As he wrote some years later: 'I had to take the land at Warrington for immediate extensions, but I only covered it with wooden buildings, and only took it on a short lease, the object of the wooden buildings being, as they were tenant's fixtures, that they were removable.' No sooner was the lease for the new land at Warrington signed than Lever, accompanied by a local architect named William Owen, was off on a search for a fresh site. 'I went', he wrote later, 'along the banks of the Mersey, on both sides of the river, taking trains to different points. Then I came across to where Port Sunlight is. I remember looking over the field gate—situated right in front of the present office door—the gate which led into the field in which the whole of the works now are. As I looked over and saw the water facilities and the railway, I said, "Here we are", and I never looked any further.' Lever enlarged, on a number of subsequent occasions, on the reasons for his choice. His expositions make an interesting study in the science of industrial location. Certain requirements had to be fulfilled. Dependent as the soap maker must be on imported raw materials, water and rail facilities were a primary consideration. The new site lay in open fields and marshes between the Mersey and the railway line from Birkenhead to Chester. 'Anything more unprepossessing than this site can hardly be imagined,' wrote the late W. L. George in his *Labour and Housing at Port Sunlight*, published in 1910. 'It was mostly but a few feet above high-water level and liable at any time to be flooded by high tides and thus to become indistinguishable from the muddy foreshores of the Mersey. Moreover, an arm of Bromborough Pool spread in various directions through the village, filling the ravines with ooze and slime; a few houses, or rather shanties, were scattered on the higher portions, whose condition as regards sanitation can easily be conjectured. It was land suitable for a dock, but it did not, at first sight, seem fitted for human settlement.' With that extraordinary intuitive sense which was to stand him in good stead so often, Lever immediately grasped the potentialities of the site. As he explained at a banquet at the Bear's Paw Restaurant, Liverpool, which followed the cutting of the first sod by his wife on 3rd March 1888, it was far enough up the river to be out of the reach of the Liverpool Dock and Harbour Dues: and these dues were a considerable item in soap costs—on a ton of tallow they might come to as much as 4s. 10d. At Bromborough Pool on the river bank, there was an anchorage where the incoming ships could tranship their cargoes to flats: then straight to the works. Compared with the arrangements at Warrington, this meant a saving of something like 8s. 7d. to 9s. a ton. And water transport gave Lever a good bargaining position with the railways. He had had painful experience at Warrington with the 'Railway Monopoly'. True, there were five railways there, but, as he explained, 'you very soon begin to learn that they are like the old Yeomanry Cavalry, which moved at the speed of the slowest man. It is not a question of the majority fixing the rates of carriage, but any alterations of a rate to any point must be unanimous on the part of the companies running to that point. The result is we are never able to get any concession.' But at Bromborough Lever was independent of the railways. He could load his own cargoes, send them to sea and round to London. 'That', he added, 'is the only kind of logic—the logic of a strong position—that I have ever found the railway companies would listen to.' The site would enable him, he reckoned, to produce soap at a cost 'below which no one can go'.

Next came the question of space. Lever's policy was to buy land well ahead of his immediate needs. He was determined not to repeat his Warrington experience. It was essential to have 'ample room for works without crowding, and plenty of space for the erection of dwelling-houses for the workpeople employed, which', he added, 'has always been our idea.' The first purchase was 56 acres, and the first priority was the building of the new works—little more than half of what is now 'No. 1 Soapery'—together with offices and wharf, alongside which the barges could bring raw material cargoes at high tide. Lever enjoyed a temporary buyer's market in land. For one thing, no one else seems to have seen the possibilities of this unlovely and unpromising site as Lever did: and local landowners were sceptical as to the success of the new venture. They were, apparently, only too willing to sell while Lever still had capital. Cheshire did not give Lancashire a very long run for its money at this point. So Lever went on buying ahead. Over a period of years, he bought an area for both works and village of almost 330 acres. In 1906, 90 acres were covered by works, railways, sidings, wharves and docks, and 140 acres by the village, while

100 acres were held in reserve. But in March 1888 this was all in the future. Lever was none too well supplied with capital. 'We shall not', he told his guests at the opening banquet, 'be able to build those houses at present simply because it will require all the capital we can spare to build our works: but that is a matter for the future.' It was not so far in the future: his idea was 'to build houses in which our workpeople will be able to live and be comfortable—semi-detached houses, with gardens back and front, in which they will be able to know more about the science of life than they can in a back slum, and in which they will learn that there is more enjoyment in life than in the mere going to and returning from work, and looking forward to Saturday night to draw their wages'. By the end of the same year, William Owen was instructed to prepare plans for twenty-eight cottages and an entrance lodge. The work began the following spring. As fast as money could be found the buying and the building went on.

Finally, it was necessary that there should be an adequate supply of labour in the neighbourhood of the factory. This, Lever could obtain from the nearby town of Birkenhead.

There was, then, only one minor disadvantage at Port Sunlight: buying land ahead of requirements meant a loss of interest on capital. The advantages in Lever's view were that the works could spread horizontally instead of vertically: this reduced the risk of fire and the cost of handling goods, provided healthy conditions for the workers, gave better ventilation in the works, better light, greater freedom from dirt and dust. Departments could be marshalled and arranged so as to give a more systematic handling of goods. Good houses and country air meant a more settled body of workers. Children might grow up in healthy conditions which would guarantee a still further improvement each succeeding generation. In all these matters, Lever was no doubt recollecting the conditions at his neighbours' factory at Warrington—Crosfield's—where some years later he observed that 'buildings piled storey upon storey, departments interlace and overlap, some are badly lighted owing to the impossibility of getting daylight into them, and in the frame room they actually have to have an arrangement by which they can take up the flooring from certain sections as soon as the frames are emptied, in order to let light into the floor below'. All such disadvantages,

Lever was determined to avoid. If Port Sunlight was the conception of a visionary, the visionary was also a business man. And nearly twenty years later, Lever could still wholeheartedly recommend that industry in general would do well to follow his own example and move out of large centres of population such as London into the country.

With the removal to Port Sunlight in January 1889 there was a further spectacular leap in production. The output in 1886 had been just under 3,000 tons; in 1887 it had more than trebled to 9,669 tons; 1888 saw it rise to 14,183 tons. The transfer of operations to the new factory necessarily delayed full expansion, and in the first full year at Port Sunlight 15,688 tons was produced.

Thereafter, with the exception of one year, 1896, output rose swiftly by annual increments which varied between 3,000 and 5,000 tons. This increased production was only possible by careful adaptation of plant and industrial methods. At Warrington, Lever had been compelled to resort to makeshifts; at Port Sunlight, improved square pans were introduced. Experiments had shown that the optimum size was a pan fourteen feet square with a capacity of thirty-three tons of finished soap. For heating, closed coils had been used at Warrington: at Port Sunlight the pans were heated by open steam coils which gave the soap boiler much more efficient control of the process. Lever himself, though he always declined to be regarded as a technical soap expert, presided over bi-monthly meetings of the Port Sunlight managers—Winser, J. S. Ferguson (a brother-in-law and an original member of the Warrington partnership), and Scott, the head chemist. The number of technical problems discussed at these meetings testifies to the spirit of scientific inquiry which Lever encouraged in his enterprise. The recovery of waste heat from condensers: the boiling down of caustic liquors in steam boilers; the reform of the glycerine department—and so on. What went on in the new laboratory was considered a State secret, and two chemists were actually dismissed for disclosing information to members of the factory staff. Lever was taking no risks with his competitors—already only too anxious to tap the secrets of the success of the new arrival. Things did not always run smoothly. There was friction between Winser and Scott. Scott was apparently jealous of Winser and Lever was hard put to it to steer a course between the two of them. Old loyalty inclined him to the side of Winser. Scott was, he opined, 'the more brilliant and energetic of the two, Winser the more thoughtful and careful'. In the end, after a dispute, Scott went, and Lever recorded in his diary his conviction that this was the only solution—'now after a few days I am quite satisfied that it is all for the best, and that with his nature it would have been difficult to get along with any degree of comfort or profit—he would have daily come more and more into competition with Mr. Winser to whom we owe more our position with regard to the quality of Sunlight Soap and therefore to the trade than we do to any one man besides.'

Most important of all Lever had to consider the market which his soap was to serve. Here the changing social situation was his paramount concern. The working classes alone had numbers sufficient to realize his ideal of making large-scale enterprise depend on a low rate of profit and a huge turnover; and rising wages had brought soap within their means. Here was a vast potential market yet only partially exploited. The working class housewife had to be convinced that soap—and not merely any soap but Lever's soap—was not a luxury or a semi-necessity but an indispensable necessity for her home.

The Lever advertising campaign really falls into two phases. In the first phase, when the market was still relatively unexploited, its object was the fairly simple one of drawing the attention of the housewife to soap and creating consumers of soap out of people who before consumed little or no soap. In the second phase, as competition increased and imitators arose, the task became the more arduous one of fighting other makers for a market which was fast becoming 'saturated'. The first phase is the time of slogans, of plates on the railway stations and hoardings, of newspaper advertising: the second is the age of the highly competitive 'prize schemes'. The two phases are never entirely separate but the emphasis is clearly differentiated.

For the first twenty years, then, Lever relied on Sunlight Soap and a large working class market, exploited by energetic advertising campaigns. His imagination grasped clearly the details of the problem and the psychology of his customers. 'In the very first handbook we issued with Sunlight Soap which was got up by myself, entitled *Sunlight Soap and How to Use It*, everything was brought down to the level of a working man's needs. The only point where I went beyond this was with instructions for cleaning pampas grass, feathers and so on, but I view these as to be found in many working men's houses, the pampas grass in a jar on the Bible in the sitting room and the feathers in the hats of the daughters.'

The famous slogan 'Why does a Woman look old sooner than a Man?' had a similar aim. It was coupled with the suggestion to 'put a man at a washing tub, let him get heated with the hot suds until every pore is opened, then let him stand over the filthy steam that comes from the scalding and boiling clothes', and obviously the subject of this inhuman experiment would be no wealthy millowner or Liverpool shipping magnate, but rather the husband of some 'factory housewife'. The pages of the *Lancashire Grocer*, from which this advertisement is quoted, are full of appeals to every side of minds made literate, but hardly educated, by Forster's Act of 1870.

The novelette, the melodrama, and doggerel verse were all pressed into service. The aristocratic beauty made her appearance in the advertisement column. In 'The Lady Gwendolin's Lament', stanzas of eight lines told how:

> The brow that once was snowy white
> Was lined by grief and care;
> The lips that once were ruby bright
> Were pale from blank despair,

and what followed therefrom. Her Ladyship visited numerous beauty specialists, but the results were most disheartening until

> At last the Lady Mary Bright
> Came laughing in one day,
> But when she saw her friend, a fright,
> She started in dismay.

Fortunately she soon recovered, 'smiles clothed her winsome face', and

> She added: 'Gwenny don't despair,
> With joy you'll quickly sing,
> To make poor women fresh and fair
> I've found the only thing.

'’Twill make your brow as snowy white,
As free from grief and care,
As when with youth your eyes were bright
And cheeks beyond compare,
This article, if you but try,
Will realize each hope.
Go send your maid at once, and buy
A box of Sunlight Soap.'

Prize schemes were the next venture, the first essay of this type of advertising being an offer of £2,000 to 'Religious and Benevolent Institutions', which were to be chosen by votes recorded on Sunlight cardboxes. When, however, Lever went on to offer '£400 in prizes' to those who most nearly guessed (again with the aid of Sunlight packing materials) the number of votes given to the winner, it became difficult to decide whether he was more concerned to give the public a chance to exercise the virtue of charity or to indulge the vice of getting something for nothing. As the schemes grew, the motive behind them became quite unambiguous: later on, Lever, referring to one just concluded, wrote that 'the winner of the first prize, the motor, had 25,000 wrappers. For them he received a motor, price £250 and I think, 9 or 11 bicycles, price £9 each; therefore you will see that he got the soap for less than nothing.' The usual method was to offer prizes to customers who collected a prescribed number of Sunlight wrappers. These facts go far to explain why this particular method of advertising became in the end such an intolerable burden on the industry that determined efforts were made to end it by agreement between the competing firms, despite the fact that it succeeded in its primary purpose of increasing the sale of soap.

Lever's devices were regarded by the old-established makers with contempt at first and very speedily with alarm, followed by imitation, tardily adopted by some but promptly by others, notably by Joseph Watson. In 1899, the older firms were much concerned over 'audacious advertising in connection with the Board School at Ipswich', and the Secretary of the Soap Makers' Association wrote to the relevant authority that he had before him 'a copy of the *Sunlight Year Book*, a book of nearly 500 pages profusely illustrated, which is being sent round to the masters and mistresses of elementary schools'. Two days later, in some agitation, he wrote again of 'a case at North Walsham, at which town the Mistress of a Board School has been distributing advertisements and prizes in connection with "Sunlight Soap", "Matchless Cleanser", and "Beecham's Pills"'. 'Absolute and immediate prohibition' was his demand: whether it was realized the records do not show.

Soap-making reputations had hitherto been built up on non-proprietary articles of the same general nature, and as Christr. Thomas, the Bristol soap maker, pointed out later on 'there is little or no difference in quality between different makes of Bar Soaps—there is a Thomas's Primrose, a Knight's Primrose, a Cook's Primrose—all the same soap. It is impossible, therefore by the nature of the case to . . . [attempt] through advertising to create a demand in favour of any one particular make.' But W. H. Lever, with his device of the branded speciality, had upset this state of affairs: he had shown how to 'create a demand', and at the same time how to break into other people's markets. No wonder the other people disliked his 'extravagant and hazardous advertising, and the offering of various prizes to both dealers and consumers'.

There is little doubt that both these things—the new method of advertising and the object advertised—which so upset the older makers had a common country of origin: America. The central pillar of Lever Brothers' edifice was the wrapped bar of soap, and in one lawsuit which Lever's brought against a competitor their Counsel told the Court that 'the plaintiffs got the idea of the wrappers from an American paper'.[1] In his diary of the American tour which he made in 1888 Lever himself recorded the genesis of the slogan 'Why does a Woman look old sooner than a Man', which he bought from Frank Siddal, a Philadelphian soap maker, and the *Lancashire Grocer's* pages teem with transatlantic material. This is mostly in the form of articles and stories reprinted from American newspapers and periodicals, but how it came into Lever's hands is a mystery. Its presence argues an intimate connection with the United States, dating from a very early period of his career.

No possible opportunity of pushing Sunlight was neglected. In 1889 Lever was involved in a quarrel with W. P. Frith, the popular artist, who objected to the use of his picture 'The New

[1] *Wigan Journal*, 13 May 1885.

Frock' as an advertisement. Lever commented publicly that 'Mr. Frith reminds me of the young lady who is asked to play the piano. She simpers and says no, and after a struggle is led to the keyboard, and plays as she really wished to do from the first. . . . My opinion is that Mr. Frith is rather pleased.'[1] Artistic pleasure or displeasure notwithstanding, the enterprising advertiser held to his course, and in 1892 visited the Academy where he 'bought a picture for the works—called "Wedding Morning" by Bacon. It is only a moderate picture but very suitable for soap advertisement.'

The idea which provoked this venture into art criticism, like so much else of Lever's advertising, reached the public by way of the printed page, but he was far from relying on that alone as a means of contact. He considered it part of his business not merely to sell his goods to the wholesalers, but to penetrate into the homes of the final users and demonstrate visibly that Sunlight had the qualities which he claimed for it. This was peculiarly the job of the 'District Agents', or as they later became know, the 'Assistant Travellers', without whom Lever would have been like a general without an army. The object of *Progress*, a magazine founded in 1899 and directed to employees and shareholders, seems to have been principally to stimulate the effort of the District Agents since exhortation and advice to the outdoor sales force make up a large proportion of the reading matter, which takes its tone from such improving precepts as 'Ding-Dong every day, every hour, every minute,—that's the way to success and happiness'.

Enthusiastic, enterprising, and, one suspects, self-laudatory District Agents are continually held up to the admiration of their less energetic colleagues. We have, for instance, the tale of the schoolmaster's cuff:

> 'Calling today on a certain schoolmaster,' writes D. A. Sutton, 'he asked me if we had a special soap for cleansing composite cuffs and collars. I thought MONKEY BRAND would be a suitable thing, so, drawing a sample out of my bag, I asked the schoolmaster for a clean cloth and a little water and also for one of the cuffs he was wearing, which was rather unclean. Mr. S. was delighted with the result.'

[1] *Pall Mall Gazette*, 18 July 1889.

No doubt he was also rather surprised, but probably not more than the wedding guests who met another of Lever's young men:

> That one can combine business with pleasure is the burden of one of D. A. Bramwell's reports. He attended a wedding party a few weeks ago, and made use of the opportunity to do a little canvassing by asking the ladies present to name what they considered to be the best soap for household purposes. There were 19 ladies present and this is the result of the voting:

For Sunlight . . .	10
,, Lifebuoy . . .	5
,, Other makes . .	4
Majority for Sunlight and Lifebuoy combined .	11

Besides these tales of enterprise, the same pages are full of education in salesmanship, particularly its finer points, such as the fact that 'showing the people that Swan Soap will float is a very good method, and especially where there are children as the latter bother their mothers to buy some'. This strategy of indirect approach was very widely applied: travellers were also told that people 'are easily humoured by little attentions such as stepping over a step that has just been washed, closing gates, and such small items as these, which, however small they may seem, generally have a great effect on housekeepers', and, of course, lead to bigger orders for Sunlight Soap.

By all these means, then, by appeals to romance, to religion, to cupidity, and to any other instinct or idea which he could press into his service, Lever thrust his goods upon the attention of potential users. His success, based as it was firmly on excellence, stood plain for all to see in the unchecked growth of his undertaking during the first twenty years of its existence. How far that success was due to advertising, and how far to other causes, is a question which cannot be exactly answered, but the importance attached to publicity by Lever may be judged from the following figures: advertising cost Lever a mere £50 in the first year at Warrington, during the next twenty years advertising costs amounted in all to two million pounds, a prodigious sum by contemporary standards. The economic principles behind advertising were explained as follows: 'Mr. Lever had always viewed advertising somewhat as a reserve of energy. The cost of advertising is not paid for by the consumer; it can only be paid for by increased sales, if increased sales result, and it may be viewed as a storage battery upon which in a time of stress . . . drafts might be made for a limited period.' So much, then, for cost, which he evidently regarded not as a fixed charge, but as something which varied with the prosperity of the business. On the function for which this money was paid, he wrote at some length to an advertising agent in after years.

> You deal with a subject of the greatest interest and one that receives generally far too little consideration, viz., that the cost of selling including the retailers' and wholesalers' profits exceeds the cost of manufacture excluding the cost of raw materials, but it seems to me obvious that this must always be the case. Under any system the cost of manufacture is kept low by modern machinery and by repetition of the same process automatically. The selling and distribution must often be an individual transaction between the distributor and the consumer which cannot be automatic. The consumer knows for instance, that to buy a sack of flour is cheaper than to buy flour a few pounds at a time, but the consumer who buys a sack of flour often loses heavily from not being able to consume the whole of the flour while the same is in the best condition and often from waste in the household if there is a sack of flour always ready to be dipped into. Economy to the consumer is a sub-division even into penny packets. Economy to the manufacturer is on the contrary principle to this, viz., aggregation and repetition. As I gather your point is to call attention to advertising it is obvious that by means of advertising the manufacturer is making less costly the distribution. The consumer of an article goes into a shop with full knowledge of the article wanted, the shopman's time is not wasted in explaining it, the manufacturer's time is not wasted in the cost of salesmen explaining the merits of the article, reducing the number of calls and the cost of each sale. Advertising is as near bringing the manufacturing conditions of repetition to the selling side of the business as possible.

This was not only a shrewd analysis of the functions of advertising; it was also an indication of the way in which the emphasis in British industry was shifting from the problems of production to those of distribution and salesmanship. In the world of the earlier stages of the industrial revolution there had been little room for advertising. In the newer world of light and secondary industries, it was often advertising which decided who was to survive and grow, who was to dwindle and disappear.

CHAPTER IV

LIMITED LIABILITY AND A NATIONAL MARKET

'... The lead of the great industries was shortening: and, in compensation, capital, labour, and intelligence were flowing away to light industry, distribution, salesmanship.'

G. M. Young, of the British economy in the later Victorian Age. Victorian England, Portrait of an Age—*O.U.P., Fifth Impression,* 1949

IN the ten years after he first started making soap, Lever increased his total annual output from 2,946 tons to 38,788 tons, and in addition to Sunlight Soap he began making an increasing quantity of other soaps. The extension of the factory and the village called for enormous capital expansion. In 1890 the new soap venture was turned into a private company with an authorized capital of £300,000. Its resources were soon outpaced by Lever's ambitious plans and he determined to seek access to a wider capital market. In 1894 the private company gave way to a public company with an authorized capital of £1,500,000. For over thirty years this company, Lever Brothers Limited, was to be the instrument of Lever's expanding activities.

The first directors of the new company, besides William Lever as Chairman, were his brother (James Darcy Lever), his father (James Lever), and P. J. Winser. The new capital was divided into seventy-five thousand five per cent Cumulative Preference shares of £10 each and seventy-five thousand Ordinary shares of the same value. In June, Lever was busy on the issue of the first fifty thousand Preference shares. By the end of the first day after the prospectus was issued, applications had been received for eighty-nine thousand shares, and when the lists were closed a day or two later applications amounted to £2,000,000 or four times the amount required. Lever's highest expectations had been surpassed but none the less he confessed to his diary that by the end of the week he was 'thoroughly fagged out'. The reason for his success in the capital market was not far to seek. Not only had Sunlight Soap established itself as a proprietary article known all over England but Lever himself and the child of his imagination, Port Sunlight, were topics of nation-wide discussion. In 1891 Mr. Gladstone had opened a new men's dining-room and recreation hall at Port Sunlight, to which he allowed his name to be given; this had put a gilt edge round an enterprise whose early days had appeared to many to bear all the marks of a speculative venture. 'In this hall,' said the Grand Old Man, 'I have found a living proof that cash payment is not the only nexus between man and man . . . I cannot but think that this day must be for you and your brother a happy day, a day for the heart to bound within the breast, a day to inspire great thankfulness for the past, more hopefulness for the future.' Mr. Gladstone made an enormous impression upon William Lever. 'I could not sleep much that night: I had to walk up and down the park thinking of him. He made an extraordinary impression.' It is perhaps not too much to hazard that Mr. Gladstone quite involuntarily made an equal impression on the investing public.

Lever Brothers had, in a short space, been transformed from a speculative risk into almost a trustee security. When, three years later, their shares appeared on the market the issue was therefore heavily over-subscribed: and so it was to continue for many years.

Like hundreds of old-established partnerships in the nineties, Lever Brothers was swept along on the tide of limited liability. But limited liability was not to spell anonymity, nor to sweep away the homeliness of the family partnership and its trusted Lancashire followers. For one thing, Lever himself took good care that the transition from partnership to company organization was effected in a way which enabled Lever to retain sole control of policy.

His instrument was the ownership of the Ordinary shares of the business. Legally this did not confer control of the business for the Ordinary shares carried no special voting rights. In practice, however, the possession of a large block and ultimately of the whole of the Ordinary share capital combined with his unique knowledge of the business gave him a moral ascendancy which he was able to maintain to the end. The Preference shareholders were only too willing to leave the problems and the risks to a Chairman who never failed to give them what was their due reward.[1]

In the early days, it is true, there were three or four Ordinary shareholders associated with the business. Even this degree of split responsibility brought Lever into conflict with his fellow holders of Ordinary shares, and it became his aim to acquire complete control of the Ordinary share capital. Lever was an autocrat who would brook no contradiction from those who served under him and almost as little from those who served with him. His colleagues were men of more modest and ordinary talents and their cautious hesitancy was a constant irritation to him. As time went on, therefore, he offered them Preference shares in exchange for their Ordinary shares on a basis which made them very willing to accept. By 1902 he could write to a colleague: 'I have sold the last of my Preference shares to my brother, so that I am no longer happy in the secure position of Preference shareholder, but am standing on the mountain top clad in the kilts and tartan of a poor Ordinary shareholder. I find the costume and position a little chilly but bracing, and decidedly exciting—very like driving a Motor Car down a hill with the brakes off, viz. that it is all very nice so long as everything goes on all right, but we never know quite what may be in store for us at the bottom or at the first corner we have to turn.' Lever thus accepted full responsibility for policy, as well as the consequences

[1] In view of its later bearing on the capital structure of the company, it will be convenient here to state briefly the essential difference between Preference and Ordinary shares. The holder of a Preference share is entitled to receive a fixed dividend at a certain rate, payable out of profits, before any dividend at all is paid to the Ordinary shareholders. The Ordinary shareholder then receives such dividend as the directors may decide to distribute, to the extent that profits permit. Thus the profits available for Ordinary dividends depend, not only on the rate of earnings, but also on the amount of the prior claims of the Preference shareholders. The Ordinary shareholder is exposed to the full force of variations in the company's profits; the Preference shareholder, in virtue of his prior claim, can normally rely on a greater degree of security of income, but, however well the company may fare, he is not entitled to any greater share of the profits than his fixed preferential dividend. Where the amount of the Preference capital is disproportionately large in relation to the Ordinary capital, the profits available for the Ordinary shareholders may, in times of adversity, be entirely absorbed by the prior claims of the Preference shareholders, or they may not even be sufficient to meet the latter. For this reason, a capital structure unduly burdened by Preference or other prior charges, may be a source of weakness to a company in difficult times. For a full discussion see Lewis G. Whyte, *Principles of Finance & Investment* (Cambridge University Press), Vol. II, Chapter 18.

of good fortune or bad, reflected as these would be in the variations of the Ordinary dividend. He, thereby, preserved in his own person many of the qualities of the family business characteristic of an earlier age. The art of delegating authority was one he never learned.

The eighties had been the years of thrift, when Lever, living modestly at the rate of a few hundreds a year in a small house in a row at Wigan, was ploughing back the balance of his £50,000 income into his expanding business. The nineties were the years of fruition. 'The Chief', as he was known to everybody, between the ages of forty-three and fifty-six was at the zenith of his powers, his energies so abundant that he could lay the foundations of half a dozen overseas businesses, continue the development of his home business, fight three Parliamentary elections as a Liberal, plan the village of Port Sunlight, buy and almost entirely rebuild the village of Thornton Hough, enlarge Thornton Manor as well as buy and alter one house in London and one in Bolton. Sir Angus Watson has given us a vivid description of Lever about this time.

> Short and thickset in stature, with a sturdy body set on short legs and a massive head covered with thick, upstanding hair, he radiated force and energy. He had piercing, blue-grey humorous eyes, which, however, flashed with challenge when he was angry. A strong, thin-lipped mouth, set above a slightly receding chin, and the short neck and closely set ears of a prize-fighter. He possessed great physical strength and a gift of sleep which was always available at his command. His dress was almost always the same. A grey tweed suit, a Victorian-fashioned collar with a carelessly worn made-up tie, and a tall grey hat. A white silk shirt, and black shoes on his small shapely feet. Hands carefully attended to, which were also small. An expression always alert but rather strained because of the slight deafness, which increased as he grew older: a man who would have been singled out anywhere.[1]

His office at Port Sunlight was in the centre of the building, raised above the level of the surrounding offices, and had walls of glass. From here he could survey the activities of the staff. Practically the whole of the business was carried in his head and was directed by his verbal instruction. Board meetings were few and formal, and such consultation as he found necessary

[1] Angus Watson, *My Life* (Ivor Nicholson & Watson, 1937), pp. 140–1.

took place at informal dinner parties held at Thornton Manor, when 'wives accompanied their husbands, and Mrs. Lever would entertain her lady guests in the drawing-room, generally far beyond the conventional limit of time, while the men sat talking over their cigars'.[1]

From the office on the bridge came an unending stream of commands, prophecies, and exhortations. Managers abroad were kept up to the mark by letters in which not only the day-to-day problems of the business but the broader issues and even the philosophy of business were set forth in the minutest and clearest detail. Autocracy was of the essence of the system and woe betide the idle or the presumptuous. The secretary who was sufficiently ill-advised to recommend certain tactics for a meeting of Preference shareholders was crushed beneath an Olympian thunderbolt. 'I have always viewed you', wrote Lever, 'as thoroughly alive to what it is correct and proper for a Secretary to take upon himself. I am always glad to have your free expression of opinion on all matters that I may discuss with you. But until I do discuss a matter with you, I think you will agree with me that it is not within your province to lay your views before me. I hope that this will be the last time on which you will venture an expression of opinion as to what course I should take at a Meeting unless in response to a request from myself that you should do so.' Conversion into a public company did not shake in the slightest Lever's conviction that the business was his to control and that its successes were his own personal achievement. Discussion of policy was limited to a small circle. Of these, in the earliest days, James Darcy Lever was the chief, though his masterful brother's diaries show that even fraternal ties were not always proof against the strain of divergent ideas and temperaments. James Darcy's ambitions were so modest that when the family fortune reached £50,000 he suggested to William that they should rest content with their winnings and retire. Illness attacked him in 1895, and from that time onwards his part in the business was purely nominal, though he did not finally resign until 1897.

In 1897 four new directors joined the board, amongst whom was Martin Harvey. Like so many successful men of his generation, he was originally a traveller, and came to Lever's

[1] *Viscount Leverhulme by His Son.*

notice through taking Sunlight on commission. He rose very high in the Chairman's favour, was employed by him on confidential missions overseas and became Vice-Chairman of the Company. In 1902 for some reason which has not come to light, he 'voluntarily of his own accord sent in his resignation to Lever Bros.' The epitaph above his tomb in Lever's graveyard of reputations was: '... one of the best Salesmen I ever encountered, but the mistake I made in the case of Mr. Harvey was because I believed him capable of much better things than being a Salesman.' The other recruits to the board in 1897 were A. J. Wolfendale, W. Y. Robinson, and Robert Barrie. The first two soon resigned their directorships on appointment to exalted positions abroad (sometimes an equivocal compliment in the Lever service) but the third—'a quiet, shrewd, and able Scotsman'—remained in office until he died in 1909. Until the retirement of P. J. Winser, Barrie did not enter the innermost circle, but thereafter his frequent, detailed, and lively reports kept the Chairman closely in touch with the state of the raw material market with which, as chief buyer, he was principally concerned. P. J. Winser, in failing health, remained on the board, and evidently in close relationship with Lever, until 1901. The absorption of the firm of Benjamin Brooke[1] in the United States brought Sydney Gross, the head of that company, on to the board, and he remained with Lever Brothers until 1910. His 'forte' was advertising and he put Lever in contact with many leading contemporary comic artists, of whom the greatest was probably Phil May. He also ran the London trade, and maintained almost daily correspondence with headquarters, writing always, as befitted the former head of a prosperous business, who had entered the 'family' of his own accord, to his 'Dear Lever'. In 1899 Lever's nephew, J. L. Tillotson, was brought on to the board. Tillotson was an enigmatic figure. By all accounts autocratic and brusque of manner, he possessed considerable ability, retained Lever's confidence for the greater part of fifteen years, and was entrusted by him with a large measure of responsibility for affairs overseas. Not the least of his contributions was to overcome Lever's suspicions of the value to the business of recruits trained in the universities and public schools. Such were the directors in key positions at

[1] See Chapter VII.

headquarters during this vital period of expansion, but there was never any doubt as to where final sovereignty lay. Lever would listen to their proposals and their advice, but the final decision always rested with him. He it was who took the risks (and they were considerable), who turned the conditions of the markets to advantage when they were favourable and devised the necessary buffers against adversity.

No department of the business was more vital than the raw material buying: raw materials formed a large part of the cost of soap and largely determined its selling price. The public company had been floated on the falling tide of raw material prices which brought prosperity to the industry in 1895. Equally, the rise in prices towards the end of the century brought difficulties which roused other makers to a chorus of complaint. With that judgement that was at once the despair and the envy of his rivals, Lever had provided against the evil day and he could write to Henry Gross, a brother of Sydney, that, although raw materials continued to advance, he was 'satisfied that we are provisioned for a siege of high prices for two years ahead of the present time, that is, until 1902 commences'. But there was no complacency about his confidence. Already, with the cool detachment of the staff planner, he was preparing for the worst that might still be in store, and he continued:

> Beyond this of course it is out of the range of human foresight to provide, but if prices did continue high for a longer period, then undoubtedly a higher range of prices of Soap would take place and we should obtain relief by an advance in prices. This latter course, however, I cannot view without misgivings, and I should want all our competitors to have advanced well ahead of us before I made any move. I do not want to break the position we have all along occupied of one fixed price and one fixed quality. We have now had fourteen years without moving our price, and during that time we have had the advantage of low prices of Raw Materials. . . . I want therefore to show the sincerity of the position we have taken up by standing for an abnormally long period the siege of high prices, and this I am confident we can do without in any way altering the Balance Sheet, beyond perhaps having to go back to a 12½ per cent Dividend on our Ordinary shares.

Undoubtedly Lever deserved his successes. While other makers were compelled to raise their prices in 1901 and 1902, Lever succeeded in maintaining Sunlight at its old price, largely by reducing his expenditure on advertising and by the shrewd policy of raw material buying described above. By 1903 the worst of the crisis was over and by 1904 he was actually able to reduce wholesale prices.[1]

The reduction was itself evidence that competition in the United Kingdom was becoming ever more intense. In 1896 the story of continuous expansion of Sunlight sales was interrupted for the first time: sales fell from over 38,000 tons to just over 36,000 tons. In all probability Lever had seen the danger, for he had already taken steps to introduce new brands which helped to offset the loss. That did not mean that the battle for the laundry soap market was to be abandoned. New advertising schemes were set afoot and the upward movement was resumed in 1897 and continued with increasing momentum. But the successes which Lever scored in these years over his competitors, spectacular though they seemed to the outside world, concealed serious difficulties which were unknown to the other soap makers.

The area in which competition was most stubborn was that covered by the Newcastle, Leeds, and Port Sunlight Branch Offices, stretching from the Tyne and Humber on the East, across to the Mersey and Northwards up the West Coast. This was the home territory not only of Lever but of several of his most powerful rivals, particularly Watson's and Crosfield's; and they were always on the watch for any tactical error which their opponent might commit. In 1897 he played into their hands.

Wrapper schemes—the exchange of soap wrappers for gifts—had been a leading feature of Lever's selling policy since 1887. In fact he claimed to have introduced them into this country. In 1897 he came to the conclusion that these schemes had outrun their usefulness because in spite of heavy outlay on prize schemes in that year the increase in sales was not more than a normal one. At the end of the year, therefore, he decided that not only would he stop advertising prizes but that he would commence 'a policy of discouragement of that system of business'. We therefore have the curious spectacle of the inventor of gift schemes trying to put his own machine into reverse. The process was not simple. The new policy produced 'the strongest resentment' and he fell back on the not altogether commendable policy of

[1] See graph of raw material and retail soap prices, Vol. II, Appendix 9.

offering prizes which, on his own admission, were 'little better than rubbish, cheap so-called leather purses proving to be made of paper and so on'. The hope was that his customers would soon get tired of applying for them and yet go on buying his soap.

In this hope he was disappointed. Good salesman and North-countryman though he was, he had strangely misjudged the mentality of his customers in the North. The mistake soon became obvious. 'All through this district', as he explained later, 'there is a thrifty class of people who save bits of string, paper, rags, old newspapers, anything of value, and a trade is done in all these articles. These people formerly collected Sunlight Soap wrappers, and looked upon the prizes as a discount off the soap.' When Sunlight no longer offered a discount worth having, the thrifty Northerners began to look for soaps that did. Their search was not unrewarded. The schemes discarded by Lever were taken up with redoubled energy by his competitors who immediately pushed 'most energetically schemes for giving prizes for wrappers as we withdrew from that method of advertising'. The makers who had protested against Lever's methods of advertising in the late eighties were now the first to seize their opportunity. Crosfield's, for example, began to run 'a highly painted elaborate horse van in Manchester delivering their prizes from door to door'. Lever described its activities:

> When this elaborate van drives up into a side street, a smartly dressed attendant jumps out, goes to the door of the cottage and knocks, the whole street is aroused and every neighbour looks out to see what the van is going to Mrs. Jones's door for. The man I understand hands to Mrs. Jones the prizes she is to have for her wrappers, with the compliments of the firm, and the pleasure it gives them to hand the prizes to a user of their soaps. The van then rattles away to a neighbouring street. The neighbours put their heads together, go and look at the prizes Mrs. Jones has had, and presumably encouraged by her example consider it good business to use the same soaps that got Mrs. Jones these prizes.

Unmistakable danger signals began to come in showing that all was not well. Whitehead, who had been with Lever as chief salesman since 1884 and who knew his Co-operatives better than most, reported in 1902 that the Co-operatives throughout Lancashire and Yorkshire sold twenty-five per cent less Sunlight in the third quarter of that year than they had sold in the corresponding quarter of 1901. He put it down to the discontinuance of prize schemes. It seemed that Lever might be hoist with his own petard.

It was true that losses were almost entirely confined to the North of England. Elsewhere, his trade continued to expand at a satisfactory rate, especially in London. Nevertheless, the 'disaffected territory' as Lever himself, assuming the language of sovereignty, called it, was his own home, where he had been born and bred, where he knew his people, and where population was thickest on the ground. And so his pride was hurt. Moreover, in 1903 he was still reaping the reward of his raw material buying policy, for prices were still high and he had a lead over his rivals. Looking ahead to the following year when he foresaw lower prices, he predicted 'a regular deluge of advertising and schemes to sell soap'. Clearly some new move was urgently called for: 'We must', he wrote to Sydney Gross, 'do something heroic in the North of England, otherwise I do not think that we should easily recover the ground we have lost.'

'Heroism' took the form of a renewed and reformed wrapper scheme. 'Instead of giving cutlery and fancy articles of doubtful value we gave our own Soaps. . . . Any Soapmaker can give cutlery, but only one Soapmaker can give Lever Brothers' Soaps, and Lever Brothers' Soaps are undoubtedly the most popular with the consumers. Another advantage in giving Soap is that it is easily converted into money. A competitor [i.e., participant] can sell to his own Grocer, and have the value of the Soap deducted from the weekly grocery bill, or in fifty other ways can easily convert the Soap into money. On the other hand, watches, cutlery, etc., are only converted into money at an enormous sacrifice in price. There is no loss in the conversion of Soap into money.' The new scheme was only applied to the smaller tablet of Sunlight—the 12-oz., on which the profit was proportionately greater than on the 16-oz. This, Lever explained, enabled him to make a good profit, even on the assumption 'that every wrapper sent out comes back for redemption'.

The results of the reformed scheme began to show almost at once, but like all gift schemes it was difficult to stop. Like them too it was subject to the law of diminishing returns, or, as Lever more picturesquely put it, it was like dram-drinking—'it appears most efficacious at first but loses its effect after a time'.

After 1903, as the market became more and more congested, these schemes became increasingly pretentious and extravagant, until they reached a point where Lever himself planned to offer '£243,500 Cash and Premiums . . . as a profit sharing bonus during 1905'. With the fall in raw material prices from 1904 to 1906 there came the period described by Lever himself as the 'era of frenzied competition'. The soap makers had placed on their own shoulders a burden the weight of which was to become intolerable when prices did begin to rise. In the North, competition—especially with Joseph Watson's—rose to new heights. 'Increased competition and lessened profits in the Soap Trade,' Barrie declared. Watson's were advertising very freely: they had a space in every paper. A week later, Barrie went to a soap-makers' meeting and afterwards repeated his note of warning—'it was not very exhilarating, and it looks as if we are in for a period of severe competition and lessened profits'.

This kind of gossip was the stuff of Barrie's life. He spent his business career chatting, watching, hinting, and acting on others' hints, and on this foundation, combined with natural shrewdness and long experience of the markets, he built the buying policy so central to his firm's success.

The nineties were years also when Lever decided to extend his range of soap and to broaden his manufacturing activities. For the first eight years, the factory at Port Sunlight had concentrated on a single proprietary article—Sunlight Soap. True there were a few 'minor' soaps, produced perhaps to cater for a local taste or to meet some special local competition: but they were of small importance. The main source of prosperity was Sunlight and Lever was fully aware of the fact. Preservation of its quality and reputation became almost an obsession with him: 'In the early days of the Soap Trade', he wrote to Barrie, 'we no more dare have altered our charge of Sunlight Soap than we dare have thought of flying.'

By 1894 Lever considered that the time was ripe to introduce his second string. This was 'Lifebuoy', a household soap containing a percentage of carbolic acid giving it disinfectant properties which were fully exploited in the advertisements. It had the advantage that it used up the residual oil left over from the manufacture of Sunlight. In a world becoming ever more conscious of the menace of microbes, it was brought before the public as a powerful germicide, and the outbreak of epidemic disease anywhere in the country was often taken as the signal for an intensive local publicity campaign. It was one of the earliest carbolic soaps on the market, and its success was sufficient to raise, within a very few years, a flourishing crop of imitators. Nevertheless, its sales were not unduly large by Sunlight standards. In 1898, after four years of life, they were 87,744 gross against 842,559 of Sunlight, and by 1906, when Sunlight had reached 1,022,917, Lifebuoy stood at 149,170 gross. These figures, comparatively modest though they might be, made it very much the most effective of Lever's supporting weapons.

Lifebuoy was followed, after an interval of five years, by 'Monkey Brand', a scouring soap which Lever acquired by his purchase of the United States soap firm, Benjamin Brooke.[1] Its celebrated advertisement—'Won't wash Clothes'—seen on the sides of the old horse-drawn trams, made it the perfect foil to the laundering qualities of Sunlight. Manufacture was transferred to Port Sunlight, and the successful progress of the soap does not seem to have been interrupted. The quantity produced was not large. The whole department in 1902 was under a man paid £2 10s. 0d. a week, and Lever said that there were about sixty-four other departments like it in his works. Nevertheless by the next year demand had overtaken the capacity of the original plant, and the department was reorganized. Special attention had to be paid to the risk that, 'anyone with a weak chest . . . ' might be 'seriously . . . affected by working in the Monkey Brand department', and Lever accordingly arranged that no man should work in the dusty part for more than a week at a time. The danger was due to the abrasive mineral which gave the soap its special properties. The Monkey's success was great enough to produce two offspring—'Refined Toilet Monkey Brand', of which the advertised uses were legion and included recommendation as a dentifrice ('occasionally' was cautiously added), and 'Vim', which was put on the market in 1904 after considerable misgiving about the name, at first thought to be too reminiscent of certain processed meat products. Its success was not immediate, but its qualities were apparently lasting.

'Refined Toilet Monkey Brand' was part of a determined effort to invade the toilet soap market which was shared mainly

[1] See Chapter VII.

by Pears', Gibbs', and the Vinolia company. The main weapon in the assault was 'Plantol', a soap entirely derived from vegetable oils which Sydney Gross with his flair for advertising romantically christened 'fruit and flowers'. Of a pamphlet prepared to boost 'Plantol' he observed: 'I am sorry to say that it is disappointing . . . forcible enough, but not elegant. . . . A pamphlet on Toilet Soap needs picturesque handling, something about the tropic climates in which the materials are produced, the care that is exercised in refining the oils, the flowers that are picked by the women of the South on fields full of colour and beauty. That is rather the line that should have been taken, and not a treatise on perspiration, sweat, and pores.'

In 1899, Lever inaugurated his second revolutionary product: soap flakes, 'milled wonderfully fine'. Their first reception as 'Sunlight Flakes' was far from warm, but after a year's trial run Lever had another inspiration. It may have come, like Sunlight, from W. P. Thompson, the Liverpool patent agent. The name 'Lux' was short and easy to remember: it suggested light and cleanliness. Within a year, and helped by heavy advertising, sales of soap flakes were trebled. Even so, they were small compared with the sales of the staple hard soaps. At the same time an attempt was being made to challenge another established maker, Hudson's, with a carbolic dry soap (really a powdered version of Lifebuoy). It was energetically pushed for some years, but it was never successful, and Lever never knew why. Probably the answer was that housewives had bought Hudson's for seventy years and meant to go on buying it, no matter what Lever Brothers did.

The failures of these otherwise highly successful years are as interesting as the triumphs. One generalization can with safety be drawn from them: they were all failures of imitative products. Lever's triumph was built on originality—Sunlight is the supreme example—and where he had nothing new to offer, in a market already overcrowded with competent and established competitors, not all his energy, optimism, and advertising skill could command success. Where he led, he conquered; where he followed, he fell.

Finally, the year 1896 saw Lever's first entry into a new branch of production—seed crushing and cattle food. In that year he decided to build the Port Sunlight Oil and Cake Mill. Although his primary aim was to produce oil for his soap works, the new mill worked up into cattle cake the solid residue left after crushing. The necessary consequence was an entry into the cattle food business, but strictly in subordination to Lever Brothers' main business of making soap. The Chairman, always a salesman, always anxious to exploit any opportunity to its uttermost, began in 1903 to devise ambitious schemes of nation-wide advertising for cattle food. He was recalled to the realities of the situation by the cautious voice of Barrie, who never allowed soap making to be displaced by any other activity from the centre of his mental horizon: 'Making money in an oil mill depends on selling at the right time and also buying at the right time. There are times when we do not want to sell very freely, and others when we do want to sell freely. This must be the case where the margin is influenced by daily fluctuations in both the buying value of the raw material, and the selling values of the manufactured products. For instance, at the present time we are really short of cake, owing to the manipulations of the raw material by the Alexandrian operators, and if we had had any more demand than the ordinary we would have been forced to go into the market just at the time when we should be holding off. Automatic selling like Soap would not work, in my opinion, in the Cake business.' These were the limiting conditions, governed by the uncertainties of world commodity markets, the necessities of soap making, and the facts of geography, under which Lever's drove a trade in oil cake which amounted to about 10,000 tons a year.

The twelve years following the foundation of the public company culminated in 1906. They had been a period of continuous expansion during which Lever Brothers had risen to the leading position among British soap makers. The activities of the business had become broader and more varied. As yet the growth had been of a fairly simple 'vertical' type, into raw material production, into seed crushing and milling at one end, into more varieties of soaps at the other. This vertical extension was still on a modest scale but the stage had been set for more ambitious things at a later date. Yet, if the picture appeared superficially satisfactory, there was undeniably a darker side to it. The rising prices of raw materials, the lavish advertising schemes, the presence of able and powerful rivals like Joseph Watson, the references to 'frenzied competition', all these were indications that the day of the expanding market was over.

CHAPTER V

COMPETITION AND COMBINATION IN THE SOAP TRADE UP TO 1906

'The history of our Association is a history of exploded agreements.'

W. D. Knight, Chairman of the United Kingdom Soap Manufacturers' Association, 1893

THE third quarter of the nineteenth century, the time of Lever's formative years, was the classic age of individualism and free competition in British industry. The historian of that industry, Sir John Clapham, has described it as 'a generally prosperous and dynamic'[1] period; a time when those ideas of imperfect competition which the early nineteenth century had inherited from a previous age were for the most part discarded. Popular economic philosophy and self-interest alike dictated a policy of unfettered competition. What was true of industry as a whole was true of the soap industry in particular. It is true that in the early fifties there had apparently been an Association of Northern Soap Makers, the object of which was quite openly to fix prices. Names later to become familiar appeared amongst its members—Crosfield, Tyson, Simpson, Hazlehurst, and Hedley—but this Northern Association was only a transient affair. It originated with the disturbance of raw material prices occasioned by the Crimean War and with the end of the war it vanished.

The long period of economic expansion, of rising prices and rising wages, which followed rendered manufacturers' associations unnecessary and it was not until the crisis year of 1867, when the business world was shaken to its foundations by the fall of the old banking house of Overend Gurney, that the idea of association was revived again in the soap industry. The Association which was formed in that year was to continue in existence, in one form or another, for upwards of sixty years.

[1] Sir John Clapham, *Economic History of Modern Britain* (Cambridge, 1927–38).

William Lever did not become a member until 1889, but even before that date his fortunes were mingled with those of members of the trade who formed the Association, and without examining the origins and the nature of the Association and the part Lever himself later played in it, it is impossible to understand how he came to control a great part of the British soap industry.

By 1867, soap makers' profits had been falling for several years and the raw material situation was reported by one firm to be 'uniformly unfavourable'. Soap makers were therefore in a mood to listen to any proposals for co-operation in the trade which would relieve their difficulties. The task of organizing such co-operation was undertaken with enthusiasm by C. J. Cross of the London soap-making firm of T. B. Rowe and Company who became Secretary to the Association. Cross was careful to stress the voluntary nature of the new Association and to avoid any suggestion of interference with the free working of economic forces. Truth to tell, the scope of the Soap Makers' Association was never easy to define and probably even its members were far from clear as to what it really was. It proceeded to deal on behalf of the trade with difficulties in the Russian tallow market, it prepared statistics of raw materials and it argued with public authorities about transport charges and Parliamentary legislation.

Cross was always anxious to stress that it had no intention of limiting individual enterprise and above all that it repudiated any attempt to fix prices. Price fixing in the full sense of the word was certainly not amongst the Association's activities at this time. It did on the other hand enable the soap trade to agree when it was necessary to alter prices and to ensure that every member took action at the same time. That, at all events, was the theory. In fact, there is abundant evidence that even this limited amount of common action met with serious difficulties. There were always individual members who stuck to the good mid-Victorian practice of paddling their own canoes. Some of them adopted the practice of 'booking forward', i.e. of offering long term contracts which guaranteed the customer against the possibility of an increase in prices, and thus put themselves beyond the reach of the Association's agreed policy. Others were apparently in the habit of accepting, after an agreed rise in price, orders sent by return of post for delivery at the old rates. The temptation to undersell and try to get business at the expense of fellow members was almost irresistible. Dispute after dispute bore witness to the failure of the Association to agree even over such relatively straightforward issues as these. It would have needed sanctions far stronger than any which the Soap Makers' Association could wield to make any substantial impression on the individualism of the soap industry.

As it happened, on the eve of William Lever's entry into soap making, that industry stood in little need of collective action to ensure its prosperity. Conditions in 1885–6 were almost idyllic. The Chairman of the Association 'compared the present condition of the trade with that of earlier times. Its importance was shown by the prominence of its advertisements at every railway station, where the word "soap" appeared to predominate. Empirical and rule-of-thumb methods had been abolished and the trade developed not only the chemist but the poet. In fact, soap had become a highly artistic article.' With the utmost satisfaction another member enlarged on the theme. The meetings of the Association had a 'marked usefulness' but of the most innocuous kind. 'By their means our competition and rivalry become like a game at billiards or cricket. Animosity was driven out and we met on "change and elsewhere like a party of friends".' This happy situation, which was to last until 1888–9, was dependent on the low prices of raw materials, and a market which was for the moment more rapidly expanding than competition within the industry. An Association which numbered among its members practically all the older English makers of substance except Pears' and Hudson's saw no cause for worry and indeed times were so good that there was some difficulty in maintaining attendance at the Association's meetings. The only hint of trouble to come was dropped by the Chairman when he referred to 'a new trouble springing up in the numerous small makers who were starting in business'. He thought members 'would live to regret their introduction but he thought they should be got into the Association'. Almost casually, at the same meeting, the Secretary inquired 'whether Messrs. Lever & Co. should be invited to become members of the Association. The general opinion was that they being buyers of soap . . . it would be better they should not be invited.'

They might keep out the man but they could not keep out his soap; soap maker or not Lever was quick to make his presence felt in the industry. His idea of a soap supplying a national market came as a shock to the older makers who were accustomed to regard their local areas as preserves upon which foreigners were not allowed to poach. In the Northern area there was a flurry as soon as Sunlight appeared; some members complained to the Association that other members were now wrapping their soaps. The offenders retorted that this was now necessary in order to compete with Sunlight. Joseph Watson's of Leeds, quick to appreciate the importance of Lever's innovations, produced a vegetable oil soap to try to meet Sunlight on its own ground. This soap, as well as Lever's Sunlight, was a source of great anxiety to Christr. Thomas & Bros. in Bristol. They in turn, their local market invaded from the North, produced their own reply in the shape of a new soap. In London John Knight's found it necessary to produce their own answer to Lever with another vegetable oil soap and this, too, found its way into the Bristol market. By 1888 it was clear that the old structure of the British soap market with its traditional partition among local makers was a thing of the past. Lever had deliberately set out to establish a national market by national advertising and where he had led others were doing their best to follow.

By 1889 it began to appear to members of the Soap Makers' Association that the supply of soap had overtaken demand. Unremunerative prices and the ever present threat to local makers from Lever and Watson gave added point to the Association's activities. It was now clear that Lever Brothers could not be broken; the Association bowed to the inevitable and invited them to join their deliberations. Those deliberations were taking on a greater appearance of seriousness, not to say acrimony. From the Chair, E. R. Cook of London commented on the 'deplorable conditions of the soap trade . . . now being carried on at a loss owing to absurd competition'. Some makers blamed one factor, some blamed another, and there was more than the usual amount of recrimination. The one thing on which most of them seemed to agree was that the trouble might in large measure be attributed to the amount of soap thrown on to the market by Lever's and by the advertising campaigns with which Lever supported his commodities. Lever himself was not in the least dismayed by his unpopularity. In January 1891 he attended the Soap Makers' dinner in London and recorded with satisfaction in his diary '. . . very pleasant evening—all London makers complained of Sunlight. Learn that Watson's soaps are not selling in London . . . it put me in good heart to see how well we stand in London.'

Throughout the early nineties the severe competition continued. One after another the members of the Association began to devise their individual remedies against misfortune. Even the conservative John Knight's were compelled to consider advertising their soaps, though they jibbed against an undignified suggestion that they should provide free steamer trips in exchange for soap wrappers. Christr. Thomas's in 1895 were still complaining of 'particularly severe' competition from the North and seeking compensation by pushing their markets down to Exmouth, into Montgomery and even to London and the North. Exports to Tasmania and Germany were not excluded from consideration. The Association itself even attempted —unsuccessfully as ever—to regulate London prices and modify expenditure on advertising. At a meeting which Lever attended, Cross pointedly asked for a resolution from members 'to deplore the practice adopted by some members of the Association in advertising gifts and other alluring baits to the public as a means of increasing their sales—believing that such a practice is degrading to the trade and demoralizing to business'; but there was no putting the clock back and appeals for a self-denying ordinance were not likely to carry much weight in a world of cut-throat competition.

Then, quite as suddenly as it had come, the crisis passed. A drought in Australia brought heavy slaughter of live-stock and a slump in tallow prices which was to last through 1895 and 1896. With raw materials cheap and abundant, the Chairman of the Soap Makers' Association could observe at the Annual Dinner in 1895 'that the present was a time of profound peace in the trade . . . and that the worst of the depression was over'. His suggestion that the improvement was mainly due to the influence of the Association was perhaps a post-prandial exaggeration. It is difficult to see in its deliberations, up to this time oscillating between occasions of optimism and mutual congratulations on the one hand and recriminations and backslidings on the other, any very ponderable contribution to the prosperity of the industry. What it did do perhaps was to provide a forum for discussion; during the ten years after 1895 those discussions were to crystallize into rather more concrete proposals for the welfare of soap makers.

The prosperity of 1895 and 1896 did not last long. By 1897 the Northern makers, who seem to have had some kind of informal arrangement which they claimed 'enabled them to fix prices and stick to them'—the North was always more frank about price fixing than the rest of the country—were complaining once again of ruinous competition from Messrs. Lever, and in 1898 Lever's agreed to move their prices upwards in harmony with the rest of the trade. The occasion was not without importance; it was the first time that Lever's had unreservedly agreed to act with the other members of the Association. Moreover the general demand for price regulation increased as the bad times continued. The Soap Makers' Association seems almost to have split into two camps—North and South—and one member even went so far as to suggest that a frontier line should be drawn between the two territories, running from King's Lynn to Gloucester. Some such assumption was at any rate tacitly accepted by members, for in 1898 the Northern makers were complaining of being undersold 'in their own territory', and threatening to retaliate by underselling the Southern makers 'on their own ground in London, to exactly the same extent as they were underselling the Northern makers on the Northern ground'.

This internecine warfare obviously could not be allowed to continue, and the Chairman of the Association in 1899 had a sympathetic reception when he put down much of the past years' losses to 'the absence of co-operation between the Northern and Southern makers which gave rise to much unnecessary competition. He considered it most desirable that some arrangement should be made for simultaneous action.' Within five days a joint committee representing North and South met in Liverpool to discuss prices and terms. Among the Northern firms elected to serve were Lever Brothers, whose influence in Northern counsels had been increasingly felt since 1898. For a time the results were favourable. Friction was lessened and North and South reached agreements on the old problems of 'booking forward', accepting orders by post after an agreed advance, and on the exchange of price lists. At last it began to appear that some sort of unity of purpose had been achieved. But the path was not so smooth as it seemed. Within two months the Southern makers were all at odds amongst themselves and engaged in a free-for-all which more than fulfilled the requirements of the most fervid apostle of free competition. That 'honourable confidence and reliance upon one another' for which C. J. Cross so often sighed seemed as far away as ever and he lamented to his Chairman: 'It is heartbreaking to think of the labour bestowed and the money spent during the last three months and all to no purpose and probably *worse*'. After more than thirty years' experience the Association seemed to be quite incapable of solving the problems which faced the trade.

It is not difficult to suggest reasons for its ineffectiveness. It was too big and there was no agreement amongst members as to its real objects beyond the vague notion that it was to promote their interests without lessening their complete economic freedom of action. Cross, the Secretary, conscientious and harassed, was getting old; he had been Secretary since 1867 and it is doubtful whether he was really in touch with current problems. Some of the London members, at any rate, had made up their minds that drastic action was necessary. Independently of the Association private negotiations had been going on between the main London firms, and in November 1900 a circular announced that proposals for new prices had been accepted by all but three firms in the South. Amongst the dissentients was Cross's own firm, T. B. Rowe & Co. The action of the Southern members was a sad blow to Cross. He had always firmly opposed the notion that the Association existed to fix prices and he regarded the action of the London firms as transgressing the unwritten economic law. 'It was always an axiom with me', he wrote, even in the year 1900, 'that the Association did not exist for that purpose.' The five London firms had 'really usurped the position of the Association altogether....' A few months later Cross resigned. His resignation was a confession that the old order was passing and a new one, incompatible with his ideas of purely voluntary association and free competition, was taking its place.

Under a new Chairman (Calderwood of Price's Soap & Candle Company of Battersea) the Association was recast in accordance with the newer ideas. It was not possible, he told the half yearly meeting in January 1901, 'to make profits without association and combination. The isolated and selfish would suffer loss. He believed the measures recently adopted would grow and secure benefit to the whole trade.' The Association itself was too large a body to exercise any effective control over the widely divergent interests of its members, spread all over the kingdom, and although the new nationally advertised soaps had breached the defences of the local manufacturers, there was still a natural tendency for groups of manufacturers to make local arrangements about prices and other matters affecting their interests. The Northern makers for example, had 'arrangements for fixing prices' and 'the Bristol houses had one fixing prices in the West'. Calderwood's idea was that London should follow suit. Thus price fixing would be done regionally, 'while the Soap Makers' Association should continue as heretofore for what had been described as imperial purposes'.

The new plan was pressed forward and, at the annual meeting of the Association in 1901, the Soap Makers proceeded to divide Britain into five parts, each region having its own members and Secretary, while a General Committee of the whole Trade supervised general policy. Firms which co-operated were supplied with maps showing the boundaries of the areas in which the various price schedules ruled. This policy of decentralization which included regional price agreements was evidently considered successful, for the General Committee did not even find it necessary to meet. And when a severe rise of raw material prices was experienced in 1901 and 1902, the machinery was thought to work pretty well, and the Association's meetings continued on 'a cordial and friendly footing'.

Quite how the machinery did work in detail, the effect it had on prices, profit and turnover, is impossible to determine. All one can say is that the frank recognition that price fixing was amongst the primary aims of association is a measure of the distance the soap trade had moved away from the principles of 'perfect competition' since 1867. By 1902 the soap makers were enjoying a sense of security against misfortune bordering on complacency. The commodity in which most of them were chiefly interested was still the old-fashioned bar soap, and it is impossible to understand the price fixing agreements arranged by the regional committees of the Association unless the continuing importance of this older trade is appreciated. The newer 'washer' soaps—Sunlight and its imitators—had rocked the older trade in bar soap to its foundations, but statistically the turnover in the older types of soap remained far larger than turnover in the new 'washer' soaps—perhaps three times as large. Having recovered from the shock and taken the measures for price fixing described above, the older firms in the industry seem to have assumed that the position had been stabilized—and that henceforth they could afford to let Lever operate in his own peculiar markets without detriment to their own trades, which were now regarded as insulated against further shock. One of the older makers put this soothing doctrine very clearly: 'Bar soaps', he said 'do not come into competition with "washers". That is a special soap sold in the lower-class neighbourhoods, and we find . . . that it does not sell in the best-class neighbourhoods. They still stick to the bar soap trade in some form or another.' Others were equally complacent. 'Messrs. Lever's trade', wrote Edward Simpson (of Hodgson & Simpson) to Crosfield's, 'is one kept as distinct as it can be from the rest of us. . . .'

This equanimity did not last long. It rested upon a mechanical theory which sorted ill with the conditions of a dynamic trade changing rapidly under the impact of Lever's continued expansion. Lever's sales of Sunlight alone had risen from just over 18,000 tons in 1890 to nearly 46,000 tons in 1900, and they continued to grow in the next five years. The comfortable theory that this growing trade could be kept distinct simply could not be maintained. The price of Lever's soaps was bound to affect the prices of bar soaps as arranged regionally. By 1903, Lever's dominant position in the soap industry was a fact which could no longer be denied and in that year he succeeded to the Presidency of the Northern section of the Association. Perhaps it was not entirely a coincidence that one of his first duties was to preside over a meeting of the whole body of the Association to consider 'the growth of the "speciality" trade in which one price was recognized from Land's End to John o' Groats'—in fact, the growth of his own trade and its immediate rivals. The result of the meeting was an agreement that the prices of these branded soaps like Sunlight were a matter of concern to the Association just as much as bar soaps. So much Lever was willing to concede, though he was far from agreeing that the fixing of his prices was anybody's business but his own. At this same meeting he aired his own views on the ethics of combination. 'He did not think it a wise policy to keep out the small makers although no one should be afraid of them. He thought that while theirs was not a combination against the interests of the public, it was the duty of the Association to secure proper remuneration for the work and experience of the individual members of the trade.' His colleagues must have been left wondering whether these ambiguous phrases were to be taken as a commendation or a rebuke.

For the time being all went well. The years from 1903 to 1905 may be regarded as the high-water mark of this transitional phase of combination in the soap industry. All the big firms were in the Association, from the difficult 'old fogeys' of Silvertown to the even more difficult newcomer of Port Sunlight. So far as voluntary combination and price-fixing agreements could secure contentment within the industry it had been secured. The picture of the industry drawn by the Chairman of the Association (H. S. Timmis of Gossage's) at the Annual Meeting in June 1905 was one of deep peace: 'The great feature to chronicle tonight,' he said, 'is that there is absolutely nothing to say. No acrimonious discussion, no charges to be brought by one firm against another. We are all working amicably together and I think it is a sign that the Soap Makers' Association is doing good work . . . and the mere fact that prices have been maintained is a proof, I believe, that although trade may be dull and many of us are not doing absolutely the trade we were doing, still we are doing trade on a more remunerative basis than we were.' . . . Price agreements had moreover ensured stability of prices even though raw material prices fluctuated. . . . 'Now, whether the market letter [for tallow] moves up or down, the price of soap pursues the even tenor of its way.'

In assessing the accuracy of these observations the historian should make some allowance for the conviviality of the occasion. The truth was that raw material prices—the principal problem of the industry—had for some time been relatively stable and such fluctuations as had taken place put no great strain on the price-fixing machinery. Indeed the very reverse happened. The soap makers' enthusiasm for combination was apt to vary in inverse proportion to their prosperity. Stability in trade had always made for instability in the Association. So it was now. A week or two after the meeting of 1905 William Lever resigned his membership. When asked for his reasons, he replied, amicably but vaguely, that 'there is no special reason at all—except that after long experience we have failed to find any benefit in continuing members . . . hence our resignation. With kindest regards. . . .' This, Edward Simpson condemned as 'meaningless'. It was not quite true. The trouble with the Association was twofold: it was only really useful in bad times, and even then it was primarily an Association to protect the makers of soap quite different from Lever's.

Apart from this flurry, however, the peace which had descended on the industry continued into 1906, and in June the Chairman of the Association was still optimistic; prices remained stable and he could see no reason to expect a change. Then in July the long calm was rudely shattered in spectacular fashion by a sudden rise in raw material prices. The dimensions of the increase were beyond the capacity of the ordinary price-fixing machinery to control, and on July 27th the representatives of the big Northern firms met W. H. Lever in Liverpool, where, as it was later recorded, 'naturally the extraordinary rise in the price of raw materials affecting the soap trade was uppermost in the minds of all these gentlemen'. The Liverpool meeting has been called the 'genesis' of the combine that followed, and with good reason; but before describing it, we must pause to consider the nature of the contribution which thirty-nine years of voluntary association had made towards the later development of the soap industry.

It had, in the first place, brought the soap makers of England together round the table and strengthened personal ties; so that in 1904 Edward Simpson of Wakefield could write to a Bristol colleague: '. . . personal knowledge of each other is a great factor in the cohesion of the soap trade. Please put up your prices and please come to the next meeting.' Two years earlier, J. J. Crosfield put the matter even more precisely when he told the Association 'that good fellowship in the trade does undoubtedly add to the value in solid hard cash to us soap makers of our Association'. W. D. Knight had been heard to say that good fellowship was 'worth 10s. a ton to the London makers', while the Chairman of the Northern section thought it was worth 'many thousands a year to its members'. The meaning of all this was that gentlemen on friendly terms did not undersell one another. That was a real advantage conferred by association, more valuable perhaps than the apparently more business-like and formal price agreements, which were made only to be broken when they proved inconvenient. Such voluntary agreements were, by their very nature, unstable. A degree of serious depression or a measure of genuine prosperity both undermined the force of this voluntary combination.

In the second place, the Association had catered primarily for the interests of the older makers of bar soaps. The manufacturers of the new branded soaps, advertised nationally, had never been in its inner councils. Lever himself had been kept out of it longer perhaps than decency allowed and had never become more than a lukewarm supporter. His attendance at meetings was far from regular; on one occasion he absented himself, preferring 'to open a Congregational Bazaar at Bolton', and in the end he resigned because he failed 'to find any benefit' in its proceedings. From start to finish he was a spectator of its proceedings rather than a participant in them. In short, the long and chequered career of the Association demonstrated, in Lever's view, the inadequacy of this type of loose-knit combination to deal with the problems of the soap trade. His observation of similar associations which had sprung up in other industries —the salt, steel, and bedstead-making industries in particular— only confirmed his suspicions. The trade association had departed from the true principles of *laissez-faire* without bringing any efficient solution of the new problems of excessive competition.

Now as we shall see, there were features about this latest crisis which threatened to make it more severe and prolonged than any of its precursors. It was clear to Lever that it called for new measures. He had already been examining the conditions of one industry which seemed to him to offer a working model for the soap trade. In the sewing-cotton industry Messrs. J. & P. Coats had amalgamated with their four chief competitors in

1895–6 and were already securing a controlling interest in smaller firms. An arrangement on these lines appeared to Lever to offer greater promise of genuine economies and industrial efficiency than the more or less good-humoured wranglings of the Soap Makers' Association, whose thirty-nine years' deliberations seemed merely to prove that the soap makers, like the Bourbons, learned nothing and forgot nothing.

Accustomed to efficiency and discipline in his own business, Lever looked for some solution which would put a term to an era of 'exploded agreements'. Where J. & P. Coats had led, he could follow. Thus at the meeting of July 27th, 1906, his mind dwelt much on the palpable inadequacy of the existing method of associations. It dwelt much less on the personal affinities and personal animosities which had been generated within the Association and which were to exert a powerful influence on his plans. It was difficult for one whose thoughts were dominated by the future to remember that there were others whose thoughts were equally dominated by the past, and who found it hard to forgive the newcomer his rapid rise to success.

CHAPTER VI

THE CRISIS OF 1906

'In the old days a manufactory would be an individual concern. Next . . . a partnership, and that was a state of affairs which continued until quite recently. Then it grew beyond the capital available by two or three joining together as a partnership, and limited companies became necessary with appeals to be made to thousands of investors, in order that still larger capital might be got together. Now we have reached a further stage again, when a number of limited companies require to be grouped together in what we call a combine, the object being concentration of capital and the concentration of effort; if these combines result in cheaper production and more abundant supply undertakings will be successful; if not they will be failures.'

William Lever addressing a Men's Meeting at Port Sunlight,
11 *January* 1903

To the soap makers who met together on the 27th of July 1906 in Liverpool, ostensibly to discuss matters arising out of their glycerine production, the 'extraordinary rise in the price of raw materials affecting the soap trade' appeared to be the most serious problem of the moment. And the problem was undoubtedly a grave one. As previous chapters have shown, it was not the first time that the industry had been in difficulties through such fluctuations. The early nineties and 1901–2 had been times of crisis. The crisis of July 1906 was different. For one thing it came with startling suddenness. In June the Chairman of the Soap Makers' Association was still looking forward confidently to a period of stable prices and trade. Secondly, the rise itself was bigger than anything that had been experienced for thirty years, prices advancing from thirty-three and a third per cent to fifty per cent and over during 1906. Finally, it became clear that this was no temporary dislocation but was likely to be a permanent adjustment of conditions in the oils and fats market. For the fact was that the demand for oils and fats for the manufacture of food had risen sharply. As refining processes improved, fats that had previously gone to the soap maker—tallow, coconut oil, cottonseed oil—were going to the manufacturers of margarine and compound lard. In short, it seemed, world consumption of oils and fats had overtaken the world supply.

In the scramble for supplies which followed, the soap makers were less happily placed than the food manufacturers, especially in the buying of vegetable oil. As yet, the margarine makers were only able to use a small proportion of vegetable oil in manufacture; for margarine had to be manufactured primarily from solid fats; they could therefore afford to bid high for what they wanted. Again, it was easier to alter the price of a foodstuff which was rapidly coming to be regarded as essential than it was to alter the price of soap, which many were still inclined to regard as a luxury. Maybe, too, the edible fat manufacturers were better organized for raw material buying than the straggling procession of mutinous soap makers.

Such, at all events, were the visible features of the situation in July 1906. Yet it was clear that the trouble went far deeper than that. Serious as the raw material position undoubtedly was, it was rendered far more serious by the economic context in which it appeared. There were two aspects—the context of demand and the context of supply.

So far as the demand for soap was concerned it is doubtful whether the soap makers themselves had much knowledge of the situation, beyond the fact that it was becoming more difficult to sell soap to housewives. Yet behind their difficulties important changes were going on. Standards of living, which had been rising from the late sixties until the nineties, had been a ladder of success for the soap makers, but now that movement had been checked, and there were even signs of a fall in real wages. Some part of the difficulties of the soap trade between 1904 and 1906 may therefore have been due to this fact. The working-class housewife, whose custom Lever had chiefly courted, was the first to feel the pinch when her husband's wage packet began to lighten. Soap, still on the margin of necessities, might well be the first commodity on the grocer's list to be cut.

The fact that the market for soap was ceasing to expand was one which the soap makers did not find it easy to accept. Since the eighties, soap and advertising had gone hand in hand. To Lever and his imitators, a market was the size they chose to make it. Except for 1896 and 1901, Lever's sales had expanded continuously. Hence the confusion of the soap makers when their expenditure on the 'frenzied advertising' of 1904, 1905, and 1906 failed to produce a proportionate result. Soap makers could not admit, even to themselves, that the spacious days were over. And, indeed, looking at his sales figures for those years, Lever could congratulate himself on considerable increases. Indeed, sales for 1905—63,024 tons—were the highest ever achieved. But they were achieved at a disproportionately heavy cost in prize schemes and Press advertising.

It took the shock of the raw material crisis to recall soap makers to a sense of reality. To Lever it was clear that the consumer must be called upon to bear his share of the burden, and as early as July 14th he had decided to alter the weight of the 16 oz. pack to 15 oz. By August 2nd the announcements of the change had been printed and by August 13th were approved by him. Trifling in itself, the matter was to be of great importance later in the year. Certainly the decision had been taken before any idea of a combine was mooted.

Closely linked with the question of price was the possibility of reducing the cost of soap by using cheaper oil. Palm oil or tallow might replace copra or palm kernel oil, but Lever fought shy of whale oil because 'Soaps in which whale oil is used have a tendency to go black in colour and also other objections such as smell'. Only the serious nature of the crisis could justify thus tampering with prices and formulae hallowed by the custom of years.

Important as they were, these changes were not sufficient to meet the situation. Capital of over four millions, including the savings of about four thousand investors as well as his own holding of all the Ordinary Shares, and the livelihood of fifteen thousand employees all over the globe,[1] were at stake. At the root of the trouble lay the condition of 'frenzied competition' and this could only be tackled by joint action among the soap makers. Above all, it was essential to impose some check on the system of 'inducements to buy' which had grown into a positive incubus on the whole industry. The old Association was powerless to deal with the new system of proprietary brands and in any case had never gone beyond fixing selling prices. It was therefore not without significance that, at the glycerine meeting of July 27th, Lever 'indicated his prognostications and gave to

[1] See Chapter VII.

each firm a printed pamphlet entitled "Combines", being a paper he had read at a meeting at Port Sunlight as far back as the 11th January 1903 and which fully explained his views'.

In that paper Lever had strongly emphasized his conviction that a combine was only justifiable or successful when it aimed to provide 'a cheaper product . . . a more abundant product . . . a better product'.[1] If the aim were merely 'to increase the profits of the masters or to bolster up decaying industries' it would certainly fail. He had pointed to Coats' thread combine as the instance of a successful amalgamation—successful because it had concentrated on economies in advertising and selling. The undeniable advantage of the large manufacturer over the small was an iron law, but '. . . any manufacturer who feels competition keen today and seeks relief in combination with other manufacturers in the same line of business, thinking thereby to avoid what he calls cut-throat competition, unless he can prove to himself that such combination will enable him to produce cheaper and to save expenses, will be simply putting off the evil day, and the firms he has combined with will simply drag each other down, down, down until they disappear. Their place will be taken by men who are producing more cheaply, with probably improved machinery and other better conditions.'[2] There is no reason to question the sincerity of these views: they were all of a piece with his conviction, reiterated year in, year out, that expanded production was vital to the well-being of capitalist, worker, and consumer. Nor was the tone of his paper merely academic. The possibility of a 'syndicate' had more than once been considered by the Association. Nothing is more probable than that in 1903 Lever had been already considering the formation of a combine as a practical possibility springing from the crisis of 1901–2 which still hung heavily over the trade.

The discussions of July were followed by a further meeting with Watson's, Gossage's, and Crosfield's on August 2nd, at which each firm produced data showing the relative value of the different businesses.

Two days later Lever and Joseph Watson met at the Grand Hotel, London. Watson was inclined to favour the idea of uniting the soap industry under the control of a parent company, largely

[1] Viscount Leverhulme, *The Six-Hour Day* (Allen & Unwin, 1918), p. 261.
[2] Ibid., p. 264.

on grounds of secrecy, but Lever stuck firmly to the scheme of an exchange of shares between companies which would bind them together. 'I think', he wrote to Watson later in the month, 'it is much sounder from a business point of view and would result in much less opposition to the amalgamation'. So far as Lever Brothers and Watson's were concerned, the danger of premature disclosures was not serious, for Lever held all his Company's Ordinary shares and Watson and his uncle held all theirs. The capital of Gossage's and Crosfield's was more widely distributed and Lever shared Watson's concern over publicity, suggesting to J. J. Crosfield that the whole matter should be kept as secret as possible, and that the information should 'rather "ooze" out than "splash" out'. It was also essential that the grocery trade should be handled tactfully.

At the meeting of August 2nd Lever had outlined his proposals. The essence of them was that the manufacturers in combination could by economies in manufacture and selling bear the burden of rises in the price of raw materials themselves rather than pass them by means of increases in the price of soap to the consumer. The 'combination' was to be achieved by a 'working arrangement' between soap makers based on an exchange of shares. Firms coming into such an arrangement would cease 'frenzied advertising' but would in general retain control over the running of their own businesses. The major economies which Lever envisaged from the amalgamation were in reduced advertising and selling expenses but there were others from combined buying of raw materials, manufacturing economies, and centralized research. Crosfield's, for example, maintained a fully equipped chemical laboratory carrying out elaborate research on raw material and other problems at considerable expense. 'Suppose', said Lever, 'that every soap manufacturer had to keep a research laboratory in active operation, trying to explore that vast dark continent of fats and oils, each manufacturer at his own expense. You can see how enormously this would add to the cost of production. . . . By coming together, joining forces, the results achieved will be eventually of the greatest value, because those findings will be applicable to every firm in the combination, and not alone to the firm making the discovery.' Gossage's agreed to join almost at once in the 'working arrangement', and while Crosfield's were consulting their shareholders, Watson interviewed Christr. Thomas of Bristol, and Ogston & Tennant of Glasgow and Aberdeen. They also agreed to come in, as did John Barrington's of Dublin.

By August 31st Lever judged—wrongly as things were to turn out—that the combine was 'an accomplished fact . . . with a combined [weekly] output of 4,500 tons, including export, but not including Lever Brothers' Associated Companies'.[1] In September, however, new recruits were still queueing up. On September 25th Lever placed his proposal before Edward Cook's of London. After a little hesitation, Cook's decided to join and two days later Lever wrote to them: 'I believe by amalgamating we shall be in a better position to serve the public well and give better value than ever, and also to better serve the interests of the distributors, both wholesale and retail. This will be the policy of the Amalgamation, and it is on this policy that the business will be founded, rather than grasping for excessive profit, which might endure for a year or two but could not be permanent.' Several smaller firms also indicated their desire to join the combine, among them Tyson, Richmond & Jones of Liverpool, the Glennifer Soap Company of Paisley, and J. L. Thomas of Exeter. Lever welcomed them as proof of his contention that the combine was not merely a strategy for major powers.

There were also abortive negotiations with several other firms—with Gibbs' of London, Isdale & McCallum of Paisley, Field's, Wilkie & Soames', and Knight's—the last three all London firms. Discussions with Wilkie & Soames' were broken off when Press attacks on the combine began. The other negotiations all broke down on one point: the firms asked too big a price for what Lever considered to be the real worth of their businesses. The outstanding case was Knight's, where J. W. Hope, an ex-employee of Lever's who had held appointments in Australia and at Port Sunlight, had become managing director after a career which could only be described as erratic.[2] Hope was evidently capable of driving a hard bargain. Against Lever's valuation of the Knight business at £300,000, Hope continued to hold out for £750,000. Lever refused and Hope

[1] For Lever's overseas companies see Chapter VII.
[2] See Chapter VII.

departed into the other camp. To the end Lever was inclined to put the blame for the subsequent agitation against the combine squarely on Hope's shoulders.

Besides the firms which joined in voluntarily on the basis of exchange of shares, the combine included, by September, two other companies which were actually bought outright by Lever's. Hodgson & Simpson of Wakefield was one of those old-established firms which had suffered severely in the period of 'frenzied competition'. Perhaps the running of the business had not been as efficient as it might have been. In the spring of 1906 they had approached Lever, offering to sell, in order to meet debts to their bankers and creditors, and in September the deal was closed at £70,000. Lever's object in buying was to enter the market for ordinary bar soaps such as Hodgson & Simpson made and which Lever Brothers up to that time had not, an aspect, perhaps, of the policy of spreading his interests and risks. Then in August, Lever, acting, as he said, 'for the Combine', bought the Vinolia Company, a toilet soap and toilet preparations business on which he had had his eye for several years. In Lever's view Vinolia was a business capable of great development in more enterprising hands, but he did not get it cheaply. On the day he completed the purchase he wrote to Barrie: 'I think we have paid too much money for it, but I think we have done wisely in taking it under the circumstances'.

The financial details of the merger were largely arranged by Lever himself. By October it was clear that the original financial arrangements which had contemplated the issue of one million more Ordinary and one million more 'B' Preference shares in Lever Brothers Limited were hopelessly inadequate to provide for the number of firms now wishing to enter the proposed combine. Lever therefore pushed on with plans to create large additional issues of capital in his own company which would then be exchanged for the shares of his new partners in the amalgamation. Lever Brothers' nominal capital was to be trebled to £12 million, divided into £3 million First Preference and equal amounts of 'B' Preference, Preferred Ordinary and Ordinary shares. Of this, £8 million would be issued to cover purchases of shares in companies: another million might be required later for trading credits. Lever steadfastly refused to be drawn into committing himself to any figures of probable earnings of the combine, depending as they did on raw material prices. On the matter of economies which could be made he was more forthcoming, and he confided to H. S. Timmis (of Gossage's) his private guess at the total probable savings which could be expected:

	£
Advertising, at least	200,000
Increased profit by combined selling, at least £1 per ton	250,000
Benefits of combined buying of Soda Ash, Sundry Supplies, Cardboxes, etc.	100,000
Benefits of combined buying of Raw Material, Oils, Tallows, etc.—not capable of estimation but certainly large	—
Economies in Agents, Travellers, Travelling Expenses, Branch Offices, management of Salesmen and Selling Expenses generally, at least	100,000
Economies in manufacture, by centring certain soaps at certain works, and mutual helpfulness in reducing cost of manufacture, obtained by comparing methods of working, say 5s. per ton at least	50,000
Actual economies	£700,000

The incidence of the economies varied from firm to firm. Gossage's, for example, did little advertising and their methods of manufacture were too efficient to allow of much easy improvement. In other firms, like Hodgson & Simpson's, there was room for economy—as much as £2 a ton—in manufacturing costs.

The estimate of these economies was no mere window-dressing. Throughout September, Lever and Watson were engaged in reducing or cancelling advertising contracts. A contract of Lever's made in June for advertisements in the *Daily Mail* at a cost of nearly £6,000 was suspended, and Watson's likewise suspended a similar contract. At the same time meetings were going on between the firms interested in the combine to consider reducing the number of agents. In Scotland, Lever's and Watson's alone maintained about twenty-four agents, out of a total of fifty employed by firms in the combine with the result that their soap prices for Scotland were much higher than those of Ogston & Tennant, the local Scottish firm, who worked with a very small number of agents. It was therefore proposed to reduce the total number from fifty to twenty. Many of the surplus agents were either inefficient or very old: others could be used in selling industrial soaps to the Scottish woollen industry. The process was to be gradual: Lever was anxious to avoid 'large volumes of men parading the country giving out disgruntled talk'. The wisdom of his policy was to appear later.

It was, of course, inevitable that news of the proposed combine should leak out; too many people were concerned in it to make secrecy possible for long. Lever was resigned to its being 'public property' in early September, but it was not until early October that Press comment began in earnest. The *Daily Mail* showed most interest, but its early comments were more or less neutral. Apparently a trifle puzzled by the whole affair, its reporters made inquiries and agreed that the leading motive was to combat 'keen competition among the makers and the dearness of raw materials'. By October 13th they had discovered that the object was also 'to lessen the costly competitive advertising and other expenses which had arisen owing to keen competition'. By the 18th, their tone was definitely hostile and an article appeared with the heading, 'Soap Trust Arithmetic—How 15 ounces make a pound'. The following day, another article included an accurate estimate of the proposed savings on advertising—£200,000—and from then onwards the attack gathered momentum. Headlines and posters rang out their fanfares—'Soap Trust Victims'—'Weights Reduced'—'Dismissal of Employees Begins'—'The 15-ounce Pound'—and so on; while cartoons added fuel to the flames. Columns appeared in the *Daily Mail* and its associated papers advising consumers which soaps to buy and which to avoid. The Soap Trust was even charged, on November 1st, with attempting to buy up the Press. The principal targets of all this publicity were first, Lever himself, and secondly his business. The cartoons portrayed him as an unspeakably repulsive and odious figure; the 'Port Moonshine' of the articles was the home of sweated labour and tyrannical oppression of master over man.

To understand the effect of all this on British public opinion it is necessary to glance for a moment at the American scene, where Theodore Roosevelt, now in his second term as President,

THE GREEDY SOAP TRUST.

POOR WOMAN—Please, Mr. Soap Trust, isn't this pound an ounce short?
MR. SOAP TRUST—Well, what are you going to do about it? You may think yourself lucky I let you live. I'm boss of the situation, and no one else can make soap except me, and I'll put as few ounces in the pound as I like and raise the price to what I like, and if you don't get out I'll call the police.

CARTOON from the *Daily Mirror*, 22nd October, 1906
(*Reproduced by courtesy of the* Daily Mirror)

was enthusiastically launched on his trust-busting policy. For more than thirty years, the movement of industrial combination had been gathering force in the United States. From profit-sharing pools the business men had moved on to trusts. John D. Rockefeller had organized Standard Oil as a trust in 1882, and that was followed by hundreds of others. In the years of prosperity round about the time of the Spanish War of 1898 some five thousand businesses were consolidated into about three hundred trusts. Along with the formation of these giant trusts went a good deal of bribery and political thuggery, but it was not so much this which outraged a lenient American public as the suspicion, voiced by Mr. Justice Harlan in the Standard Oil case, 'that the country was in real danger from . . . the slavery that would result from the aggregation of capital in the hands of a few . . . controlling, for their own advantage exclusively, the entire business of the country, including the production and sale of the necessities of life'.[1] The attack was taken up by Congressmen, Senators, Presidents, and the result was the famous Sherman Anti-Trust Act of 1890. That Act had failed to check the activities of Rockefeller, Carnegie, Pierpont Morgan, E. H. Harriman, and the others. Hence Roosevelt's decision to reinvigorate the Act, and it was at about this time that big business was being discredited by the attacks of the 'muck-rakers' on the Standard Oil Company, the beef trust, and the railroads; a sugar trust was found to have swindled the government out of four million dollars in customs duties and by false weights. All this was echoed in the British Press and formed an inevitable background to the comments on the doings of the Soap Trust. No opportunity was missed of suggesting parallels between the alarming history of what Mr. Dooley called 'heejous monsthers' and the new 'octopus'. Trusts and their activities made good copy in 1906.

The attack by the Northcliffe newspapers was certainly successful. By November, it was clear that the effects on the sales of the associated firms—especially Lever's—were serious and ominous. At a meeting in Liverpool on November 23rd, Watson and Crosfield proposed that all idea of a combine should be abandoned. Lever himself and his fellow directors withheld their votes on the issue though Lever was resigned to dissolution and to a reversion to former prices and weights. The working arrangement had completely dissolved and Lever was left facing the most serious crisis he had experienced so far. Sales in November were sixty per cent below those for the same month in the previous year: and since the possibility of higher prices had disappeared with the combine, profits on these reduced sales were lower than ever. Worst of all, the frenzied

[1] Morison and Commager, *Growth of the American Republic*, Vol. II, p. 143.

competition of the pre-trust period returned in an even more severe form than before. In an effort to economize, the Building Department, which since 1890 had been busy extending the Port Sunlight Works and Village, was closed down and all constructional work stopped. Lever's £10 Preference shares fell by £2 a share, total depreciation of nearly half a million. The Ordinary shares, being held by Lever himself, were not quoted on the Stock Exchange, but were valued before the crisis at £30 per £10 share. By December, in Lever's own estimate, they had been depreciated by £10 per share.

Not all the trust firms suffered so severely. Crosfield's could report that 'our own orders are keeping up in a manner which has quite surprised us', Gossage's trade 'was quite up to average if not better', but of course these firms had kept in the background and in any case Gossage's had never done much advertising. As Lever wrote rather bitterly to Joseph Watson: 'I think it is natural that your firm and ours should feel the shrinkage for the simple reason that we have borne the brunt of the attack. . . . It is one of the ironies of the situation that yourselves and ourselves, that of the United Kingdom have spent most with the newspaper Press, come in for most of the attack. Those firms like Messrs. Gossage, who have never spent a penny in advertising, have never received any. In fact, I doubt whether the Editor, sitting on his stool in his office, has ever heard of Gossage's name.'

All this made it clear that Lever Brothers' reputation, built up by advertising expenditure estimated at over two million pounds, had been gravely damaged. The hopes of effecting economies, on which the Trust had been based, had vanished; profits on much reduced sales had themselves been cut, while fixed charges of production had to be borne by a smaller volume of business. In the autumn of 1906 there was only one bright spot. The 'outside' makers, who had benefited by the *Daily Mail* attacks on the 'trust' makers, were overwhelmed with orders, but having only inadequate supplies of raw material were compelled to apply to Lever's and others for their needs. At the end of October, Barrie wrote jubilantly to Lever: 'makers outside the Combine will pay anything at all for *spot* materials and the market is simply ablaze'. At the prices they had to pay for oils these anti-trust businesses were run at a loss.

One maker 'wished to goodness these newspapers would stop the agitation, as he was getting too much unprofitable business from it'. Another 'was flooded with inquiries and propositions, but has refused them all, stating that he does not want their trade' . . . and so on.

Raw materials, and such by-products as glycerine, provided some little consolation in an otherwise gloomy situation. One of the most serious aspects—and its real gravity was not to be revealed till later—was the effects of the Press agitation on the working-class consumer. C. F. Huffam, of Crosfield's, was under the impression that the effects were largely confined to the middle classes and that the working classes had paid little attention to the *Daily Mail.* That may have been true in the early stages, but the Co-operative Societies were sensitive to the suggestion that they were buying from a trust, and through them the reluctance to buy trust soaps was transmitted to their consumers. Here were the seeds of more trouble and more competition.

Lever, convinced that there had been nothing unworthy in his motives or actions, and equally certain that the driving motive behind the attacks was not concern for the public welfare but chagrin at the loss of advertising income, began to consider legal action. His first inquiries were not promising. The first K.C. to be consulted delivered 'a long-winded and hesitating opinion' and tried to dissuade him from action. Lever was not satisfied. He went back to his solicitor, George Harley. Harley, imperturbable and courageous, enjoyed Lever's confidence as few other men ever did, and Harley's advice was that the case should be laid before F. E. Smith. Smith was summoned from Oxford to London and asked to produce an opinion by the following morning. He ordered a bottle of champagne and two dozen oysters, worked through the night, and at 8.30 the following morning wrote: 'There is no answer to this action for libel, and the damages must be enormous'.

Lever lost no time in acting on Smith's opinion. The brief was drawn up by Harley's firm, Simpson, North, Harley & Co., in close conjunction with John McDowell, Secretary of Lever Brothers Limited, and on the 15th of July 1907 Lever went into action against the Northcliffe Press at Liverpool Assizes before Mr. Justice Lawrence. It was a battle of giants, but an unequal one. For Lever Brothers, Sir Edward Carson was supported by Mr. Horridge, Mr. F. E. Smith, and Mr. E. G. Hemmerde. On the other side Mr. Rufus Isaacs was supported by Mr. H. E. Duke, Mr. Norman Craig, and Mr. F. H. E. Branson.

Even before the case opened, Lord Northcliffe realized that his newspapers had overreached themselves. On July 11th he offered Lever public apology and agreement 'to refrain from all further comment' in his papers. But Lever's blood was up and he flashed back to Sidney Gross: 'I like the cheek of the *Daily Mail*—it is simply colossal. They have had their detectives round Port Sunlight, and no doubt myself also if I only knew, for the last eight or nine months and have been interviewing every discharged, disgruntled, dissatisfied malcontent that there is or ever was in Lever Brothers' employ any time during the last twenty-two years. They have raked in all the scrap heaps and refuse heaps they could find. If they had discovered anything that would enable them to still further bully and browbeat us they would have had no suggestion of settlement. They now come forward and offer agreement to refrain from further comment. I suppose they mean "attacks". I consider this about as great an insult as they can offer because it is quite obvious that either they themselves are feebleminded or they think we are feebleminded, and especially myself. Neither Lever Brothers nor myself are quite so feebleminded as the *Daily Mail* evidently consider.'

Carson was no less confident of his ground. He had already made up his mind that he could destroy his opponent's case in two days. 'This libel, gentlemen,' he began, 'is of a very exceptional and serious character, deliberately carried on for several weeks, and was made with the object of smashing up Lever Brothers. It is a libel which has been persisted in up to the present moment. . . . The plaintiffs' complaint is that the defendants, having made up their minds to smash the Combine, instead of attacking it in a fair way, have stooped to methods of libel, which have rendered Mr. Lever and his company liable to be branded as men with whom no honest man could have any dealings in this country. The first and most serious charge is that the plaintiffs sold their soap in such a fraudulent manner as to deceive the public as to the weight of the soap. The next charge is that the plaintiffs, in consequence of the Combine, have dismissed large quantities of employees. Another charge is that they have cornered all the raw material in the market. Messrs. Lever Brothers are also accused of having, along with others, attempted to bribe and buy the Press, and it is suggested that the attempt had to be abandoned because high-class and patriotic papers like the *Daily Mail* refused to be bribed. A number of the libels also contained hostile criticism of certain brands of the plaintiffs' soap, and alleged that unsavoury fish oil has been used in their manufacture, which they have fraudulently concealed by scenting it. After suggesting that the conduct of the plaintiffs in the matter of the Combine tends to the oppression of the poor, the libels finally shake the foundations of the plaintiff company by alleging that the Lever Preference shareholders, by certain manipulation, are to be got rid of for the benefit of Mr. Lever himself.'

Carson then put his case. Lever was the pioneer of pure soap, the model employer who from small beginnings had built up one of the great businesses of the world. The alteration in weight had been made, in conformity with trade practice, before the combine was thought of. Weight had never been guaranteed —it was impossible to do it—but in fact great care had been taken to notify both retailers and public of the change.

The scheme for the combine had a fair and logical explanation in the increased cost of raw materials. Then he passed to the question of damages. 'If you find', he said, 'that Messrs. Lever Brothers are not robbers and swindlers, fraudulent traders and all the rest of it, and if you find that all the other charges are untrue, what are the damages to be given to them? The damage is incalculable. . . . No money can wipe out the sufferings of weeks and months during which the charges were hurled against the business of Lever Brothers. You must, without shirking, try to assess something that will be compensation for what has been done. For the rest, up to the time of the issue of the writ, the plaintiffs' trading losses have been £40,000. Those losses have continued. The *Daily Mail* have not only admitted, but gloated over, these losses that have been caused by them. But that is a small part of the total loss. The whole company has been shaken from top to bottom. Two million Preference shares have been reduced in value £1 apiece, with a loss, to those who held the shares, of £200,000. On the Ordinary shares it is impossible to say what the loss has been. The whole concern had been shaken up as if by an earthquake. Then you have to ask yourselves how the goodwill of the company is to be restored, and at what price. It has to be rebuilt to some extent, and that can only be done by a verdict of the jury.'

Finally, with a wave of the hand, Carson directed Lever into the witness box, 'And now, gentlemen,' he concluded, 'I have put my first witness—my client, Mr. Lever—into the box: let my learned friend, Mr. Rufus Isaacs, cross-examine him to his heart's content, and, when his time comes, I hope he will be able to follow my example and do the same, and call as his first witness his own client, Lord Northcliffe. I hope he'll be able to play cricket with us.' Carson knew his client. Not all Isaacs's subtlety could make any impression on Lever, who was quite as much at home giving evidence in the box as he was taking the chair at a shareholders' meeting or opening a chapel bazaar.

The following morning found Isaacs offering £10,000 to settle out of Court. Carson and Lever treated the offer with contempt and the case proceeded. The court was treated to the curious spectacle of Counsel for the defence bargaining for a settlement as it has been said 'like a buyer at an auction'.[1] The offer rose from ten to fifteen, to twenty, to thirty, forty, fifty thousand pounds.

'What do you say to that, Mr. Lever?' asked Carson. 'That's a substantial offer,' said Lever, 'I'll take it.'

So ended one of the great *causes célèbres* of the day. Lever's victory owed much to Carson and Smith. Few people knew how much it also owed to the brilliant and intransigent Ulsterman who was Lever Brothers' Secretary. This was the first, but by no means the last time that McDowell's untiring work behind the scenes was to lay the foundations of legal triumph for Lever. Besides the £50,000 agreed in regard to the *Daily Mail*, substantial sums were added to cover the libels in other papers. In all, Lever Brothers received £91,000 in compensation. The sum was enormous by contemporary standards. Neither Counsel nor solicitor had held out any hope that a jury would award as much. Nevertheless in some quarters it was held that Lever had given in too easily, and indeed two years

[1] E. Marjoribanks and I. Colvin, *Life of Lord Carson*, Vol. 1 (Gollancz, 1932–6).

later Lever himself estimated his total losses from the affair at 'considerably over half a million'. His reasons for not facing a protracted argument in Court over compensation were sound enough. He did not want 'two or three days' wrangle with all the books of Lever Brothers displayed in open Court, showing the districts in England where the trade had suffered, the kind of customers who had taken most offence such as Co-operative Societies particularly. . . .' He was probably right. The libels had done enough damage: the effects were to be felt for years to come. The sooner the question could be closed the better.

One thing was clear. The libels and the publicity had put an end to any hopes of rationalization in the soap trade for some time to come. '. . . unfortunately, I am positive,' wrote Lever to Ogston, 'in the lifetime of the present generation, it will not be possible to again come together. I see not the slightest prospect of any attempt in that direction.' And so far as voluntary movement was concerned he was right. Amalgamation was to come but it was to be piecemeal. Nor was his other hope, that '. . . there will be a more friendly feeling amongst us all as the result of this coming together . . .', fulfilled. Reaping where they had not sown, the other firms in the combine proceeded to make satisfactory, but in Lever's eyes dishonourable, settlements with Northcliffe. Watson's settled for £60,000—£30,000 in cash and £30,000 worth of advertising space in the *Daily Mail.* Such bending before the storm did not improve their relations with Lever, embittered and enraged as he was against the Press which had treated him, as he considered, so shamefully. Then came the question of how the costs of the lawsuit were to be shared between the members of the combine, with further cause for friction. Out of the failure of the project of union had come disunion. The atmosphere of friendly rivalry of the old Association, which Baillie Knight had estimated to be worth '10s. a ton' to the soap makers, was to give place to bitter animosity. Henceforth, the industry was to be sharply divided, in Lever's mind, into the sheep and the goats. In this new struggle for existence the motto was to be every man for himself —and Lever take the hindmost.

CHAPTER VII

OVERSEAS DEVELOPMENTS

'If I had concentrated on both sides at Port Sunlight [production and selling], I could not have spread the sale of our product beyond the United Kingdom, and we get enormous strength on the selling side in England by our knowledge of selling and advertising in overseas countries, especially in the United States. I owe much more than I can ever tell to the fact that thirty-five years ago, namely in December 1888, I began to open up overseas businesses. It reminds me of the quotation, "What should they know of England who only England know".'

Lord Leverhulme to his Son, 1923, *quoted in* Viscount Leverhulme by His Son, *p.* 57

THE British exporter's task was nowhere easy in the eighties and nineties. The easy conquests of the third quarter of the century were over and everywhere the British industrialist watched uneasily as tariff walls rose against him. For an article such as soap there were special difficulties. Both in the old peasant countries of Europe and the lands of the frontier in America and the Dominions, domestic manufacture of soap was common, and this was rapidly being supplemented by high-quality soap made in local factories. Moreover the very nature of Lever's speciality meant that it could only be sold in countries with a reasonably high standard of living. Its virtues and its superiority to ordinary soap could only be explained to a literate and receptive audience. So it was perforce to civilized communities that Lever turned when considering the future of his export trade. Yet it was here that local competition was likely to be strongest and tariffs most troublesome.

In 1889 he was prospecting in France, Belgium, and Germany. 1890 saw him in Canada. During the summer of 1892 he was touring Western Europe again. After a short return to England he was off on his first world tour—America, Canada, New Zealand, Australia, Ceylon. Two years later he crossed the Atlantic again and late 1895 and the early months of 1896 were spent in South Africa, Tasmania, Australia, and Ceylon. Visits to North America and Europe followed in 1896 and 1897. In 1898 he concentrated on Switzerland, Germany, and the United States. In all these journeyings, Lever kept two objects clearly in mind. The first was to explore export markets where the produce of Port Sunlight could be sold. The second was to investigate possible sources of raw materials; for the rising demand for fats and oils in Western Europe was already beginning to cause him some anxiety. While touring Samoa and Ceylon he noted the possibilities of copra production. In Australia he attended sales where tallow from the sheep stations was being sold. In 1894 he bought an oil mill at Vicksburg 'in the very heart of the Mississippi and Yazoo valleys' cotton plantations'. His original motive in buying Vicksburg was to transport its oil to Port Sunlight. But it did not take him long to learn that this was impracticable and Vicksburg was soon disposed of. The following year he established at Balmain, on the Sydney harbour front, an oil mill for crushing copra from the South Sea Islands. It was the first oil mill to be built south of the Equator. The outcome of these journeyings must now be described in greater detail.

In September 1888, while the Port Sunlight works was still being built, he left for New York to arrange for an American agency. America had a great fascination for Lever throughout his career. His salesman's eye saw a great potential market in a country whose population had doubled between 1860 and 1886. But Lever was not only interested in America as a market; he was fascinated by the whole panorama of American life. The vigour and efficiency of American business methods made an enormous impression on him. His later speeches and writings are full of tributes to the organization and high productivity of American industry.

His main concern was to gauge the American market for Sunlight: to do this he had to test the strength of the local competition and study local methods of distribution. It needed no lengthy investigation to show that there were formidable difficulties to be overcome if an imported soap were to be sold in competition with the large American soap makers, including Procter & Gamble of Cincinnati. Formidable though the difficulties were, Lever refused to be dismayed by them. He was confident that he could secure a foothold in the populous Eastern States. It was otherwise in the West, where he immediately recognized insoluble problems: 'I do not think

California at present will be of much use to us on account of high freight and other expenses, the purchasing power of money being less here than in New York, but the principal drawback is the thinly populated state of the country. . . . Also there are already twenty soap makers in San Francisco, to add to which all the Eastern soap makers send their soap and are represented out here—all do a little and no one man much—with only 1,500,000 of population we could never sell enough to pay expenses.'

The task of building up an agency for a special commodity like Sunlight in a distant country was both novel and formidable. It was hardly surprising that progress in America was disappointing in the early years. Close personal attention was the only solution and for the five years from 1894 to 1898, Lever made an annual visit to the United States. The journey of 1895—'dull, wet and rough weather'—temporarily took the edge off his usual optimism and soon after arrival he wrote to his father: 'It [the American business] is the biggest undertaking I ever had on hand and I fancy it has depressed me.' A few days sufficed to restore his natural ebullience. A. J. Wolfendale, who had been the Director in charge of outdoor advertising in the United Kingdom, had been appointed manager of the New York agency. 'Am delighted', Lever wrote in his diary on 26th March 1895, 'with the way everything is going in New York—Mr. Wolfendale is just the man for the position.' After a visit to the South he was back in New York in April dealing with advertising problems: there was, he wrote, great difficulty in introducing a new soap 'but my confidence that we can do it is as great as ever—or greater'. By May 20th he was able to record that his New York staff was complete. It consisted of a manager (Wolfendale), a head clerk, a lady stenographer, a boy, three travellers, and three agents, and salaries ran from $4 a week (the boy) to $8,000 a year (the manager). Lever left for home in good heart, confident of Wolfendale's ability to run the business. 'I leave a good man in him and I feel our interests are safe.' It was, in fact, a critical phase for the American business. Sales were still small and practically confined to the Eastern States. But in spite of severe competition, sales continued to grow until the next phase of the business—the purchase of an American factory—was reached.

Farther north, in Canada, the difficulties seem to have been somewhat less though he had to face a strongly competitive industry. On his first visit there in 1888, he listened to encouraging reports on the popularity of English goods—'all Canadians prefer English goods and will take them at high prices'—and in Winnipeg he met a grocer who 'sells Pears' soap quite extensively. . . .' In spite of a tariff, therefore, he was encouraged to set up an agency in Montreal. At its head was an old boyhood friend—Alfred Robinson—who had settled in Canada a few years previously. The Canadian business did not prosper as well as he had hoped, but he did not lose faith in his manager though his frugal eye noted that 'Alf's home was, if anything, better than his position warrants but not better than it will warrant I hope'.

Nevertheless, everything promised well in 1892 for the future of Sunlight in Canada: from the manager down, the staff were in good heart for the future. Some administrative rearrangements were necessary. The main agency was moved to Toronto, and subsidiary agencies at Halifax and St. Johns (New Brunswick) placed under Toronto—'so that now Toronto office is head of all and controls all—I believe the arrangement will work well and hope it may—there is no other way of working the country than this. . . .' And if any further evidence of his confidence in Canadian progress is required it can be seen in his purchase of land in Toronto for building a factory: it was not opened till eight years later. In the nineties all seemed to be well enough with the Canadian trade.

The first world tour in 1892–3 included a visit to Australia and New Zealand. At Auckland Lever was greeted by J. P. Gray who had already been in Australia and New Zealand as an agent for some four years. Pursuing the same routine as in America, he set to work to study the local distributive trade. The situation was evidently patchy. He found among the wholesale and retail grocers 'a general apathy and indifference to Sunlight affairs that is not a good sign. . . .'

Evidently these comfortable traders were not displaying the interest in Sunlight sales which Lever thought desirable. He was not long in deciding on a solution. The same evening he 'went into question of prices with Mr. Gray at night and arranged a new basis under which Sunlight can be sold here'.

This was as much as could be done at Auckland and Lever moved on to ten days' sightseeing which included volcanoes, hot springs, and a retired cannibal who described from memory the taste of his victims as 'very like pork only nicer'.

Work started again at Wellington where he 'arranged Sunlight business on the new basis satisfactorily'. From Wellington, he passed on to Dunedin where he 'found Sunlight well introduced and selling freely'. As the year was running out he sailed for Hobart, cheered perhaps by a visit which his companion Mr. Gray paid to a grocer in Invercargill 'who had just received five cases of Sunlight [and] said it was the only soap that had a steadily increasing sale'. Tasmania did not detain him long and he was soon in Melbourne, where he 'went to see agents in morning, and found them unwilling to push the soap so decided to appoint fresh agents'. After producing this simple and characteristic solution he passed on to Sydney, where he called on several wholesale grocers, who reported sales of Sunlight good but complained of the small profit. 'A very good sign' was his comment. With that, he was off to Brisbane to call on his local agents. 'Did not much care for them,' he wrote. 'Their manner was not that of calm business and they do not pay their accounts regularly.' Everywhere he gave minute attention to the arrangements for agents and travellers, himself negotiating prices and salaries and defining territories. As in Canada and the States he carefully noted the effects of tariffs—complicated in Australia by the fact that the as yet unfederated colonies had separate tariff systems. In South Australia, for example, he observed that Sunlight was charged duty at fourpence a pound, whereas if the soap were stamped in South Australia he would only have to pay the laundry-soap duty of one penny a pound. These difficulties apart, the development of Australia undoubtedly promised a good commercial opening. Since the sixties material advances, though uneven, had been substantial. The population was increasing steadily and the tendency was for the great cities—Melbourne, Sydney, Adelaide—to grow at the expense of the country. It was a land 'almost empty of villages . . . ruled by a few great cities'.[1] Sydney itself and the other cities on the seaboard provided a substantial market for soap sales, but beyond lay a vast, empty country where orthodox

[1] Sir Keith Hancock, *Cambridge History of the British Empire*, Chapter XVII.

salesmanship was of doubtful value. A salesman's 'tour' might take the best part of two years. Long journeys and the tough customers of the remote markets called for stamina and resource. The gold-fields of Western Australia proved an unexpectedly profitable field for the soap travellers. Here large numbers of men and very few women were living and the laundry problem was acute. To have brought water over three hundred miles to the settlement was a triumph of engineering skill but the water supplied was hard and brackish. Sunlight, designed to lather freely in any water, found a new popularity in Kalgoorlie.

Meanwhile Lever was developing plans for an attack on the markets of Western Europe. Throughout Western Europe in the second half of the nineteenth century, an increase of population had gone hand in hand with industrialization and the drift from country to town. In the century between 1800 and 1900, the population had roughly doubled—from perhaps two hundred to four hundred million people. The increase had been most marked in Germany, but Holland, Belgium and Switzerland had all experienced considerable expansion. Only in France had the movement been checked. After Sedan, the French population became almost stationary, and perhaps it is no accident that Lever's progress was slowest in France and most rapid in Holland and Germany. Everywhere the drift into towns was a marked feature of the new age. England had led the way but in the latter part of the nineteenth century the movement was most rapid in Germany. By 1900 more than half Germany's people lived in cities. In some degree the features which had marked industrialization in England were reproduced in Europe. Everywhere, except in France, wages rose until about 1900, but many of those who benefited by the rise had to live in conditions of squalor and overcrowding. The old Europe had gone the way of the old England. These were the vital facts and figures on which Lever confidently based his plans for Western Europe.

It was in 1888 that he had first met a man who was to be closely connected with him in the development of the continental companies—F. H. Lavanchy Clarke. Lavanchy was a Swiss, ingenious, imaginative and eloquent. As a young man he had been fired with ambition to become a missionary, had gone through some alarming experiences with the Red Cross in the Franco-Prussian war of 1870, and later developed a great interest in the problems of the blind. From helping to establish schools for the teaching of Braille he had turned his energies to raising money for the blind and had conceived the idea of founding a company for making and hiring out automatic slot machines, a percentage of the profits to go regularly to the blind. It was in connection with this company that he met W. Whiteley, the head of the well-known London store, who put him in touch with Lever. And for several years, Lavanchy helped to build up the trade of Sunlight in Switzerland, bringing to the task a tireless energy and a flair for advertising comparable to Lever's own. Two examples of his methods are worth quoting: an annual almanac, written largely by himself, with jokes, cartoons, moral tales, competitions and the inevitable appeal for the blind—for Lavanchy never forgot his philanthropic duties—the whole reminiscent of Lever's own *Lancashire Grocer*; and one of the first types of apparatus for giving cinematograph shows, entry being restricted to those who could show a coupon obtainable by buying a carton of Sunlight.

Lavanchy's most famous stunt, however, was a *Fête des Blanchisseuses* held on Easter Monday 1889 on the Lake of Geneva. All the washerwomen from the Lake towns were invited and transported by steamers together with large and enthusiastic crowds of spectators to a rendezvous, where a large banquet concluded the proceedings. With his great leonine head, aquiline nose, his long black hair brushed back from his temples and overhanging his collar, and a wide-brimmed hat, Lavanchy looked more like a virtuoso than a business man. And indeed he was no ordinary business man. His brain teemed with advertising schemes. Lever's business in Europe was to owe much to Lavanchy's restless talent, and the missionary fervour which he brought to the humdrum problems of commerce.

As his representative in Holland, Lever chose a very different type of man. A. P. van Geelkerken was in business in London as a general commercial agent when Lever met him in 1888. At the end of the year he left London for Rotterdam and opened a small agency for Sunlight. The Dutch trade was a success from the very beginning. From a mere 3,765 cases in 1889, sales rose by 1904–5 to over 125,000 cases. Some of the success was due to the efforts of the painstaking van Geelkerken, some perhaps to social and economic conditions—a high standard of living combined with a high degree of urbanization. Sunlight was launched in Holland with the same fanfare of advertising trumpets which had proved so successful in England. The Dutch railways were plastered with blue and white enamel signs: the Dutch Press asked its readers why a woman grew old sooner than a man, and the Dutch polders grew an unaccustomed crop of hoardings twelve metres long and three metres high, 'painted with fanciful subjects'.

Nor was this all. Samples of Sunlight Soap and a book by Barnum, the Yankee circus magnate, entitled *How to Become Rich* were distributed from a blue, red, and yellow wagonette by two men 'dressed in a blue uniform, rain cape and cap, piped in red and on the cap in gold letters, "Sunlight Soap"'. Their success in the towns, we are assured, was great, but in the villages the less sophisticated peasantry took them for members of the still unpopular Salvation Army, and Lever had his martyrs no less than General Booth.

All this propaganda was doubly necessary. In the first place, Lever was never without competitors, both English and Dutch, who included on the one hand the familiar names of Hazelhurst, Goodwin, Cook, and Wheen, and on the other, notable amongst many, that of Van den Bergh. This latter firm made 'Stuiver Zeep' and 'Sultana'; not to be outdone by their English rival and his Barnum inspiration, they paraded through the astonished streets of Rotterdam a real live elephant bearing a Sultana. Secondly, and more important, Lever had to combat the established habits of the Dutch housewife. She washed her household laundry with soft soap dissolved in boiling water, both of which she bought very cheaply at a local shop, and she stoutly resisted the efforts of Lever's missionaries to convert her to the easier but more expensive 'Sunlight way'. Sunlight she persisted in regarding rather as a toilet luxury, which did not fit in at all with Lever's doctrine of small rates of profit on large sales. The educational problem was still acute after twelve years of effort, for in 1901 Tillotson wrote to van Geelkerken: 'The main point is—how can we best teach the public how to use the Soap in the Laundry, especially by the adopting of the Sunlight method. We know that the habits and customs of a nation are hard to overcome—still, new methods of transit, living and working are being introduced almost every day, therefore why not new methods of washing.' Although the Dutch market had its problems, the major problem of the tariff was not amongst them: Holland clung to free trade longer than any other country except Britain. While therefore Lever did his best to give his business in Holland a local complexion by forming a Dutch selling company, Lever's Zeep Maatschappij, the soap that was sold there continued for many years to come from Port Sunlight.

Belgium very early attracted Lever's notice. It was highly industrialized and thickly populated, thus providing the essential foundations of his trade. Early in 1889 he established an agency in the Place de la Bourse in Brussels. The first general manager, who was to remain as head of the business until 1917, was Ernest Brauen. In the early days his way was hard. 'We note', wrote Lever Brothers in the spring of 1889, referring to Sunlight Soap, 'that you have instructed your travellers to sell it as a Household soap which we think is very wise, as being packed so entirely different from anything there is at present in Belgium, might lead people to believe that it is merely a toilet soap.' Faced with this difficulty, which was common in continental countries, the Brussels management only achieved small sales, and in order to stimulate them the advertising technique which had been developed in England was applied in Belgium. Watches were offered in exchange for soap wrappers, and the usual profusion of Press notices, showcards (bearing reproductions of Royal Academy pictures), and other printed propaganda were showered upon the Belgian public.

Just as in other countries, Lever had not only to overcome the resistance of Belgian consumers, but also to combat the 'excessive competition' of other soap makers who were protected against the foreigner by a fairly stiff tariff, and as long as the export trade lasted this handicap remained. Under these circumstances it was inevitable that the business should show a loss in its early years, for it could only be carried on at all under the burden of expensive advertising and tightly calculated prices, but Lever persevered with his design. By 1900, eleven years of effort produced results sufficiently solid to warrant the foundation of a separate Belgian Company, the 'Société Anonyme

Savonneries Lever Frères', under the Presidency of Ernest Brauen. By 1903 Brauen was speaking of 'greater and greater prosperity', of *brillants résultats*.

In France, Lever found himself up against the competition of a soap industry which was really a by-product of the great oil and fat market of Marseilles. Frenchmen used an inferior household soap which was cheap and it was a long time before Lever was able to make any impression on the market. Nor was progress in Germany, where an agency was opened in Hamburg by Ernest Brauen's brother in 1889, any more rapid.

Thus, with the single exception of Holland, the European markets in this early phase seemed to present even more formidable obstacles than the American and Empire markets: but Lever stuck doggedly to his task. There were more ways of killing a cat than one and his imagination was far from exhausted.

From Export to Manufacture

By 1890, agencies had been established on the Continent, in America and in the Empire to sell Sunlight, but Port Sunlight remained the home of its manufacture. This phase of the business did not last long and by 1900 the agencies had been replaced by factories producing for local needs in Australia, Canada, the United States, Germany, and Switzerland. Factories were contemplated in other European countries as soon as the volume of trade warranted it. This policy of replacing export by local manufacture did not go unchallenged. The Conservative Tariff Reformers were the first to open the attack. Lever was accused of robbing English workmen of work. Later the argument was appropriated by the exponents of Socialist economics. The capitalist, they said, was side-stepping the rise in wages in England by seeking higher profits where wages and living standards were low. Applied to the Lever policy of overseas expansion, there was no justification for the accusation. The fact was that, just as in England Lever was thrusting his way into an industry dominated by powerful competitors with established reputations, so, abroad, he was compelled to challenge existing native manufacturers supported by Government policy and national sentiment. Far from being easy victories these overseas ventures were the fruit of heavy risks knowingly undertaken.

The general problems were similar everywhere—tariffs, local sentiment, and transport costs. The fact that raw material imports were generally much more lightly taxed than manufactures gave a powerful stimulus to the policy of establishing factories behind these tariff walls, especially as the remittance of profits raised no problems. Money still knew no frontiers. Hence the force of the argument which Lever was never tired of using, 'Suppose . . . the World was free trade, and soap could be imported with merely the question of freight . . . there would be no need to manufacture soap in Germany, and no need for the establishment of Associated Companies'. Lever dealt with the whole question of tariffs in a speech made in 1902.

> The question of erecting works in another country is dependent upon the tariff or duty. The amount of duties we pay on soap imported into Holland and Belgium is considerable, and it only requires that these shall rise to such a point that we could afford to pay a separate staff of managers with a separate plant to make the soap to enable us to see our way to erect works in those countries. When the duty exceeds the cost of separate managers and separate plant, then it will be an economy to erect works in the country so that our customers can be more cheaply supplied from them.

Undoubtedly foreign tariffs had much to do with the changing character of the British export of capital about 1900. Britain had been exporting capital for the best part of a century. But now British investment in commercial enterprise and industrial manufactures abroad began to grow as it had never done before. In this movement, Lever was in the van: but he had to pay the penalty of the pioneer whose privilege it is to let others profit by his experience. A second, but scarcely less powerful motive behind the establishment of works abroad was the necessity for dealing on the spot with eccentricities of local taste. In the States for example, Baltimore had 'a large German, Jewish and coloured population; of the 680,000 inhabitants about forty per cent are coloured' and their tastes ran to cheap soaps 'such as two cents and penny [1c.] bars', while Monkey Brand, owing to persistent advertising fifteen years before, was 'as staple as granulated sugar'. In Pittsburgh, the salesman was confronted with a local preference for a tar soap called 'Grandpa's Wonder' while throughout the Eastern States there was a violent prejudice against the smell of Lifebuoy. One man said he had seen grocers hand samples to some of their customers and say: '... there is something you ought to use' and 'the woman would take the sample of Lifebuoy, smell it, and throw it across the store'. Even Lifebuoy sales however invariably increased during the summer months 'on account of the intense heat'. The Negro population provided its own peculiar problems and a salesman from the deep South said, 'It was a sort of fad in New Orleans to buy everything two for five cents, not only soaps, for there are no pennies in New Orleans. For instance a coloured woman will come into a store and lay down a nickel and she will get a cake of soap and glass of soda water for it, or she will lay down a nickel and get some soap and hair pins.' The Negroes were also 'very much interested in anything to be given away free with soap', but they were by no means alone in that.

Germany too was a market with its own problems. In the North, East, and greater part of Western Germany, hard soap of the Sunlight variety was not used at all. Potash soap was the local choice in general but every town appeared to have its special likes and dislikes.

Germany also raised in an acute form another problem facing the British trader pushing into foreign markets—native dislike of the foreigner. To some extent this was present everywhere and even the establishment of a local factory did not provide the complete answer. Even van Geelkerken, who on other occasions treated his chief with the greatest respect, in 1902 wrote a letter smarting with resentment over British policy in South Africa, concluding: 'No more as English people will be governed by French or Germans or Dutch, no more will Dutch, French or Germans be governed by British and no treaty like England compelled the Dutch to pass in 1813 will surrender a colony from one sceptre to another like a herd of sheep. We do not consider ourselves the property of a king or diplomat.' No doubt such incidents as these were in Lever's mind when he said in 1902 to representatives of his Belgian and Dutch businesses: 'I want you to continue your efforts a little longer until we can put a Works down in your country and you are able to call upon your customers and say to them: "This soap is made in Belgium for Belgian people" or "This soap is made in Holland for Dutch people".'

Quite apart from these obstacles, the exporter had to face formidable rivalry from native manufacturers. Nowhere was the problem more acute than in America for nowhere were manufacturers more ingenious in pushing their goods. A. J. Wolfendale had only been in charge of the New York Office for a few months when he sent home a report to Port Sunlight. It dealt almost entirely with rival firms, their sales and their advertising, which included everything from gift schemes and advertising plates to plain imitation ('American Sunlight Soap' and 'Daylight Soap' put out by a combination of Brooklyn retail grocers). Both Australia and Canada had well-developed local industries supplying relatively restricted markets by the middle years of the century. As railways were laid and populations grew these areas were linked up, and by the time Lever arrived, in the nineties, he had to join in a fiercely competitive 'fighting trade'. Here in the Dominions was all the sophistication of salesmanship and perhaps less of the gentlemanly atmosphere of the home market.

In Europe, competition was everywhere severe. Germany, whose tariffs were high, was a market which could virtually only be tackled from the inside. And prospects were anything but rosy. Dr. Aufschlager, an investigator sent on reconnaissance in 1897, warned Lever strongly against a German factory. Total German production was estimated to be about 210,000 tons a year, soap works were numerous—in Bavaria there was said to be 'a soapery in every village'—and the larger makers' products were 'not inferior to Lever's'. That was enough to make Lever determined to invade the German market: and wiser than his advisers he never lost sight of the cardinal fact that the German population was growing rapidly. From 44,000,000 in 1870 it had grown to 66,000,000 by 1906 and was increasingly gathered in the large towns. Nor did Lever share his advisers' high opinion of the German soap industry and its technique. Legal difficulties were overcome: Ludwig Stollwerck, an experienced German business man, became Chairman of the German business.

Markets in the smaller countries were hardly less difficult to conquer. In Switzerland the introduction of Sunlight brought a prolonged battle over tariffs with the Swiss soap makers. The end of the struggle (which involved seven visits by Lever to

Switzerland between 1896 and 1898) was that a soap works was erected at Olten in 1898.

The moral of all this was plain: as soon as the volume of trade warranted it, a local factory was opened. The policy was not, as opponents alleged, an irresponsible search for higher profits: it was inevitable if the struggle for foreign markets was not to be lost before it was begun. But the mere establishment of branch works was not in itself a complete answer to the problem. Each one presented its own difficulties of management and organization. The art of building up a large complex of overseas enterprises was new and full of surprises. One thing, however, was clear to Lever: these overseas factories could not be administered from Port Sunlight. There must for each factory be a separate limited liability company responsible not least for any debts or losses the business might suffer. 'I should never entertain for one moment', he wrote in 1901, 'any suggestion of opening a single branch works outside the United Kingdom unless as a preliminary thereto a separate company was formed for working such business. In my opinion, this is a *sine qua non*. For similar reasons many shipping houses in Liverpool make each separate ship a limited company.' Responsibility must rest with the local management. No other system would work. The difficulty was to find managers who combined enterprise with reliability. What is surprising is not that he met with some failures but that he had so many successes.

The methods by which the new companies were financed varied from country to country. The object was in every case the same: to give Lever Brothers a sufficient preponderance of voting rights to ensure full control of policy. In America, where Lever purchased two existing factories, at Boston and Philadelphia, the vendors retained a considerable interest but after the consolidation into one company (Lever Brothers Company) the whole capital was held 'within the concern'. On the Continent, the original agents were sometimes compensated by the issue of shares for the termination of their earlier contracts. Thus in Switzerland, Lavanchy Clarke received four-tenths of the Ordinary shares as payment for his monopoly rights for the sale of Sunlight in Switzerland. There was also a handful of outside Preference shareholders, but Lever Brothers' total holding maintained a comfortable lead over the combined holdings of all the other shareholders. In the German company at Mannheim there were eleven other shareholders, including three members of the Stollwerck family, but here again Lever Brothers' holding was almost twice that of the others. In the Australian Company, Lever Brothers held the whole of the Ordinary and Preference shares. It is this heavy capital outlay on the overseas companies which in part explains the expansion of the capital of the parent company from one and a half to four and a half millions between 1894 and 1906. The fortunes of the overseas businesses will be followed in detail later. It is sufficient here to note that in 1900 there were five. Sydney and Toronto were the largest, each with an output of 92 tons a week. Mannheim came next with 81 tons a week, followed by Olten with 67 tons. Philadelphia was the smallest, producing 31 tons a week. None of them was big by home standards of production, nor did they bring any immediate reward to the parent company, for all their profits were ploughed back into the businesses themselves for many years.

As the overseas factories expanded criticism of Lever's policy grew. 'English workmen were being robbed of work': these were the years of Lever's excursions into politics as a Liberal and his opponents did not fail to make the most of their opportunity. But Lever refused to be intimidated. 'There is not a word of truth in it,' he thundered to the shareholders. 'If we had not these works abroad we should not have this trade, and the best proof I can give of this is that no English soap maker ever had a soap trade in Germany till we put a soap works there. No English soap firm had a soap trade in France until we came and built works there. No English firm had any soap trade in Belgium until we came and built works there. I could say the same for U.S.A., the same of Canada, and the same of Australia. Therefore we have never taken any trade from England. . . . In 1895 we employed at Port Sunlight directly less than 1,500. In 1911 at Port Sunlight and elsewhere in the United Kingdom directly employed by Lever Brothers exclusive of any employed at our associated companies, we employed over 6,000 . . . so that this policy, instead of making less work in the United Kingdom, is making more.' In this last claim he was on less solid ground, though he would have been justified in claiming that his overseas policy had done nothing to retard the growth of Port Sunlight. And about his general argument as to the necessity of replacing export trade by overseas factories there can be no possible doubts. The individual histories of the overseas companies provide striking confirmation that only by some such policy could foreign trade in soap be captured, retained and expanded.

The New Factories

The building of the factories overseas only solved the first problem of selling soap abroad. It got Sunlight over the tariff wall but it did not do more than that. A multitude of problems still remained to be tackled. The best answer to the charge that overseas expansion was a search for an easy life and cheap profits lies in the history of the new companies themselves.

Wolfendale's agency was still small when in 1897 Lever began negotiations for the purchase of his first American manufacturing company—the Curtis Davis Company of Boston. After the purchase the company was reconstructed, Lever taking three-fifths of the capital and the other partners the remainder. Along with the factory went the rights in Welcome soap, which were to prove a valuable asset. Two years later Lever bought Benjamin Brooke's of Philadelphia, the property of Sydney and Henry Gross. The Gross brothers belonged to a family of American Jews of Austrian origin, and Sydney was to play a prominent part in the subsequent history of Lever's.

Almost immediately Lever reorganized his new American concerns. The Boston company was responsible for trading in the New England States; the Philadelphia company became the selling agency throughout the rest of America. Evidence of the difficulties of the American market, which in these years brought continual reorganization and a series of resignations, can be found in the report of a conference of salesmen which took place in New York in 1903. Neither of the Lever staple products, Sunlight and Lifebuoy, was going well. A Brooklyn salesman could report that the grocers in his area 'positively refuse to stock Sunlight because of it being such a slow seller'. Lifebuoy was disliked because of its smell; and possibly Lever's policy, based on English experience, of concentrating on the retailer and the public and ignoring the wholesaler got him into further difficulties. Perhaps too the quality of Lever's American-made soaps was not all it might have been for Edward Wainwright, over from Lancashire, twice reported unfavourably on the colour and texture of the Boston-made Sunlight.

A general gloom hung over the North American scene, where we have the remarkable spectacle of Lever employing private detectives to find out whether his New York manager was doing enough work, nor were affairs in Canada, where the Toronto works started production in 1900, in much better order. Here 'Alf' Robinson had been put into the presidency and evidently his capabilities were not of the highest. P. J. Winser, visiting Toronto in the autumn of 1900, sent home a damning report: 'Toronto was a great disappointment. . . . Business seems to go along at its own sweet will, without proper guidance and the part of it managed by the agents (in Winnipeg, British Columbia, and Nova Scotia) seems better managed and more successful than that directly controlled by Toronto, while the poor sales (*per capita*) in Toronto and Ontario generally show there is something radically wrong with their methods.' In Winser's view the policy of local manufacture might appeal to local patriotism in Toronto and afford some help there, but not in other areas. The only remedy was a clean sweep and Alf Robinson made way shortly afterwards for Joseph Meek. Meek's reign was successful but short for he was quickly moved on to a similar post in Australia, being replaced in Canada by A. C. Knight. These were years of rapid transformation in the Canadian soap trade. By a process not unlike that which had been going on in the United Kingdom for the previous twenty years, local markets were giving way to national markets, and free-for-all competition to amalgamation and absorption. With the first acquisition of associated companies there begins a new phase in the development of the Canadian business. By 1906 the North American organization had been trimmed for action. It only remained to increase the sales.

The Australian tariffs varied from a highly protectionist one in Victoria to a nominally free trade system with a revenue tariff in New South Wales. This had influenced Lever powerfully in the choice of Sydney as his headquarters. The internal tariffs were swept away by the establishment of the Commonwealth but the external tariff remained and with it the incentive to develop an Australian factory. In 1900 the first Australian factory took its place at Balmain beside the mills built five years earlier, on a site where access to raw materials was combined with other advantages. Transport was always Lever's first concern and Balmain had a water frontage to Port Jackson whence raw materials could be brought right into the works by water. There was coal at Newcastle and Kembla. In 1900 even ocean-going ships could unload direct on to the wharf and when later they became too large, raw materials and manufactures could still be handled by lighter. At Balmain, in fact, Lever might congratulate himself on finding a down-under reproduction of the Port Sunlight site. J. P. Gray, who had been with the Australian business for ten years and stood high in Lever's opinion, was put in as first chairman of the new company. Gray had under him J. W. Hope[1] as manager of the oil mill and works manager of the factory. Hope combined with dislike of subordination an embarrassingly accurate judgement of his superior's capacity and it does not seem to have taken him long to realize that Gray was by no means a brilliant chairman: not so brilliant, for instance, as he himself might be if he were given the opportunity. He took occasion therefore to quarrel over certain charges incurred in the building of the works, particularly the rates paid to a firm of contractors called Gray Brothers with which the Chairman was connected. This apparently earned him nothing but a sharp reprimand from Lever, but meanwhile evidence was accumulating to show that Gray's management was unskilful. When P. J. Winser arrived in Australia towards the end of 1900, Gray offered him his resignation but asked for delay before it took effect because 'he felt certain he could get into the Senate, which would give him £400 per annum'.

The new Chairman was Joseph Meek, who was to hold the office for twenty-two years. His appointment was the first move in a complete reorganization, which was designed to strengthen the discipline in the Australian business. This was doubly necessary for Sydney was particularly important in the supply of raw materials to Port Sunlight. Tallow and other materials were bought through Sydney over a long period of years; but careful guidance and tutelage of the pupil company were regarded as essential both by Lever and Barrie who, as chief raw material

[1] See Chapter VI.

buyer, was vitally concerned with the health of the Australian Company.[1]

The Swiss trade was the first to reach dimensions which justified the building of a factory. The site, chosen with all Lever's usual attention to transport facilities, was at Olten, half-way between Zürich and Basle. 'Olten in Switzerland', wrote Lever a year or two after its foundation, 'is a great central rail-way junction—a sort of Swiss Crewe—equidistant from the large towns of Zürich and Basle.' The factory was designed to produce 67 tons a week and Savonnerie Helvetia, the company floated in 1898 to work the plant, had a capital of two million francs (about £80,000). Lever Brothers took a controlling interest but the balance of the Preference shares were spread amongst a group of Swiss business men interested in the venture. Lavanchy became secretary and manager. The separation of capital and management led almost immediately to quarrels: Lavanchy, who not unnaturally had come to regard the Swiss business as his own creation (which it largely was) and was in any case not good at compromise, was soon at loggerheads with his Swiss colleagues, and in March 1899, before the Olten factory was in full working order, he resigned. The loss of his talents was fortunately not permanent though when he returned some years later it was to Lever's French business.

Those native Swiss manufacturers who had done their best to keep out Lever's soaps before 1899 were slow to admit defeat. Evidently they considered their best vantage point for making further trouble was that of shareholders and by 1901 a proportion of the balance of shares had fallen into their hands, causing Lever some misgivings as to the amount of information he might safely give the shareholders regarding the progress of the business. What with the disturbance caused by Lavanchy's departure, teething troubles in the new factory and Swiss competition, the first two years might well have given rise to gloomy forebodings. A small profit in 1898 gave way to heavy losses in 1900. There was a small profit in 1901, and thereafter business revived. Even so, the bill for dividends was too heavy to be met and Lever Brothers had to make a substantial loan to keep Olten afloat. By 1903, however, the Swiss business had settled down comfortably.

[1] See Chapter XII for later developments.

The establishment of the Swiss factory in 1898 was followed by the founding of a German company, Sunlight Seifenfabrik, in the same year. In 1900, disregarding the gloomy prophecies of his advisers, Lever opened his works at Mannheim. Once again, transport facilities played a large part in determining the site. 'The Mannheim Soapery (Germany)', he wrote, 'has a siding connection with the main line of railway running through the city—in fact, it has a frontage of over 500 feet to that line: besides which it is on the Rhine.' At Mannheim Lever was in the heart of industrial Germany.

The capacity of the Mannheim factory (81 tons a week) was modest in relation to the vast potential market. But Lever was conscious of the strength of the opposition, political as well as economic, that he might encounter. He was wise to start in a small way. Even so, the reaction of the German soap makers to this foreign invasion was swift and sharp. Internal rivalries were sunk in a concerted effort against Lever, and an advertising battle followed. Some sort of compromise was reached in 1901 and until 1903 there followed a period of quiet consolidation. Under the Chairmanship of Stollwerck, the Managing Director was H. O. Beck, a German for whose ability Lever had considerable respect. Beck was certainly enterprising and ambitious, but jealous and quick to sense a slight if anyone else earned favour or reward. For the moment his flair for aggressive advertising stood the new Company in good stead.

By 1903 Mannheim was making money but it was evident that the advertising truce was working to Lever's disadvantage. Beck therefore embarked on a new advertising campaign which caused the soap war to break out afresh. The new campaign began *pianissimo*, articles in German newspapers appearing 'not as an advertisement but in the form of an impartial editorial utterance apparently written by some scientific contributor to the newspaper'. One of these 'impartial utterances' contained a remark which the German soap makers conceived to be derogatory to their products, and their trade paper, the *Seifenfabrikant*, took the matter up.

In addition to stirring up the hornets' nest of his competitors, Beck also upset his Chairman, Stollwerck, who felt that the advertisements had made unnecessarily pointed comparisons between Sunlight and the native soaps and that his articles were insufficiently cultured to appeal to the educated classes. A voluminous correspondence between the two men followed, in which Beck defended himself against the charge of vulgarity. 'The tone of all our advertisements . . . is as refined as our object will permit, which is to impress the public at large, the masses, the innumerable army of consumers. Language which will do so must be expressed in a positive form, any milder way would be regarded as a weak attempt of saying something without the courage of one's convictions. I am fully convinced that, whatever is said in our advertisements can be backed up by facts and we have not to be afraid to displease anyone.'

The dispute must have had a familiar ring to Lever. He was quite used to dealing with over-enthusiastic travellers whose method of selling his goods was to disparage other people's. Hence the tone of his reply: 'I am gratified that you are taking up a definite position with regard to meeting the opposition from soap makers in Germany. I believe that your policy will be "the strong hand in the glove of velvet", but that the strong hand will be courteous but firm. In any case all new firms like the Sunlight Seifenfabrik have to fight for their existence in the early days—Lever Brothers had to do it.' By 1904 Lever was well launched into his campaign to capture the German market. As in England, the objects of advertising were twofold: to create new consumers, and to attract existing custom away from his rivals. But the task in Germany was more difficult than in England. Wages and standards of living were lower: the German housewife was given to using soft soap or low-grade bar soaps and powders. Sunlight was apt to be regarded as a toilet soap rather than as a laundry soap. Demand for Sunlight was still relatively sluggish, and, to stimulate trade, Lever recommended the introduction of wrapper schemes. In July 1904 he was able to congratulate Beck on a successful quarter's trading. Nevertheless it was evident that a stiff fight lay ahead in the German market.

In Belgium, Ernest Brauen had, by 1904, raised his trade to a point where the volume warranted putting up a Belgian factory. Building was commenced on the site chosen for the factory at Forest-Midi, a suburb of Brussels. The site was far from ideal; it was wet and boggy, but it was cheap and it had the advantage of being situated within ten minutes' tram drive from the Midi station in Brussels; it had a siding connection with the main line running between Brussels and Paris; and it was near the Charleroi Canal. In July 1905, the new factory was ready. Two thousand workpeople from Port Sunlight were transported across the Channel, and driven in wagonettes from Brussels to Forest to watch the proceedings. At the appointed time 'le Burgomestre de Forest, au cours d'une inauguration solennelle, ouvre une vanne d'admission de vapeur et déclenche ainsi l'activité de l'usine de Forest'.

SUMMARY

There is no marking time in the march of events which gives the historian an obvious opportunity to survey progress overseas. On the whole, 1906, a turning point in home development, is as convenient as any other date for a stock-taking overseas. By that time the volume of trade had justified the building of factories in a number of foreign countries and Dominions: elsewhere, it was approaching that point and factories were planned though not erected. There was a steady trickle of engineers, soap boilers and accountants from Port Sunlight to the overseas factories, several of which were faithful reproductions of the parent factory in lay-out and general methods. All the new overseas companies were having teething troubles but a few were beginning to show a profit though as yet those profits were being ploughed back into the businesses to finance further expansion.

At the annual meeting in 1906, Lever reminded the shareholders that the growth of the new companies called for further capital. 'I am reminded', he went on, 'when I think of them that the only comment we have ever had upon them at these Meetings has been, "Don't put too much money in these associated companies". Well, we have got to help these children, they are growing, and it would be a little difficult to follow this advice with them.'

It has sometimes been assumed that the diversion of British capital from home to overseas and even from European to Dominions and tropical areas at this period can be quite simply accounted for by a reference to the desire of British investors for easy profits. Evidently one lot of shareholders at any rate were less enthusiastic about this economic baby-farming than some

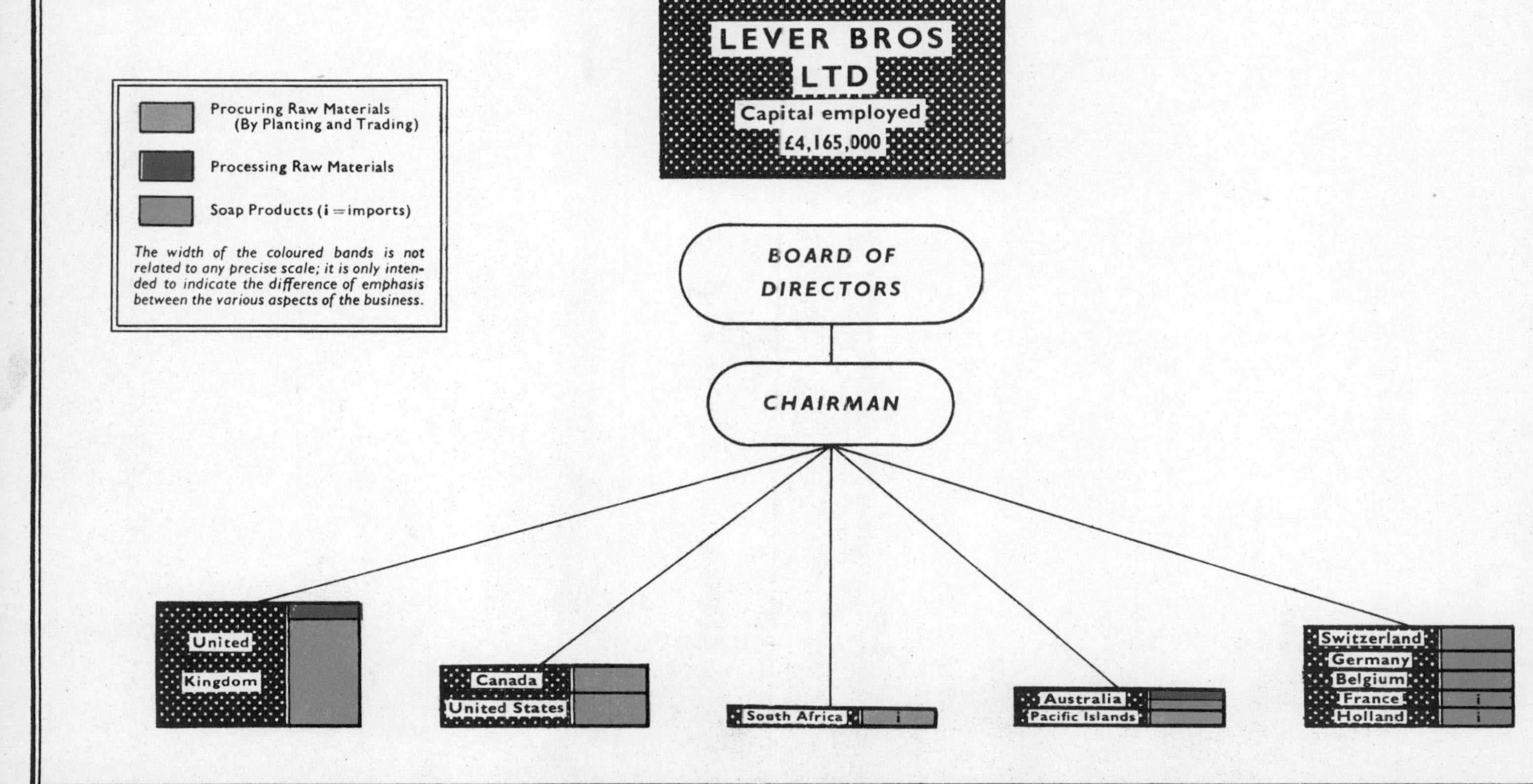
THE LEVER BUSINESS IN 1906
A DIAGRAMMATIC IMPRESSION
Procuring Raw Materials (By Planting and Trading)
Processing Raw Materials
Soap Products (i = imports)
The width of the coloured bands is not related to any precise scale; it is only intended to indicate the difference of emphasis between the various aspects of the business.
LEVER BROS LTD
Capital employed £4,165,000
BOARD OF DIRECTORS
CHAIRMAN
United Kingdom
Canada
United States
South Africa
i
Australia
Pacific Islands
Switzerland
Germany
Belgium
France
Holland
i
i

historians have supposed.[1] The shareholders had a truer picture than the historians of the difficulties of making these new projects pay. The capital locked up overseas was about £1,000,000, roughly a quarter of the capital of Lever Brothers, Port Sunlight—and even Lever himself was prepared to admit that the proportion was now large enough. He therefore proposed to form a company to take over the shares of the associated companies overseas. The prime object was to limit the proportion of Lever Brothers' capital invested in the overseas companies; but it was more than that. Abortive though the proposal was it was the first recognition of the fact that Lever Brothers was no longer a United Kingdom affair but a world affair of which the overseas businesses were an integral part; and of the need for some kind of centralized financial control of those companies.

[1] See, for example, Cole and Postgate, *The Common People*, pp. 486–7, where an interpretation of the motives for capital export is given which is, to say the least, oversimplified.

PART II

THE DIFFICULT YEARS 1906–14

CHAPTER VIII

THE WAR IN THE SOAP TRADE 1906–14

'The last four years our fleet has had to be steered through fogs, round sunken rocks and over sand banks represented by the *Daily Mail* attack—high priced materials—virulent competition from the whole Soap Trade—not always fair . . . '

W. H. Lever in a letter to Joseph Meek, 23 August 1910

FOUR years after the *Daily Mail* attack, Lever wrote a long letter to Joseph Meek, the head of the Australian business and one of the few men with whom he was on really intimate terms, in which he described the course of business during that interlude of difficulties. The letter is couched in nautical language: himself he saw as the 'Admiral of the Fleet'—'never once leaving the bridge' and varying his orders to suit the vicissitudes of weather and battle. His imagery was not inappropriate. The days of the friendly rivalry—the 'game of cricket'—were over. As so often happens after the failure of a coalition, the underlying hostilities emerged sharper than before: tempers were frayed and nerves were on edge. But that was not all. The whole economic setting had changed. Between 1891 and 1907 the total production of soap in the United Kingdom rose from 260,000 tons to 353,000 tons. From then on until the outbreak of war the market remained pretty well stationary; consumption per head had reached its limit for the time being. At the same time new bidders from the margarine industry were sending up prices in the raw material markets. The isolated crises of high prices were becoming more frequent. What had once been acute was becoming chronic.

In the immediate shock at the failure of his plans, Lever was reduced to resigned Shakespearian quotation: 'The robbed that smiles steals something from the thief. He robs himself that spends a bootless grief.' But the mood did not last long: it quickly gave way to active resentment at the wanton damage caused to his business prosperity and his personal reputation. 'I consider the old highwayman of one hundred years ago', he wrote angrily, 'was a gentleman to the modern newspaper proprietor. . . . My spirit rebels against letting my business drift into where blackmailing methods and corruption prevail as in the English Press. . . . I am strongly and resolutely set to discover other methods of conducting our business entirely free from the English Press which to my mind wreaks [*sic*] with corruption as is not fit for a respectable firm to advertise with.' It did not improve his feeling towards his late allies to find them patching up their quarrel with the Press. When he noticed Joseph Watson's advertisements reappearing in the *Daily Mail*, he remarked to Sidney Gross, 'Well, they are not the first curs that have turned to lick the hand that whipped them'. Lever's annoyance was understandable. Besides the trading losses which resulted from the *Daily Mail* attacks, Lever Brothers had to bear unaided the heavy costs, legal, accounting and administrative, of the abortive 'Working Arrangement', for one after another the other firms repudiated their obligations. Ogston & Tennant alone remained faithful, but Lever's blood was up: declaring that he would not penalize one firm for its honesty he set out to foot, as best he could, the bill for £70,000.

Whatever the rights and wrongs of the actions of the other members of the abortive combine, they could at any rate claim with every justification that they were facing bad times. Lever himself had every sympathy with what he called 'the junior firms of the late Combine', remarking to Gross that he would 'dearly like to be able to help them in some way'. Edward Cook was one and there was 'another little firm at Liverpool similarly placed, namely Tyson & Co.'. Neither of Lever's acquisitions during the period of the Working Agreement could be said to be in good fettle. Hodgson & Simpson were certainly in deep waters, mortgaged to the hilt, and probably only saved from public failure by Lever's purchase. Vinolia, he regarded as an orphan of the storm deposited on his doorstep by his late colleagues. Even the bigger firms were not much happier. Christr. Thomas's and Gossage's were in difficulties, and only Crosfield's of Warrington increased their sales between 1905 and 1913, a fact which helps to explain why relationships with Crosfield's loomed so large in Lever's policy in these years.

But Crosfield's were more than just soap makers; their strength lay in their pre-eminence in chemical research, especially into vital raw materials, and their prosperity hardly nullifies the general impression of hard times. These were described vividly by T. A. Cook in a letter reporting the proceedings of a Soap Makers' Association Dinner in 1909: 'We had before us a letter from the smaller Scottish makers complaining bitterly of the state of trade. The London makers, none of them, had a word to say: and in twenty-five years of my experience of the trade, I never knew members so depressed and miserable as they were last night . . . all agreed that they were suffering.' The cause of the suffering was not far to seek. It might be summed up as too many soap makers, too few customers, too many buyers on the raw material market. 'The situation,' wrote Lever, 'needs no half sheet of notepaper and a stubby pencil to work out. Raw materials are practically the dearest for the last twenty years—soap the cheapest for the last twenty years.' Raw material prices had not touched such levels since the early eighties. The change had been brought about largely by the 'enormous increase in the consumption of margarine'. The margarine churner was beginning to use refined vegetable oils in preference to animal fats and what was more could afford to pay higher prices for his materials than the soap maker. 'The Soap maker', wrote Lever in 1910, 'has no chance against the Butterine Maker. The Soap maker gets £24 a ton for soap containing sixty-three per cent of fatty acids and the margarine maker £60 a ton for eighty-five per cent fatty acids . . . there is practically no good oil or fat but what the margarine maker can make into excellent food.'

In the old days a situation such as this would have brought the soap makers round a table to discuss friendly means of mutual defence. But that was all over and done with. Lever himself was quite adamant: he would have nothing to do with the Association. It was 'quite obvious' that 'every member of the Soap Trade was out "on his own" whether in buying or selling' and his strong view was that Lever's must act 'in a friendly way' with the trade but not attend any more meetings at any rate for some time, keeping a free hand as to the best way of conducting their business. Nor was Lever the only one to stand out: John Knight's and Watson's were also out: only Crosfield's and Gossage's among the large firms remained faithful.

Not only had competition amongst existing firms been intensified but one important newcomer had appeared. The Co-operative movement had never been entirely friendly to Port Sunlight and the *Daily Mail* charges had not improved relations. During the crisis of 1906 their soap factory had been overwhelmed with orders and the unexpected flood of business had set the C.W.S. off on a search for a new works. By 1909 two new factories had come into operation. The C.W.S. output of soap was more or less doubled. The inroad into Lever's trade was no temporary phenomenon.

Nowhere was the impact of the 1906 crisis more serious than on Lever's own trade. True, it could be shown that it affected only one brand of soap, but that brand was Lever's principal one: Sunlight had suffered its first setback. The loss was especially severe in London which accounted for four-fifths of the total decrease in sales. Coming to the London office was like 'coming to a cemetery' compared with the old days of bustle. The situation was a depressing one but Lever was not slow in coming to his decision on policy, hard though that decision was. Broadly, what was entailed was a policy of cutting advertising while maintaining prices and accepting the consequence of reduced sales. Lever realized that a new advertising policy was required. The more discerning customer must be courted. There were to be no more prize schemes ('even though Sunlight goes spark out') because 'the higher the position and standing of the user the less demand there is for prizes even on a laundry soap'. Previously he had been catering for 'two classes of consumers . . . the class that wanted quality and were careless about prizes, and the class who wanted prizes and were careless about quality'. Now the first class must be cultivated, even though sales would never get back to their old peak. (He was right to resign himself to that: they never did before 1917.) Thus to Lever the moral was plain: 'Reduce the price and double or treble sales, result loss. Maintain price, sales drop fifty per cent, result profit.'

Such were the sober calculations as regards the old type of trade. But undoubtedly Lever never intended to be content with a contraction of his business. Already his mind was evolving new schemes for new lines of business. Here lay another difficulty: new enterprises meant new capital, but Lever

Brothers' credit had been severely shaken by the crisis. Buildings in process of completion at Port Sunlight had to be stopped. 'We could not get 1d. of cash,' Lever wrote of this period later. A capital issue in 1907 had to be undertaken on very disadvantageous terms. A quarter of a million was raised at six per cent but Lever had to pay five per cent for underwriting, and only about two-thirds of the issue was applied for. It was a sorry state of affairs to one who remembered the days when the public had clamoured for five per cent shares. Nor was it only the investing public who had lost confidence. Even in 1908 an official of the Liverpool Branch of the Bank of England had 'definite information' that Lever's were 'in very great straits' and the Bank refused to discount two of their bills for £36,000. Energetic action by Lever and Barrie soon convinced the Bank of its mistake but the incident was significant. Up to the end of 1908, Lever calculated his losses arising from the 1906 proceedings at £367,000. By the end of 1909 they were estimated at 'over half a million, including the amount received for damages'. In addition to this, the raw materials required for production were costing about a million pounds a year more than before.

So much for the debit side of the account. There was another story to be told, and a brighter one, of progress overseas, where increased trade more than balanced Lever's losses. In fact, in 1909, the Chairman was able to tell the shareholders that profits from the Associated Companies would be sufficient to pay all dividends on Preference Capital for the parent company after allowing for all repairs, renewals and depreciation for all the companies. Truly, the policy of 'spreading the bases out broadly all over the world' had amply justified itself.

The problem that still remained was the provision of capital to finance the increased cost of production and the new businesses which Lever wished to acquire. The first acquisitions were more or less involuntary. The purchases of Hodgson & Simpson of Wakefield, and of the Vinolia Company, were part of the larger scheme that had failed. Lever had no wish to be left with the shares on his hands but his late allies could not be persuaded to co-operate—a further cause of bad blood—and in the end Lever kept both companies as a means of breaking into new trades.

Vinolia he used as a weapon of attack on the toilet soap market, though it was long before results were encouraging.

Hodgson & Simpson's business was used as a means of entering the export trade in bar soap—largely the province of Crosfield's and Gossage's. The Wakefield factory was closed and manufacture transferred to Port Sunlight.

This first move was forced on Lever but it set the fashion for what followed. Whereas in the first twenty years of the company's existence many associated companies were formed overseas, none was acquired at home. In the eight years before the Great War, while overseas development continued, existing English soap businesses were acquired at an ever-increasing rate. The combine which the *Daily Mail* had defeated in 1906 took the field again, more slowly but none the less steadily, in the years that followed. What Lever could not build by one means he set out to construct by another. General conditions in the soap trade, already described, were no doubt largely responsible for the partial diversion of Lever's attention from overseas to home development. With the sales of Sunlight seriously affected by the 1906 agitation and by the voluntary abandonment of wrapper schemes, Lever in 1907 was anxious to find some compensating product. Soap powders had already attracted his attention, but his own venture into that particular field had shown no very encouraging results: the combined production of flakes and powders at Port Sunlight was only 1,400 tons per year out of a total national production of 45,000 tons.

R. S. Hudson's business was soap powder. The business had grown by 1900 to imposing dimensions, with works at Bank Hall, Liverpool, as well as at West Bromwich, an annual production of over 18,000 tons, and a hold on the housewife which Lever found quite impossible to loosen. The firm was buying soap stock from Gossage's at the rate of two or three hundred tons per week, and paying for it sums which during the forty years that the connection lasted amounted to about £2,500,000. The business was still conducted by the founder's family, though concern with politics was already beginning to overshadow the claims of soap, a fact which is perhaps reflected in the steady fall of sales from 19,204 tons in 1899 to 17,681 in 1907. For this business, amid the financial difficulties of 1907–8, Lever paid £1,000,000 and the results were immediately apparent in the Lever 'family's' sale of flakes and powders, which leapt to 20,000 tons in the year of the purchase (1908).

By this transaction Lever established himself in a new branch of activity, which at first he explored cautiously—'I do not propose', he wrote to Sidney Gross, 'to make any change in the management of the business, at any rate not till I understand it better than I do at present.' Nevertheless there was room for improvement, which no doubt Lever had perceived before he paid this huge price. Hudson's powder was of a low fatty acid content and was mainly used for dishwashing. In 1910 'Rinso', an improved soap powder, appeared on the market under Hudson's name, but manufactured at Port Sunlight, not at Bank Hall. Soap powders of high detergent value were already popular in Germany, and Germany was probably the source whence Lever borrowed the idea for Rinso. Its appeal was to the housewife who wanted to save herself the labour of scrubbing the clothes; clothes were soaked in solution overnight. Hence its promise: 'We work while you sleep'.

The advantage gained by Lever Brothers was a sad blow to Gossage's, since the manufacture of soap stock for Hudson's produce was at once taken out of their hands and transferred to Port Sunlight. The seriousness of the loss may be gauged from the figures already quoted, and Gossage's took immediate but ill-advised steps to counteract it. From knowledge in their possession of Hudson's secret but not patented methods of manufacture they started to produce a soap powder of their own, and with it they did their best to attack the sale of the original commodity. A legal action followed, and after a hearing of thirty days in St. George's Hall, Liverpool, Hudson's won. The heavy damages and costs incurred in this case, combined with the loss of their trade with Hudson's, must have rocked the foundations of Gossage's stability, and without doubt influenced their decision to sell out to Brunner Mond in the following year, with results which profoundly affected the course of Lever Brothers' history.[1]

Throughout 1909 Lever marked time. Trade was still far from recovery. 'We can put all the profit there is in soap at present in our eye without danger of permanent injury to the eyesight,' he remarked in that year. But already while he was reorganizing the businesses which he had acquired, he was planning ahead. The transfer of the toilet soap manufacture of Vinolia and the export soap manufacture of Hodgson & Simpson

[1] See Chapter IX.

to Port Sunlight meant that the existing 'soaperies' were 'too crowded altogether'. A new, fourth, soapery was therefore necessary. Additional mills for crushing oil seeds were also required: here was a means of turning high raw material prices to advantage. 'When materials are dear,' he told the shareholders in 1908, 'of course oil milling does well.' Overseas, too, new projects were taking shape. A soap works was planned for South Africa and another for France.

To finance these projects, Lever set out to raise fresh capital. In March 1910, Lever Brothers' authorized capital was increased from six to seven million pounds. Three months later it was increased again to nine millions and before the end of the year it stood at fourteen millions. Of this, some six and a quarter millions had been issued: with tremendous plans for expansion at home and abroad, Lever was determined not to leave himself short of elbow room. In addition to the Ordinary capital (all of which he held himself) he also created a special class of Preferred Ordinary shares which were to be instruments for the buying of companies.

With these increased resources, Lever set about the rebuilding of the combine adumbrated in 1906. Speaking to Sir John Brunner in 1911 he explained 'that he had not bought any business (except Hudson's) that was not included in the so-called "Combine" in 1906; that he was determined that none of those firms should suffer from having been associated with him; that in taking them over he had commenced with the smallest and that he had in the same spirit made an offer to both Gossage's and Crosfield's'. Some of his acquisitions of 1910–11 were small, like Barrington's of Dublin, an old firm which for some years before had made a modest profit on a production of about thirty tons a week; or Tyson's of Liverpool, of whose misfortunes he had written sympathetically in 1907. Others were not so small. By the end of 1911 he had control of Edward Cook's of Bow, which was no doubt a relief to his hard-pressed London trade, and of Christr. Thomas's with its widespread West Country goodwill. At the same time his foreign enterprises steadily spread across the continents, so that to all outward appearances the Lever undertaking had emerged stronger than ever from the depression: such, certainly, was the impression which the Chairman did his best to build up at the annual shareholders' meetings, and the success of his efforts is evident from the class of person who put money in the business. Speaking of a proposed new issue of capital in 1912, 'Sir William[1] . . . felt that in the case of the particular class of Shareholder who subscribed to our issue, the [Balkan] war would make little or no difference at all. It would be different with Colonial or other big Loans, which would not appeal to the speculative man at present, but it would make no difference to a man who was looking out for an investment for his savings.'

All this expansion of capital and manufacture was evidence of returning confidence; and indeed Lever seems to have thought, in the late summer of 1910, that the worst was over. Concluding his nautical homily to Meek in Australia he wrote: 'And now Full Speed Ahead and let's hope we keep clear of another repetition of our last four years'. His hope was not to be fulfilled. A few months after he had written to Meek, a conflict broke out between Lever's and the great chemical firm of Brunner Mond & Company, which in many ways was to dominate Lever Brothers' history for at least six years. It was a conflict so full of intricacies that it requires to be examined in a separate chapter: one of the several dangers which Lever apprehended was that Brunner Mond & Company might enter the soap trade as the most powerful of all competitors. The risk was perhaps as strong an incentive as any he could have been given for pressing on with his design for controlling a larger and larger share of the existing soap firms.

So the process continued, and one by one well-known names from the old Association were added to the Lever list. The first was that of Hazlehurst's, acquired by outright purchase from the United Alkali Company in 1911. Then, between 1912 and 1913, Lever drew within his orbit four more firms. Two of them were small—Isdale & McCallum of Paisley and Richard Wheen's of London—while two were amongst the largest—Joseph Watson's of Leeds and John Knight's of London. None was purchased outright, but a substantial holding was acquired in each. The aim of all these transactions was to limit competition or increase sales: Watson's had long ruled the soap market of North-East England, while Knight's held sway in London. Knight's, in particular, had recently introduced their 'Castile'

[1] Lever was created a Baronet in June 1911.

toilet soap, aimed at that very middle-class trade with which Lever had lately become concerned.

One competitor he did not attempt to buy—the Co-operative Wholesale Society, whose manufacture of soap had received a stimulus from the anti-trust agitation of 1906. Many of the local societies, never particularly friendly to capitalist soap makers, had given up stocking their products: managers and assistants in their shops were instructed, when asked for private makers' soaps, to reply that they did not stock them and to offer instead soap made by the C.W.S.

Lever was seriously perturbed by the strength of the C.W.S. The Co-operative Stores, with their profits from groceries and other goods, were in a position (so he thought) to undersell the private soap maker. Moreover, it seemed to him that they were trying to reap where they had not sown. Manufacturers who had spent large sums of money, as he had, in creating a demand for a particular brand of soap were entitled, in his view, to expect that shopkeepers would fulfil the requirements of customers who demanded advertised products. Whatever the merits of his view, it had no basis in law and when Lever somewhat optimistically brought an action against the Masborough Society's shops, alleging that they were passing off C.W.S. products as his own, his evidence failed to prove his case and the action was lost. Lever thereupon appealed, adumbrating his theory of the obligations of shopkeepers. But here he overreached himself. The appeal failed and the Master of the Rolls remarked that he regarded the action as 'an attempt by the plaintiffs to compel the defendants to stock their soaps or to abstain from selling their own soaps . . . a somewhat audacious claim to a monopoly without warranty in law'. Lever recognized his error and resigned himself—quite wrongly as it was to turn out—to the conviction 'that in the long run they [the C.W.S.] would make all the soaps they sold'.

The result of these direct acquisitions between 1906 and 1913 was to concentrate under Lever Brothers' control a large share of the British soap market. By 1914 the production of the Lever group of soap companies was about double that of Lever Brothers in 1906, accounting for perhaps 125,000 tons out of a total production (for home consumption) of some 335,000 tons. But even that was not the whole story.

CHAPTER IX

THE CONFLICT WITH BRUNNER MOND
1911–14

'The question between these two great concerns, Lever's and Brunner's, at that date, was who was to be top dog, and the validity of the Normann patent would clearly be a deciding factor.'

Horatio Ballantyne, A Memorandum on Litigation over Normann's Patent

THE spring of 1911 saw Lever matched against a worthy adversary. Starting as a jockeying for position in a market for a subsidiary but indispensable raw material—alkali—the quarrel rapidly spread until it involved all the major issues in the soap industry. It became in fact a struggle in which the whole question of access to raw materials and the control of the home and export trade in soap was at stake. An essential requirement for the manufacture of soap was caustic soda—every 100 tons of soap needed about 12½ tons of caustic against 66–7 tons of oils and fats.[1] Caustic soda accounted for perhaps one-tenth of the costs of soap production. For the manufacture of his caustic soda, Lever obtained soda ash from the firm of Brunner Mond and Company. By the late nineties Brunner's had built up a combine of great power. At home, their only competitor was the United Alkali Company, which used the older Le Blanc process, a far inferior one to the Solvay process used by Brunner's. Abroad their position was secured by an alliance with the 'Solvay Group' of manufacturers which effectively divided the markets of Europe and America.

Brunner's thus held a very strong bargaining position: on the one side a unified alkali industry, on the other, a disunited and highly competitive soap industry. Brunner's had not been slow to see their strength: their contracts with the soap makers—Lever's included—ran for a period of years, during which alkali was to be supplied at a fixed price. As early as 1903, Lever had

[1] See also Chapter II.

become aware of this dangerous weakness in his defences. He had even taken precautions against the growing danger of monopoly by putting down his own caustic plant, only to sell it to Brunner's when the contract fell due for renewal in 1904. Once again in 1907, when the contract had come up for renewal, Lever had to agree to an arrangement palpably disadvantageous to himself. For almost ten years, he had to bind himself not to manufacture caustic for general sale. In return, Brunner's agreed not to sell their goods to any other soap maker at lower prices than they charged Lever (Crosfield's alone excepted by virtue of an old agreement). Thus to the high price of fats and oils was added an onerous and, to Lever, humiliating agreement controlling the supply of his main subsidiary raw material. The most noteworthy omission from the agreement was that while it strictly bound Lever not to go into caustic manufacture it said nothing to prevent Brunner's from going into soap. Evidently, it was a contract dictated by strength to weakness. Nothing else would have induced Lever to accept such terms.

It was not until 1911 that Lever saw a favourable opportunity of redressing the balance of power. In that year there came on the market an estate at Lymm in Cheshire of 1,700 acres, under which lay valuable salt deposits suitable for the manufacture of alkali. Quite apart from the salt, the estate seemed a reasonable investment, and the transaction was concluded in April 1911. There was no secrecy about the deal. Brunner's could hardly regard it as anything less than a warning that there would be hard bargaining at the termination of the current contract. The challenge was quickly taken up. For many years there had been a very intimate relationship between Brunner's and the soap and chemical firm of Crosfield's. During Brunner Mond's early days, old John Crosfield had assisted them with both money and ability: for some years he was their chairman. In the autumn of 1911, Brunner's bought not only the Ordinary capital of Crosfield's but also the Ordinary capital of Gossage's of Widnes. How seriously Brunner's took Lever's threat may be judged from the heavy price they were prepared to pay for these businesses shares to the market value of more than £2,250,000, equivalent to Brunner's whole issued capital. They were no doubt impressed by the speed at which Lever was building up in his industry a position which threatened to equal their own in the alkali industry. Lever in turn must have been equally impressed by Brunner's move. At a single stroke they had acquired two firms which were the next largest soap makers in the United Kingdom to the Port Sunlight works. Together, Crosfield's and Gossage's production equalled Port Sunlight's output, and constituted about one-sixth of the total national production.

To the hard facts of business, there were added certain personal considerations which did not make the situation any easier. Gossage's production had fallen steadily since 1900: but they had valuable connections, especially in the export trade, which with Brunner's backing might be formidable. And Gossage's had no reason for friendly feeling towards Lever's, who had not only deprived them of their lucrative contract with Hudson's,[1] but had not hesitated to cast aspersions on their business methods in the legal proceedings which followed. Crosfield's had likewise been in low water in 1906 but by 1911 the business had been restored to prosperity. About 1890 they had taken over from Brunner's an able German chemist, Dr. K. E. Markel, who had developed for them a flourishing trade in chemicals. Most serious of all, Crosfield's had bought a patent taken out by another German chemist, Dr. Normann, for converting certain oils into hard fats—the hydrogenation process. By 1909 this process was already recognized as having vast potentialities. Not only could Crosfield's sell licences to other firms to operate the patent but they themselves had brought the process to a point where they could manufacture a hundred tons of hardened fat weekly. In the existing scarcity of hard fats which bore particularly hardly on the soap maker, such a process was a priceless asset. Liquid oils, hitherto unusable by soap and margarine manufacturers, might now be turned to good account. But Crosfield's possession of a master patent raised highly disturbing thoughts. If they could establish a monopoly in fat hardening, Lever would be at the mercy of Brunner's for his supply of hardened fats as he already was for his supply of soda ash.

To make matters worse, relations between Lever and J. J. Crosfield, the chairman of Crosfield's, could not have been more

[1] See Chapter VIII.

strained than they were on the eve of the Brunner purchase. In public speech and in private correspondence with Crosfield, Lever had kept green the memory of how he had been left to bear unaided the expenses of the debacle of 1906. So when the transfer to Brunner's took place, Crosfield showed his resentment by securing from Brunner's an undertaking that in no circumstances should the Crosfield shares be sold to Lever's without his knowledge and, presumably, consent.

Thus, in the autumn of 1911, the outlook for Lever's was gloomy indeed. Profits were being squeezed between rising costs of production and shrinking markets. Lever's move in buying the salt deposits had proved a boomerang. Two of Lever's most formidable rivals had been enticed into the camp of an adversary who already dictated terms on one type of raw material and now seemed fairly on the way to monopolize supplies of another. But there is no evidence that Lever was in the least daunted by these unexpected setbacks. On the contrary, when Sir John Brunner and his son, Roscoe, met Lever—now Sir William—at Liverpool late in 1911 to discuss the Crosfield-Gossage purchase, they met with a spirited reception. The object of their visit was to seek help in the conduct of their new soap business, of which they confessed their ignorance.

With some asperity, Lever pointed out that they were now his competitors, and went on to counter-attack by suggesting that their entry into the soap trade was a breach of the 1907 agreement and that he was thereby released from his obligation not to manufacture alkali for outside sale. In support of his argument Lever referred to the clause which bound him to reveal to Brunner's the amount of alkali which he sent to the Continent and claimed with justice that he could not be expected to give this confidential information to his competitors in trade.

Brunner was quite open about the motives for his action. He said that he had never contemplated entering the soap industry until Lever's bought the land at Lymm. Then he had begun to look to his defences. 'Lever Brothers', he said, 'had purchased a number of soap businesses; excepting Gossage's and Crosfield's there were not many left in the United Kingdom; and they [Brunner Mond & Co.] had bought these two businesses for their protection, as the supply of alkali to the soap trade was a large part of their business and they viewed the possible loss of that market as a very serious thing for them.' The interview ended in frigid politeness with Sir John disavowing any wish to fight Lever's and Sir William reiterating that his company was entitled to be free of the restrictive clauses of the 1907 Agreement.

The primary object of Brunner Mond's policy now was to force Lever's into renewing their contract in a manner which would bar them effectively from making use of their newly acquired resources in the alkali industry. Early in 1912 they brought forward a suggested bargain. The home trade and export sales of Lever's, Crosfield's, and Gossage's might, they said, be arranged to the mutual benefit of all three parties by means of conferences between their directors. This arrangement, however, must be based on a new alkali contract, in return for which Brunner's were prepared to sell to Lever's the shares in Crosfield's and Gossage's and agree for all time not to compete in soap, oils, and fats. But for the inconvenient undertaking given by Sir John Brunner to J. J. Crosfield, all might have gone well, but here was an insuperable obstacle: and after several meetings Brunner finally wrote that the sale was out of the question: the directors of Gossage's and Crosfield's were 'against the proposal'.

Thereafter, throughout the summer of 1912, negotiations languished. Lever's ostentatiously took legal advice on their interpretation of the 1907 Agreement: Brunner's remained polite but distant, and J. J. Crosfield could be coaxed no nearer to allowing Brunner's to sell to Lever's their shares in Crosfield's. 'I see no great difficulty', he wrote to Sir William, 'in a friendly working agreement being come to, and I should personally welcome it, but beyond this we are not prepared to go.'

The battle was shifting to another part of the field. Crosfield's, and behind them always Brunner's, were preparing their attempt to set up the Normann patent as the only legal process for hardening fat in England. After Crosfield's had bought the patent, they had been forced to spend several years in rendering the process workable; meanwhile other investigators had been at work upon the same problem, because it was not difficult to see that any method of reducing the prevailing high price of soap makers' raw materials would find a ready welcome. By 1912, therefore, several different hardening processes had been developed and patented, and it was necessary for Crosfield's, if they were to establish their desired monopoly, to set up Normann's process as a master patent and so force the holders of other patents to pay a royalty if they wished to put their property to use.

Lever's, though slower than their rivals to appreciate the importance (or perhaps the possibility) of hardening, were not very far behind. Crosfield's opened their attack in December 1911 by starting an action against Techno-Chemical Laboratories Ltd., the owners of the rival Testrup patent, for infringement of the Normann patent. Lever's had no great faith in the Laboratories' ability or even intention to defend their rights—probably they suspected a half-concealed willingness to sell out to Crosfield's rather than take the case to Court. Possibly to forestall such a move, they themselves took a licence under the Testrup patent and undertook the defence. The agreement was concluded on 19th July 1912, and preparations for the battle began. Lever's had never embarked on a more critical contest. If they lost, control over a vital raw material would pass into unfriendly hands, so that nothing less than their commercial independence was at stake.

The prime purpose of the hardening inventions was, of course, to provide substitutes for the various natural hard fats traditionally used by the soap maker and the margarine maker. Of these, tallow, though threatened in its pre-eminence by the coming of tropical vegetable fats, such as coconut fat, retained much of its ancient importance. But tallow was dear and scarce in 1912 and vegetable oils were even dearer. The soap makers fixed their hopes on whale oil. It was cheap and comparatively plentiful, and lent itself to the hardening process. Unfortunately there was considerable public prejudice against the use of 'fishy' materials in soap, and Lever would not risk the use of whale oil in Sunlight, though 'he had no objection to its use in Lifebuoy. The carbolic in Lifebuoy would destroy any smell there might be. . . . We could not play with goodwill articles such as Sunlight, Hudson's and Lux, or we might find ourselves before we realized it robbed of the fruits of years of advertising and of the large amounts expended for goodwill.' On the other hand there was no objection to hardened fat being used in the cheaper soaps and powders. Moreover, even in Sunlight itself,

Lever was prepared to countenance the use of hardened cotton oil: it was only whale oil which he consistently excluded, despite the not unreasonable remark of one of his directors (not made in the chairman's presence) that if hardened whale oil 'was good enough to eat, surely it was good enough for any soap'. Apart from its prohibition in Sunlight, however, hardened whale oil would obviously afford valuable relief in these other directions. With such prizes at stake, it is easy to understand why the struggle over the patents was embittered, hard and long.

While the legal batteries were mounted, negotiation went on spasmodically, and tempers rose. Lever met Roscoe Brunner and F. W. Brock (a director of Brunner Mond's) and high words passed. When Brunner offered a new alkali contract which would allow Lever's the liberty of manufacturing caustic, the violence of Lever's answer took his breath away. 'Sir William replied that he objected to being made to sign contracts and shown how he should manage his business. He was not a clerk in Brunner Mond's office to be told to make a contract.' Brunner, evidently shaken, replied 'not at all, that they had no intention of taking away from him his high position'. Sir William himself reported the interview to the board, and said 'that on no account would he agree to an Alkali Contract'.

During the winter of 1912–13 Lever Brothers' directors, with their chairman away in Africa, were faced with the necessity of deciding whether or not they should buy the foreign rights in the Testrup patent. The ownership of the various hardening patents was very involved; it was divided between a big German oil milling concern, Bremen Besigheimer Ölfabriken (B.B.O.) in Germany, the firm of Schichts, the biggest soap maker in Austria-Hungary, the soap maker Fels in America, and Richard Curtius G.m.b.H. in most other countries.[1] The B.B.O., the Curtius Group and the Techno-Chemical Laboratories were inter-connected; it was chiefly with the B.B.O. that negotiations were carried on. Besides owning the patent itself, the B.B.O. had special knowledge of the preparation of catalysts and a secret process for the treatment of low class oils which would be valuable and perhaps indispensable to any buyer of the Testrup rights. The price asked for the whole matter—patents, secrets,

[1] See also Book II.

and all—was £100,000, and the sellers saw not the slightest reason to consider a lower sum, either for the whole or any part of it. So the bargaining began, with Lever's in none too strong a position. As one of the directors, J. L. Tillotson, pointed out: 'If we did not get in now we might have a big group against us with Crosfield's in league with the B.B.O. and Testrup . . . at present we were in splendid isolation and there was no question to his mind that we would gain very valuable information from the B.B.O. people, especially with regard to the refining of oil for all purposes. At present Procter & Gamble,[1] Jurgens', Schicht's[2] and Crosfield's were all in touch while we were "ploughing the lonely furrow" and it was important to us that we should acquire the rights of the B.B.O.' This opinion was supported by George Harley, Lever's solicitor, who advised purchase 'even though it did cost £100,000. . . . ' These arguments prevailed: in February 1913 the price was paid and the rights were bought. Then in March, thanks largely to the convincing technical evidence given on Lever's behalf by their chemical consultant, Horatio Ballantyne, judgement was given for the defendants in the Testrup case and the Normann patent was declared invalid. This put an end once and for all to Brunner Mond's hope of a permanent victory over Lever's. Instead of being able to dictate to Lever's the terms on which they should be suffered to conduct their business, Brunner's found it politic to approach their triumphant antagonists with proposals for establishing a community of interests.

Brunner's first proposal was that they should exchange Ordinary shares with Lever Brothers, but Lever was in no mood to agree to a move which would have given his rivals a say in the running of his business. On the contrary he intended that any arrangement arrived at should give Lever's control of the two soap businesses, and in return he was prepared to conclude a perpetual alkali contract which should bind the whole 'Lever family'. After this exchange of views, little time was lost in bringing the negotiations to a head. On 7th May 1913, at the Hill, Hampstead—Lever's London home—preliminaries of peace were signed in the form of Heads of Agreement. Since

[1] Procter & Gamble were, with Fels, one of the biggest soap makers in the United States.

[2] For Jurgens' and Schicht's see Book II.

Brunner's were still bound by their obligation not to part with the Crosfield shares, and since Lever was determined not to surrender any control of his own business, it was not at all easy to devise an agreement which should achieve the desired end of establishing a community of interests with effective guarantees for its preservation. The ingenious provisions of the document settled the matter for the time being although containing, like many treaties of peace, the seeds of future war. The essence of the agreement was that in return for placing a large block of their Cumulative Preferred Ordinary shares in the hands of a Trustee, Lever's were assured of a substantial share in the profits of Crosfield's and Gossage's. With this agreement in his pocket Lever was prepared to sign a new contract for the supply of alkali. It provided that the 'Lever family', except the European and North American companies, should purchase all their alkali from Brunner's, and that in Europe and North America they should give preference to Brunner Mond and their allies, in return for which Brunner's promised to 'use their influence to secure for Lever Brothers and their Associated Companies preferential treatment'. Lever's were still barred from selling alkali to anyone outside the 'family', but the restrictions were not so all-pervading as those of 1907. The price to Lever's of alkali was agreed: there can be little doubt that the agreement represented an important gain by Lever's over their competitors.

Next the new contract categorically prevented Brunner's from acquiring any further interests in the soap trade without the consent of Lever's. In return, Lever's parted with the salt bearing portion of the Lymm Estate to Brunner's at a price which represented neither profit nor loss. Finally, all litigation between the parties was to be dropped. Causes of dispute were eliminated, mutual obligations were undertaken, and sanctions were provided to ensure that they were observed. The new alliance controlled not far short of half the production of soap for home consumption in the United Kingdom and had a firm grip on the export trade. It controlled besides, all the necessities for soap-making success—raw materials, manufacturing capacity, technical ability, commercial skill, all were there—and nothing was needed but confidence and goodwill to set in motion an industrial engine of impressive power. Unfortunately nothing was yet settled over the development of the new fat hardening processes and the use to which they might be put. Here was another bone of contention.

Hydrogenators Limited

The immediate effect of the Testrup judgement was to put an end to the idea that any one firm was to monopolize the new process of fat hardening. A number of firms now had different versions of the process all equally valid. Brunner Mond (through Crosfield's)—Jurgens', the margarine manufacturers of Oss in Holland (who had obtained the manufacturing rights of the Normann process from Crosfield's)—Joseph Watson of Leeds—Van den Bergh's, margarine manufacturers of Rotterdam—Schicht's in Austria—Procter & Gamble in the United States—all these firms had the process and the necessary plant to operate it.

So far Lever's had only the process; the plant had still to be built or purchased. Now, there was in Norway a fat-hardening plant built in 1912 by De Nordiske Fabriker (De-No-Fa, for short) to work another rival process. Half the capital of De-No-Fa was in the hands of the Bremen Besigheimer Ölfabrik. After protracted bargaining, Lever's succeeded in buying out the B.B.O. and obtained a fifty per cent interest in the Norwegian plant. Lever's thus put themselves on a level with the other fat-hardening firms.

Lever was now ready to begin bargaining. With him stood Joseph Watson. On the other side were Crosfield's, Schicht's, Van den Bergh's and Jurgens'—with Brunner Mond in the background. The interests of the principals were sharply divided. Lever's, as we have seen, looked upon themselves as *buyers* of hardened fat whose main concern was to see it sold as cheaply as possible. As Lever himself put it, their direct policy was 'to foster such schemes as would work up to ourselves as soap makers. The more hardened fat available the better. . . .' To them hardened fat was an essential raw material. The desired end was that it should be available cheaply and in plenty. Jurgens' on the other hand were manufacturing five hundred tons of hardened fat a week. Since the amount which could be used in margarine was still very small, they intended to sell most of this at the highest price possible to soap makers. Crosfield's attitude was less clearly defined. As soap makers they ought (as

Lever's men did not fail to point out) to take sides with the buyers, but as pioneers in the fat-hardening process they naturally wished to make the utmost profit out of their knowledge; moreover they were by no means so firmly wedded to soap making as Lever's—they had, in fact, committed bigamy with the chemical industry. To all this they added hostility towards Lever and friendship with Jurgens', who had been one of their earliest customers for a Normann licence, and the result was a distinct bias to the sellers' camp, especially since they 'had always looked forward to huge profits from hardened fat'.

The object of the negotiators was to seek some common policy which would profit both the buying and the selling interests. It was not difficult to see that the chances of bridging the gap were highly problematical, but optimistically a proposal was mooted for a joint company, Hydrogenators Limited. It was to be promoted by all the parties concerned in fat hardening and was to hold all their rights for mutual profit and defence. A spark only was needed to touch off an explosion which might wreck the negotiations and Lever's provided it. The establishment of the De-No-Fa alarmed both Jurgens' and Van den Bergh's because they saw the new company as a potential supplier of cheap raw materials to their competitors, and when Lever's bought their holding in De-No-Fa the same thought came into the minds of each; it was voiced by Henry Van den Bergh in conversation with Clarence Knowles, Lever Brothers' director in charge of raw materials: 'The first question Mr. Henry Van den Bergh, the head of the firm, put to me about the De-No-Fa was—had we secured sufficient shares to give us the controlling interest? What he meant by controlling interest he explained was—should we have the power to close the place down altogether or of restricting them in any way we thought proper?' Henry Van den Bergh's inquiry was premature, to say the least of it. Had he waited a little longer, he might have been able to work his will on the De-No-Fa, for Lever's had offered to transfer their shares to Hydrogenators Ltd., when that company should be formed. Sir William's reaction was swift and violent; he cabled from Toronto: 'VIEW SUGGESTION CONTROL POSSIBLY CLOSE DENOFA [IMPOSSIBLE] LEVERS WITHDRAW OFFER SHARES WHATEVER ARRANGEMENTS

MADE DIVISION PROFITS AND LOSSES THIS FINAL UNCHANGEABLE.'

Thus commanded, two of Lever's officials, Knowles and McDowell, with the solicitor Harley, went to a meeting of Hydrogenators' promoters held on 9th October 1913. Knowles announced that Lever's offer to sell the De-No-Fa shares to Hydrogenators was withdrawn. 'Up to that moment everyone at the Meeting was beaming and happy but when he made his statement it acted like a bombshell. It produced long faces and volleys of questions from every side of the room.... Evidently our decision was very upsetting to all present.' Lever's men remained unmoved by protest or argument; anger mounted on the other side. 'Mr. Jurgens picked up his papers remarking "that finished it, I won't go into Hydrogenators", and he seemed to be in dead earnest, but he relented and took his papers out again, though little mollified, for he burst out that "if it had not been for Lever's making a contract for 3,600 tons of oil the De-No-Fa would have been smashed before this and . . . they would have smashed De-No-Fa and further that they could still smash them if it were not for the further contract we [Lever's] had made with them".' His tactics failed; seeing their failure he said mildly 'that there was no reason why, if we all helped, the De-No-Fa could not be made a most gigantic success'; his side withdrew all threats, and the meeting ended quite amicably. Nevertheless, Crosfield's, Jurgens', and Van den Bergh's asserted that, unless the Lever offer were renewed, they would withdraw from Hydrogenators. Jurgens' great fear was that De-No-Fa, besides spoiling their prospects in Scandinavia, would interfere with the promising business in hardened fat which they were building up in Germany. 'They were afraid of competition from the De-No-Fa,' as Knowles told Lever's Policy Council, because 'although the duty in Germany was £6 per ton the De-No-Fa could still send their product into Germany and compete'. The threat was the more dangerous because the De-No-Fa product was especially suitable for edible purposes, so that besides interfering with Jurgens' trade in technical fat it would cut directly across their margarine interests. Yet again, they competed for supplies of raw material, and Knowles added that 'Jurgens' were more anxious to smash the De-No-Fa in order to put them out of the market for whale oil'. Nevertheless, they were anxious that the Hydrogenators' negotiations should not break down entirely, and so too were Van den Bergh's; but after the meeting of October 9th there was little real prospect that Lever Brothers would join in the formation of Hydrogenators. With their interest in the established patent rights and their agreement with the De-No-Fa, Lever's were far better placed than Jurgens', cabined within Germany and menaced by invasion. They could afford an attitude of friendly detachment.

The other side were not deceived by their opponents' genial affability. On 22nd October 1913 they prepared documents for the formation of Hydrogenators without Lever's, and the new Company was publicly launched, on 5th December 1913. Lever's were perturbed to discover that one-third of the capital was held by Brunner Mond's, who had never suggested taking any financial share in the earlier project, but had been content to rely on their control of Crosfield's. Brunner's latest move thus gave them an important stake in a second source of raw material supply to the soap trade.

The formation of Hydrogenators Limited emphasized Lever's isolation from the other firms in the oils and fats world, but it did not seriously threaten the strength of their position, which was further reinforced by an agreement reached with Procter & Gamble in America in May 1914. This treaty represented a considerable diplomatic victory for Lever's, since Procter & Gamble, who held a licence from Crosfield's to work the Normann process, had hitherto been regarded by Lever's as members of the hostile coalition.

Despite the gulf which was now fixed between them, the soap and margarine makers found that it was impossible to carry on their affairs efficiently without co-operation in some matters, and one of these was the supply of raw material for fat hardening. Although by no means the only substance suitable for hydrogenation, whale oil was the most important, and already by 1913 it was evident (though not so painfully evident as in later years) that world demand considerably exceeded supply. To meet the situation, the principal buyers took to meeting in conference and dividing the available quantities between themselves in agreed proportions. The conferences were no less acrimonious than other meetings between Lever's and their associates: on one occasion Knowles reported to the Policy Council that Mr. Kingdon [of Crosfield's] 'was most aggressive . . . and was really very rude to him', which the chairman's red pencil 'noted with great regrets'. In spite of these lapses, the conferences continued and hardened into the so-called Whale Oil Pool for distributing world supplies of whale oil amongst the leading buyers—Lever's, Watson's, Crosfield's, Jurgens', Van den Bergh's, Schicht's and De-No-Fa.

Such were the arrangements, abortive as well as successful, devised by the leading European consumers of oils and fats to meet the emergency caused, first, by the increased demand for hard fats and, secondly, by the inventions designed to supplement their supply. Reduced to its essentials, the story is one of an attempt to set up a monopoly controlled by one concern, of the shattering of that monopoly, and of the subsequent attempt by parties sufficiently interested in its benefits and powerful enough to assert their influence to rebuild it, so as to share its advantages amongst themselves and with no one else. With such issues in the balance—either free access to cheap raw materials or no access at all—it is not strange that the lesser soap makers of England should have been ready to enter the Lever combination, which throughout the warfare steadily increased in size.

The New Alliance and the Export Trade

The skilful conduct of the battle with Brunner Mond's had brought Lever substantial advantages both in the matter of access to raw materials and in a promised limitation of dangerous competition. There was another advantage to be hoped for, and it was all the more desirable in face of the continuing stagnation of the home market for soap. Foreign markets had expanded substantially since the beginning of the century. From some 47,000 tons in 1901, soap exports from the United Kingdom had risen to about 80,000 tons by 1911. This increase had been largely shared by the two firms whose profits were now to be divided between Lever's and Brunner's. Gossage's were in the lead: their export trade, rising steadily, reached a figure of some 40,000 tons by 1913, just under a half of the total United Kingdom exports. Crosfield's share was smaller than Gossage's—about 13,500 tons or about sixteen per cent of the total. Apart from the Lever 'family'—controlling some thirty per cent—the other exporters were negligible.

Here lay the great value of a working arrangement with Crosfield's and Gossage's. Between them they held a commanding position in the export trade: and in 1912–13 there were high hopes of a vast increase in exports. Established markets could be extended and new ones explored. Tillotson reported optimistically on progress in China: in Russia, according to the director in charge of the export trade, the sanguine E. V. Salaman, 'they were beginning to get orders everywhere': here, Sunlight and perfumery had a big future. So, soon after the Heads of Agreement were signed,[1] discussions began among the three firms which covered the whole field of export policy—standardization of qualities and packs, advertising, prices, and consultation on raw material buying. All this led up to the possibility of an agreement to divide the export trade throughout world markets on an agreed basis and in particular to form a joint company to exploit the trade in China. General discussions gave way to Export Conferences where the new allies attempted to reduce principles to practice. It was more easily said than done. While Lever was writing expansively cordial letters to Sir John Brunner enlarging on the theme of 'avoiding friction and avoiding unnecessary expenditure' and 'on the greater pleasure . . . and greater happiness we shall have in pursuing our daily duties . . .' others, further down the line, were less content. The general understanding was that 'healthy rivalry' might continue between the allies but not 'cut-throat competition'. The trouble was that no one could decide where the one finished and the other began. The Lever representatives on the Conferences began to object almost at once that Crosfield's were not 'playing cricket' over standardization of soaps. It was even thought prudent at one Conference to appoint umpires to mediate between Salaman (of Lever's) and Jones (of Crosfield's) and try to settle differences. Nevertheless some results were achieved. Very detailed 'Draft Principles for the Regulation of the Export Soap Trade' were worked out—covering prices, terms, and conduct of trade, much on the lines of the old Soap Makers' Association agreements. They never got beyond the draft stage. In South Africa, where the three firms were competing against severe

[1] See pp. 132–3.

local opposition, Lever's took a large interest in the Natal Soap Works. Most important of all was the proposal to build a joint works in China. Imports of English soap into China were very considerable—in 1912 well over 10,000 tons. Of this, Gossage's had some seventy per cent and Lever's the remaining thirty per cent. The trade was large enough to suggest to Lever the possibility of building a joint factory.

But already rifts were becoming apparent in the alliance. From September 1913 onwards, Lever became conscious of a 'marked change' of attitude on the part of the Crosfield management. The truth was that J. J. Crosfield was rapidly coming to the conclusion that he and his firm were merely being used as pawns in the game between Brunner's and Lever's: conscious of the high standards achieved in technical matters by his firm, he was more and more reluctant to co-operate with Port Sunlight. Lever seems to have made genuine attempts to meet his wishes. Crosfield's were offered assistance on advertising and selling methods—they were hardly strong on either—and in a desperate effort to break the deadlock over China, Brunner's were offered the appointment of all seven directors of the proposed company. But the suspicions of nearly thirty years afflicted others besides the Crosfields themselves. There was, Lever thought, a 'nervous dread' amongst the higher staff that they would lose their jobs if Lever's took control. 'I do not know', he went on, 'why this dread should exist. Lever Brothers have sixty-four Associated Companies; we have no good men to spare and we never willingly part with a good man.' Nevertheless their anxiety was understandable. It was another manifestation of that normal love of liberty and the old ways which Lever so often praised in the abstract but found it difficult to admit in the concrete.

All this rancour combined with legal delays and the outbreak of the First World War to obstruct the formation of the China Manufacturing Company. Before it became possible to take up the threads again, trouble had broken out between Brunner's and Lever's once more.

The Brunner-Lever conflict had demonstrated most of the classical features associated with large-scale combination—the desire for economy, for price-fixing, for limiting competition, even—in the case of the alkali contract—for monopoly. At the same time it had illustrated how powerful were those forces less commonly appreciated by the economist—the interplay of human personalities and ambitions. Lever's determination and diplomacy, backed by the skill of able lawyers and scientists, had defeated the attempt at a monopoly of raw materials. In retrospect the history of a business, like a man's own life story, is apt to take on an appearance of inevitability. Yet if there is any discernible reason why this business rather than another became the giant of the industry it must surely be sought in the qualities of the men who directed it—in the tenacity of Lever himself, in the legal skill of McDowell and Harley, in the technical and forensic ability of Horatio Ballantyne. From dangerous insecurity in 1912, Lever's had raised themselves, in twelve months, to a position of enormous strength.

CHAPTER X

THE ENLIGHTENED CAPITALIST

'And now I venture to assert . . . that still no employer-capitalist with a true feeling of brotherhood can be quite happy in the fullest sense in the enjoyment of wealth (the product of his own hard work, intelligence, self-denial and thrift, every penny earned without committing injury to any man, and the acquisition of which has resulted in enormous benefits to his employee-workmen) without feeling a strong sense of dissatisfaction with present industrial conditions and a strong desire to improve them so that the employee-workmen may be raised to a much higher level in social well-being.'

Lord Leverhulme in a paper read to the Royal Society of Arts, 13 *February* 1918

THE speeches and papers which Lever poured forth over a period of years represent an attempt to formulate a rational defence of an improved and modified capitalism as an economic way of life. In the system he propounded relations between employer and employee took high place as a factor in industrial peace and prosperity. The basic fact in that relationship must continue to be the wages system. It was, he told the Royal Society of Arts in 1918, a convenient system, logical and practicable. It gave the employee-worker a form of income as stable as could be devised. It was perfectly sound and just in its basis and principles.[1] In practice, however, the wages system alone was not sufficient. The profits of industry were the fruits of the exertions of labour and the risks and policies of capitalists. Day in, day out, Lever had preached the doctrine of ever-expanding production, against the timidity of fellow-capitalists and the fears of ca' canny workers. Somehow the workers must be brought to see that industrial prosperity was their interest as well as the employers' and the only solution was to reconsider the division of the profits of industry which resulted from the joint labour of employer-capitalist and employee-worker.

How could this be done? One thing was plain to him. Mere benevolence, deriving from no principle other than a sentimental

[1] Viscount Leverhulme, *The Six-Hour Day* (Allen & Unwin, 1918), pp. 302–3.

feeling of sympathy for the worker, was worse than useless. 'There could be no worse friend to Labour', he remarked in an address in 1909, 'than the benevolent, philanthropic employer who carries his business on in a loose, lax manner, showing "kindness" to his employees; because, as certain as that man exists, because of his looseness and laxness, and because of his so-called kindness, benevolence, and lack of business principles, sooner or later he will be compelled to close.'[1] He was only repeating what he had been saying for thirty years: that there was no room in a properly run industry for the kind of charity which was an insult to the working man and bad business into the bargain.

Lever had thus decided that charity as an economic lubricant must be rejected. He had then turned to consider a more orderly and principled system for a more just division of the rewards of industry. There was, for example, the profit-sharing system introduced by Leclaire in his house-painting and decorating business in Paris in 1842. Events after Leclaire's death showed pretty clearly that the success of the experiment in its early days was due to Leclaire and not to his system. Study of other schemes led Lever inevitably to the conclusion that they were all equally unsatisfactory. Reviewing the situation later in life he summarized his objections to them. Labour had to be assured of its weekly wage. It could not afford to stand the losses which might have to be faced in any business, however well conducted. The Trade Unions had—rightly in his opinion—never set any value on profit sharing. In practice, such schemes had proved short-lived; on an average—this was in 1909—their life was a mere five years and in that year only forty-nine such schemes had survived.

With this melancholy record before him, Lever set himself to find some more satisfactory method of profit sharing, and he hit upon the idea of what he called 'prosperity sharing', a plan which combined the notion of profit sharing with another project which had long occupied his thoughts—the provision of better housing and amenities for the workers. Lever was prepared to defend private capitalism as a basis for industry with all the eloquence he could muster but he was honest enough to see that the social conditions of the urban worker were often an

[1] Ibid., p. 64.

indictment of the system. Hence his campaign for better housing, which coincided with the efforts of a number of contemporary social reformers.

Port Sunlight

The genesis of Port Sunlight was the result of the meeting of these two streams of thought—profit sharing and housing reform: the motive, as Lever said, to build houses, with gardens back and front, where the workers could live and know something more of life than going to and from a factory and drawing wages on a Saturday night. The whole site of three hundred and thirty acres was to provide for both works and village. By 1890, twenty-eight model houses were complete and others were in process of building. 'The Style . . . of this neat and cheerful village', wrote an observer, 'is Old English, and in process of time, as the village develops, it will be pleasantly demonstrated that it is quite practical to erect a large number of industrial dwellings without habitations being, as is so often the case, hideous in design and grieving in aspect.' The villas were laid out with sloping lawns, gardens back and front and gay with geraniums and roses. Eight years later, the number of cottages had risen to two hundred and seventy-eight. Architectural styles had multiplied, Flemish and Dutch coming in to supplement Old English and a visitor remembered that two cottages 'are actually reproductions of Shakespeare's cottage at Stratford-on-Avon, with quaint nooks and corners and fascinating gables'. The streets were laid out to reproduce on a small scale the Continental boulevard, bordered with elm and chestnut trees. Five hundred workers' children were educated in the Port Sunlight school. Girl workers—always a high proportion of labour in the factory—were provided with classes in cookery, dressmaking, shorthand, and so on, in the village institute which was equipped with a reading room and canteen. Amenities for the male workers were provided in Gladstone Hall.

Lever himself was the driving force behind the development of the village, endowed as he was with an extraordinary natural talent for surveying and an absorbing interest in architectural problems. Expert advice was sought continually and the cottage designs were the work of a whole team of architects; but the first plans were his own and in all his travels he was on the lookout

PLAN OF PORT SUNLIGHT

on which William Lever, in 1912, noted plans for the future.

(*Reduced from* 10¾ *x* 12¾ *in.*)

M

for new ideas. It is not without interest that in these years he made several visits to Delft,[1] where van Marken, one of the leading Dutch industrialists and social reformers, had himself built a model village on lines very like those adopted at Port Sunlight. Nearer home there were other models—one not more than a mile from Port Sunlight—Price's Candle Works model village: while at Bournville, George Cadbury began to build his garden city in 1895. To Lever 'the life of the people, in all town planning, must be the first consideration' and he believed that the life and convenience of the people could be achieved 'without any sacrifice to beauty or inspiring vistas'.

By the time W. L. George made his comprehensive survey of Lever's experiment in 1909 the acreage of the village had increased to 130 acres and there were 720 houses, about 700 of which were occupied by Lever's employees. There were broadly two types of cottage—the kitchen and the parlour type. The parlour type had a large living-room and one bedroom more than the kitchen type. Otherwise there was little to choose between the houses. In a number of ways, the designs showed liberality and a vision far beyond the average contemporary ideas on working-class housing. Basements were abolished and every house had a bathroom. W. L. George, at the conclusion of a sympathetic but not uncritical account of the architecture of Port Sunlight, concluded that 'taking them all round the cottages are the best possible for a working man'.[2] Certainly, compared with the drabness of urban working-class housing elsewhere, they were a paradise.

The theory behind the experiment was, as has been said, the theory of 'prosperity sharing', a variant on the idea of profit sharing, the advantages of which were bluntly set out by Lever himself in an interview in 1903: 'If I were to follow the usual mode of profit sharing I would send my workmen and work girls to the cash office at the end of the year and say to them: "You are going to receive £8 each; you have earned this money: it belongs to you. Take it and make whatever use you like of your money." Instead of that I told them: "£8 is an amount which is soon spent, and it will not do you much good

[1] See Book II for the account of how the Delft factories and village came to be associated with Unilever.

[2] W. L. George, *Labour and Housing at Port Sunlight* (1911).

if you send it down your throats in the form of bottles of whisky, bags of sweets, or fat geese for Christmas. On the other hand, if you leave this money with me, I shall use it to provide for you everything which makes life pleasant—viz. nice houses, comfortable homes, and healthy recreation. Besides, I am disposed to allow profit sharing under no other than that form."'

The financial basis of this somewhat dictatorial benevolence was set out in the Village Account, which was published each year. The Capital Account for 1907 showed an outlay to that date of nearly half a million. The Maintenance Account showed an Expenditure which consisted partly of current costs of upkeep—repairs, improvements, administrative expenses, etc.—but largely of the interest payable on the capital which it had taken to build the village. Income consisted of rents but again largely of the same item of interest on capital (roughly £25,000) brought into the income side as a contribution by Lever Brothers towards the sharing of prosperity. Even with this contribution, rents were not low, though they were not unreasonable. The kitchen houses varied from 5s. to 6s. 3d. per week (including rates); the parlour houses from 7s. 6d. to 10s. The majority of the workers did not pay more than 6s. a week in rent or rates—on an average a quarter to a fifth of the weekly wage. (There was a guaranteed minimum wage of 22s. a week but most workers earned more.)

All in all, there was no doubt that working and living conditions at Port Sunlight reached a very high standard. Men worked a 48-hour week, girls a 45-hour week. The works themselves were built on a single-storey system and well-lighted. Medical inspection and treatment was provided. Special precautions were taken against dirt and accidents. The workers' co-operation was sought in such matters as improving output, simplifying or improving industrial processes, and reducing accidents. Canteens where cheap meals could be bought were built for both male and female staff. Recreation for leisure time was provided by public institutions: by 1909 Port Sunlight had a theatre and concert hall, a library, a gymnasium, an open-air swimming bath, a men's club and a number of voluntary societies for furthering interest in literature, music, and art.

The results, as recorded by W. L. George, were certainly remarkable. The Port Sunlight birth-rate considerably exceeded

English averages. Particularly striking was the preponderance of large families amongst the higher grades of workers. More than half the children of these grades of workmen were in families of more than four children, a convincing testimony of the general impression of contentment and security in the village. The sense of community was strong, standards of health and morality high, industrial and social relations good. So far as output was concerned, the experiment had worked well—men well-fed, well-housed, and cheerful were able to produce more in their 48-hour week than their fellows who worked longer hours under bad conditions. Quality, even more than quantity, reflected the success of the scheme. Management, however efficient, could not be ubiquitous: a great deal depended on the sense of responsibility of the individual worker and the management was satisfied that any reputation the firm might have acquired for quality 'was due almost entirely to the fact that the men will not allow flaws to mar their work'.

So much for the material side of the experiment. Clearly it had been to a very large degree successful. But there were less ponderable matters in which it was much more difficult to assess results. Powerful, and in many ways subtle, as Lever's mind was, he was perhaps at his weakest in dealing with the finer shades of human rights and preferences, and it is at least doubtful whether he appreciated the problems of social relationships which were involved. Nothing could disguise the fact that, benevolent as the scheme was, it was despotic benevolence. Lever's own statement, quoted above, was confession of the fact, frank enough. Despotism—or at any rate heavy paternalism—made its appearance at many points. It was perhaps not unreasonable that at the winter weekly dances girls over the age of eighteen might 'submit the names of men to the social department, which issues invitations to them unless there be reasons that militate against them'. It was less justifiable that the tenants' front gardens should be controlled and looked after by the central management; though again there was the excuse that individual tenants had used their gardens for fowl runs and refuse heaps 'while the family washing was unblushingly exposed on the railings'. These were minor but not unimportant examples of the perpetual struggle between the claims of order and liberty. And at Port Sunlight in 1909, order usually won. As W. L. George put it: 'It is quite clear that absolute democracy cannot reign in the village so long as the financial basis of the scheme remains unaltered; thus, the directors, Messrs. Lever Brothers, must retain absolute control over local conditions'.[1] And he proposed that meantime an advisory Village Council should be set up to give the villagers a voice in a more democratic form of government.

Other critics were more outspoken. 'There is a type of man', wrote Lever rather irritably, 'who sees in Port Sunlight and in everything we do, from the building of a church to an Arts and Crafts Exhibition, an advertisement for soap. My experience is that such people are better avoided. It may be that Port Sunlight by being talked about becomes a soap advertisement but it was never so intended at its inception, and if it had been so intended and had been so worked, it would have utterly failed in its object. It would be like some painting in a theatre—made to look like nature but deceiving no one.' The irritation is understandable; it is the irritation of an honest man who sees his motives wilfully distorted. Yet the criticism was inevitable. Lever had himself, with the best of intentions, created his own dilemma. If he did nothing for his workpeople, he ranked himself with the most backward of employers; if he contributed to their welfare, it seemed that his contribution was doomed to be regarded as salesmanship. For it was not only his opponents who made the criticism. Even so staunch an admirer as Angus Watson could write that 'the whole village was dominated by the spirit of soap. All its occupants were employed in the industry; not only were they engaged in it all day, but it was a constant source of conversation at night. You could no more escape from its influence than from the odour (not at all an unpleasant one) permeating it from the great factory plant. The Chairman, the management, and the workpeople alike were caught up with the fever of the progress of this great enterprise; there was little time to talk or think of anything else. There was an air of urgency about it all; one felt that everyone was stimulated to the utmost to take a hand in creating the material prosperity that was flowing into its centre like a torrent.'[2]

[1] W. L. George, *Labour and Housing at Port Sunlight* (1911).
[2] Angus Watson, *My Life* (Ivor Nicholson & Watson, 1937) pp. 137–8.

The dilemma was inescapable—at any rate for the time being. And nowhere was it clearer than in the matter of the village church. Convinced of the futility of theological dispute, Lever sought the solution to the religious problem by vesting the church which he built for the villagers in the Congregational Union. And the service itself was as undenominational as it could be made. In practice the move was not unsuccessful in the sense that religious disputes were apparently avoided. W. L. George observed with some satisfaction that the congregation contained Anglicans and Nonconformists as well as Unitarians and some agnostics. It is difficult to share his satisfaction at a policy which attempted to remove *odium theologicum* by enforced latitudinarianism. Even a minister at one time quartered at Port Sunlight could confide to Angus Watson: 'I sometimes feel that I am intended to be an advertisement for Sunlight Soap more than for the Kingdom of God'.

Radical Liberal though he was, Lever found it hard to avoid the temptation to create a kind of twentieth-century feudalism of his own, an industrial counterpart of the great landed estates of the thirteenth or the eighteenth century, with Port Sunlight as a principality in which the works replaced the castle or the manor house, and with factory hands instead of villeins or copyholders. The paternal regime was not without its good points, but it could hardly be expected to recommend itself to working men at large, who had not escaped from the domination of the squire to fall under that of the manufacturer. 'No man of an independent turn of mind', wrote the Secretary of the Bolton Branch of the Engineers' Union to Lever in 1919, 'can breathe for long the atmosphere of Port Sunlight. That might be news to your Lordship,[1] but we have tried it. The profit-sharing system not only enslaves and degrades the workers, it tends to make them servile and sycophant, it lowers them to the level of machines tending machines.' The accusation was exaggerated; but it represented an extreme type of a criticism which was brought against the paternal despotism of the village from its earliest days up to the time when the inhabitants refused to buy at the local Mac Fisheries[2] because they felt the firm was trying to dictate to them where they should spend their money.

[1] Lever was raised to the Peerage in June 1917.
[2] Mac Fisheries were acquired by Lever Brothers in 1922.

The problem was set out inadvertently but unmistakably in a letter which Lever himself wrote in 1901. 'The private habits of an employee', he wrote, 'have really nothing to do with Lever Brothers providing the man is a good workman. At the same time', he continued, 'a good workman may have a wife of objectionable habits, or he may have objectionable habits himself, which make it undesirable to have him in the village... it is not a matter of a man being dismissed from his employment, but merely being granted or refused a house in the village.' The problem could not be more clearly posed, and the very form of its exposition indicates that Lever himself, individualist though he was, had failed to grasp the delicacy or the importance of these problems of social obligation which he had set himself.

Yet it is possible to be too critical. The Port Sunlight experiment was a bold venture, a conception with vision, imagination and a genuine concern for human welfare. Its gains were great and its influence beneficial. We may perhaps leave it for the moment with W. L. George's word of sober confidence. 'The rock upon which Port Sunlight might split does not loom very large on the horizon; I mean paternalism—a danger which is always to be feared by social schemes conceived and conducted by a man or a very small group. . . . Glorified pauperism is the end of many generous schemes; Port Sunlight is exposed to the danger but it is likely to escape it.' Time was to show that while the material benefits of the village could be increased and improved, the dangers arising from its original constitution could be mitigated and reduced. Port Sunlight stands as a monument of which any man might be proud.

Co-partnership

In the dark days after the *Daily Mail* crisis, building operations at Port Sunlight had to be suspended. But trade difficulties did not deter Lever from further attempts to stimulate the interest of his employees in the business, and it was in 1909 that he decided to introduce the system he called Co-Partnership into the business. 'In my opinion,' he told an audience in November 1909, 'ordinary profit-sharing has been proved and found wanting. Prosperity sharing is very good, but does not go far enough. Now, then, we come to a possible adoption of Co-Partnership.'[1]

[1] Viscount Leverhulme, *The Six-Hour Day* (Allen & Unwin, 1918).

He did not enlarge further but the reason for the innovation is not far to seek. In the earlier period Lever Brothers' business had meant Port Sunlight. But from 1908 onwards, the policy of acquisition meant that Lever had employees in other factories, several of them in built-up areas where the Port Sunlight experiment could not be repeated. It became necessary, therefore, to consider some form of profit sharing which could apply not merely to Port Sunlight employees but to workers employed in subsidiary companies wherever they might be situated. He had, in fact, been considering a scheme on some such lines for almost twenty years. As early as 1894 he had drawn up a scheme under which a block of Ordinary shares was to be placed in trust for the benefit of the employees but, quite apart from legal difficulties which arose, Lever did not like the parting with the control of policy which the experiment involved. The success of the policy of bold expansion was, in his opinion, due to his position as sole Ordinary shareholder. Small holders of Ordinary shares were inclined to obstruct any proposals for the future involving risks. So the Ordinary shares were all bought back again.

Still Lever continued to search for some system which would increase the sense of common effort and aim between the three components of industry—capital, labour, and management. Ultimately he found his working model in the oldest working arrangement of all—the ordinary partnership, as exemplified, for example, in the fishing industry. 'Men in the old days', he told a meeting of employees on 25th February 1909, 'entered a firm as errand boys: they worked up to the desk; then to the management; and were finally taken in as partners and made their positions. An account was then opened in their names in the books of the firm, and an arrangement was entered into that they should have a definite share of the profits. Under the old-fashioned partnership arrangement the partner who had provided the capital was invariably credited with five per cent on his capital; so that the first charge against profits was five per cent upon the capital of the undertaking; after that the balance was divided in some proportions agreed upon between the partners.'[1]

The problem was to adapt this old arrangement to the conditions of modern industry, and especially to avoid the weakness of the ordinary profit-sharing scheme where the employee was

[1] *Viscount Leverhulme by His Son.*

only concerned in profits and not at all in losses. The essence of Lever's new scheme was that the co-partner should know that 'if there is no dividend for the Ordinary shareholder, or if there is only five per cent for the Ordinary shareholder, he knows that there is nothing for him'.[1] This object he tried to attain by creating a Co-Partnership Trust in Lever Brothers Limited, of which the directors were to be trustees. Instead of co-partners holding shares, they were to hold 'Co-Partnership Certificates' which had no money value but entitled the holder to an annual dividend. To qualify as a co-partner, an employee of either sex had to be not less than twenty-five years of age, and to have completed five years' service with the Company. There were four classes of co-partner: Directors, Management, Salesmen, and Staff, and in each class the total issued certificates were not to exceed one-quarter of the whole.

A special class of Preferential Certificates was also created to cover the needs of retired employees or the dependants of employees who died in service. The profits of the Company were in future to be distributed as follows: first the claims of Preference and Preferred Ordinary shareholders must be met: next came a dividend of five per cent on Ordinary shares, followed by a dividend of five per cent on Preferential Co-Partnership Certificates: the remaining balance was then to be divided between the Ordinary shareholder and the co-partners on an equal percentage basis. The scheme was to be controlled by the Trustees but a Co-Partnership Committee of twelve was set up, three members being elected by each of the following groups of Co-Partners—Management, Salesmen, Staff, and Preferential Certificate holders. Thus, from the beginning, the co-partnership scheme had an element of democratic management which had been lacking from the Port Sunlight experiment in its earlier days. It is doubtful whether such a scheme could have been operated if there had been large numbers of Ordinary shareholders because it would of necessity have had the effect of depreciating the market value of the Ordinary shares through lessening their rate of dividend.

Again, as with prosperity sharing, there was a moral flavour to co-partnership. One of its main objects was to stimulate production and, on being admitted to co-partnership, the employee

[1] Viscount Leverhulme, *The Six-Hour Day* (Allen & Unwin, 1918).

was to sign an undertaking that he would not 'waste time, labour, materials or money in the discharge of his duties, but loyally and faithfully further the interests of Lever Brothers and its associated companies and his fellow co-partners to the best of his skill and ability'. If the holder were guilty of neglect of duty, dishonesty, intemperance, immorality, wilful misconduct, flagrant inefficiency, disloyalty to his employers or any breach of his undertaking, his certificates were liable to be cancelled. It was a curious mixture of the ethical principles of the Band of Hope and the precepts of Samuel Smiles. Excellent as the intentions were, they involved an interference with the private lives of employees in the interests of the business which went beyond what twentieth-century opinion was prepared to tolerate.

For the facts of modern industry made it impossible to reproduce the conditions of primitive partnership. As Lever himself truly remembered on one occasion 'modern industrial conditions, with thousands and tens of thousands of workmen, and in at least one industry a quarter of a million workmen, under one oligarchical rule, are intensely anti-democratic, and as such violate the gregarious instincts of humanity'. Not all the artifices of salesmanship nor the sincerity of a score of speeches extolling the benefits of co-partnership could disguise the fact that co-partnership could not restore what industrial development itself had obliterated. A glance at the balance-sheet showed that the co-partners' dividends were really a drop in the bucket. By 1912 there were nearly two thousand co-partners. Certificates had been issued to the amount of £350,000 (nominal value). The dividend was ten per cent and the amount to be divided some £40,000. The average dividend was therefore in the region of £20 per head: and allowing for higher dividends for the higher ranks of staff, it is evident that a good many employees must have earned much smaller dividends.

What the ordinary working man's expectations from co-partnership really were is vividly brought out in a letter from Joseph Meek in Australia which, spurning verbiage, goes to the very heart of the matter. In Australia, Meek explained, the Wages Board System was in operation. Awards were revised every three years and the revision was invariably upwards.[1]

[1] See Chapter XII for further information about Joseph Meek.

Meek calculated that at the very least his workpeople could reckon on a gain of £5. 4s. a year. Against this, the most that the lowest class of co-partners (Class D) could hope for from co-partnership would be 32s. which, as he said 'will not overbalance the Wages Board System; and unless co-partnership does overbalance (not merely supplement) the Wages Board System, it is not good'. He therefore thought that unless the Class D co-partners could see at least £10 per man at once the scheme would do more harm than good to Lever Brothers in Australia. Moreover the fact that co-partners' dividends might in bad times be wiped out altogether would be a further disadvantage because such failure would inevitably be attributed to 'the folly of the man at the top'.

He went on to say that 'I feel the whole strength of this scheme is the amount per annum (not the scrip value) that would be drawn by Class D. If it does not meet with the enthusiastic approval of Class D it has missed the mark. The working man of Australia is quite a different man from the working man of England. . . . Where the co-partnership scheme with £2 or £3 per annum will meet today the working man of England—it would be detrimental applied to the working man of Australia. The Australian makes more money, he spends more money, and what is more important, he has not the keen sense of saving against the future such as you find amongst the bulk of the workmen in Great Britain. On the other hand, he is great on Friendly Societies, and Insurances.'

The alternative proposed by Meek was that instead of the co-partnership scrip the Class D co-partners should receive an Insurance Policy for £100 payable at the age of sixty or at death with the premiums paid so long as the man remained in Lever Brothers' employment. The policy ought to be payable to the man or to his wife and his children. He said, 'You may not take children into a co-partnership scheme—but they are the background of human life. If a man and his wife had no children and had enough to live upon for the remainder of their lives—many would cease work—it is the children that are the driving power in life generally.'

Meek carefully avoided criticizing the introduction of the scheme into the United Kingdom, but there is no doubt that some of his blunt criticisms applied, though perhaps to a lesser degree, here too. It might be true, as Lever said, that 'the wages system has broken down as a sole and only solution' but certainly the Trade Unions remained suspicious of the palliative that co-partnership offered. One reason for their attitude emerged after a strike in the Port Sunlight Oil Mill in 1911. Lever attached no great importance to the disturbance, and was willing 'to let bygones be bygones'. Nevertheless, it was not without significance that he considered that the affair offered 'an opportunity to bring forward the relationship of co-partners to the Firm at such times as a Strike so that we may have a precedent created for future reference should any serious situation arise in the future when we may require the position of co-partners to be clearly defined'. Nor was it without interest that in the following year Co-partnership Certificates were granted in recognition of help given during the strike of 1911. How, in fact, was the co-partners' undertaking to be interpreted in relation to strike action and Union membership? Did a strike constitute 'neglect of duty . . . wilful misconduct . . . disloyalty to . . . employers . . . or a breach of the undertaking'? Again, one is tempted to ask whether the author of co-partnership, sincere as his motives were, fully realized the delicacy and difficulty of the problems of industrial relations, involving as they did human rights and aspirations as well as material benefits. Perhaps that very optimism which carried him so far as a producer and a salesman may have tempted him to gloss over the deeper problems of employer and employee relations. For these were real problems of human relations which could be solved, if solved at all, by the qualities of patience and understanding rather than the quality of courage: and William Lever was stronger in the latter than in the former.

At the same time, one must not disregard the evidence of those who should have been in a position to know the effects of the scheme. Thus Lord Leverhulme's biographer writes: 'Speaking as one who has had the opportunity of studying at close quarters the progressive effects of my father's policy, I can, without hesitation, describe it as successful, for it has instilled into the working lives of the employees a spirit of comradeship which has evidenced itself on many occasions and in many directions'.[1]

[1] *Viscount Leverhulme by His Son.*

The limitations on the scheme are nevertheless fairly obvious. Profit sharing schemes of various kinds have continued to appear in industry with varying degrees of success since 1909: they have not, however, done more than modify in a small degree the normal wages system. The real change in social relations has come about through welfare, insurance, health, and housing schemes sponsored by democratically elected public authorities, while industry has contributed higher wages and better working conditions. To that extent Lever was perhaps attempting a task that was beyond the powers of the individual employer. He could scarcely avoid becoming at least the petty interferer, at most the giver of moral law. The dilemma was inescapable. The founder of co-partnership could inform the Manchester Athenæum during a speech on co-partnership that 'The British workman has a profound distrust and dislike of paternalism': but the fact remained that in this 'Partnership' the function of control and maintenance of discipline remained with capital: there was to be no delegation of supreme authority from the management. That was reasonable enough but it was a measure of the distance which separated the days of co-partnership from the days of those early business partnerships which Lever had taken as his model. The fact was that the business now comprised one employer and a large number of employees. By introducing co-partnership, the employer (who was also the sole Ordinary shareholder) robbed himself annually of an amount which by 1912 was about £40,000. The employee earning say £100 a year, gained annually something between 30s. and £5 a year.

Co-partnership was only practicable in this business because the voting power of the Ordinary shares lay with one man: and it should not be forgotten that this particular industry was favourably placed in its relation to labour compared with some older industries. Labour costs were low in the soap industry. The co-partnership scheme had the virtues and vices implied in one description of it: 'The scheme amounted to an annual gift out of his [Lever's] own pocket as sole Ordinary shareholder'.[1]

Later experience of the risks and complications of economic and social planning has made it possible to view those early schemes of Lever's in better proportion. It was, we can now see,

[1] *Encyc. Brit.*, 14th Edition. Article on Leverhulme.

unreasonable to expect that all the problems of industrial relationship could be solved by one man with two schemes. Inevitably their success was limited. But the real value of those schemes did not lie in the immediate degree of success or failure which they achieved but in the new attitude and heightened effort which they represented. In an industrial era still suffering from the necessarily hasty improvisation of earlier decades, Lever's model factory and village, his treatment of his workers—standard wages, a pension scheme and a score of welfare schemes—were an attempt to embody enlightenment in a system. Despotic the management might be, but it pressed most hardly on the upper layers of society. The directors suffered the slings and arrows: the workers enjoyed the benevolence. For this was not only an enlightened régime but an efficient one. Lever rejected the idea of a workman being appointed by his fellow workmen to sit on the board of directors as futile and sentimental, but he could tell the Institute of Directors in 1913 that every one of his own directors had graduated successively through the works, the office, or the salesmen's department, and had gone through the ordeal of sitting on a number of works committees as well. Other things being equal, Lever liked to find a place in his business for the local boy—the old Lancashire names were to remain obstinately prominent throughout the firm—but it was up to the local boy to make good. Nor, in spite of the growth of the business, did Lever allow financial considerations to lessen his concern for consumer or workman. The quality of Sunlight remained his obsession, Port Sunlight and its people his favourite creation and his delight. There lay the wider importance of Lever's business: in an age when the study of industrial relations was in its infancy, it demonstrated that efficiency and success could be combined with social health and humanity and even suggested that there might be some essential connection between the two.

CHAPTER XI

IN SEARCH OF RAW MATERIALS

'The large soap maker in ten or twenty years from today who has not behind him a raw material scheme must go under no matter what be his advertising. Advertising will I believe be a dead letter in soap by then. Mere investments in planting schemes will be no use: the soap maker must own the raw material scheme and have it as a background to his business.'

Joseph Meek to W. H. Lever, 4 *October* 1910

'The Congo is the land to teach one patience.'

William Lever in his Diary of the First Congo Tour (1913)

MANY factors combined in the later years of the nineteenth century to divert the stream of British capital and enterprise from European to non-European investment, from temperate to tropical areas. In Europe, industrial competition was growing and capital investment not only in Britain but in Europe generally was less profitable than it had been in the third quarter of the century. In the nineties, proposals for the protection of British industry went hand in hand with ideas of imperial preference. These in turn were stimulated by better communications and transport. Distance was no longer the bogey it had once been. Looked at against the broad canvas of world economic development, Lever's tropical enterprises form a part of the contemporary movement to open up new markets in the Empire and the tropics. To that extent, Lever was a man of his time. It was the Age of the *Jungle Books*. There were in addition cogent reasons inherent in the soap industry itself why these tropical excursions should take place at this time.

The nature of the raw materials required by the soap maker made him peculiarly conscious of the importance of foreign supplies. And the quality of Sunlight, depending as it did on imported vegetable oils, made Lever from the beginning alive to the problem of raw materials. Round about the turn of the century, the fear of being 'squeezed' for these materials by the merchants and brokers became almost an obsession with him, and in the projects for winning raw materials that followed there was probably a large element of defensive strategy.

Pacific Prelude

The start of Lever's planting adventures really dates from 1901 when, on a voyage from Sydney to Vancouver, he decided that the time had arrived when the mills at Sydney should be supplied from their own copra plantations in the South Seas. A fellow passenger on that journey was John T. Arundel who interested Lever in a company largely of his own creation and which traded in phosphates. Arundel's company, the Pacific Islands Company, was short of money and Lever proposed that he should personally take £25,000 in the Company on condition that the Company would sell to Lever Brothers for £25,000 the whole of their interests in the coconut islands in the Pacific. All told, the Company held about 51,000 acres from the British Government on a ninety-nine year lease. The upshot of the negotiations was that two new Companies were formed in place of the single old one. The original business was carried on by the Pacific Phosphate Company. It turned out to be a most successful venture and Lever never regretted his investment. The second Company was Lever's Pacific Plantations Limited, which was incorporated in England in 1902. Harold Greenhalgh and George Fulton, two Port Sunlight men, were immediately despatched to the South Seas to report on the prospects of more intensive development. Fulton then remained in Sydney to manage the business, while Greenhalgh returned to London to report on what he had seen. It soon became evident that the undertaking was going to involve commitments of quite a new kind. Trade between the islands and the transport of copra to Sydney necessitated a ship, and Lever Brothers bought the S.S. *Upolu* (1,141 tons gross). From the old company they inherited a pearl shell industry which they tried, though with scant success, to continue.

No sooner had the new venture been launched than world conditions turned against the producers. Raw material prices which had been very high during 1902 slumped towards the end of that year. Lever attributed the drop in copra prices to 'the large corn crop in the United States' and to 'the opening up of the West Coast of Africa by railways which have brought

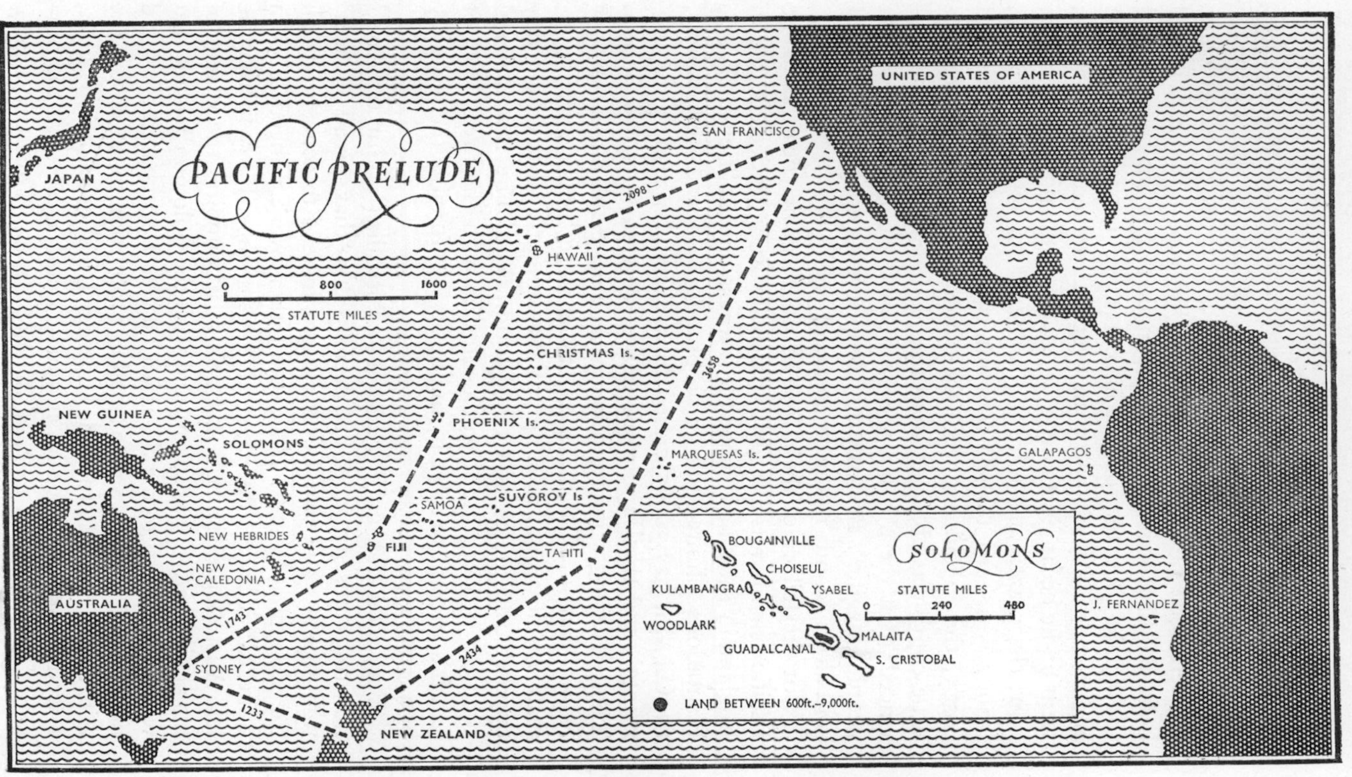
PACIFIC PRELUDE
JAPAN
UNITED STATES OF AMERICA
SAN FRANCISCO
2098
HAWAII
0
800
1600
STATUTE MILES
CHRISTMAS Is.
3658
PHOENIX Is.
MARQUESAS Is.
GALAPAGOS
NEW GUINEA
SOLOMONS
SAMOA
SUVOROV Is
NEW HEBRIDES
FIJI
TAHITI
NEW CALEDONIA
AUSTRALIA
1743
2434
SYDNEY
1233
NEW ZEALAND
J. FERNANDEZ
SOLOMONS
BOUGAINVILLE
CHOISEUL
KULAMBANGRA
YSABEL
STATUTE MILES
0
240
480
WOODLARK
MALAITA
GUADALCANAL
S. CRISTOBAL
LAND BETWEEN 600ft.–9,000ft.
N

enormous quantities of palm oil and palm kernels to the coast'. He was not long in coming to the conclusion that his newly bought islands would be losing money for many years to come at their 1902 rate of production of 337 tons of copra. He still believed that the islands could be made to pay but he confessed to Arundel that 'the road we have to travel is both a longer one and a more difficult one than ever I imagined. . . .' As 1903 went on he became steadily more aware of the difficulties before him: the plantations were too scattered for effective working, labour was hard to get, communication was infrequent and costly, the subsidiary pearl shell industry was a failure, very little copra was obtained from the plantation. He became convinced 'that there is not the profit in the copra business that people imagine'. By 1914 the company, accepting defeat, had sold all its islands in this area except one.

But the failure of these first efforts to grow coconuts in the Pacific Islands was already apparent by 1905; indeed Meek, in England in 1904, had gained the impression that 'Lever's Pacific Plantations Limited was to be practically abandoned entirely, the Oil Mill [at Sydney] closed down except for soapery requirements', and that he himself was to be transferred to Boston. The prevailing school of thought at Port Sunlight, headed by Robert Barrie, held that plantations were 'outside our legitimate business and . . . simply an investment'. Meek vehemently opposed the policy of total abandonment. The raw material problem was urgent: it would not die with the breakdown of Lever's attempt to solve it, and he argued forcibly the necessity of a fresh approach.

Very soon after his first arrival in Australia ('within ten days,' he wrote himself), Meek had decided that 'that spread out area' was hopeless and that Lever's ought instead to concentrate on the Solomon Islands. His protest then went unheeded, even unheard, at home: but now came his chance. Early in 1905 he left Australia in the S.Y. *Victoria* to reconnoitre the islands of his choice and 'I was so satisfied with the Solomon Islands that when I went out to the Solomon Islands I purchased all round me and the amount was so small in proportion to the cost of the trip that I had determined, knowing I had exceeded my limit, I would take over the lot if you did not agree with the purchase'. He went on to New Britain, Papua, Thursday Island,

Celebes, Java, and the Straits Settlements, but nothing that he saw in any of those places shook his conviction that the Solomons were the place for Lever's new plantations, and as a result of his recommendations the L.P.P.L. company bought 51,000 acres of land, ships, and a number of trading stations in the islands which, as Meek pointed out, offered the advantages of harbour anchorages, good rainfall, cheap labour, and proximity to Australia.

Work began on the new property at once and in 1906 the first plantings were made with seed nuts brought in the Company's ship *Upolu* from Samoa. No marketable results, of course, were possible for some years: in the meantime the trading stations were turned to account. Copra was bought: so also were ivory nuts (shipped to Germany for the manufacture of buttons) and turtle shell. As the estates came into bearing it became necessary to increase the Company's fleet: in 1910 and 1911 four ships were built or bought, of which the *Kulambangra* (2,005 tons gross) was considerably the largest. She carried 2,000 tons of cargo and twenty passengers: she did the voyage between the Islands and Sydney in seven days, and upon her, evidently, the Company mainly relied for its existence. The smaller ships, between 140 and 170 tons gross, were required for recruiting labour and for general communication between the scattered islands.

The development of Lever's in the Solomons naturally brought them into contact and sometimes into conflict with Government departments. The acquisition of land was not here, as it was to be in Africa, a cause of friction, for the Company obtained freehold or leases of 999 years. In the matter of labour supplies they were less fortunate. The declining native population were little inclined to work: as soon as they had satisfied their very limited desire for imported luxuries the islanders lost interest in plantation employment, and it was necessary for the little ships to go ever farther afield, to less civilized islands, in search of recruits. Lever's answer to the problem was simple: 'I do not see', he told his shareholders, 'why we cannot bring as labourers to these beautiful Islands Hindoos from the teeming millions of India.' The Government of India, unfortunately, could not agree, and when Meek went to India in 1911 with offers of free land to tempt settlers he was repulsed. After years of fruitless wrangling, Lever expounded his view of the case to Captain C. M. Woodford, at one time Chief Commissioner in the Solomons and one of his rare official allies:

> I cannot understand the attitude at the Colonial Office, but these interlacing Government departments such as the Colonial Office and the India Office are very difficult to influence for the good and progress of those portions of the Empire where they feel a little in conflict. I am sure that Kulambangra is quite an ideal spot for Indians, and from there as time went on they would spread all over the Solomon Islands [which was no doubt exactly what his antagonists feared]. We should have an increasing population instead of as at present a decreasing population. Land is valueless without men and women to live on it. It seems a pity that such good fertile rich land, as far as my knowledge goes the best in the Pacific for coconut growing, should lie unused in this way.

He ended on a note of resignation:

> We must however be patient. Probably their nerves are a little strained at present with the War. When we get to the 'piping times of peace' again, we can have another try.

Managers had to be engaged as well as labourers, and here too difficulties arose. They must be men adaptable to life in trying and isolated conditions who could be trusted to serve the Company faithfully without detailed supervision. To provide the necessary incentive Lever toyed with several schemes, among them a proposal to grant life leases to managers of plantations, coupled presumably with a plan for allowing them a share of the profits.

'Under this lease', he had written to Meek some time previously, 'a capable manager would have a splendid opportunity, and he would have every inducement to keep down expenses of planting, otherwise he would be unable to make the undertaking sufficiently profitable.'

Meek did not agree and evidently in the end his views prevailed, for by 1913 the managers were engaged on a salary basis. But Lever was not altogether to be denied an outlet for his unorthodoxy, and he formed four companies to work estates owned by L.P.P.L. Half the shares were held by the L.P.P.L. Company and half were held by the managers. The men engaged under these terms were nearly all Australian bushmen.

When Lever visited the islands in 1913 he was greatly impressed by them: 'They are sober and hard-working and used to a solitary life far from town or city life. They can live in comfort, not to say luxury, where a city man from most places would grouch and grumble, sulk and starve. They have a natural love and aptitude for the life—they are full of little ways that enable them to adapt themselves to their island life.' Their inventiveness he particularly admired, and certainly Lever had need of all the inventiveness he could command from his subordinates, for they had first to clear the bush and then establish the plantations, and at that time little was known about the planting of coconut palms: most of the knowledge had to be obtained from experience. The estates grew from the original 51,000 acres of 1905 to 300,000 (three per cent of the Islands' total area) in 1913, of which about 30,000–35,000 acres was in cultivation. There were about sixty natives on each plantation, and on the whole territory there were 1,500 head of cattle, each of which could do two men's work in keeping down the grass, besides ploughing and draft work. From less than a hundred tons in 1906, copra production rose to over a thousand tons in 1913. Small though these figures were, with only ten per cent of the acreage yet under cultivation the possibilities of expansion were vast. It was nevertheless only a beginning: as Lever himself confessed: 'Our task in the Solomons is child's play to our task in the Congo Belge.'

Africa

From the beginning of Lever's raw material adventures Africa was in his thoughts; early in 1902 an investigator was gathering information for him from the West Coast, whence he reported 'an inexhaustible supply of Palm Oil and Palm Kernels in the hinterland there only awaiting development and the opening up of markets'. It was evident to Lever that there was 'ample margin for lower prices in all these products before the supply is checked', and he was supported in his opinion by the fact that he was 'in two West African Companies neither of which paid any dividends for many years, but have now begun to pay very handsomely'. In 1903, Harold Greenhalgh followed in the footsteps of the earlier explorer. Lever's early African excursions were all directed towards British possessions.

Unfortunately the Colonial Office received his overtures with frigid suspicion.

The controversy between Lever and the colonial officials was prolonged. The question turned upon the conditions of occupation and use of land; it was the settled policy of the Colonial Office that the native populations of West Africa under British rule should in general have secured to them rights to hold their ancestral soil without disturbance, to cultivate it as they would, and to do with its produce what they thought fit. These principles did not conflict with the interests of the ordinary European merchant trading in Africa, who was concerned merely to carry on commerce with the natives. They were supported, moreover, by a formidable weight of experience, which did not encourage the alienation of native land. The policy was firmly grounded on the economic convenience of the Occupying Power and the welfare of the subject races.

Lever challenged it on both counts. He saw that the production of the materials in which he was interested, by native methods, was miserably inefficient and he believed that if he were once allowed to proceed with his plans he could improve the efficiency of the industry out of all recognition. But to do so he must introduce scientific cultivation of the oil palm, and mechanical milling of its fruit, for both of which he required the grant of extensive rights over large tracts of country for long periods of time. The most the Colonial Office would offer was a twenty-one year lease in Sierra Leone, of which Lever scornfully remarked: 'If the Government had offered us a twenty-one days' lease we might have been wise in buying a wheelbarrow or two, but that would be about the extent of the capital we could wisely expend on a twenty-one days' lease. On a twenty-one years' lease we could go further, but, after all, it would be comparatively a very small amount of money that we would be justified in expending holding only a twenty-one years' lease. I sometimes wish', he continued, 'that all native chiefs in the British Colonies, in Africa at any rate, were made dukes. In my opinion we should then take the sensible view that this land was theirs for development and the advancement of civilization, and just as we will not tolerate a duke keeping his land for his own pleasure, or to lock it up, and have passed laws that make this impossible in the United Kingdom, so I can never understand why a black man should be allowed to assume a different attitude, and neither develop his own land nor allow other people to do so.'

He was equally unimpressed by the arguments in favour of tribal organization. Natives should be treated as 'willing children', housed, schooled, doctored, and moved from place to place as might be required. Above all, they should be taught the value of regular habits and of working to time. Under such a régime, how could they fail to become both healthy and industrious, and how then could they fail to be happy? These arguments, not always couched in terms either diplomatic or respectful, failed utterly to convince the Colonial Office of its error. With the exception of Joseph Chamberlain, to whose wisdom Lever, normally a bitter political opponent, had to pay reluctant tribute, no Colonial Secretary would grant the long leases which were demanded, and Chamberlain's grant did not apply to Africa, but to the Solomons. Prevented, therefore, from developing his plans within the British Empire, Lever turned his eyes beyond its borders. In 1909 opportunity came his way.

The Belgian Congo

The Belgian Government, newly committed to its work of salvage and reconstruction in the territory of the extinct Congo Free State, sought the assistance of British capitalists, and as its spokesman sent to England Dr. Max Horn who 'addressed the principal Chambers of Commerce . . . , and . . . called upon the late Sir Alfred Jones, the Chairman of Elder, Dempster & Company, at the time the outstanding figure in the trade of British West Africa'. Sir Alfred, who had once been British Consul-General in the Congo Free State, passed Horn on to Lever, and so set in train an enduring association between the two men.

The land policy of Belgium in the Congo differed strikingly from that of Great Britain in her possessions, and Horn intimated to Lever that his Government would be sympathetic to the idea of a long-term concession. No policy could have been more to Lever's taste, yet he was not at first attracted by Horn's proposals, because the distance of the suggested scene of operations from the sea, and the primitive nature of Congo communications which, apart from the railway between Matadi and Leopoldville, were restricted to river steamer and jungle footpath, called up visions of exorbitant transport costs. Nevertheless, in 1911 L. H. Moseley, late of the Bank of Nigeria and an expert on conditions in West Africa, together with an engineer, H. Beckwith, went to the Congo on reconnaissance. Moseley's report was sharply critical of social conditions and of official incompetence and obstruction. He suspected that the hindrance proceeded less from natural ineptitude than from the jealous inspiration of vested interests, whose representatives from the outset watched Lever's plans with unfriendly solicitude.

But Lever was deterred neither by the formidable natural obstacles to the project, nor by the opposition of local interests. His friends, after all, were more powerful still, for he had the support not only of the Government but of King Albert himself, who had inherited all his uncle's enthusiasm for colonial development and a good deal of his power. With this backing, and evidently convinced in his own mind that probable but distant advantage outweighed certain and immediate difficulty, he entered into treaty, almost like a sovereign prince, with the Belgian Government, and on 14th April 1911 a convention was signed with the colony of the Belgian Congo which brought into existence 'La Société Anonyme des Huileries du Congo Belge'. Thus Lever, in the sixtieth year of his life, burdened already with the direction of a world-wide business, undertook a task which was little less than the reorganization of a principality.

In 1911 the administration of the Congo Free State was far from popular with Liberal opinion in Europe. In the early years of this century resentment against the regime ran high in Europe and America, and nowhere was feeling more bitter than in Great Britain, where disapproval of Leopold II's conduct was a strong motive behind the King's decision to hand over his creation to the Belgian State. Lever, therefore, if he wished for the favour of public opinion, could scarcely have chosen a more unpropitious setting for his operations, since the reputation of the Congo Free State had not, in 1911, had time to lose itself in that of the Belgian Congo.[1]

The system of forced labour employed by earlier concession companies had depopulated large areas of the country.

[1] It is only right to add that though there was much to criticize in the Congo, by no means all the criticism was either fair or well informed.

L. H. Moseley, on his reconnaissance in 1911, remarked of several districts that the country was deserted, and added the highly significant comment that near Lusanga, although the population was in reality plentiful, they 'prefer for safety to keep away from the highways of the white man until sure of security'. The numbers, state of mind, and willingness to work of the native population were of the highest consequence to Lever, for without a plentiful labour supply his plans must fail. The pioneers who established Leverville, Lever's first settlement near Lusanga, found that the local tribes were eager to come and work, but it was not so everywhere. The natives lived in varying degrees of savagery, from cannibalism to Mission-cultivated sophistication, but they were not normally dangerous to white men, and Lever, when he visited the Congo, decided that they were grossly maligned by the white man who 'is always speaking of the "lazy nigger". He is a child and a willing child but he wants training and handling with patience.'

The white population of the Colony contained a large element of a dubious character. Conditions of life were not such as normally to attract men who could earn a living at home. The climate, as tropical climates go, was perhaps not one of the worst: on the hills between Matadi and Leopoldville and at Lusanga, where Leverville arose, it was quite good. Nevertheless, malaria and sleeping sickness, abetted by filth and the multifarious minor pests of the tropics, did their work, and the mortality rate was high. The general standard of housing and sanitation may be judged from Moseley's description of Matadi as it was when he landed:

> Our quarters are stuffy and hot and there are about fifty other white passengers *en route* to the Upper River staying here. They are of all kinds and classes and the atmosphere is by no means a healthy one for any young men we may later send out, yet this is the best place in the town. . . . The stench tonight from the town is abominable. There appear to be no latrines and the natives use all the unused small areas of rock, etc., in the town. There are no lights in the town and it is most dangerous at night climbing the steep rocky streets and crossing the Railway.

The permanent accommodation provided by large companies for their officials was often extremely rough. Against this squalid background the Jesuit missions stood out in sharp contrast. The

Order had established itself at various places in the Congo, and at the station at Wombari the Fathers taught the native children 'useful work' and 'have really wonderful farms, breed sheep and poultry, make bricks, do carpentry, engineering, building and have even a brewery'.

Lever's new principality, then, was a country still suffering from the reputation of an unpopular administration, and which, at the time when he entered it, had barely begun to feel the effect of the new Government. In the face of all the difficulties he accepted a concession which his critics did not hesitate to describe as an unprincipled monopoly. He knew better and, justly indignant, wrote to L. H. Moseley: 'The word "Concession" conjures up in the mind of most people a "tom tiddler's" ground where the happy concessionaire merely has to stoop and pick up the sovereigns. You and I know, and all the staff of the Huileries know, that this is not the case in the Belgian Congo. In fact we have to take great risks, use an enormous amount of Capital, and tax our energy and strength to get this business on a sound commercial footing.'

The legal foundation of the Huileries du Congo Belge was the Convention of 1911 between Jules Renkin, representing the colony of the Belgian Congo, and Sir William Lever, representing Lever Brothers Limited. It was ratified by the Belgian Parliament before signature, and so acquired statutory force. It was more than an ordinary commercial contract; it was a State document and as such it brought Lever Brothers out of the business world and into that of international politics. The rights and duties of the new Company were partly commercial, partly administrative: that is to say, it was required to shoulder heavy social responsibilities as a necessary condition of conducting its primary business.

The Company's main operations were to be carried on in five areas of palm-bearing 'domainal land', which were to centre on Bumba and Barumbu on the Congo, Lusanga on the Kwilu, a point situated forty kilometres to the south of, and on the same meridian as Ingende on the Ruki, and Basongo on the Kasai, and were to stretch for at least sixty kilometres round these points. Within six years an oil mill was to be set up in each area to process not less than 6,000 tons of fresh fruit per year, gathered from the natural palmeries. The huge areas of the

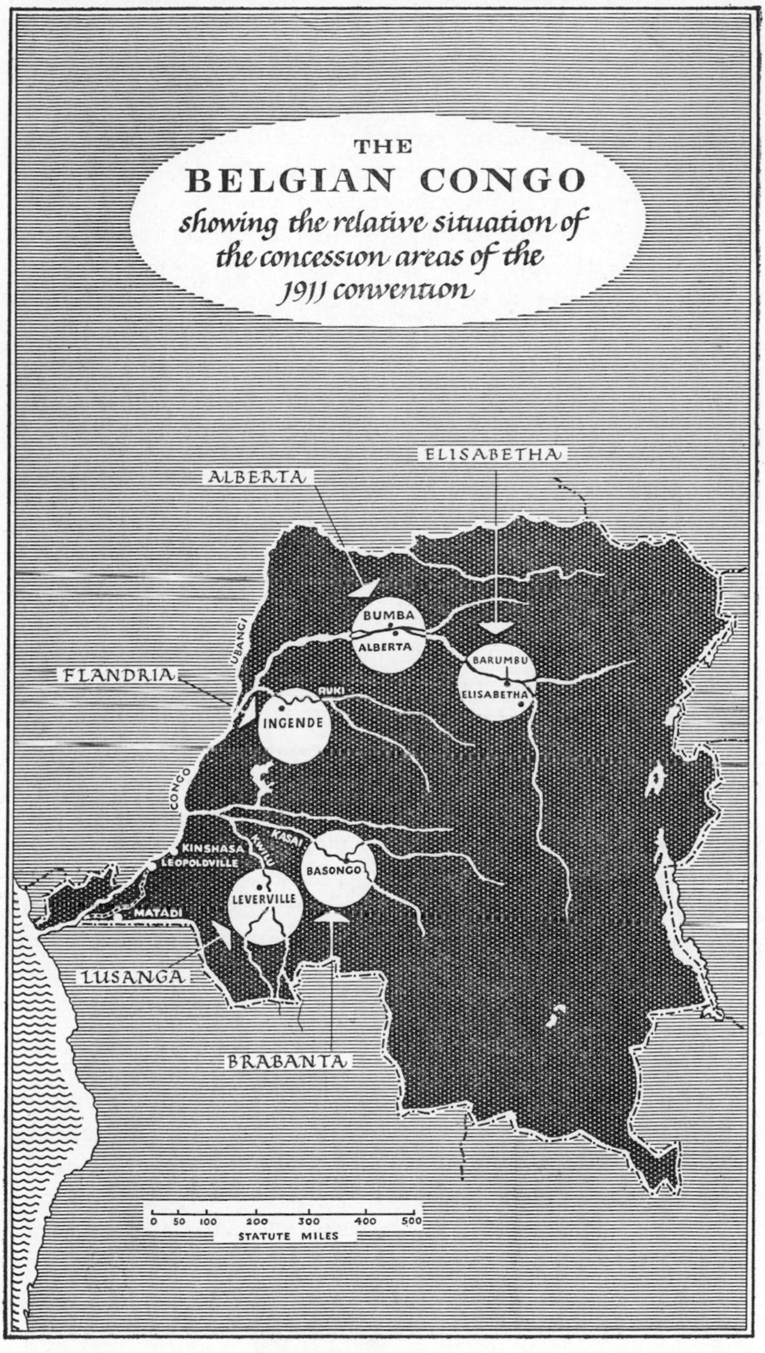

THE

BELGIAN CONGO

showing the relative situation of the concession areas of the 1911 convention

ELISABETHA
ALBERTA
BUMBA
ALBERTA
UBANGI
BARUMBU
ELISABETHA
FLANDRIA
RUKI
INGENDE
CONGO
KASAI
KWILU
KINSHASA
LEOPOLDVILLE
BASONGO
LEVERVILLE
MATADI
LUSANGA
BRABANTA
0 50 100 200 300 400 500
STATUTE MILES

original concession were not to be occupied totally and permanently. In each of them where, at the end of the sixth year, the obligatory mill had been erected, the H.C.B. were to have the right to choose, within ten years from the Société's foundation, up to 75,000 hectares of palm-bearing land or, if by that time they disposed of sufficient equipment in any area to treat at least 15,000 tons of fruit, they might take up to 200,000 hectares, provided that the total of land chosen in all areas did not exceed 750,000 hectares. The land, in the first instance, was to be held on lease from the colony. On the 1st of January 1945, provided the necessary obligations had been fulfilled, the land chosen was to pass into the freehold possession of H.C.B., subject to the payment of ground rent at the same rate as before.[1]

The country in which H.C.B. were to operate was, as we have seen, entirely wild and undeveloped; it lacked all modern means of communication except river steamers, one railway, and an exiguous Government telegraph and telephone service up the course of the Congo itself. The Société was therefore empowered to establish in its own areas at its own expense 'routes, canaux, chemins de fer, télégraphes, téléphones, et autres voies de communication qu'elle jugera nécessaires à son exploitation', and also harbour works along the waterways. These facilities, so far as the Société's business allowed, were to be available, upon payment, to all; Government and military rights were especially defined and protected. The other major 'political' provision stated that the Company 's'efforcera d'améliorer la condition des populations établies à proximité de ses usines et de leur assurer des soins médicaux'. In pursuance of this obligation at least one school and one hospital, with a doctor, qualified in tropical medicine, were to be established and maintained in each area at the H.C.B.'s expense.

As well as safeguarding the physical well-being and cultural development of the native inhabitants, the Convention also looked to their economic interests. Natives employed for the gathering and delivery of palm fruit were to be guaranteed a minimum daily rate of pay, exclusive of their rations, and the Société was to encourage the circulation of money—the value

[1] The articles dealing with the choice of land and the terms under which it was to be held were very materially modified in later years.

and use of which were as yet very imperfectly understood—in the districts where it worked.

The national trade and industry of Belgium and her colony, and the employment of Belgian citizens, were very carefully safeguarded. Half the Société's servants were to be of Belgian nationality. One third of its imported material (except that manufactured by Lever Brothers or their associates), and a quarter of its trade goods were to be bought in Belgium; its ships were to be of Belgian register and to sail under the Belgian flag. After 1932, for every 50 hectares of land held at least one thousand kilograms of oil were to be exported annually through a Congo seaport.

No sooner was the Convention published than it was assailed by business men in England, Belgium, and Germany as an unwarrantable monopoly, and by philanthropists as an unscrupulous invasion of native rights. Lever himself never denied that the concession endowed the new concern with very extensive privileges, but he did deny emphatically that it set up an unfair and injurious monopoly. Ever present to his mind were the enormous risks he ran, with other people's money, in attempting such an enterprise in such a country. There was no justification for the enterprise unless the capital were secured in such a manner as would allow him to develop without interference from rivals unburdened by responsibilities such as his. He put his point of view forcibly before Horn when, writing of the prospects of success, he said:

> I have . . . foreseen . . . that if we fail the 'wiseheads' will wag their beards gravely—'they always said so'—and that if we succeed the same 'wiseheads' will attempt to rush in through the gap in the wall we have made, and attempt to overrun our Concession or to prevent us from reaping the reward of our courage, enterprise and risk by declaring that our rights must be cancelled, and our concessions opened to every Tom, Dick and Harry who like to copy our methods and trample over our orchards. The inrush of a herd of wild elephants would be trifling to the inrush there will be to the Congo if we prove a success. The world is big enough for everyone, and the Congo is not in any way a small slice of it, and there will be room enough in the Congo for rapid development on the lines we shall have proved to be successful for everyone who wishes to go, and all I ask is that our rights as provided in the concessions should be respected.

Neither did he admit the arguments of those who accused him of defrauding the inhabitants of the legitimate use of their tribal property, reducing them from independence to the status of mere wage-labourers. Capital investment was essential if the colony were to develop from its existing state of primitive barbarism: such capital investment must be properly secured by the grant of adequate rights, and in any case he had undertaken to do so much for the well-being of the peoples affected that his benevolence towards them could not reasonably be called in question. His conscience was quiet, and he could write to Horn:

> We shall want the natives to live in comfort and happiness, cultivating their own ground in their own way, and making any use they may wish by native methods of palm trees within our area, as provided in the Concession.

The Convention once signed, development was pushed ahead with Lever's characteristic energy. He was determined that oil should be produced from a mill in the Congo within a year from the conclusion of the agreement. The first area to be developed was that centring on a site near Lusanga on the Kwilu, which was henceforth to be known as Leverville, and in the summer of 1911 a thousand tons of cargo, mostly machinery, arrived at Matadi. The difficulties were enormous. The tiny railway, with its 2½ foot gauge, was utterly inadequate: its carriage capacity was about thirty tons a day and there was practically no provision for handling heavy freight. Neither the railway company nor the Government authorities at Leopoldville were prepared to exert themselves unduly to assist the new arrivals, and it was only by the combined manual labour and technical ingenuity of the H.C.B. staff that the material was successfully transhipped from sea to railway at Matadi, then from railway to river at Kinshasa, and was finally landed at its destination some hundreds of miles from the port of arrival.

The site of Leverville itself required considerable tailoring, because it was a hillside dropping straight down into the river, and 'many thousands of tons of earth had to be shifted to make the present flat plateau'. Fortunately native labour in the district was not difficult to recruit, though apart from one or two tribes the population was 'poor, underfed, ravaged by sickness and inter-tribal warfare, and all were cannibals'. The white supervising staff were lodged in temporary quarters of varying degrees of discomfort: their food, supplied with a total lack of imagination from Liverpool, was unpalatable to Continental members of the staff and monotonous to all, and the feeling of insecurity was such that three Europeans deserted in a stolen canoe. Besides the erection of the mill itself under all these impediments, the collection of fruit had to be organized. It was soon found that the price calculated by the home management was too low to attract native interest, and also that the available population was not large enough for the double task of collection and construction; recruits would have to be brought in from outside, which would involve problems of housing and feeding. Nevertheless the thing was done. The first machinery was despatched on 12th August 1911, and the first consignment of palm oil reached Antwerp on 20th March 1912. Soap made from this oil by the Lever factory in Brussels was ready—three months after the landing of the first material at Leverville. In April, with appropriate ceremony, a casket made from Congo ivory, containing the first tablet of this soap, was presented by Sir William Lever to the King of the Belgians.

Lever himself, with his wife and staff, set out for the Congo in November 1912. On board the rivercraft, Lever settled down to his daily routine: 'Rise at 5 a.m. shave, Cup of Tea at 5.15, Cold Bath at 5.20, Breakfast 6.30, Lunch 12, Afternoon Tea 4, Dinner 6.30, Bed 9. Writing letters, Diary, etc., early morning, Oils and Fats Committee 8.30 a.m.' The tour was comprehensive. It included all the areas granted under the concession: it involved arduous journeys by land, weeks of cramped life aboard the small steamer, and it lasted until March 1913.[1]

The first major problem which claimed his attention was that of native labour. Population was not always sufficient in the areas where it was required: labour therefore had to be imported. But this could not be done indiscriminately: apart altogether from the question of housing and training these immigrants, there was also the fact that feeding habits differed from district to district; in the Kwilu, for instance, the inhabitants would only

[1] It is perhaps worth noting that even at this early date Lever made arrangements to have moving pictures taken of the tour. A few film sequences of scenes on board the steamer have survived, and form an interesting and rare example of the film as a historical record.

eat prepared manioc, whereas in other places they would eat rice or maize. 'This problem of labour', he wrote in his diary on Christmas Eve, 'has grown as an ominous dark cloud', and a few days later he set out what was really the central difficulty:

> The fact is, the native has few wants, a little salt and a little cloth are his indispensables. After this, beads, brass rods and other luxuries. Chief Womba at Leverville can be taken as an example. Twelve months ago he and his people were poor and few in number, and were keen to bring fruit. After 12 months or less of selling fruit he is rich and lazy, has 10 wives, and his village is about 4 times the size it was, but he gathers little or no fruit. . . . The Palm tree is in these parts the Banking account of the native and he no more thinks of going to the Bank for fruit for money when his wants and ambitions are supplied than a civilized man would. His bank is always open when he wants to draw on it.

Besides the difficulties inherent in the nature of his task, Lever had to combat the inevitable errors arising from inexperience. 'I am continually getting rude shocks', he wrote in his diary, 'on the subject of our extravagance in Capital Expenditure, the result of our gross ignorance of the building material and capabilities of the Country', and he went on to commend the good sense of other business men who, instead of importing costly stores from Europe, exploited to the full the abundance of the forest. It also became apparent to him that the experience of others was no reliable substitute for his own, for of the Société's steamers, built after a pattern which had been approved for use on the Congo for many years, he wrote bitterly, 'If anyone can devise a new error in boatbuilding after seeing our Congo Fleet he will deserve a patent for it'.

The Congo was much the greatest single enterprise that Lever had undertaken; its full reward could not be reaped for many years. Before he left for England, Lever summed up his impressions:

> Words cannot tell the value to myself and, I hope, to our business, of this journey, I feel more confidence in our great undertaking than ever, although the difficulties are greater than I judged. We have got hold of something we can employ all our talents and energy upon for the next quarter century and still find plenty to do. Our title will not only depend upon the terms

of our Concession, our strongest hold will be our plantation work, and without such work being done our concessions are valueless. There are still many things to be done, but I can see our way clearly and given our usual loyalty from ourselves and staff to the obligations we have undertaken and our success, great and boundless, is assured.

Most urgent was the framing of the programme for the following year and the designing of an administrative organization to supervise it. Liverpool was to be the headquarters but local control was to rest with Moseley, as a director of the Société, with his H.Q. at Kinshasa. An English manager, Sidney Edkins, at Leverville, was to have charge of that area and Brabanta: a Belgian, H. de Keyser, was to have command of Alberta and Elisabetha. As soon as possible units were to be set up which, at full strength, would have a total annual capacity of 100,000 tons of palm fruit:

Mills	
At Alberta . .	20,000 tons p.a.
Elisabetha . .	20,000 ,, ,,
Basongo (Brabanta)	10,000 ,, ,,
Leverville . .	50,000 ,, ,,
Ingende . .	?
	100,000

Lever did not expect 100,000 tons to be achieved during the first year, but probably nearer thirty to forty thousand tons, and 'the central idea of the above programme is to get as much machinery shipped as possible this year to provide cargo for our stern wheelers, launches, tugs, and barges, so that 1914 may see us with a fair output of oil'.

Kinshasa, Leverville, Alberta, and Elisabetha were to be pushed ahead first. Kinshasa, besides being the administrative headquarters for the operations of the Société as a whole, was also a terminal point in the bulk transport and storage of oil. Wooden casks, on Edkins's suggestion, were abandoned: a tank yard and pumping station were built, and the Société's barges themselves were turned into tankers. Workshops, power-driven machinery, and warehouses were also erected at Kinshasa on orders given by Sir William during his visit. The other three areas mentioned above were those of the palm estates which gave prospect of the earliest success. One 1,000-ton mill each was to be built immediately for Elisabetha and Alberta; Leverville was to have two. Brabanta and Flandria had both been rather disappointing to the hopes raised by early reports: they were therefore to be left until Edkins had had a chance to explore them more thoroughly.

This programme, of course, did not go through without a hitch. The administrative organization was soon altered. Edkins had given ample proof that he was endowed with all the courage and resourcefulness of the true pioneer. Accordingly he was given a roving commission with plenary powers to act in any area where he might for the time being find himself and from this time onwards was effective head of the organization. Edkins was faced with a succession of shortages—shortages of staff, shortages of materials, shortages of everything. But steadfastly refusing to admit defeat he improvised, improvised again, and pushed on. Thanks largely to his enterprise, progress by the end of 1913 was fairly satisfactory. Moseley reported that Kinshasa was 'in a fairly straightforward condition, and . . . there was nothing seriously wrong'. At Leverville, he hoped Sir William would consider 'that matters are progressing as quickly and as favourably as can be expected' and 'at Alberta the mills should be finished and ready for work very shortly, and early in the new year, Elisabetha should also be in the producing stage'. The administrative problem was still far from being solved—'There has unfortunately been considerable trouble with certain members of the staff and . . . the general systems of Accounts and Stores were far from being anything like properly organized'.

Indiscipline amongst the staff was worrying other minds than Moseley's. Early in 1914 Horn wrote that 'there appears to be urgent need for a strong man or two—leaders—at Alberta and Elisabetha. I fear the conditions there are very much like anarchy; there seems to be a great deal of discontent and strife amongst the white staff.'

Amid such tribulations the work went forward. Railways were laid, and new towns arose round the mills. Explorers pushed into the unmapped forests. Above all, the 'agriculturists' set about their task of taming the jungle. The plantations which were established in the Congo were not new foundations, but rather a development of the natural growth of the forest. Trees and vegetation, other than palms, were cleared, and the palms themselves were cleaned, thinned out, or planted up as might be necessary. At first, on expert advice, the policy was clean-weeding, but later this process was found to be harmful: it was replaced by the planting of leguminous cover-crops which were mulched into the soil.

Lever had intended visiting the Congo again in 1913 or 1914, but other business claims, and then the outbreak of war, interfered with his plans. The war, by impeding the supply of merchandise, plant, machinery, and agents, seriously hampered the planned development of the concessions. Nevertheless, by 1914 a great deal had been achieved, though tangible results were still small.

The Belgian Government was not the only one prepared to offer more lenient terms than Whitehall in the matter of African plantations. About the same time as the Congo concession was going through, Lever was examining an optimistic report on a large expanse of territory—some six million acres—owned by the French Compagnie Propriétaire du Kouilou Niari (C.P.K.N.). '. . . the country was very beautiful, with beautiful lakes in the interior, well-wooded and almost like English park land. . . .' In this demi-paradise were supposed to dwell some 25,000 natives. Encouraged by these glowing reports, Lever sent J. T. Irvine, a Liverpool broker who was brought into the business to strengthen the raw material side, to Paris to negotiate. Irvine succeeded in bringing down the price to £70,000, and at that price the land changed hands.

Then came the awakening. Irvine was sent out to investigate and brought back a depressing story. Out of the six million acres, only some 10,000 were suitable for planting. This attenuated coastal area was hemmed in by a barren range of mountains. Communications were almost non-existent. The population was scanty and quite inadequate for even a limited development of the area. Experience bore Irvine out in his contentions. It proved to be quite impossible to grow palm trees. A succession of alternative projects followed—groundnuts, minerals, and cattle rearing—but all proved impracticable. From the beginning the C.P.K.N. was a dead loss.

British West Africa

In the Solomons, the Congo, and—theoretically—in French Equatorial Africa, Lever could buy or lease land on which to grow palms. In British West Africa he could do neither. The policy of the Colonial Office compelled him to buy the palm fruit and palm kernels from the Africans. He had, therefore, to enter the ancient and none-too-reputable Coast Trade. The background to the trade—still not far distant—was the slave traffic, and its traditions lingered. Tropical medicine had scarcely touched the fringe of the problems of health in these climates, and a man needed powerful incentives to attract him there. The job of the company agent in Africa in those days was to make an agreed margin of profit for his employers; what he could make for himself was largely his own business. The trade itself was barely out of the barter stage. European manufactures, particularly ironmongery and Manchester cotton goods, were exchanged for African produce—palm fruit and kernels, timber, minerals, ivory. In Nigeria, which was above all the land of the oil palm—it included the territory of the 'Oil Rivers Protectorate'—competition between the European trading firms had been free and fierce up till 1900. But in that year the Niger Company, the African Association, Alexander Miller, Brother & Company, and the Company of African Merchants signed a pooling agreement: markets were divided; each party remained independent, but a 'Committee of Control' was set up to co-ordinate operations. After this agreement the African Association first began to pay large dividends. The alliance was by no means popular among its competitors on the Coast, but after its guiding spirits, in an interview with Joseph Chamberlain, had satisfied the Colonial Office of the purity of their intentions there was no official interference. The Gold Coast was likewise 'regulated' after 1905 between the African Association, Miller's and F. & A. Swanzy. The only serious threat, all along the Coast, came from a number of independent German firms who were supplied with abundant 'currency' in the shape of cheap German hardware.

Into this strange and hazardous world Lever launched himself in 1910, at the age of nearly sixty. He knew next to nothing of the merchandise trade, the surest source of steady profits; produce prices and profits fluctuated, at times wildly. Lever's interest, of course, lay in the produce side. Indeed, he was impelled to enter the trade by his conviction that the only solution to the soap maker's difficulties lay in the increase of the world's resources of oil seeds. That conviction was shared by many others in the oils and fats industries—by Crosfield's, the C.W.S., and Jurgens', all of whom were adventuring in one or another part of Africa at this time. Lever's first step was to buy W. B. MacIver & Company Limited, a Liverpool firm trading in Nigeria, mainly in timber. Unlike some of their competitors they were not prosperous, and they lacked capital. The acquisition gave Lever an entry to the Coast trade and above all a man with experience of its ways. This was W. K. Findlay, Chairman of MacIvers, who became responsible for the conduct of Lever Brothers' West African interests. Two more purchases followed in 1912: Peter Ratcliffe & Company, who traded to Sierra Leone, and a more or less bankrupt business called the Cavalla River Company in Liberia. In the years up to the war, Findlay did much to develop the trade in kernels: new areas were opened up, where Peter Ratcliffe & Company bartered textiles for kernels. Throughout Nigeria palm fruit and palm kernels came from the natural palmeries; there was no systematic cultivation. The natural palmeries were farmed out by the chiefs to favoured families. The produce was then sold by the chiefs to the various European companies.

Equipped with plantations and trading companies, Lever passed to the second part of his plan. Not only was the fruit to be gathered in West Africa but processed there too. Two kinds of oil were involved: palm oil from the juicy pericarp of the palm fruit and palm kernel oil from the kernel encased in the hard nut at the centre of the palm fruit. The native method of extracting oil by hand from the pericarp was undoubtedly inefficient. It was not only that the amount of oil extracted could be raised by between fifty per cent and ninety per cent if modern machinery were substituted for the old hand method: the quality could also be improved. As for the palm kernels, local mills—or so Lever argued—would avoid wasting shipping space in carrying nuts to Europe. The oil could be transported in casks. So kernel crushing mills were erected in 1910 at Opobo and Apapa (Lagos) in Nigeria. Later, in 1912, Lever succeeded in getting grudging permission from the Colonial Office to put up a mill at Yonnibannah in Sierra Leone for crushing kernels and for extracting

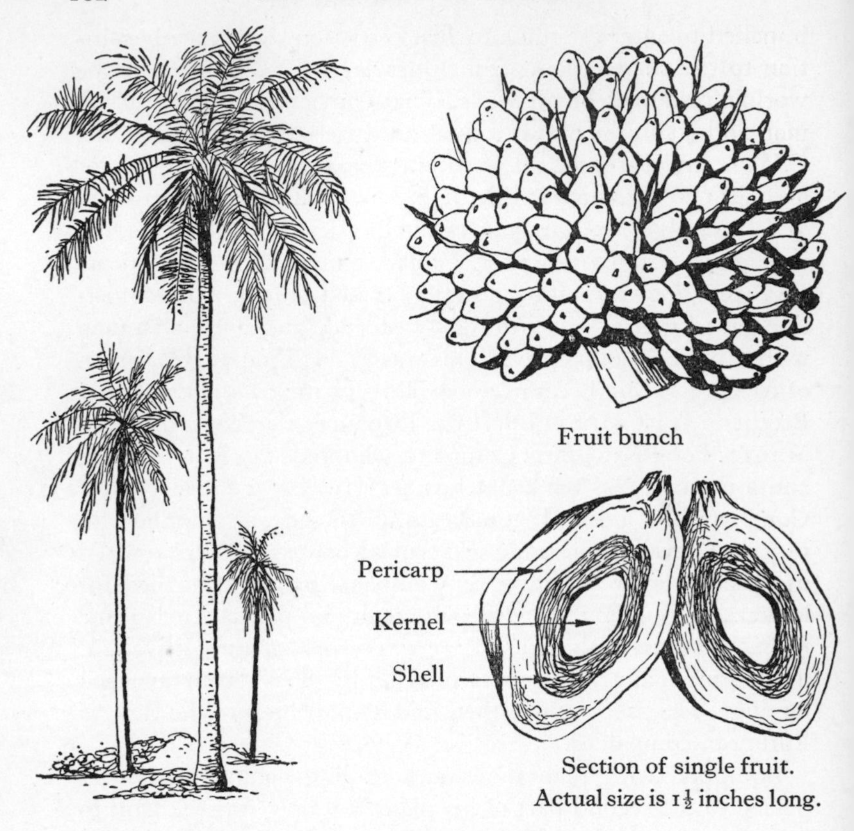

THE NATIVE PALM

oil from the pericarp of the oil nut. (At the same time another mill was set up in the C.P.K.N. territory at Kakamoeka.)

Lever still had many unpalatable truths to learn about the economics of the African trade. The project for oil mills in Africa was his first lesson. Experience showed that the idea simply did not work. The mills—unlike European mills—were wholly dependent on local supplies of nuts. The natives knew when supplies at the mills were running low, held back supplies and put up their prices accordingly. Nothing was saved on freight: shipping in casks proved inordinately expensive so that by 1914 Lever embarked on what must have been the earliest experiment on record in transporting edible oil by tanker. The oil cake could not be sold in Africa. High salaries had to be paid to European staff to manage the mills. Local labour was disastrously incompetent. In the September quarter of 1913 the Nigerian mills lost nearly £13,000. All told, West African Oils Limited, the milling company responsible for these plants, lost over £50,000 in 1913.

Policy and Profits in the Tropics

By 1912, Lever had broadly three types of interest in the tropics. On the plantations of the Solomons, he was himself the producer: in the trading companies of West Africa, he was only a purchaser—a middleman trader: between these stood his Congo business. Its function at this stage was to enable European capital and skill to be applied to the improvement of natural methods of production and processing.[1] The agglomeration of these interests called for new organization, and in that year the control of all Lever's foreign interests (not only of the raw material companies) was removed from Port Sunlight to Liverpool. There, on the fourth floor of the Royal Liver Building, J. L. Tillotson presided over a staff some hundreds strong. The scene which the newly formed administration surveyed by 1914 was not altogether a happy one. About a million and a half pounds had been sunk in the African businesses alone. One of them—the French affair—was a dead loss. The Belgian Congo showed no profit. The oil mills had lost over £50,000. Only MacIver's and, in the Pacific, the Solomons' plantations showed small profits. The Solomons alone were making a net addition to world production of raw materials, and even their contribution was a drop in the ocean.

Lever's motives in entering the raw material business can only be understood if they are placed against the general background of the pre-war decade. These were years when, as a soap maker, he watched anxiously as raw material prices continued to rise. In some years a steep increase was followed by an equally steep decline, but by 1910 prices were well above the 1900 level and it seemed that they were not likely to fall below a figure some thirty per cent to forty per cent higher than that level. A number of factors had contributed to the rise; of these Lever's

[1] The development of cultivated plantations in the Congo was a much later innovation. See Book III, Chapter II.

mind seized firmly on two. He was convinced that the growing demand, especially by the margarine makers, was remorselessly driving up prices and he hoped by increasing world supplies of raw materials to bring them down. He expressed this quite clearly in a letter to Robert Barrie written in 1904. 'For years now this market [nut oils] has been becoming a more and more difficult one. . . . The recent use of copra oil for edible purposes increases our difficulties. There is no corresponding increase in production. We want the market as much overdone on copra as the tea market is overdone on tea. . . . We are the most interested in this question of any firm in the world, and we have got to make some attempt to relieve the position. It is all a question of whether the supply should be ten per cent below the requirements or five per cent above the requirements. If ten per cent below the requirements, prices will rule high. If five per cent above the requirements, prices will rule reasonably and in our favour.' As the decade advanced Lever also became deeply suspicious of the combines and rings among the raw material dealers who, he thought, were conspiring to the disadvantage of the manufacturer. And to this was added the fear that other manufacturers might also take measures to secure their supplies by themselves entering upon raw material producing.

Such were the main motives for attempting to secure his own supplies of raw materials. Behind Lever's plans one may discern an idea of the advantages to the manufacturer of the industrial structure known as the vertical combine. The classical view of these advantages may be stated briefly by saying that through a vertical combine a manufacturer might obtain his raw material supplies at the production stage: he would thereby cut out the middleman's profits. The advantage would be enhanced when the middlemen were combined together to raise prices, for the manufacturer would be independent of the market; to the financial advantage would be added a strategic advantage. In a vertical combine the raw material companies would supply the manufacturing companies directly and at cost price. The manufacturing companies, furnished with cheaper raw materials would then be at a competitive advantage over their rivals: they would be able to decrease their selling price, expand sales and thus increase their profits, or alternatively, they could sell at the same price with a greater profit.

In real life, however, this simple theory of the advantages of the vertical combine broke down on two points—price and quantity. Although Lever extended his raw material schemes from the Solomons to the Belgian Congo and to the acquisition of trading companies in British West Africa, it was clear that he could not get raw materials in sufficiently large quantities from his own companies to supply even a significant proportion of his steadily expanding factories. Indeed, in replying to his Chief's letter quoted above, Barrie had cautioned him against any large-scale development of plantations. 'The difficulty always seems to me to be,' said Barrie, 'that no appreciable quantity of product can be produced by any one concern, and if an appreciable quantity was produced the undertaking with its allied industries would be much greater than the making and disposing of soap from such material.' In spite of this counsel, Lever pressed on with his schemes, encouraged, no doubt, by the enthusiasm of Joseph Meek who, deeming that 'the large soap maker should have behind him a raw material scheme', felt that 'the Solomons were the keystone to the future'.

By the time Lever bought the West African trading companies he must have realized the practical impossibility of producing even that 'five per cent above requirements' which he had hoped would make prices 'rule reasonably and in our favour'. But he may well have hoped that his raw material companies could offer enough competition to keep prices from rising still further and could prevent rival interests from obtaining too great a hold on the market. Strategic rather than financial advantage had become his aim.

Just as the raw material companies could not produce a sufficient quantity of raw materials, so also were they unable to produce materials sufficiently cheaply. The development costs of the plantations were always much higher than at first anticipated. We find Lever complaining at the end of 1916 that '. . . after sinking money in the Solomon Islands for fifteen years we are still unable to make money out of copra'. And when once the plantations were developed it was found that they, like other associated companies, to be run efficiently had to be run as separate and independent enterprises.[1] There could be no efficient management of the plantations unless its products were

[1] See Chapter VII.

sold at a profit. And only by selling the product according to what it would fetch, that is, at market price, could the management be certain that the plantations were a paying proposition, and not subsidized by other members of the group. If this was true of the plantations it was even truer of the trading companies with their dual function of selling merchandise and buying produce.

It was some time before the force of these arguments was appreciated. Thus the general policy up to 1914 seems to have been that the raw material companies should supply the soap factories directly and at cost price. As late as August 1916 we find Lever stating that: 'The basis I prefer for one Associated Company to charge another is, cost price plus a margin for contingencies'. Here we must anticipate by a few years to carry the argument to its conclusion. Under war conditions it was often found that the raw material companies could sell outside the concern at higher prices while the concern companies bought a substitute material at a lower price. By persevering, therefore, in the 'vertical combine' policy Lever would not only have failed to secure any competitive advantage over rival manufacturers but would also have risked depriving his raw material companies of the profits which they would have been able to win by selling their produce on the open market. In 1917 a central buying department for the whole concern was established under Clarence Knowles. It was 'to buy materials for works and oil mills . . . , to sell surplus raw materials . . . , to consult with Findlay and Greenhalgh on markets for West African and Congo produce . . . , and to give close attention to the interchange of oils and fats, as the market values varied'. By 1920, the reversal of policy was complete, for it is clearly laid down in the Policy Council Minutes of November 1920 that: 'The Chairman had decided that if our West African companies had surplus material on offer at prevailing market prices the purchases were [to be] made from them'.

The original theory upon which Lever's raw material enterprises were based had to be modified as his business grew in size and complexity. But, once launched upon the raw material venture, for him there was no going back and indeed Lever was in no way deterred from going forward and extending his activities in the raw material field. For to Lever business was never solely a matter of profit and loss rationally calculated by reference to a balance sheet. His needs as a soap maker had first taken him to the tropics but if his ambitions had been limited by soap the task of empire building would not have detained him long: it never detained Joseph Watson or the Van den Berghs. Lever was held by the sheer fascination of the scene. The great colonial enterprises of the seventeenth and eighteenth centuries had never been 'business' in its narrow sense; they were the work of adventurers as well as of city men. In Lever the two types combined. In him the rationality of the business man was blended with the restless ambitions of the explorer. Expanding business brought not merely bigger profits but more opportunities for adventure. 'My happiness', he said once, 'is my business. I can see finality for myself, an end, an absolute end; but none for my business. There one has room to breathe, to grow, to expand, and the possibilities are boundless. One can go to places like the Congo, and organize, organize, organize, well, very big things indeed. But I don't work at business only for the sake of money. I am not a lover of money as money and never have been. I work at business because business is life. It enables me to do things.' Certainly, among the many things he did, few were to have consequences of greater lasting benefit than his bold venture into the Congo. To the very end, his Congo enterprise was to retain a hold on his energies and affections only equalled by his feeling for his first creation at Port Sunlight.

CHAPTER XII

OVERSEAS FACTORIES

'When we go to a country and put up works there, we cannot immediately get a return on that capital. Trade is small, advertising and other expenses are large and it takes some little time.'

Sir William Lever at the Annual General Meeting of the Shareholders; 5 *March* 1914

POTENTIALLY the most important of the separate Lever businesses already established in continental Europe by 1906, was that at Mannheim. The rapid growth of the German population had always attracted Lever's interest and in 1907 he was still occupied with it. 'The business in Germany', he noted, 'has grown in the last two years at a very great rate and shows signs of continued growth. The population of Germany is 66,000,000, and the population of the United Kingdom is 44,000,000. The soap trade in Germany is in a much more backward condition than the soap trade in England; in fact, there are a very limited number of really up-to-date firms in the laundry soap trade in Germany.' He went on to suggest the issue of another Mk 2,000,000 (£100,000) of capital, which he intended should be held in Germany 'to give us more friendly feeling . . . and a better backing than we should have if the whole of the capital is held in England'. 'The Company', he concluded, 'is thoroughly sound and the trade progressive and, I think, our prospects in Germany as far as the German market is concerned are superior to our prospects in any part of the world, not excepting even the United Kingdom.'

Whatever may have been the condition of the German laundry soap industry, there was no lack of inventive talent in other branches of the trade. In particular the Germans had been active in developing the manufacture and use of soap powders, powders that is in which soap was mixed with crushed or powdered soda and sometimes a bleaching agent. For the manufacturer it had the advantage of being cheaper to make than 'pure' soap; it kept better in the shop; and the housewife was saved the labour of rubbing and scrubbing, for the powder dissolved easily in water and clothes were either soaked or boiled. In 1910 Lever bought a half interest in one of the biggest soap powder businesses in Germany, 'Dr. Thompson's Seifenpulver' which operated at Wittenberg and Düsseldorf. This was the product from which Lever may very well have borrowed the idea for his own Rinso which was launched about the same time in England. 'Seifenpulver' gave Lever a useful weapon for meeting an attack which affected the soap market not only in Germany but in Switzerland and Belgium too, and was to become more important as time went on. This was the competition of Persil, a soap powder with a strong bleaching action, marketed by the German chemical firm of Henkel. Lever explained his strategy as follows: '. . . the best way to meet Persil is by an article of the Rinso type, with Rinso advertisements, viz: "We work while you sleep". It is quite obvious that Persil has captured that section of the public which is prepared to go to greater labour in boiling their clothes. It leaves Dr. Thompson's Seifenpulver out to capture that section of the public which usually soak their clothes overnight and require a soap powder of a very high percentage of fatty acids.' The Seifenpulver business, when Lever's bought it, was doing very well. The terms were based on an average annual profit of Mk 1,500,000 (about £75,000), and for 1910 they reached Mk 1,800,000, 'which', as Lever remarked, 'was most encouraging for the future'. There was, further, the advantage that the manufacture of soap powder depended to a large extent on 'chemicals . . . not liable to market fluctuations'. They could be 'contracted for by the manufacturer years ahead, being natural products of the ground merely influenced by the price of fuel and labour'. This fact, at a time of high oil and fat prices, no doubt helps to account for the remarkable increase in the production of soap powders in other countries besides Germany.

Austria-Hungary held out to Lever temptations almost as great as Germany. Industry was not so highly developed, but the population was large. Unfortunately, in the Georg Schicht concern of Aussig, he had formidable opponents. Their soap business in Austria was older than Lever's in England: they thoroughly understood the complicated marketing conditions of the 'ramshackle Empire', and they were sufficiently up to date both in technique and administration to hold their own against any invader. Nevertheless, in 1908 a Lever company was floated in Austria. Lever's soaps were still imported from England but in order to enjoy the difference in the tariff on soap in bulk and soap in cartons, the Sunlight was brought in in slabs, then cut, stamped and packed in the basement of a private house in Vienna.

In 1912 Lever's carried their attack on Schicht's a stage further by opposition in the English Courts to registration of the word 'Schicht' as a trade mark. Their case was founded on the confusion which might arise with 'Sunlight' by reason of the similarity of the lettering. They won, but it was a doubtful victory, for Schicht's in Austria at once took proceedings against the mark 'Sunlight', basing their contention very largely on the decision of the English judge.

While this legal comedy was in progress, Lever decided that combination might hold out greater hopes of gain than competition. Certainly it could hardly make things worse, for his company was losing between £7,000 and £9,000 a year in Austria. Accordingly, in 1913 Lever met the brothers Heinrich and Georg Schicht in Vienna with an offer to buy half the capital of their company (30,000,000 Austrian Crowns). Strongly placed as they were, the Schichts saw no reason to part with more than a third 'without experience of the advantage from a community of interests'. The negotiations broke down, and when war began Lever's in Austria were left with an unprofitable business on their hands and a lawsuit which they lost on appeal in 1915.[1]

The only remaining large European country where Lever's had trade sufficient to warrant the construction of a factory was France. A company was formed at Lille in 1905 but, probably as a result of the financial weakness following the *Daily Mail* attack, no move was made towards building works until 1910. In that year, S.A. Savonneries Lever was incorporated, with a capital of eight million francs, to replace the earlier foundation, and building began in October. 'Our trade [in France]', Lever had written earlier in the year, 'is going ahead at such a great rate.'

Lille was in an industrial area where there was greater hope than elsewhere in France of finding the kind of working-class customer who had formed the market for Sunlight in so many

[1] For the history of the Schichts see Book II, Chapter XIV.

other countries. It had one disadvantage; it was not well placed for supplying the rest of France. There he was up against the competition of the Marseilles makers. The Marseilles industry, a by-product of the great crushing mills of Marseilles, made a cheap soap with which it was difficult to compete. To deal with it Lever decided to buy his way into the trade. In 1913 he started to negotiate with two small Marseilles firms. They passed into Lever's control in 1914, and by the outbreak of war Lever Brothers found themselves with three French factories, each controlled by a separate company. Geographically, and in form, it was a pattern less tidy than that of, say, Belgium or Holland. Owing to the peculiarities of French law, and perhaps of French temperament too, it was to grow untidier still as time went by, and it presented difficult problems of control.

Of the older Lever foundations—Belgium, the Netherlands and Switzerland—the Belgian business, by 1906, had emerged from its early vicissitudes, and was settled on a course of increasing prosperity which was not interrupted until 1914: the 1913 figures showed Belgium as far and away the most profitable of the continental markets. In the Netherlands, by 1912, Lever considered that 'we had the hard soap trade', and van Geelkerken remarked at the same time that Van den Bergh's 'had for years desired to amalgamate with us', so it would seem that the situation was fairly well in hand. It had so far been unnecessary to put up a factory, although the requisite land had been bought at the turn of the century, but Van den Bergh's decision in 1912 to build a factory themselves caused Lever to say that 'we should have to consider the whole matter', and the Vlaardingen factory was opened in 1915. To these older foundations were added new ones. Norwegian and Swedish companies were formed in 1910. By 1913 Norway had made some progress, but Sweden still showed a loss.

Together with the European countries it will be convenient to consider the Japanese venture of 1910. Alone in Asia, Japan was a developing industrial power, with all that that implied in the conditions of life of her increasing population. 'There is no doubt', wrote Lever in 1909, 'that whoever enters into Japan in its development state will greatly benefit by having a secure foothold in the early days.' He went on, 'The volume of our trade in Japan at present does not justify soap works there', but nevertheless in the following year he took the preliminary step of founding a separate company, and in September the building of a factory at Tori-Shindon near Kobe commenced: it was opened by the Provincial Governor early in 1913.

The importance of Japan was not confined to the manufacture of soap. It would also make a very convenient centre for fat hardening, and for the supply of hardened fat to the works which it was proposed to erect, jointly with Brunner Mond's, in China. It seems, in fact, that in 1914 Lever's looked upon Japan as their future Far Eastern base. Because of Gossage's hold on the Chinese import trade it was not convenient for Lever's to erect works independently in China, but in Japan the situation was very different. The total British imports of soap were no more than 374 tons in 1908, falling to 54 in 1913 (no doubt because Lever's factory was by then in production), and of these small figures Gossage's share varied between 4 and 16 tons. It seems reasonable to suppose that the Tori-Shindon works were built at least as much to supply China as Japan, and Lever's were anxious to secure the largest possible share of the China trade. But this was another long-term project, and the last accounts published before the War showed heavy losses in Japan and a small loss in China.

The story of Lever's European development is largely concerned with attempts to defeat the tariff legislator. In these early stages a single factory was usually sufficient to handle the volume of business which Lever felt he could achieve. By comparison with his turnover in the United Kingdom the average turnover in the Continental markets was still relatively small. Therefore, France excepted, the Lever organization within each country remained fairly simple. In the great expanses of North America, South Africa, and Australia, the problem was different. It was not sufficient to build one factory; if business were to develop on the scale of Lever's ambition, other factories must be built or bought so that the whole of the area could be adequately covered. The result was that in the Dominions there developed, and in the United States but for special limiting circumstances there almost certainly would have developed, complex organizations which resembled far more closely the concern in the United Kingdom than the simple one-country-one-company pattern of Europe and Japan.

During the first ten years of the twentieth century the tide of immigration flowed strongly into Canada and towards the Western prairies. The Canadian Pacific Railway and the other trans-continental lines which followed it transformed a nomadically peopled wilderness between the settled East and the Pacific Coast into an inhabited region which provided the necessary basis for the growth of national instead of provincial industry. The more enterprising Canadian soap manufacturers saw the possibilities of the situation. Private firms were turned into limited companies, and by the familiar process of competition and combination, concerns were built up which dominated far larger areas than the immediate vicinities of their original works.

Lever saw the opportunities and understood the methods as clearly as any of his competitors: with a prosperous population, and a market in the Middle West open to all comers the prospect was inviting. Nor were raw materials lacking: there was tallow in plenty at Toronto, Calgary, and Winnipeg. He began operations near his base, with the purchase in 1906 of Pugsley, Dingman & Company of Toronto, which Lever described as having been 'one of our most serious competitors'. The Company's main product was 'Comfort', a soap which seriously menaced the progress of Sunlight, no doubt because the Canadian housewives followed the American example and preferred a large tablet of filled soap rather than a small tablet of pure soap. Pugsley, Dingman's method of competition, as described by John Pugsley himself, was to lower prices rather than raise them in times of difficulty, with the idea that trade thus gained from less courageous competitors would be retained when conditions were easier again. There is strong reason to suspect that by 1906 this policy, after some years of success, had finally brought him very near to disaster, probably because the rise in raw material prices of that year was sharper and more prolonged than he had anticipated. However that may be, the share control of the company when Lever bought it was vested in the National Trust Company of Toronto, which almost certainly means that it was having difficulty in meeting its liabilities. It seems, however, that Lever's faith in Pugsley's ability was not thereby shaken, for he joined the Board of Lever Brothers (Canada) in 1907.

Lever's intention for his Canadian associated companies was camouflaged concentration of effort: he explained the principle to A. C. Knight who had gone from Port Sunlight to take charge of the Canadian business: '. . . the policy, it seems to me, we ought to follow is that whilst keeping each business clear, separate and distinct in the eyes of the public and consumers of soap, that we concentrate as much as we can the manufacture and other arrangements'. Factories acquired were to be kept going, but all expansion was to be concentrated on Lever's own works. This was the policy followed when the death of William Strachan, a soap manufacturer of Montreal, gave Lever's the chance of buying his business from his executors. A. C. Knight and two other Lever men became officials of the company, the head office was transferred to Toronto, and the Montreal premises were sold to the Canadian Pacific Railway. Lever was extremely pleased with the transaction: '. . . another strong competitor in Montreal', he wrote later, 'died and we bought that business on extremely favourable terms, almost ludicrous terms. We paid $100,000 for the business, and sold to the Railway Company the premises which we did not require for $75,000 leaving us only $25,000 to pay for the business, exclusive of stock and book debts which the Executors realized themselves. It has proved a very good little business to us, as the trade has already doubled since we took it over and promises to be an extremely profitable purchase.'

The Toronto and Montreal purchases gave Lever's a secure base in Eastern Canada from which they could advance westwards. Here they had to face Manlius Bull, who had ideas of his own on the foundation of a national Canadian soap business. Bull's business was at Winnipeg, where he incorporated Royal Crown Soaps Limited in 1902. In 1906, Knight approached him with proposals for purchase, but Bull had a shrewd (Lever called it 'exaggerated') idea of the value of his business, and the negotiations fell through. Bull went on to buy in 1908 a company in Vancouver and another in Calgary which gave him a commanding position in the prairie provinces and British Columbia.

A foothold in the West was essential if any Dominion-wide business were to be established; but Bull knew his strength: he did not finally come to terms until 1911, some five years after he had first been approached, and there is nothing to suggest that

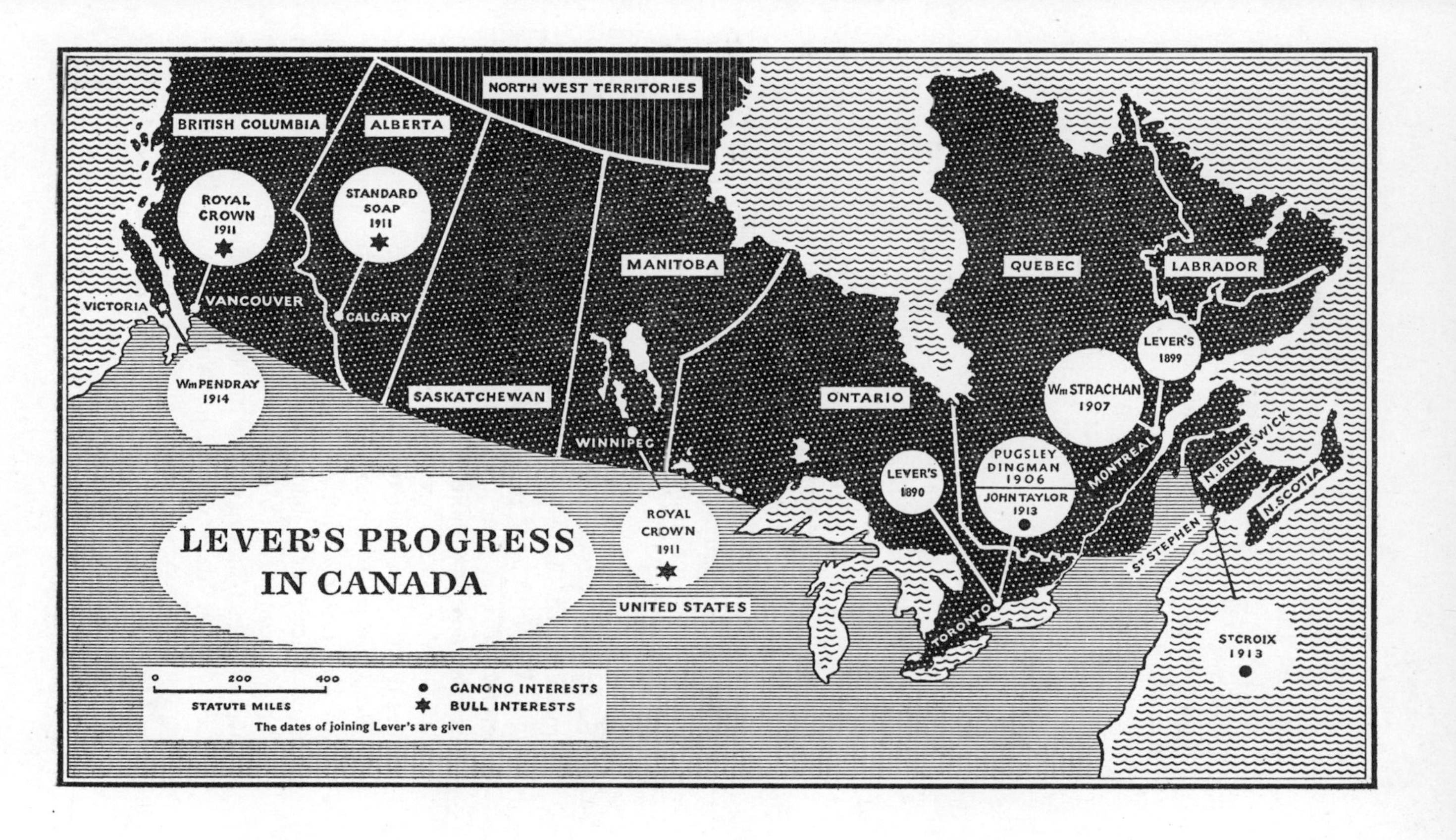
LEVER'S PROGRESS IN CANADA
NORTH WEST TERRITORIES
BRITISH COLUMBIA
ALBERTA
SASKATCHEWAN
MANITOBA
ONTARIO
QUEBEC
LABRADOR
N. BRUNSWICK
N. SCOTIA
UNITED STATES
VICTORIA
VANCOUVER
CALGARY
WINNIPEG
TORONTO
MONTREAL
ST STEPHEN
ROYAL CROWN 1911
STANDARD SOAP 1911
Wm PENDRAY 1914
ROYAL CROWN 1911
LEVER'S 1890
PUGSLEY DINGMAN 1906
JOHN TAYLOR 1913
Wm STRACHAN 1907
LEVER'S 1899
ST CROIX 1913
0 200 400
STATUTE MILES
GANONG INTERESTS
BULL INTERESTS
The dates of joining Lever's are given

he did so then because his position had seriously deteriorated. Times for the soap maker no doubt were hard—a Canadian Soap Makers' Association had been formed in 1910, and association is nearly always a sign of tribulation—but there is no reason to suppose that Bull negotiated with Lever's otherwise than as an equal. Immediately after the purchase he became a managing director of the Lever company. He had charge of Western operations until he retired in 1925. After the Bull purchase the Lever network stretched right across Canada and by means of local manufacture they could meet competitors on their own ground unhampered by transport costs. In the remaining years before the war they buttressed themselves still more strongly by the acquisition of the Ganong and Pendray interests in the East and West respectively. J. E. Ganong was the head of an old loyalist family which owned the St. Croix Company in St. Stephen, New Brunswick. The St. Croix Company was amalgamated in 1912 with another family firm, John Taylor & Company of Toronto. The businesses were combined under a holding company, Canadian Soaps Ltd., which Lever acquired in 1913 during his transatlantic tour of that year. Ganong himself succeeded A. C. Knight in the presidency of Lever Brothers Limited of Canada in 1914. In 1914, the Pendray business at Victoria, British Columbia, was also acquired.

So by 1913 Lever had built up a chain of works stretching across Canada. There was one in St. Stephen, three in Toronto, one in Winnipeg, one in Calgary, one in Vancouver and one in Victoria. In that year the Canadian businesses were far and away the most profitable of Lever's overseas enterprises. Sales, at nearly 26,000 tons, were twice those in South Africa and six times those in the United States or Australia.

Despite early prospects, the history of the Australian company was far from happy, and in 1906 only two years had passed since Lever had completed a drastic reorganization which he considered necessary for the future success of the business. The Chairman, who had been in office since 1902, was Joseph Meek. Meek was an ex-printer, a man of retiring disposition but strong character, who actively resented interference from Port Sunlight and had no hesitation at all about telling Lever his exact thoughts on any problem that might arise. In October 1906, Lever was complaining of 'continual criticism and wranglings' with Meek. The immediate cause was Meek's operations as a buyer of raw material, but the real trouble lay deeper—in the failure of the Sydney business to expand as Lever thought it should.

Lever pointed the road which the Australian company must follow if that expansion were to be achieved: it must cease to be 'an entirely isolated concern'. Head and shoulders above its competitors stood the powerful Kitchen group which, employing the varied talents of a numerous and able family, had built up formidable strength both geographically and economically; towards this concern schemes of union or conflict must inevitably tend. The centre of Kitchen's trade was in Victoria, where since 1856 the family had been established at Melbourne, first as candle makers and then as soap makers also. They had amalgamated with their principal Melbourne competitors in 1885 to form J. Kitchen & Sons & Apollo Company Limited, and in the same year had formed a similar composite concern, the Sydney Soap and Candle Company Limited, to exploit the markets of New South Wales.

Melbourne-Sydney was reinforced by the steady absorption of competing companies, a process which, beginning in Victoria in the seventies, gave the concern by the early nineteen hundreds wide interests throughout the Commonwealth. From 1894 onwards they had also an extremely valuable link with London, where John Hambledon Kitchen had an agency business, which kept them in touch both with the London money market and with technical progress in Europe and America. They did not overlook the ancillaries of a soap maker's business: in 1902 a plant was erected by the Melbourne Company for the extraction of coconut oil, which made it unnecessary for them any longer to buy the material from Lever Brothers at Sydney. From oil extraction they proceeded along the same road as Lever's towards production of oil seeds: about 1903 they started a scheme for the growing of cotton seed in Queensland, and four years later launched into coconut planting in Papua. What Lever's, Crosfield's, and the C.W.S. of England could afford was by no means beyond the scope of Kitchen's of Australia. They gave further proof of versatility by successful extensions during the late nineties into the sale of kerosene, in 1910 into fertilizers, and in 1913, the last year of independence, into margarine.

Beside this large and growing business, Lever's in Australia were for years relatively small and static. Production in 1913 was actually less than the planned output for 1900, just over 4,000 tons a year. Lever wrote in 1912: 'I am rather concerned about the position in Australia. We do not seem to grow there as I should like. We do not seem to make good our position in either South Australia or Victoria. I am rather inclined to think that in these countries like Australia, with long distances . . . separate centres of soap manufacturing is the soundest policy.' Soon afterwards the opportunity for which he was waiting presented itself. 1913 was a bad year for Kitchen's, and 'my idea', he wrote, 'would be to come to some working arrangement on some basis or other with all the principal soap makers in Australia and New Zealand'. Early in 1914, Lever went out to Australia and in March of that year amalgamation with the Kitchen interests was arranged: at about the same time Burford's were absorbed; they had been troublesome competitors in South Australia both to Lever's and Kitchen's for many years.

The Kitchen family, except for two members, were at first hostile to an amalgamation with Lever's, but eventually all but one came round to the view of the two members who wished to sell. The terms of the agreement left Kitchen's with substantial independence in the running of their own companies. A Central Management Board was set up, on which were represented Lever Brothers of Balmain, the Kitchen interests and Lever's Pacific Plantations, but the idea, Lever explained, was 'to keep the distinct individuality clear, or partially clear. The Imperial Tobacco Company, Messrs. Coats' Thread, and many other instances I could give, have been conducted on these lines. It is much more certain, safe and sure, and enables competition from outsiders to be met more effectively. Therefore, there is no intention on the part of Lever Brothers to merge Lever Brothers or Messrs. Kitchen or Messrs. Burford together.'

Lever's had been exporting to South Africa since 1890 but it was not until 1910 that they decided to build a factory. No doubt political instability in South Africa accounted to some extent for their hesitation, but the economic situation was also less promising than in the other Dominions. Although the growing industrialism in the mining areas seemed to offer reasonable

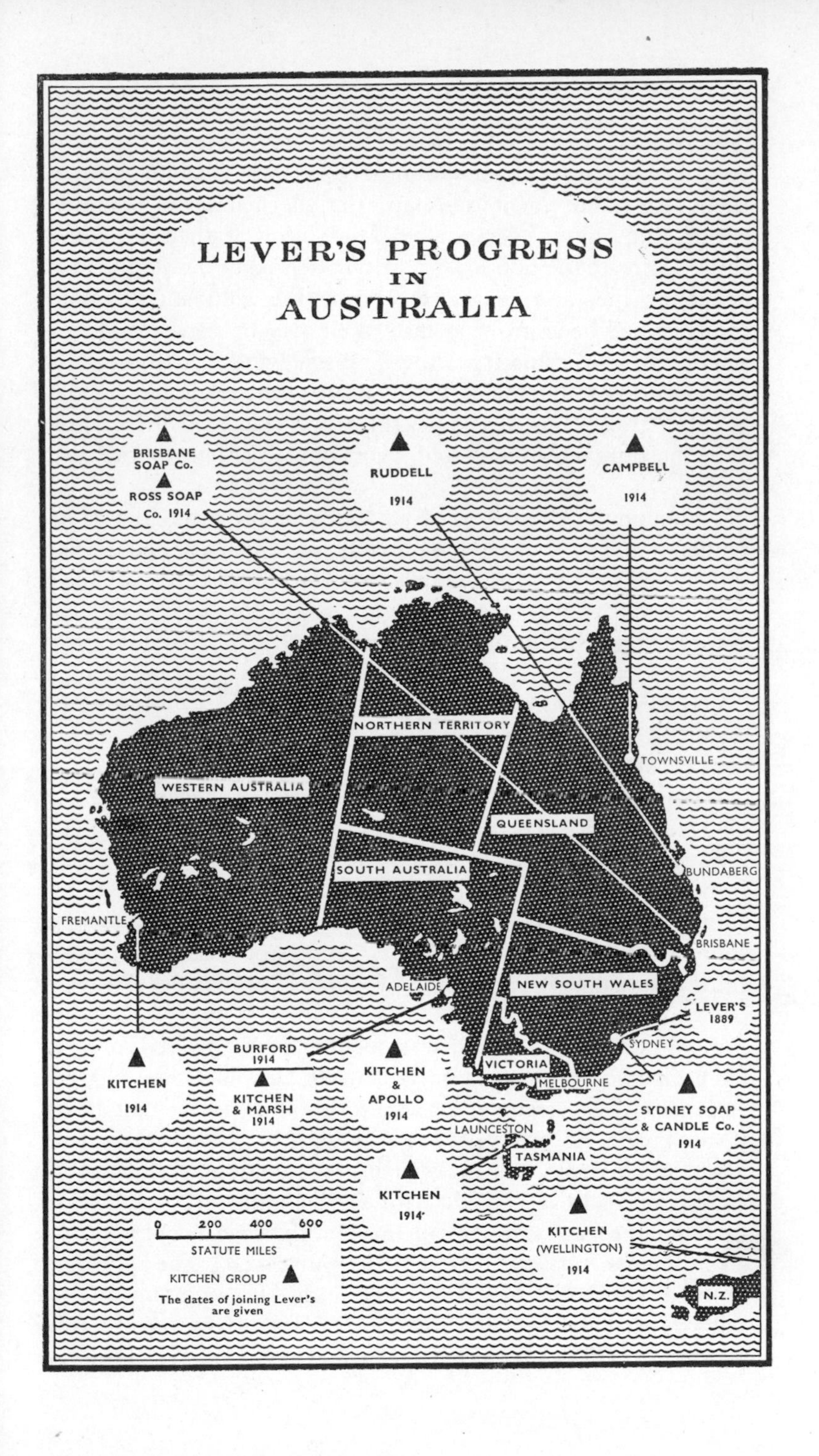
LEVER'S PROGRESS IN AUSTRALIA
BRISBANE SOAP Co.
ROSS SOAP Co. 1914
RUDDELL 1914
CAMPBELL 1914
NORTHERN TERRITORY
WESTERN AUSTRALIA
QUEENSLAND
SOUTH AUSTRALIA
NEW SOUTH WALES
VICTORIA
TASMANIA
TOWNSVILLE
BUNDABERG
BRISBANE
FREMANTLE
ADELAIDE
SYDNEY
MELBOURNE
LAUNCESTON
LEVER'S 1889
KITCHEN 1914
BURFORD 1914
KITCHEN & MARSH 1914
KITCHEN & APOLLO 1914
SYDNEY SOAP & CANDLE Co. 1914
KITCHEN 1914
KITCHEN (WELLINGTON) 1914
N.Z.
0 200 400 600
STATUTE MILES
KITCHEN GROUP
The dates of joining Lever's are given

opportunities to the soap maker, yet there were vast areas of veldt where a scanty population of conservative habits provided their own requirements of soap after the manner of primitive rural communities everywhere. The Union of 1910 did something to create the political security essential to development of economic life, and in the meantime the gold and diamond industry had been growing fast. Well over half the world production of gold came from the Transvaal and over three-fifths of the world production of diamonds was centred in the Union of South Africa. The big cities of Cape Town, Durban, and Johannesburg clearly offered promising markets to the soap maker.

Although the Union brought stability, it also brought a strong tendency towards economic separatism which created serious difficulties for the British soap exporter. As Lever explained: '. . . local soap works are springing up there at a great rate and competition is becoming very keen. South African colonists are at present mad upon local industries and are not only giving protection by duties but they are giving advantages in railway rates and very serious advantages, viz., in many cases fifty per cent rebate on goods manufactured in South Africa.'

After widespread reconnaissance, a site was chosen in 1910 at Congella outside Durban and the factory was opened in the following year. Congella had many advantages—a deep water frontage, good roads, railway transport, and cheap coal, but the country was too large to be served adequately from one factory, so in the same year Lever obtained control of a soap company in the Transvaal which gave him a Johannesburg factory 'in a very good location'. Still he felt the need for a factory to serve the Cape Town market which was separated by hundreds of miles from his two existing plants, and when he was in South Africa early in 1912 he arranged for a factory to be built at Salt River, Cape Town. He was very pleased with his choice. Salt River was 'right in the middle of the artisan population' while a railway siding 'offered every facility for the manufacturer'. Evidently he felt it necessary to explain his South African policy to the shareholders. 'It may look a little unnecessary', he told them in 1912, 'to have three works in South Africa . . . but when I tell you that it takes the management four days to come from Durban to Cape Town and a day and night in the train from

Johannesburg to Durban, and when you consider that local management is generally required to be right on the spot, it is the only way really in which you can conduct the business.'

Nevertheless, all was not well. The high hopes which Lever entertained early in 1912 were dashed by the discovery in June that the business was showing a heavy loss. The new works were running far from smoothly, and competition was troublesome. To some extent the arrangements made with Crosfield's and Gossage's over the export trade[1] alleviated outside competition and the figures of soap imported into South Africa fell away sharply. Internal competition on the other hand remained serious and up to 1914 the few small purchases made had done little to mitigate it. The principal competitor was the New Transvaal Chemical Company of Johannesburg which, as Lever said, 'stood at the gate of South Africa and was keeping our profits down'. The company was formed by Dr. Schlesinger and his brother, Caesar. Dr. Schlesinger was a formidable opponent; he had been chief metallurgist to the Transvaal Republic and his connection with the Rand and 'influence in Government quarters' had encouraged him to set up a business which did a large trade contracting for candles for use in the mines. From candles, the Schlesingers had branched off not only into soap but into many other things—into the manufacture of manure, into whaling, fat hardening, and chemicals. It was their prosperity in the various chemical branches of their business which made them such dangerous rivals as soap makers, for in the soap trade they were prepared to undercut and go on undercutting.

Even in 1911 Lever had bought a considerable block of shares in the Schlesinger company in the hope of reaching 'a working arrangement' but the Schlesingers were still too prosperous to be interested in selling their business outright. After 1912, however, they had heavy losses in their whaling and fat-hardening ventures and gossip had it that adversity put relations between members of the management under some strain. Lever, therefore, greeted the arrival of the Schlesingers in England in 1913 with some interest, especially when the rumour was conveyed to him that 'they were in deep water and Dr. Schlesinger is here either to sell to you or to raise more capital'. He was to find that they were not in such extremities that they were prepared to

[1] See Chapter IX.

accept the first offer, and when agreement was finally reached late in 1914 the price he had to pay was heavy. 'We are certainly', said Lever, 'paying more for this business than we did for any other business in view of the importance of the business to round off our interests in South Africa.' Moreover the difficulties of management which would arise from the complexity and strangeness of the New Transvaal Chemical Company's various activities gave the Lever directors pause before they came to their final decision. They were eventually persuaded by contemplating the extraordinary strength which the acquisition of the New Transvaal Chemical Company would give them in South Africa.

That some 'rounding off' of Lever's interests was necessary was certainly indicated by the state of the finances of the South African Companies in 1913. In spite of sales three times as large as in Australia—some 13,000 tons as against 4,000 tons—profits were small—less than £5,000 as against more than £31,000 in Australia. No doubt Lever had these facts clearly in mind when purchasing the New Transvaal Chemical Company.

The United States presented, as Lever realized from the outset of his soap-making career, the conditions which he sought for the establishment of a successful and expanding business. It had a large and growing population with a high standard of life, to which his goods could be introduced over a well-developed system of communication. Once inside its tariff fence, the manufacturer could contemplate a vast area without any further obstacle to free trade. In all these respects it resembled and excelled the British Dominions: one might expect, therefore, that the development of the Lever business would follow a similar course, and that a network of associated companies and factories would grow in the States as it did in Canada, Australia, and South Africa. Yet in the years of expansion with which we are concerned nothing of the kind occurred. Lever Brothers remained a single company with a single factory, at Cambridge near Boston in Massachusetts.

The answer probably lay in the strength of American competition. In soap making alone there were the great companies of Procter & Gamble, Colgate's, and Fel's, to name only three of the largest, but they were perhaps not Lever's most serious opponents. There were also the meat packing concerns, which

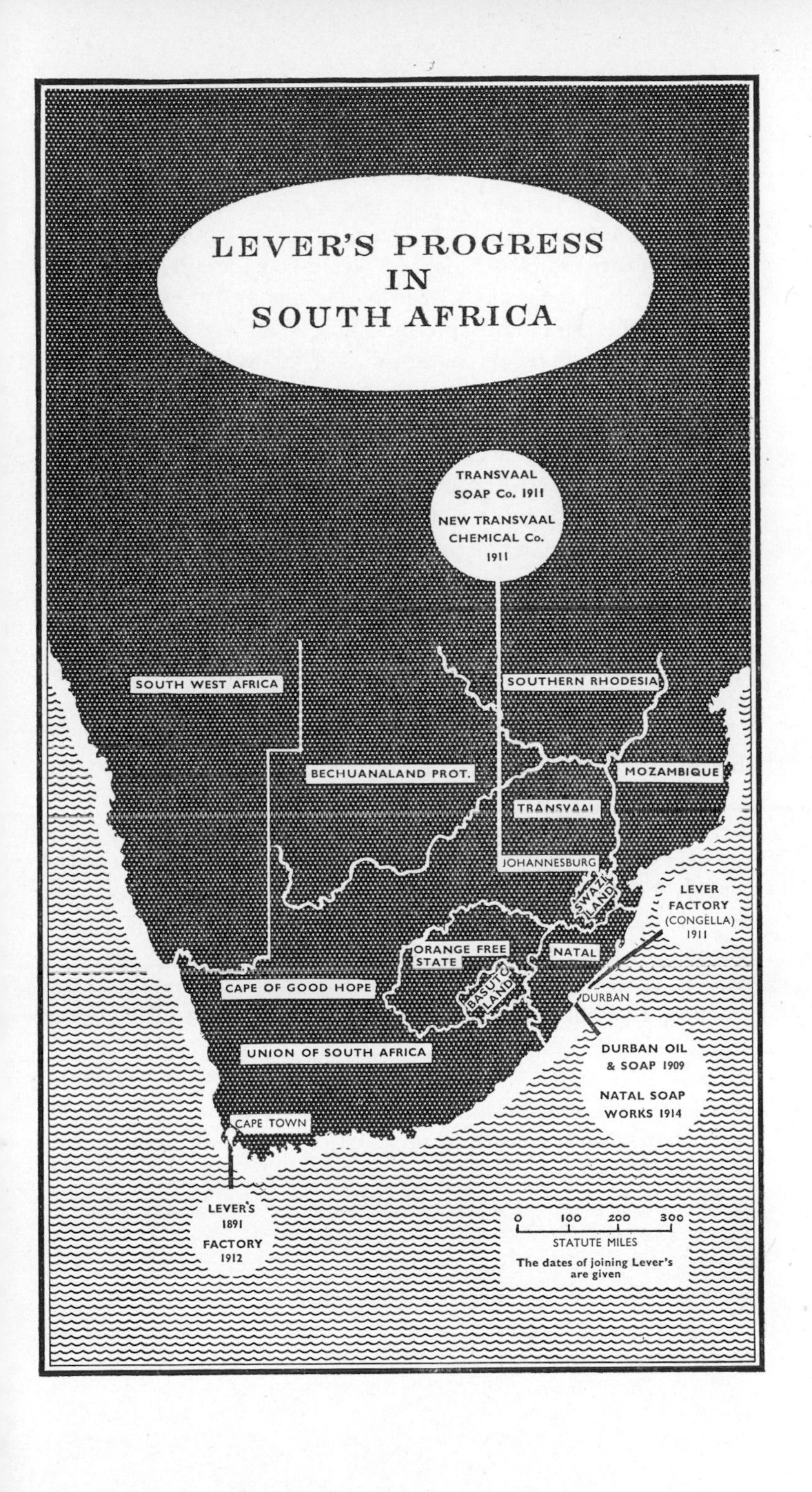
LEVER'S PROGRESS IN SOUTH AFRICA
TRANSVAAL SOAP Co. 1911
NEW TRANSVAAL CHEMICAL Co. 1911
SOUTH WEST AFRICA
SOUTHERN RHODESIA
BECHUANALAND PROT.
MOZAMBIQUE
TRANSVAAL
JOHANNESBURG
SWAZILAND
LEVER FACTORY (CONGELLA) 1911
ORANGE FREE STATE
NATAL
BASUTOLAND
CAPE OF GOOD HOPE
DURBAN
UNION OF SOUTH AFRICA
DURBAN OIL & SOAP 1909
NATAL SOAP WORKS 1914
CAPE TOWN
LEVER'S 1891
FACTORY 1912
0 100 200 300
STATUTE MILES
The dates of joining Lever's are given

made soap as a sideline, and the effect of competition from a rival whose principal business was elsewhere than in the soap trade has been shown in considering the New Transvaal Chemical Company of South Africa. The great meat packers—Armour's, Swift's, and Cudahy's—were considerably more formidable than the South African Company, and they possessed apart from their size another redoubtable advantage: they handled one of the world's principal supplies of tallow. Moreover when hydrogenation threatened to depreciate the importance of tallow, they were quick to see the possibilities of the new process, and, try as he might, Lever was never able before 1914 to come to any arrangement with them for the pooling of patents. Nor could he come to terms with the large milling interests, such as the American Linseed Oil Company, the American Cotton Oil Company, and the Southern Cotton Oil Company, which again were uncomfortably strong: the American Linseed Oil Company, for instance, had the backing of John D. Rockefeller.

Unless the Lever Company could find some means of extending its operations beyond the range of its factory at Cambridge, it must remain virtually a prisoner in New England; the size of the country made it very difficult to exploit the national market from that one centre alone. There are indications that quite early in his career as an American manufacturer Lever realized the necessity of dispersing his operations; about the turn of the century he had plans for a factory in California, but they came to nothing. Things were not made easier by the obstinate refusal of the American housewife to appreciate Sunlight Soap. The truth was that Americans preferred quantity to quality. They could buy satisfyingly large bars of filled soap and they were not going to be persuaded that they got better value for money in the relatively niggardly tablets of 'pure' Sunlight. In spite of all the wiles of the advertiser 'by 1912, the sales of Sunlight had receded to about one-third of their peak volume which was reached in 1901'.

Lever's had an answer in 'Welcome', the original Curtis Davis soap which was sold in bars large enough to please the American taste for size. 'Welcome Soap', Lever told Gross in 1907, '... has not had anything like the advertising that Sunlight has had, yet we have sold more Welcome soap in the last twelve months than ever in the history of Welcome either in our own hands or the hands of our predecessors.' They had also Lifebuoy which, from 1902, steadily increased its sales so that in 1912 its volume was more than three times that of 1902 with most of its business coming from certain sections of the so-called 'General Territory' (outside New England) where it was in good demand among factory, mill, and mine workers, as well as among the general public. In their other products, Lever's sales in 1912 were proportionately about level with those of Sunlight: Brooke's Crystal and Monkey Brand had both fallen away by about two-thirds from their peak of 1900. The total of all sales was less than 200,000 cases, which compared miserably with the 48,000 cases of Sunlight sold on its first introduction into the country seventeen years before.

To the rescue came Francis A. Countway. He seems to have been the first among Lever's managers in the States who realized that if the Company were to make headway two things would have to be done: the markets outside New England would have to be more effectively exploited, and the range of products would have to be drastically overhauled. Before 1909, marketing in the States was based on a division of the country into New England and the rest, or as it was known in the trade the 'General Territory'. In New England, ten to a dozen Lever salesmen were regularly employed: in the 'General Territory' only enough men were maintained to cover the jobbing trade periodically. It was, in fact, an organization strongly reminiscent of the early days in Australia—and most of the business came from jobbers and direct-buying retailers, besides a few selling agents maintained by the company. Countway realized the system's weaknesses with peculiar clarity, and in 1909 he altered the whole organization outside New England by having Lamont, Corliss and Company of New York appointed sole selling agents in the General Territory. They had branches at Philadelphia, Buffalo, Chicago, and other key cities and were equipped to furnish better services for jobbers and retailers. Countway also was satisfied to join fortunes with the jobber in the marketing of Lever goods, and set out to repair the damage done by Lever's initial mistake of deliberately attempting to play down the jobber's importance; his policy paid. New England he regarded partly as the advertiser's laboratory. When publicity devices had been tried out there, under the close supervision of the Cambridge office, they were passed on, if successful, to Lamont, Corliss for exploitation in wider fields.

When he became General Manager in 1912, Countway at once decided that, so far as the United States were concerned, Sunlight was best left to die peacefully. He put his main effort behind three brands: Welcome, Lifebuoy, and Lux, of which the last two were considerably the most important.

The beginning of Countway's management coincided more or less with the crisis of the hydrogenation struggle.[1] In America a satisfactory settlement was hardly less vital to Lever's than in Europe for it was the only other continent where the process was likely to be immediately exploited on a large scale, and unless some treaty could be made there might be endless complications in America itself and in the export markets of the world. Procter & Gamble had had a licence from Crosfield's for the employment of the Normann process for some years, and they were in 1912 preparing to defend their rights against all comers, who included, besides Lever's, the great packing concerns and the milling companies. As soon as Lever's base in Europe was secure, he hastened to America, where he was in the autumn of 1913 while the discussion of Hydrogenators Limited was going on in England. Reconciliation of the jarring American interests was difficult, but there emerged on 5th May 1914 an agreement between Lever's and Procter & Gamble under which 'The Hydrogenation Company' was to be established to hold hydrogenation patents belonging to both parties. On Lever's side, the arrangement helped to secure the position of their own hydrogenation patents and protected them from attack by a powerful soap-making rival.

By 1914, it would seem that Lever's in America had concluded that the volume of trade to be had did not yet warrant a chain of factories such as they had built up in other large countries. Boston could supply the manufacturing capacity required while outside New England sales could be most economically handled through the Lamont, Corliss Agency. But at the head of the business there now stood an American executive who understood more thoroughly than his predecessors the psychology of the American consumer. That there was great business to be done in America could not be doubted, but in 1914 America was still the land of promise rather than the land of achievement.

[1] See Chapter IX.

CHAPTER XIII

PROMISE AND PERFORMANCE IN 1914

FAR from improving after 1910, as Lever had hoped they might, conditions in the soap trade continued to grow progressively more difficult. At the root of the trouble lay the old difficulties—high priced materials and too much competition. The only method of dealing with the former was by opening up new supplies of fats and oils and this Lever was doing in the Solomons, in the Belgian Congo, and by purchasing various businesses trading to Africa. Competition was being reduced by the purchase and absorption of competing firms in the home market and by the development of the export trade, by the establishment of factories in foreign countries and the Empire, and by the purchase of competing manufacturers overseas. All this would bear fruit in time but the harvest was slow to ripen. The demand was for capital and ever more capital. Without capital, businesses could not be bought, plantations could not be established, the bills for stocks and machinery could not be met.

When, therefore, the directors met in June 1912 to estimate the prospects for the year they found the outlook not altogether encouraging. The home trade was difficult though roughly up to expectations, but overseas there were some black spots. The Mannheim Company, the biggest potential source of profit in Europe, had fallen below its estimates and in South Africa the new Company showed a loss. The Chairman therefore set about examining various economies. Advertising was to be cut down, selling staffs reduced, hardened fat production increased and so on.

The difficulties were tided over but still the following year brought no improvement. It brought instead fresh demands for capital, and Lever's decision to issue fresh capital early in 1914 brought him into head-on collision with J. K. Greenhalgh, his Finance Director. In appealing to the public, Lever argued from past profits, neglecting to bring to their notice what Greenhalgh considered to be the full facts of the current situation. In particular Greenhalgh thought that the Chairman should have made public the fact that in 1911 the Company had only been able to maintain advertising at its usual level by realizing assets in the shape of Pacific Phosphate shares. Sir William declined to agree. 'The worst that could be said was that in 1911 we spent more on advertising than we were justified in doing, but our Auditors and others had been consulted and we were told that we could spend it.' But Greenhalgh's conscience continued to trouble him and before long he tendered his resignation from the Board asserting bluntly, 'that as Financial Director he considered that the Company were asking for further capital before the profits justified it'.

Sir William responded warmly to the challenge; he said, very emphatically, 'that he would never have gone to the Public even for the present £500,000 if he did not consider that the Company were in a sound position. In fact he thought that they were stronger today than they had ever been.' In support he produced evidence—the observations of competitors who confessed that they were unable to shift the Lever products from their popular pedestal; the evidence of history—briefly, that he had never let the investors down in the past and was not going to now. 'He did not care for fifty Auditors' certificates—they would never make Dividends. It was after all a question of ethics and not certificates, and if the Company could get a million pounds next January he had no hesitation that it would be safe with the resources of forty Associated Companies and the development work which was in hand.' Unconvinced even by a novel theory of Cabinet Government advanced by the chairman ('John Bright had gone out of the Cabinet because war was declared[1] but Sir William did not think there was any reason for him to do so'), Greenhalgh stuck to his decision to resign though he later accepted nomination as Lever's personal Deputy Director, a position which relieved him of any responsibility for policy decisions. The difference of opinion between Greenhalgh and Lever was vital at this stage of the development of the business. Greenhalgh was a man of the highest integrity. The issue to his accountant's eye was clear. Performance, not promise, was the only justification for borrowing money from

[1] The reference was presumably to Bright's resignation in 1882 on account of the British naval bombardment of Alexandria.

the public. To Lever, on the other hand, the question was one of well-grounded faith. Without Greenhalgh, the Company might have been less stable than it was; but without Lever there could have been no progress.

In the last quarter of 1913, it began to look as if Greenhalgh had been right. The cost of raw materials had risen in this single quarter by an amount which represented some £3 per ton of soap. Profits from by-products such as glycerine had fallen with a decreasing soap output, and there was a proportionate rise in the weight of overhead charges. Administrative expenses had almost doubled since 1910 and fuel costs were increasing alarmingly. The home market was becoming saturated; Lever himself had put his finger on one of the chief causes when he referred in a letter to the *Financial Times* to the higher cost of living amongst the working classes. To add to Lever's worries the Export Department only made about half the profit that it had shown in the corresponding quarter of 1912. In the Export Trade and Overseas there were 'exceptional losses' in Japan and in West Africa. The hard truth was that in 1913 'the trading profits were not sufficient to pay the dividends and . . . it was necessary again [as it had been in 1911] to draw on extraneous sources'. The 'extraneous sources' meant Pacific Phosphate shares, which were realized in order to meet the bill for dividends. Without this assistance Lever would have had no option but to pass the Ordinary dividend, and to have done that at this stage when more capital was continually required might have been disastrous.

Thus on the eve of the war the story was still one of rewards postponed. Sales of soap in the United Kingdom were lower than in 1913. The overseas factories were not progressing according to programme. The Belgian Congo was not yet in production and the French Congo business was losing money. Trade in Japan, China, South Africa, Sweden, and Austria, was showing losses; in the States, it was just about breaking even. Meanwhile Lever's issued capital had risen steadily, and that capital included an ever-increasing proportion of Preference shares carrying the serious burden of a fixed interest rate. The authorized capital of the whole concern stood at £30,000,000 and of the issued capital of just over £13,250,000, £2,000,000 represented Ordinary shares held by Lever himself. That briefly was what the pessimist or the cynic would have seen as a picture of the business in 1914. Lever saw a different picture—a picture of a growing complex of businesses under his control, providing nearly half the soap used in the United Kingdom, and facing only one serious native competitor; controlling, through the alliance with Brunner Mond's, a sure supply of alkali; through Crosfield's and De-No-Fa, the knowledge and equipment for large-scale fat hardening; through Lever's, the vast potential resources of the Congo and the Pacific and a chain of valuable factories and businesses scattered throughout the Old World and the New. Time, Lever was convinced, was on his side. If only he could hold out the harvest would be rich indeed. It was to come more quickly then he could have guessed.

PART III
BUSINESS IN WARTIME
1914–18

CHAPTER XIV

INTRODUCTION

'We all expected that the war was going to make employment very bad. The war has proved us all to be very bad prophets.'

Lord Leverhulme addressing representatives of the Liverpool Trades and Labour Council, 23 *November* 1917

BETWEEN 1885 and 1914, the growth of Lever Brothers had proceeded more or less unchecked: even the crisis of 1906 and its aftermath proved after all to be only a temporary halt. From being merely one of a number of soap-producing firms, Lever's had become first of all *primus inter pares* and, later, by a process of absorption, the controlling element in a complex of British soap companies and a chain of daughter companies in Europe, America and the Dominions. In 1914, the total sales of the Lever 'family' in the United Kingdom amounted to more than 236,000 tons. The total estimated national consumption of soap was round about 385,000 tons, so that Lever's share of the total trade amounted to sixty-one per cent. The sales of the American and Dominion companies came to another 50,000 tons while the sales of the European companies stood at about 25,000 metric tons.

Alongside this primary organization, there was the secondary growth of raw material projects in West Africa, the Belgian Congo and the Solomons. Undertaken originally with the idea of augmenting supplies of raw materials to Lever's own factories, they already showed signs of establishing for themselves a separate identity, though they were necessarily linked, and were to remain so, to the general business of soap production.

In 1914 then the Lever business still remained essentially a soap-producing concern. It remained also as nearly as was possible for its size a one-man business, in the sense that all major decisions and a surprising number of relatively minor ones depended not merely on the consent but upon the initiative of the chairman. In some senses, the growth of the business and the coming of new men had emphasized his isolation. As early as 1908 he had confessed: '. . . to none of the new staff is it possible for me to get quite as close as to the old . . . I am more standing alone in the business of Lever Brothers than ever'. True, the growing complexity of the business was reflected in an increase in the board of directors. In 1906 he had been assisted by three; by 1914 by nine. Most of them probably did little more than modify Lever's personal dictatorship in matters of detail. The most independent of them, J. K. Greenhalgh, had, as we have seen, resigned over precisely this issue. Amongst the few who had any real voice in policy making was John McDowell, to whose brilliant handling of legal issues Lever already owed much. Like most of his colleagues, McDowell went in some awe of his 'Chief', but such was the keenness of his brain and the quality of his advice that Lever was compelled to listen to him. Others were less fortunately placed. There was, for example, J. L. Buchanan, a technical expert of great competence and a man given to plain speaking, who finally paid the penalty for his frank criticism of Lever's financial policy—he was made Chairman of an associated company. Perhaps the only other voice Lever was prepared to listen to in matters of general policy was that of George Harley, the Company's solicitor and the last of Lever's close personal friends connected with the business. Various Councils met regularly to study problems such as sales, publicity, finance, accounts and the works and they reported to a committee of the whole board, known as the Policy Council. Theoretically the Policy Council wielded the power of final sanction, but in reality it was subject always to the overriding influence of the chairman.

The degree of control exercised over the associated companies varied widely. Separate Group Boards were formed to look after their interests but in the last resort the degree of control was bound to depend on the size of the financial stake which Levers had in the company concerned. Control over capital expenditure was the real test; companies wholly owned by the parent concern were entirely subject to Lever's will. But the large, partially owned companies preserved a considerable measure of independence. At one point in 1915 Lever could observe that all exchange of information between Watson's and Lever's on all subjects had ceased, and of John Knight's that on matters of capital expenditure 'they never consulted us'. Nor had there been much in the way of 'rationalization', i.e. the closing of small factories and the transfer of their production to larger plants. In his early years Lever had been a convinced rationalizer, and even in 1906 he had closed down two small factories in England and one in America and transferred their production to Port Sunlight, but as time went by he changed his mind. Comparative figures for manufacturing costs in large and small factories, he discovered, were 'always misleading'. He would have done 'infinitely better' to have kept on the small factories, for quite apart from costs there was the factor of goodwill; 'a soap business', he wrote very late in life, 'must have an individuality founded upon its centre of manufacture apart altogether from the question of railway rates in distribution which would in many cases be increased by closing the works and moving to, say Port Sunlight'.

For many reasons, therefore, the control of the 'family' remained loose. Its centre was still Port Sunlight and from his office there Lever exercised a personal influence which for the time being made up for the lack of formal administrative organization. During the period which follows, however, the evidence accumulated that a change of system could not be long delayed.

CHAPTER XV

THE SOAP BUSINESS

LEVER himself had for many years recognized that hostility towards Great Britain existed in Germany, and had taken it into account when he considered the development of his business there, but the thought of war he never seems to have seriously entertained. Moreover when war came, the true measure and scope of the catastrophe were not easily nor quickly realized. The idea of 'total war' was only born slowly in the minds of Lever and his generation. England's wars in the past had been fought on a principle of limited liability: the fighting was the business of the professional armed forces of the Crown; the civilian's part was to pay and get on with his job. Hence the cry of 'business as usual' and Lever's own remark that 'war was only a passing phase of business life'. In the early days he expected the phase to pass fairly quickly, and although he recovered from that delusion sooner than many, the duration of the war was no more accurately foreseen by him than had been its outbreak. Only gradually were the economic implications borne in upon him—the loss of several Continental businesses, the shortage of capital, labour, and raw materials, the growth of Government interference in industrial affairs, the increase of employment and purchasing power as well as the social changes which resulted from these things.

The most immediate effect of the war on Lever Brothers was to cut them off from their highly profitable business in Germany and their less profitable business in Austria, and very soon afterwards from their factories in Belgium and Northern France also. Lever accepted the loss of the German business philosophically: 'He felt', he said, 'that in any case during the war we would not get our profits out of Germany'. The shares in the Mannheim Company were sold (with the permission of both belligerent governments), and for the first time the control of a Lever business, with its trade marks, passed out of Lever Brothers' hands: the financial settlement was left until the peace.

He was less easily reconciled to the loss of his trade in enemy-occupied territory, and for some time tried to persuade the Government to allow him to export to these areas. To the objection that soap sold in this way would find its way to the Germans he had a typically ingenious answer ready. The only interest (so he argued) that a belligerent power could have in the soap industry lay in the production of glycerine. The more soap Britain made the more glycerine its Government would have. The same applied to Germany, and if some German consumption was supplied by Britain, there would be a corresponding decline in German soap output and therefore in German glycerine production. On balance it would therefore pay to go on exporting soap to the Continent and to accept the risk that some might find its way to Germany. As he put it, 'it would make the Germans clean but it would not make them better fighters; they could not eat it, therefore it would not nourish them, in fact as fighting machines they would not be affected at all, and whilst we know that soap may have a good effect on health I do not think that life in the trenches or the battlefield, notwithstanding constant washings can be affected very much by the question of what soap is issued, whether good soap from England or poor soap from Germany'. It was not a very convincing argument and it is hardly surprising that it failed to convince the Government.

At home, it was not long before the capital shortage made itself felt. By February 1915, the Government had taken power to control the issue of capital and, if permission for an issue were sought, they might, in Sir William's words, 'ask a lot of questions and wish to make an inspection and generally interfere with our business'. Rather than accept this he decided to 'continue the policy of sitting tight and of keeping expenditure down'. Expenditure absolutely necessary must of course be faced but there must be no extravagance. Share issues were not altogether impossible. The Issued Capital rose during the years 1914–17 (both inclusive) by £2,817,742, but this amount did little more than cover the cost of entry into the margarine industry[1] and the increased cost of raw materials. It made modest reading when compared with the £7,000,000 increase which had taken place in the four years before the war. Therefore, although

[1] See Chapter XVI.

during the war the building of the combine did not entirely cease, most of the purchases were relatively small. The most important exception was the purchase of Joseph Watson's remaining shares which were offered and taken, at characteristically short notice, in July 1917. By the agreement for the sale, Watson was barred from re-entering the soap trade, but he was left in sole possession of the shares in Olympia Oil and Cake Mills Company Limited, a fact which Lever was later to regret.[1]

Apart from this overriding difficulty of capital shortage, conditions of business during the first two years or so of the war were not radically different from those of peace, although difficulties both in labour supply and in transport began to make themselves felt. Some raw materials of relatively minor importance were rendered scarce by the interruption of trade with Germany, but the major oils and fats were almost embarrassingly plentiful for precisely the same reason, since the British blockade had seriously interfered with the operations of the German crushing industry and had diverted supplies of oilseeds to England. In these circumstances there were two courses open: either to let stocks run down as the market fell, or to store against a time when supplies might not be so plentiful. Lever's chose the first course; the Dutch margarine makers, it may be noted, chose the second.[2]

The first important sign of a change was the unexpected requisitioning by the Government, on the 6th of August, 1915, of soap makers' stocks of glycerine at a price which was considerably less than Lever's idea of the value of the commodity and which remained unaltered throughout the rest of the war. To do him justice, he did not grumble—much. The gunners' need was obvious, and he was prepared to do his part in supplying it. But perhaps the main significance of the Government's action was its proclamation of the principle that soap making, vital in those days to the munitions industry, must in time of war submit to control for the good of the State. The principle once admitted (and Lever, individualist though he was, did not dispute it), the practice might be indefinitely extended.

Soon after the Government took over the glycerine there began to be signs that the raw material abundance was coming

[1] See Book II, Chapter XIII.
[2] See Book II, Chapter X.

to an end. In November 1915, Sir William wrote to his son of 'the high cost of raw materials and the entire reversal in the position soap makers find themselves in', and of 'the fact that it will be extremely difficult for us to make any further advance in the price of soap'. During 1915, Lever Brothers had made enough profit to pay fifteen per cent on the Ordinary Capital, though they had only paid ten per cent and kept the rest 'for purposes of strengthening the business', and he had evidently thought that much the same situation would arise in 1916 but 'this position is now entirely reversed, and it is quite obvious that we shall have to conserve any surplus profits there may be during 1915 to meet the high prices of raw materials for 1916'.

It became obvious that the Dutch margarine manufacturers in choosing to store raw materials rather than let their stocks run down had followed the right policy: Lever, while complaining bitterly about the motives and results of his rivals' activities, prepared to follow their example. It became obvious to Lever that with severe shortage sending German oil and fat prices up to fantastic heights 'the minute peace is declared neutral countries such as the United States, the Argentine, Brazil, and elsewhere will ship everything to Germany and nothing to the United Kingdom. Prices of oils and fats, therefore, are bound to have an immediate and overwhelming advance the moment peace is declared and unless we have stocks to tide us over many months when peace is declared we shall be in great difficulties, but the question of holding these stocks is not a policy that should be known to our competitors.' While the soap makers' raw material difficulties deepened, the demand for their products grew. 'I am of opinion', wrote Sir William in 1916, 'that we must at an early date begin plans for new additional soaperies. I believe the increased demand has come to stay owing to the higher rate of wages being paid in the United Kingdom.' But the most compelling pressure came not from the public demand for soap so much as from the increasing Government demand for glycerine. At the beginning of 1916 the soap makers were suddenly told that the munitions shortage was very serious and that the Government would require in 1917 more than double the quantity produced for the previous year. Lever's first instinct was to say that the suddenly demanded increase was impossible of fulfilment, 'but', he went on, 'this must not be the attitude with which we approach it'. He told John Gray, his Managing Director at Port Sunlight, that they must make plans for a higher output not 'based upon any possible sales of soap but merely imagining that the sale of soap was a secondary consideration, the production of glycerine being the main consideration'.

Fortunately, it proved unnecessary to regard the sale of soap as 'a secondary consideration'. By the beginning of 1917, orders were coming in so fast that Lever was urging Gray to consider temporary manufacture in buildings that were already standing: he had in mind disused cotton mills in Bolton, Wigan, or other Lancashire towns. If enough soap could not be boiled by Lever Brothers themselves, then contracts must be made with other firms to boil it for them, and he added, 'I would not limit myself to Associated Companies'. When Salaman reported arrears of orders piling up in the Export Department, Lever's mind flew back thirty years to his Warrington days:[1] 'The position of course is becoming very acute. I have not yet abandoned all hope that we can yet put rings round some of the pans. I do not care whether these rings are wood or iron, either would do, so that we could get more soap made . . . we are in such an awful position that unless we do something to get more soap we are going to lose all the benefit that the present conditions have given us for recovering our lost ground. A ring round the pans apparently would increase the pans' output by about twenty-five per cent at least . . . now twenty-five per cent added to the present output would put us straight in a few months.' The results were evident by the spring of 1917: 'I was greatly pleased', he told his son, 'with the statistics Mr. Gray put before me last week which was the largest output in our whole history, but we want to get several hundred tons a week more. . . . I am very anxious about our pulling up the arrears of orders. We are thousands of tons oversold and we really want some seven hundred tons of soap more per week to keep level.' Figures for the completed year showed that in 1917 the Port Sunlight Company had produced more soap than ever before: its total sales were 65,710 tons against 63,024 tons for 1905, the only previous year when sales had risen above 60,000. Other companies in the group could show comparable results: with the noteworthy exception

[1] See Chapter III.

of John Knight's (who anyway were not yet fully associated) nearly every member of the 'family' sold more soap in 1917 than they had done in the years immediately before the war.

Here was the first sign of a substantial expansion of the market for many years. Lever himself and others had no doubt of the underlying cause: higher wages had brought higher working-class purchasing power and some of the extra money had been spent on soap. Wage rates were not the whole story: a great deal of overtime was being worked, and unemployment had almost disappeared. Many more women were earning during the war than before it, and women were always the soap makers' best customers. These civilian purchases were, of course, swollen by Government buying on behalf of the Services and by the flourishing state of the export trade, neither of which was directly related to the condition of the working classes.

This great increase in production was achieved at the time when the U-boat campaign was at its height, and when, consequently, the supplies of any industry which depended on imported raw materials were increasingly imperilled. The soap industry, because it provided glycerine, was one of the last which could be allowed to run short, but the only authority which could hope to ensure that it would not run short was the Government. Therefore, as the raw material situation grew more acute, so State control of the industry grew closer. Early in 1916, Sir William met 'the Committee connected with the Admiralty, dealing with oils and fats' which put forward a proposal for the British Government 'to requisition the whole of the supplies of oils and fats and oleaginous substances and to deal with them themselves for the use of consumers within the British Empire'. Lever welcomed the idea, not least, perhaps, because it would deal a blow at the 'hoarded stores' which his Dutch competitors had laid down in England. But it was only in the spring of 1917, after many months of hesitancy, that a really thorough scheme for the control of oils and fats took shape. Like other schemes in other industries, it was to be worked largely by members of the trades concerned. A Joint Trades Committee was formed under the presidency of Sir William Lever; it included representatives of the soap and candle trades, the margarine makers, the oleaginous seed and nut crushers, and the feeding stuffs makers. At about the same time the Minister of Munitions prohibited by Order dealings in oils and fats except under licence. 'It was believed', Clarence Knowles told the Policy Council, 'that the proposed scheme of control would ensure supplies of raw materials, but . . . while maximum prices had been fixed, there was nothing in the Order that had been issued that prevented hoarding . . . there was nothing . . . to compel holders of stocks of raw materials to sell.' With the provision and distribution of raw materials in their hands, there was nothing to prevent the Government from establishing a control of the soap industry far more complete than any that could be attempted by a mere private capitalist like Sir William Lever. In the summer of 1918, impelled by a mixture of motives, strategic, economic, and political, the Government proceeded towards the logical completion of their policy. They set up The Soap Makers' Federation, which though in form a voluntary association of manufacturers, was in fact an engine of official compulsion. Its contemplated activities included the distribution of raw material, the fixing of prices, and the 'rationalization' of productive capacity. It was hardly born before the Armistice brought about its premature death, but its very inception demonstrated the change brought about by four years of war in Englishmen's notions of the functions proper to their Government.

Not only raw materials were scarce. The war from its very earliest days, so far from causing the mass unemployment which had been feared, had brought about an acute shortage of labour. In March 1915, Gray told his colleagues that 'the labour problem was . . . difficult and the quality of the labour is very much below what it was before the war. Many of our best men had gone to the war and their places had been filled by inferior men.' The problem could not be entirely solved by the employment of women for, as Gray said, 'many of the jobs on which women had been engaged had not proved to be economic propositions. . . . He instanced cases which required two women to do one man's work at a cost of 72 shillings as against 58 shillings for a man', and the Company found itself short-handed 'for the duration'. The drain of men to the war and the urgent need to keep the essential industries (of which soap was one) in full production, placed the workmen who remained at home in a bargaining position of unprecedented strength, especially since the Government was far readier to grant wage increases than to contemplate industrial unrest. Under the pressure of a mounting cost of living, this strength was not left unexploited, and throughout the war Lever Brothers, like other firms, were presented with periodical demands for high wages which, in their prosperity, they were not seriously unwilling to grant. The cost of living pressed not only on the labourer or the factory hand, but on the office worker too, and he, lacking a tradition of collective bargaining, did not fare so well. Long before the end of the war the labourer's wage had overtaken the clerk's. By June 1918, the lowest wage for an unskilled labourer was 54s. whereas the lowest wage for a clerk was 48s., and the Policy Council felt the necessity of levelling the one up to the other.

The Lever businesses abroad were affected, to a greater or less degree, by most of the forces operating at home. Governments everywhere clamoured for glycerine; in many countries wage rates and the cost of living rose; in most, Government control made its appearance. With the important exception of the American company there is no very great expansion to record during the war years: the shortage of new capital had its moderating influence abroad as well as at home. Moreover, the building of the 'subsidiary combines' in Australia, Canada, and South Africa was well advanced by the beginning of 1915, and Lever could rest more or less content, as he explained in August of that year:

> I am this year dealing with Co-Partnership with all our Associated Companies, both English, Colonial, and Foreign, on a basis that is now possible owing to the greater security we have and hope to have on profits. I have not been able to do so earlier because until we had arranged with certain firms in England, and until I had arranged with certain firms in South Africa, Canada, and Australia, obviously we might be at any time compelled to take on a policy of fight when profits would disappear.

Events in Canada quickly put an end to any idea that Lever's were now isolated from the shock of competition. In 1916 Procter & Gamble built a factory at Hamilton, Ontario, and a new and unwelcome phase was opened in the hitherto prosperous Canadian business. 'Prior to the advent of Procter & Gamble soaps on the Canadian market', as three touring directors reported, 'the concerns in which we have acquired an interest practically controlled the soap interests, either in their individual units or as advisers to the smaller soap makers.' By 1919 this situation had been altered so drastically as to provoke Lever into remarking 'More resin in Sunlight won't put the Canadian business right. It is not more resin in Sunlight but more genius in Canadian business.'

Other countries were less exposed to the intrusion of powerful newcomers and in general the Lever managements were able to spend the war years in consolidating and in working out solutions to problems of co-operation within the group. These problems arose most urgently in the three Dominions and in France since in each there were both original Lever foundations and acquired interests running in double harness, distinct from one another but linked by remote control from England. So greatly had the overseas network been elaborated in the years immediately before the war that the single company organization survived only in Holland, Switzerland, Japan, and the United States. Holland and Switzerland, being both neutrals, preserved their businesses unhampered by invasion or enmity, but although they escaped the German army they suffered from the naval blockade —Holland so severely that the factory at Vlaardingen, completed in 1915, never came into use during the war at all; the trade was maintained, as far as possible, by imports from England. The Japanese company, remote from the European conflict but affected nevertheless by its influence, wiped off its early heavy losses (£100,000 by September 1915), and in 1917 began for a brief period to make money.

In the United States, the outbreak of war found Lever Brothers losing money. With the war came a tide of prosperity and the opportunity Countway was waiting for. His American competitors had nothing with which to meet his campaign to sell Lux throughout the United States, and Countway pressed his advantage home before they had time to prepare a reply. He was enthusiastically supported from across the Atlantic: all his demands for money were met, if not from the parent company's resources, then from Lever's private fortune or from borrowing in America, and production mounted week by week and year by year: from 9,000 cases in 1914 it rose to over a million before the war was over. By 1916 he had also doubled the 1912 turnover of Lifebuoy. The importance of such success in America could hardly be over-estimated, for in America was the largest and the richest market that Lever could hope to capture. In the gloom of 1920 the Chairman was to be able to comfort himself with the thought that the efforts of Countway had converted annual losses of £20,000 into a profit of over £300,000 a year.

Besides their manufacturing interests overseas Lever's were deeply concerned with the development of their export trade, the importance of which has been indicated previously. In this field Lever's had no rivals but their semi-allies, Crosfield's and Gossage's (known collectively, even in legal documents, as 'Crossage's'). Unfortunately the old acrimony showed itself wherever the two sides came into contact, but nowhere more clearly than over the proposal to found a joint factory in China. The possibilities of the Chinese market had been in the forefront of Lever's mind at least since 1913. In that year his son visited China in the course of his business training and reported to his father that: 'The soap trade in China offers enormous prospects and there is no reason why almost the whole of it should not be in the hands of the joint company'. A vast population would have to be educated to use soap, but there was no competition and raw materials were available in tremendous quantities. Despite these glowing prospects, the preparations for starting the new company dragged on interminably, and were still incomplete when, early in 1915, the brothers Crosfield resigned from the board of their company. Lever at once pressed for representation on the board of Crosfield's and Gossage's. His claim brought Lever Brothers once again into direct conflict with Brunner Mond's, and transformed the matter of the China company from an affair of outposts into a major engagement. Brunner's would have none of his proposal, and the chairman of Crosfield's intimated that 'sooner than see Lever's representatives on the Crosfield Board he would resign his Chairmanship'. Realizing, apparently, that no agreement with Lever's would be possible over the China problem, Brunner's reverted to a proposal for another company in China in which Lever's share would have been limited to a financial holding shorn of any control of policy. Lever in turn refused to participate and in September 1917 issued a writ against Brunner Mond for breach of the 1913 agreement. Nevertheless, within a few days of the action being brought to trial the parties had come to terms, which provided for the sale by Brunner's to Lever's of half the Ordinary shares in Crosfield's and Gossage's and for the appointment by Lever's of one third of the directors of those companies. The exact details of the agreement are not important since it was never carried out, but although it brought no final settlement of the Lever-Brunner quarrel it did establish a temporary truce and, perhaps more important, pointed the way to one of Lever Brothers' largest post-war acquisitions, namely that of the entire businesses of Crosfield's and Gossage's.

The First World War ended almost as unexpectedly as it had begun. Towards the end of 1918, Lever's, with the rest of the soap trade, were resigned to extended Government control, to soap rationing, and to the manufacture of standard soap. But at the same time they were prosperous—too prosperous their enemies said—though they defended themselves by saying that the high price and large profits of wartime had been forced on them by the rising cost of raw materials, and that whatever excess profit they had made and been allowed to keep would disappear when raw materials began once again to fall in price. However that may be, the Ordinary Dividend, which had only with difficulty been declared at ten per cent in 1914, stood at fifteen per cent for 1917, and reached seventeen and a half per cent in the following year. Prosperity was general in the business world, and there seemed no good reason why it should not continue: indeed much the reverse, for would not war-deprived England and devastated Europe consume all and more than all that could be made? Besides, after four years of steadily more irksome control business men were ready for unfettered adventure. Lord Leverhulme[1] especially had chafed under the restrictions imposed by the shortage of capital and, although he realized that difficult years lay ahead, he was only too eager to resume the process of expansion.

[1] Lever had been raised to the Peerage on 4 June 1917; he was created a Viscount on 11 November 1922.

CHAPTER XVI

THE MARGARINE BUSINESS

'We drifted into the margarine business because of its close connection with oils and fats for the soap kettle. We drifted into West Africa, and the Congo, and the Solomon Islands to supply ourselves with oils and fats. Finding that these oils and fats were even superior for margarine than for soap, we naturally diverted to and developed margarine manufacture.'

Lord Leverhulme, 23 *May* 1918

The idea of going into margarine manufacture had been in the minds of Lever's directors for a year or two before 1914; the outbreak of war gave the necessary impetus to it. For nearly half a century the food consumed by the British people had come increasingly from overseas. The growth of the German navy constituted a threat to these supplies which could not be ignored. Butter from Denmark and margarine from Holland were amongst the supplies likely to be cut off first. The Government, therefore, inquired at once whether Lever would manufacture margarine and by October 1914 plans were well in hand. There was no doubt about his eagerness. He told the directors that 'the present was the opportunity of a lifetime, as we could sell all that we could make at our own terms . . . his policy would be at first not to go in for too big an output of margarine, but to get a big profit until we felt our feet . . . he did not think there would be any difficulty in selling. Van den Bergh's and Jurgens' had a trade of 75,000 tons a year and we had this to cut into . . . the margarine business would work in well with the soap business as it would enable us to use up any high class raw materials we bought to better advantage and the residue we could use up in soap better than the margarine maker.' He added that the proposition 'would help us to get a better price for our Congo oil', and J. L. Buchanan remarked that 'it would put the oil mills on their legs'.

The scheme was that Lever Brothers and Watson's should buy from the Maypole Dairy Company[1] a margarine works at

[1] For the story of the Maypole Dairy Company see Book II, Chapter XIV.

Godley in Cheshire. Before a final decision could be taken three main questions had to be considered: the financing of the purchase, the supply of refined oil to the factory, and the probable nature of relations with the other principal partner to the enterprise, Joseph Watson. Lever characteristically ignored counsels of financial caution. The supply of refined oil he could not ignore, it was to come from his own refinery at Bromborough, near Port Sunlight, and from Joseph Watson's refinery, The Olympia Oil and Cake Company, at Selby, at the rate of about 200 tons a week from each. The third problem was Mr. Watson.[1] His masterful independence was only too familiar to Lever and his directors. If the joint arrangements were not completed he was ready to start making margarine on his own. Any risks which partnership might entail were to be preferred to the alternative of leaving the field to Watson alone. Planter's Margarine Company Limited was therefore set up early in November 1914, as a joint enterprise by Lever's and Watson's. The Maypole were only too glad to be rid of Godley which in fact was becoming obsolete. They suspected, moreover, that if Planter's could not buy an existing factory they would build themselves a new one which would face them with even more formidable competition. Not that Lever went into the contract blindfold; as he generously put it:

> I think Sir George Watson and the Maypole Dairy Company ought to be congratulated on having got rid of their Godley Works at such advantageous terms. I always felt at the time that they had much the best of the deal and had obtained more than a full price for the undertaking, and I rather rejoiced at this because there was no cause for irritation in the matter. Human nature is so built that if in a deal of this character the pendulum sways either to one side or the other there is always some little resentment and I hope this was entirely avoided between the Maypole Company and Planter's by the excellent terms the Maypole had obtained for their Godley business.

Linked with the sale was an agreement for co-operation between the new company and the Maypole. In return for help with supplies of suitable oil the Maypole Company agreed to instruct Planter's in the making of margarine, and to allow

[1] Joseph Watson of Leeds, not to be confused with Sir George Watson of the Maypole Dairy Company.

them the use, within the United Kingdom, of any invention employed by themselves in the manufacture of margarine. Efficient refining was of the first importance and only by some such assistance could it be ensured that the new venture would start its operations as well equipped as possible.

The Godley factory was in the charge of K. V. Hansen, a Dane by birth, who had previously been in the Maypole's service, but to his chagrin the direction of policy was reserved to Lever's and Watson's. Selling was Lever's responsibility; buying Watson's; a joint committee of the two companies met fortnightly in London. For some time all went well. But the characters of the two leading men were too strong and too similar for peaceful co-operation. By the summer of 1915 it was clear that one would buy the other out, though which would buy and which would sell was not immediately determined. The diplomacy that followed contained more than the normal amount of bluff and counter bluff but finally in July 1915 the Planter's business passed into Lever Brothers' control. It had by then an average weekly output of 257 tons, against a total production in the country which Lever's themselves estimated, later in the year, at 2,295 tons weekly. It was already the second largest producing unit in the United Kingdom, but the largest, the Maypole, was far ahead with about 1,200 tons. This was by no means the whole story, for during 1915 imports from the 'Dutchmen' were steadily rising towards their wartime peak; as yet they had no factories in the United Kingdom. It was in the sale of the more expensive, branded qualities, rather than in that of the cheap qualities sold without a name that the bulk of the money, though not the bulk of the trade, lay. Sir William told his son late in 1916 that 'more than half of what we sell is the cheap quality on which we lose money', and this remark explains his eagerness, from the very start, to work up for Planter's a trade in good quality branded margarine. The fact was that the scarcity of butter in 1916 had created an entirely new type of demand. For the first time in history the consumption of margarine in the United Kingdom exceeded that of butter—and exceeded it moreover by 100,000 tons. 'I hear on all hands', Lever wrote in 1915, 'that there is an enormous demand from the public—possibly an entirely new public—for one shilling margarine. By a new public I mean not previous users of margarine. . . . The one shilling margarine consumption is entirely taken off the consumption of butter.'

The mark which he chose—not perhaps his happiest inspiration—was 'Plate', and with 'Plate' he set out to challenge the Dutchmen. There seems little doubt however that, in its early days at least, 'Plate' was not outstandingly good. In November 1915, after some weeks' trial, Hansen reported that 'Plate margarine does not seem to be an unqualified success . . . people can detect . . . the vegetable fat . . . and for that reason people think that it is only an improved, perhaps not even very much improved, form of the Maypole Margarine', to which Sir William replied: 'I have been waiting for these complaints ever since I received samples, and also from the ominous silence in speaking of the quality by many of the friends to whom I have sent samples. Friends are not often candid critics and therefore when quality is doubtful and silence ensues, the only interpretation is that no good word can be said for quality.' He went on to admit that 'I am sorry I have not sufficient experience of the margarine business to form an independent opinion that would be of any value': a significant admission, and one that he would never have made in connection with his soap business. As matters stood, he need perhaps have looked no further than his own household for an 'independent opinion'. Always an ardent salesman of his own wares, he had very early introduced Planter's margarine into the economy of his various households, and very soon there had been rumbles of discontent below stairs—in February 1915 he wrote that 'the London staff of domestic servants are under the impression that they will either be poisoned or very much degraded as human beings if they eat margarine'. At the end of 1916 the matter came to a head: 'I may say I have had a mutiny in the domestic staff at the Hill because I laid down the rule that we must eat Plate margarine. I have not heard whether it has subsided, but I had to interview the whole staff in the dining room yesterday morning before leaving. Several of the maids had told the Housekeeper that they would rather leave than eat the margarine and of course I have to insist upon the margarine being eaten. I have not heard of any of the maids leaving but, of course, it is a little early yet for me to have heard.' Nevertheless demand was brisk and expanding, so that in the last quarter of 1915 profits were sufficient to wipe off entirely the initial losses of the first eight months' trading. There were losses again in 1916, but after that, for the remainder of the war, profits were large, though fluctuating, and sufficient to wipe out earlier losses. And whatever might be the opinion of Lever's friends and servants about the quality of his margarine, his competition was sufficiently strong to worry the 'Dutchmen', who both approached him more than once during 1915 and 1916 with the idea of buying him out of Godley. But as yet times were too good and prospects too fair for Sir William to think of any such thing.

The production at Godley was worked up from a total of 13,372 tons in 1915 to 27,235 tons in 1917. These figures placed Planter's high up on the list of English manufacturers, but it left them far behind the Maypole and the two great importers. This was by no means a position which Lever felt content to occupy permanently: Godley had only been a nursery: it offered no scope for expansion on the scale which he desired. Next door to Port Sunlight, at Bromborough, was a site large enough to accommodate the factory he had in mind: 'In every way a model Works, walls inside tiled, and so on, everything bright and clean,' and having, of course, a productive capacity commensurate with the scale of Lever Brothers' activities elsewhere.

From the start, the new factory was intended to produce 1,000 tons per week, and during 1916 work went forward on a first unit of 500 tons. Rising demand and pressure from the Government soon combined to make Lever dissatisfied with the original scheme, and before it was completed far larger things were in his mind. On the 9th of August 1917 the Policy and Tactics Committee met to consider a proposal which 'entailed doubling the present margarine works at Bromborough and putting down a refinery to deal with Bromborough and Godley requirements, and laying down also of a new oil crushing and extraction plant . . . on a rough estimate the cost of the scheme would be £1,500,000 . . . this expenditure would cover oil crushing plant to produce 1,000 tons of oil per week; refining plant to deal with that quantity of oil; fat splitting plant in connection with the by-products; and plant to give an additional output of 500 tons per week of margarine. The total output when all the extensions had been completed would be 1,500 tons per week', and this estimate was very shortly raised to 2,000 tons. Two days later the Chairman personally explained his advocacy of the scheme: '... we were profitably in margarine to-day, and if we were not in it to-day our position would be less strong. Margarine manufacture fits in well with soap manufacture, and it fitted in well with our developments in West Africa which were going ahead at a great rate in spite of the war.' It was true that it would be necessary to capture some of this trade from competitors but this he was confident he could do. The Dutchmen might have their chain of multiple shops but that policy 'would be advantageous rather than the reverse for Lever Brothers. By being tied to multiple shops the tendency was for a manufacturer to be restricted to his own shops and to lose his wholesale trade, and the last people to be crushed out of business would not be the multiple shops nor the co-operatives, but the small shopkeeper.' He was confident too that there was a large market for margarine as yet unexploited in the United Kingdom. 'In some countries on the Continent', he went on to say, 'the consumption of margarine per head of the population was twice as much as it was in the United Kingdom, and there was therefore room for expansion.' Neither was he daunted by the prospect of a battle for raw materials; Lever Brothers had their African sources.

On these arguments a decision was taken which committed Lever's to creating a very large and expensive organization to challenge rivals who had long been established in the trade. Nevertheless, for the time being all the signs were fair. Hansen wrote of 'these trying conditions when we can only manufacture less than half of what we could sell', which sufficiently indicates the prevailing briskness of demand. The Dutch competitors were increasingly harassed by official interference with their import trade and had scarcely completed their plans for manufacture in England. There were growing difficulties of raw material supply, rationing, and Government control of the industry; since the spring of 1917 with the Allied shipping losses running to more than half a million gross tons a month the expansion of the home industry was an urgent necessity.

By the end of the war United Kingdom margarine production had been built up by the united efforts of Government and manufacturers from about 78,000 metric tons annually in 1914 to nearly 238,000 metric tons in 1918. To this total, at the end of the year, Lever's were preparing to add their enlarged contribution, for after many vexatious delays in the building, their new factory at Bromborough at length went into production a few days before the Armistice. Jurgens' and Van den Bergh's had both begun manufacturing in England, and the Maypole had reached a point where, for the purposes of a Government return, its utmost production was estimated at 2,400 weekly tons. On the outskirts of the trade were a great many small makers who had joined in the scramble, and it was to their products that Lever severely attributed much of the public discontent with the quality of wartime margarine. That production, in the latter months of the war, was not overmatched to demand is proved by the fact that early in 1918 margarine was rationed: it remained to be seen whether or not peace and butter would replace war and margarine.

CHAPTER XVII

RAW MATERIALS

By 1914 one of the reasons for Lever's anxiety to secure his supplies of raw materials was becoming obvious. The West African trade, on which he so largely depended, had settled down, after a period of sharp competition, into a system of 'working arrangements' between the surviving companies. He might well feel that without the organization which he had built up since 1910, he would have run the risk of being threatened by the oils and fats merchants in much the same way as he had already been threatened by the producers of alkali. In the other great department of raw materials supply—fat hardening—there had been the same necessity for Lever Brothers to have a process and a plant of their own if they were not to be dependent on a limited number of possibly hostile suppliers: they had accordingly fought the battle of the patents in 1912–13 and acquired a half interest in the De-No-Fa Company of Norway. Thus, by 1914 Lever's had taken decisive measures to defend their interests in both the branches of the oils and fats market which chiefly concerned them, but their ventures were yet young and it remained to develop them.

As we have seen, Lever Brothers' greatest raw material venture was the Huileries du Congo Belge.[1] It was inevitably unprofitable for the first years of its existence, but it was hoped that 1917 would see the enterprise turn the corner. To that end, the Congo was allowed as large a share as possible in the limited amount of new capital available to Lever's during the war. 'It is obvious', as Sir William told his son, 'that in the development of a country such as the Congo we cannot suddenly pull up and cut off all capital expenditure without courting disaster.' Harold Greenhalgh, the director in charge of operations in England, was persistently optimistic. But, in fact, the story in the Congo was one of slow progress. The difficulties were the same as they always had been: the African mentality, unreliable reports of palm areas, disappointing white staff, obstructive officials, with the added wartime vexations of capital shortage

[1] See Chapter XI.

and delay in the provision of essential supplies. Others besides the Huileries du Congo Belge were exploiting the resources of the Congo. From 1911 to 1916 the colony's total exports of palm kernels rose from 7,000 to 22,500 tons per year, with the greatest increase, as might be expected, between 1914 (8,000 tons) and 1916 (22,500 tons). Palm oil exports rose too, but not so strikingly; they were 2,300 tons in 1911 and only 3,900 tons in 1916. The great bulk of the kernel trade was in the hands of merchants who had no mills. Now part of the H.C.B.'s concession was that they should erect mills and export palm oil. They were already fulfilling their obligations to the best of their ability, but the work of development could only proceed slowly.[1] There was however no reason why Lever's should not extend beyond their original concessions and go into general trading with the prospect of much quicker returns. This was the genesis of the Société d'Entreprises Commerciales du Congo Belge (SEDEC for short) which from 1917 proceeded to make handsome profits out of the purchase and export of palm kernels, and the sale in the Congo of European merchandise. How welcome this successful trading was, as a set-off to the continued expense of H.C.B.'s main activities, is obvious.

Towards the end of the decisive year 1917, Harold Greenhalgh reported progress on the plantations; of the five great areas planned, three—Elisabetha, Alberta, and Leverville—were well up to schedule. The fourth, Flandria, was proving swampy and treacherous. The fifth, Brabanta, was still 'a dangerous area' not yet occupied by the Congo Government themselves.

[1] H.C.B. ANNUAL PRODUCTION

Year	*Palm Fruit Production*	*Palm Oil Tons*	*Palm Kernels Tons*
1912	2,953	384	118
1913	4,921	639	196
1914	7,874	1,020	315
1915	10,878	1,519	402
1916	18,047	2,400	749
1917	22,593	3,434	1,586
1918	26,908	4,491	2,206

Both palm oil and palm kernels are obtained from the palm fruit; the oil from the juicy pericarp of the fruit and the kernel from the hard nut in the centre of the fruit. The kernels were extracted from their outer shells by the Africans and shipped to Europe to be crushed for oil and cake.

This sounded well enough, but enthusiasm was modified by the reflection that the Congo was not yet covering its expenses, much less paying any return on capital outlay. And indeed two more years were to elapse before Greenhalgh was able to claim that it was doing so.

Whereas the H.C.B. was principally concerned with plantation and milling, and only secondarily with trade, the Lever Companies in West Africa were first and foremost mercantile: they bought and sold; but the most considerable of them neither grew nor processed fruit. The principal problem they raised in wartime was that of shipping, and Lever, as will be seen, spared neither trouble nor expense to solve it. If it could be solved the profits that could be made on the West African Trade would be far higher than in pre-war days—to be more precise anything from 400 per cent to 800 per cent higher. It is not surprising, therefore, that the various trading concerns which Lever's had taken over between 1910 and 1914 should have been both vigorous and profitable during the war. Even the Cavalla River Company, which Lever had once described as 'a business on the rocks' was by 1916 'round the corner'. MacIver's themselves were prosperous and expanding: their timber concessions, for instance, were enlarged during 1915 and 1916 to a total area of about 1,000 square miles, while their trade in groundnuts was built up from a few hundred tons in 1914 to 3,000 in 1915 and in 1916 they hoped 'to increase this quantity three-fold, if the report we hear as to the crop turns out to be correct'. 'Our goods Cash trade', W. K. Findlay reported at the same time, 'continues to improve and our monthly sales run from £12,000 to £15,000 . . . quite apart from barter trade.' Only Ratcliffe's of Sierra Leone had not been profitable, but even they had a balance on the right side by the end of 1916.

Encouraged, perhaps, by trading prosperity, and certainly in need of high quality oil for margarine, Lever in 1916 revived the coast mills. Foreseeing the shortage of raw materials, he was determined to draw his supplies from as many sources as possible, even at the risk of loss: '. . . it is much more important', he wrote, 'for both Godley and Liverpool to get a large quantity of palm kernels and ground nut oil than any question of mere accountancy in charging the products. Obviously we must see that we are on an economic basis, but whatever loss, if there is any loss, that the Mill shows must be set against the difficulties of obtaining supplies in England without advancing the market. I am satisfied that with the present high rates of freight, crushing on the Coast ought to be profitable. . . .' Unfortunately, he did not foresee that it would become impossible to ship the oil to Europe: that produce would pile up at the mills for lack of transport, and that after the war, when losses were running at the rate of £15,000 a quarter, there would be no alternative to closing the mills altogether because tropical produce, from being scarce and expensive, was to change into a drug on the market.

Three more businesses—John Walkden's, the Bathurst Trading Company, and King's of Bristol—were brought into the Lever West African group during the war, so that, by the time of the Armistice, operations were very widely dispersed along the Coast. Even after this expansion, however, the activities of the Lever African companies were small by comparison with those of the giants of the African trade—the Niger Company and the African and Eastern Trade Corporation.

The West African merchant during the war had no great difficulty, as we have seen, in buying produce cheaply on the Coast and selling it dearly in England; his most serious problem came between the two operations, for sea transport was scarce and expensive. The trouble was not entirely due to the war. The West African sea route was dominated by one shipping line: Elder Dempster's. By 1916 Lever's had made up their minds to go into shipping themselves. Their first move was to bring their steamer the *Kulambangra* from the Pacific for the Coast trade, but they had much larger future plans than that. If Lever's were to be independent of Elder Dempster's, four or five steamers would be necessary. Ships were expensive to buy but the profits on shipping were very high. Over and above any immediate profits, however, Lever's would be assured of carrying capacity to deal with their exports to Africa and their raw material imports from Africa. The only risk was that Elder Dempster's might take reprisals by entering the soap trade themselves but Lever's directors 'did not consider this serious . . .'

Towards the end of March 1916, Lever's began negotiations with Herbert Watson & Company of Manchester for the purchase of their fleet of six ships. They would give an annual cargo capacity of about 80,000 tons of which Lever's could take up about 8,675 tons outwards and 43,000 homewards themselves. There were several difficulties in the way: outward cargo might not be easy to come by; the Government might requisition the ships (they had already requisitioned two); the purchase money would have to be found at a time when money was extremely short; Elder Dempster's would certainly dislike the purchase and might cause trouble not only on the African route but also in other parts of the world. Nevertheless, the deal was closed, and for the sum of about £380,000 Lever Brothers became the owners of the six Watson ships.

It was a difficult trade which they thus entered, particularly in wartime. In the first place, none of the Lever directors knew much of the details of ship management: they had therefore to engage an outside firm to manage their fleet for them, and they were occasionally afflicted with an uneasy suspicion that perhaps they were paying too much for the services rendered. They therefore asked the advice of Mr. Gilbert Wheaton Fox, a Liverpool sugar broker who understood these matters, and very soon he became the only part-time director on the Lever Board. Then, even when they had bought the fleet, they were not its ultimate master, for in May 1917 the Government took control of the West African shipping trade (through a committee of the owners concerned) in order to ensure that private interest should not override national advantage in the allocation of tonnage. But the most difficult problem which they had to face was the replacement of lost ships. In June 1917, the *Delamere* was sunk: in October, two more ships went down. There arose immediately the question whether to replace at inflated wartime prices, or wait until after the war. Fox was in favour of waiting, for he foresaw a 'tremendous fall in freight' after the war, and his views sufficiently impressed the directors to persuade them to defer a decision from month to month. However difficult it might be to formulate future policy, the fact remained that for the present the venture was financially successful. In October 1917, when it had been operating for about eighteen months, Clarence Knowles summed up its results:

> Our fleet had enabled us to bring from West Africa large quantities of produce that would not otherwise have come

> forward, and that helped our markets generally for raw materials. MacIver's warehouses had been blocked at the time we entered into shipping, but with our ships MacIver's were able to go ahead and buy produce that they would not have been able to buy if we had not had the ships. It had further to be borne in mind that to-day's prices for the steamers would show a big profit, and in a word, good results had been more real than apparent. On broad principles the steamers' purchase had been a great success.

The Chairman was no less convinced of the wisdom of owning ships.

If the wartime history of Lever's African projects was happy, that of the Pacific Plantations was less so. In 1916, while general prosperity was reported on the Coast, Lever was compelled to admit that in the Solomons he was 'still unable to make money out of copra'. Meek, in Australia, still retained his faith in the project which he had been so largely responsible for launching. Coconut planting was 'the Gold Mine of the next twenty years, though it will have its ups and downs'. For a time, comforted by late wartime profits, Leverhulme allowed himself to be persuaded, though he continued to reflect uneasily on the problems of labour and cost in the Pacific.

Scarcely less important than the provision of tropical produce was the manufacture of hardened fat, especially after Planter's Margarine Company was added to the Lever organization. Lever's had secured themselves before 1914 by their contract with the De-No-Fa Company in Norway, by which they bought crude whale oil, the Norwegian company hardened it, and Lever's bound themselves to buy back a guaranteed quantity of the finished product. In March 1915, the Government refused to allow the shipment of oil to Norway. By 1917, the Government had taken over the distribution of whale oil in Great Britain and it was allocated to the three main hardening concerns as follows:

Lever's	47·4%	later 40%
Crosfield's . . .	31·6%	later 35%
Watson's (Olympia Oil and Cake Company) . .	21%	later 25%

The disruption of the De-No-Fa arrangements, combined with the steadily rising demand from Godley, made it important for Lever Brothers to expand their own hardening plant at Bromborough as rapidly as possible. The Chairman pressed for an increased output with his accustomed energy: by October 1917 the original target of 1,000 tons a week was reached; but by the end of the year the Chairman had once more raised his demand. He wrote: 'We are not at all exaggerating the demand there will be for hardened fat for edible and technical purposes when we aim at a total output of 2,000 tons per week.'

PART IV

CRISIS AND RECONSTRUCTION

1919–29

CHAPTER XVIII

MERIDIAN FRENZY AND ITS AFTERMATH

'I had a fancy to go and take a look at the city throngs, and I must admit that things are going so wonderfully and so beyond all Expectations that one stands paralysed and as if bound in chains—this was how it struck me yesterday—it is like nothing so much as if all the lunatics had escaped out of the Madhouse at once.'

From a letter written by a Dutch stockbroker in London to his correspondent in Holland at the time of the South Sea Bubble, January 1720

THE war ended as suddenly and unexpectedly as it had begun, leaving behind it a situation full of danger. For the first time in history, governments were faced with the problem of restoring to normality an economy every section of which had been distorted by the demands of war. People were optimistic and unreasoning, impatient to be rid of wartime controls so that they could get on with the work of replenishing not only capital goods but all those personal necessities and luxuries which they had been so long denied. Everywhere there was the itch to spend—to spend the wartime savings that had accrued to war workers, the bonuses granted to demobilized warriors and the profits earned by industrialists. Prices everywhere had risen during the war. At the time of the Armistice prices in Britain were about one hundred and thirty per cent above their pre-war level. Elsewhere in Europe they were higher.

Bowing to popular demand and sharing in the general optimism, the Government removed many of its controls and the replenishment boom swiftly and irresistibly assumed dangerous proportions. Prices rose even more steeply between 1918 and 1920 than they had done during the war. Early in 1920, the British wholesale index stood at 310. In France and Italy prices were twice as high, while in Germany the figure stood at just under 2,000. One of the least healthy aspects of the situation was the rush for capital. Businesses were bought up by men who had no interest in them except as a vehicle for capital appreciation, were recapitalized at inflated figures and sold to a gullible public. The banks themselves were swept along on the stream of popular optimism and provided loans on a scale which only added to the dangers of the situation.

Leverhulme himself shared to the full the prevailing mood of optimism. Although wartime restrictions had hindered the expansion of his businesses, the war itself, by increasing the purchasing power of the working class, by creating a shortage of butter and a huge demand for glycerine, had conjured up enormous possibilities of expansion. A month before the war ended he was brushing aside counsels of caution. 'As to people's talk, a well-known Liverpool man said 25 years ago that my ideas were too big at £1½ million Capital—so I cannot take these pessimistic views as of any value as a forecast for the future. My capital has always been planned for the future, not the immediate present, and I am convinced I am not too sanguine.' It was useless for the directors to argue, and on 30th January 1919, Lever Brothers' Authorized Capital duly mounted from £40,000,000 to £60,000,000, but of this total only about one third had so far been issued. By the middle of the year the figure was again raised—this time to £100,000,000. What were the plans Leverhulme had in mind which could justify such vast capital increases?

There was, first of all, the situation in the soap industry in Great Britain. In 1918 Leverhulme had perhaps half the soap trade in Britain—it is impossible to be more precise than that. His theory as to the future prospects of the industry was expressed laconically at this time: '. . . with increased wages comes increased spending and soap will get its share.' Of the two dozen or so producers who controlled nearly ninety per cent of the trade, his business was far the largest. With one of his competitors, the C.W.S., negotiation was clearly out of the question, but there were others over which he dearly wished to exercise full sovereignty—Crosfield's, Gossage's, John Knight's. His reasons were not primarily economic; indeed they were hardly economic at all. Leverhulme had a long memory. Perhaps he still remembered 1906.

Secondly, there was the margarine business. Planter's had entered the post-war period quite prosperous. The demand for butter substitutes seemed likely to continue indefinitely. K. V. Hansen, Planter's manager, estimated the country's requirements at from 6,000 to 8,000 tons weekly. When the existing plants were fully developed, Planter's capacity would be about 2,500 tons a week. In addition, Leverhulme had plans for a factory between Bath and Bristol to supply the West Country, another at Renfrew, and possibly one in Ireland. If production began to outrun demand, he was confident he could capture trade from competitors. He had done it with soap; why not with margarine?

Abroad, there were boundless possibilities. Even before the war, plans had existed for a soap company in New Zealand. To this was added a project for an Italian company. In Scandinavia, where neutrality had brought prosperity and an unprecedented rise in the standard of living, fair prospects seemed to beckon. The Norwegian fat-hardening plant De-No-Fa, in which Lever's already had a fifty per cent holding, provided a base for operations. Soap factories in Denmark and Sweden would act as an outlet for certain grades of hardened oil produced by De-No-Fa.

All these manufacturing developments would in turn increase the demand for raw materials. Moreover, the war itself, by nurturing the growth of margarine factories in Britain, by cutting out the German oil milling industry and by diverting the stream of West African produce to Britain, had wrought a major change in the structure of the raw material buying organization and the seed crushing industry. Undeterred either by those who thought his schemes too large or those who doubted the soundness of his economics, Leverhulme prepared for action when it should become possible. He would go into oil milling: for the British oil-milling industry, greatly expanded during the war, was handling an unprecedented variety of oil-bearing seeds and enjoying large profits from its new customers, the margarine factories. Soap, margarine, oil milling—each led back to the tropics or the whaling grounds. He would, if opportunity offered, increase his existing stake in raw material production. Such, one may imagine, were the more or less rational calculations which led Leverhulme to increase his capital. But behind the rationalism lay motives less explicit but not less powerful. 'I work at business', he said in 1914, 'because business is life. It enables me to do things.' The urge to do things had not been blunted by four years of war or the approach of old age—he was now nearly seventy. Indeed, there were bigger things to be done now than ever before.

The drive to extend Lever's control over the remaining sections of the British soap industry began with a renewal of litigation against Brunner Mond's. Under the terms of settlement which ended the litigation of 1917, Lever's had been given a half interest in Crosfield's and Gossage's, the two large soap firms which had earlier passed under Brunner Mond's aegis.[1] The alliance had never been cordial, and the terms of agreement had never, in Leverhulme's view, been satisfactorily observed by the other party. In March 1919, therefore, he went to law once again, alleging that the directors appointed by Lever's to the board of Crossage's (as the combined firms were known) had been improperly prevented from learning anything about the secret technical processes operated by Crossage's. He therefore asked the Court for a declaration that Lever Brothers were entitled to an equal share in the running of Crossage's with Brunner Mond's. This the judge refused to grant, saying that 'for a long time he failed to understand what the claim was in this case'. It was evident that the alliance could not continue. Either Brunner's or Lever's must be sovereign. Leverhulme was determined that sovereignty should be his. Brunner Mond's were no less determined to exploit the strength of their legal position, and when the Ordinary Capital of the Crossage business finally passed to Lever's control in October 1919 it was at a cost of £4 million. (For some two-thirds of its £900,000 Ordinary shares, Brunner Mond's had paid just over £2¼ million in 1911.) The prize was great, for Crosfield's brought into the Combine a great soap business and a unique fund of technical information, but the cost was heavy.

In the months that followed, other large soap firms followed Crossage's into the Lever combine on equally lavish terms. Price's Patent Candle Company's output of soap was not large, even when the production of their associate firm D. & W. Gibbs was included, but their main business of candle making made them a competitor to be reckoned with, especially in South Africa, where they competed for valuable contracts with the mines, and in China. Leverhulme's offer was too attractive to refuse and they were added to the family in October 1919 at a

[1] See Chapter IX.

price which included an honorarium for disturbing the directors so generous that, as one of Price's directors put it, 'I am afraid they will all avail themselves of it'.

One more large private soap business remained—John Knight's of London. Lever's had had a stake in Knight's since 1913,[1] but not such as would give them anything like firm control of the business, at the head of which stood Leverhulme's bitter rival of 1906, J. W. Hope. Pocketing his pride, Leverhulme again made an offer which proved irresistible. He had opposed in the past any combination with Messrs. Lever Brothers, Hope told his shareholders, '. . . therefore he assured them that if the offer they had received was not of such a tempting nature he would not for one moment have brought it forward, but they must look at things as they were'. And, with more prudence than many of his contemporaries, he warned the shareholders that their business was 'nearing the peak of high profits. . . . ' The shareholders accepted his advice and in April 1920 Leverhulme achieved his purpose: the control of John Knight's.

These were not the only soap companies which Lever Brothers acquired in 1919 and 1920, but they were the largest, and their acquisition marks a definite point in the development of the business. After many years and at great cost, Leverhulme had at last grasped the prize of which he had (as he saw it) been robbed in 1906: undisputed leadership of the British soap industry. He did not, it was true, control more than about sixty per cent of the national production, but even that degree of control was sufficient to give rise to anxiety in some circles. Lever's had such control of the soap industry, it was said, that they could fix prices to suit themselves, which naturally meant the sacrifice of the consumer. It was in response to such allegations that the Government set up a Committee to inquire into soap prices as it had done with regard to a number of other commodity prices.[2] (The price of household soap in 1920 was 11d. a pound, as compared with 3½d. in 1914—an increase exactly corresponding to the rise in the British wholesale price index in the same period.)

[1] See Chapter VIII.

[2] It was a sub-committee of the Standing Committee on Trusts. The Chairman was Sir William Beveridge.

To a large extent Leverhulme conducted his own defence before the Committee. He told them that 'he considered the terms [of his purchases] were justified by the assets and potentialities of the businesses, and that resultant economies would meet the increased commitments'. He pointed out that if he had not followed costs down immediately, neither had he in the past followed them up. His prices and profits were fair. He not only denied that his companies had charged unfair prices: he denied that they could even if they would, for the forces of competition would quickly operate to frustrate any such plan. Soap making was a simple process and exaggerated prices would quickly bring new manufacturers into the market as well as imported soaps from the United States. And, indeed, even as he spoke, plans were maturing amongst the oil millers to enter the soap trade, and the C.W.S. were expanding their production. Nor was it to be long before American soaps were to invade the British market. It was, however, hardly possible for the Committee to accept Leverhulme's arguments. They were bound by their terms of reference to take the short view. By the time they came to their deliberations, costs of raw materials had fallen. Why had the price of soap remained static? Leverhulme's evidence was by no means unconvincing. He emphasized the complexity of calculating costs and profits in a time when all prices were fluctuating and explained the necessity of using up stocks bought at heavy cost. But the Committee were left with the conviction that soap prices were too high. They therefore ordered that they should be reduced at once, best household soap being cut from 11d. to 9d. a pound.

On a short view, the Committee were probably right. For Leverhulme's real justification lay in a conception too visionary and impalpable to have much appeal for a committee immediately answerable to an irritable public opinion. There is not much doubt that the cost of soap to the public at this time included a contribution towards the cost of keeping afloat a number of other ventures very dear to Leverhulme's heart—particularly his West African projects. The conception underlying his economic policy was that the fortunes of the manufacturing side of his business were bound up with the fortunes of his raw material ventures in a swings-and-roundabouts relationship. When raw materials were cheap and plentiful, the consumer of soap and margarine would reap the benefit of cheap prices. When costs rose, the position would be reversed. In any case, consumers would benefit from the economies of large-scale production and Lever Brothers' risks would be spread. The trouble in 1920 and 1921 was that the storm had broken on the raw material ventures with such appalling fury that these predictions were temporarily falsified. For this once, the home consumer was being asked to pay in order that Leverhulme's conception of his business might not be utterly destroyed. It was faith versus reason: the long view against the short. On any rational calculation—and there were not lacking many ready to offer such prudent counsel—Leverhulme would have been well advised to cut his losses in West Africa and get out while he could. Against this, Leverhulme could only pit his faith in the ultimate rightness of his policy in Africa. Here, he was convinced, he had not only a personal asset but a national asset of incalculable value. That was a view which could only be held privately: it was too much to expect politicians and publicists to accept it. Ultimately Leverhulme was to be proved right and his critics wrong. The reader will decide for himself whether the facts justified the secrecy in which Lever Brothers' affairs were shrouded in these years.

In many ways, the raw material ventures of the post-war period looked like a natural continuation of Lever's pre-war policy of securing his supply line. The attempt to buy the big Olympia oil mill at Selby in Yorkshire from Joseph Watson seemed a policy naturally descended from the old Vicksburg project or the building of the Port Sunlight oil mill. Possession of Olympia would have given Lever Brothers milling capacity to cover half their total requirements of oil: a valuable link in the chain. In the event, Lever's were outbid by Jurgens' and were left to buy the much smaller Barton & Waterhouse mill at Hull as a consolation prize. Olympia remained to serve as a counter in a later and bigger game. For the moment it was only symptomatic of the tendency to vertical concentration in the industry. The purchase of the Southern Whaling and Sealing Company was in line with the same policy. Based in South Georgia, this company had an average annual production of four to five thousand tons of whale oil. With the growth of their margarine production, whale oil was essential to Lever Brothers. Leverhulme had no hesitation in buying the company, even though he knew nothing about whaling and even though it cost him dear—£4 for each £1 share. The politics of the world of oils and fats were bitter and complicated, as the history of the Hydrogenators Limited and the De-No-Fa purchase had demonstrated.

Following close upon these projects, the purchase of the Niger Company in 1920 may be considered merely a logical extension of the same policy, and indeed a more natural extension, for Lever Brothers had already a nucleus of trading companies in West Africa—MacIver's, Walkden's, King's, and Ratcliffe's—in addition to their Pacific and Congo plantations. What distinguished the Niger purchase from the earlier raw material projects was the scale of the company's operations, the vast sums involved, and the circumstances of the purchase which might well have brought the whole Lever edifice down in ruins.

The immediate impetus to this further extension of Lever's raw material ventures is not difficult to discern. The growing complex of manufacturing businesses called for a secure supply of oils and fats. To be secure, that supply had to be protected against the competition of other buyers and sellers. By 1919 a rough estimate would put the total annual demand of the Lever factories in Britain alone at a figure not far short of a quarter of a million tons. Their raw material companies in the Pacific and in Africa were not capable of supplying more than a small fraction of this demand. Hence Leverhulme's interest when, late in 1919, suggestions were mooted (apparently by the Niger Company itself) that he might be able to purchase a company which in that very year had handled nearly 100,000 tons of oil seeds.

The Niger Company was in truth no ordinary company. It traced its ancestry back to the United Africa Company, created by an amalgamation of the various trading interests on the Niger River which was accomplished in 1879 by one of the most remarkable men in the recent history of the Empire. George Taubman (he reverted to the paternal name of Goldie in 1887) has been described as 'the founder of Nigeria'; his title is not likely to be disputed. A slim, fair man, with piercing blue eyes, Goldie shunned publicity and remained throughout his life a firm believer in what he called 'the Chinese policy of silence'. From his arrival in 1877 he set himself, in face of contemporary opinion at home, to consolidate and secure British interests on the Niger. Goldie quickly decided that only a royal charter, conferring on his company the full support of Government in relation to the whole valley of the Niger, could enable him to fulfil his task. His first application in 1881 was refused on the grounds that the United African Company did not command the necessary capital. He thereupon launched the National African Company with a capital of a million sterling. Then in 1884–5 Germany called the West African Conference in Berlin. 'The scramble for Africa' had begun. So rapid had been Goldie's progress that at that conference Lord Salisbury could claim that 'the whole trade of the Niger basin is at the present moment exclusively in British hands'. The British Government declared a Protectorate over a large area of Southern Nigeria and in 1886 granted Goldie's Company a royal charter. It imposed on the company the duty to govern and preserve order, to discourage and ultimately abolish slavery, to levy customs to defray its administrative expenses, and to trade (though not to establish any monopoly). The vast territory in which the new chartered company (renamed the Royal Niger Company) was to operate was carefully defined. Its coastline extended from the Forcades River to the Nun mouth of the Niger and its treaty rights covered both banks of the Niger with its tributaries for a distance of about ten hours' journey inland, over the whole of the Sokoto and Gando Empires and over 'all the various independent pagan countries on the Benue up to a distance by water of almost one thousand miles from the sea'.

The Royal Niger Company's situation was not altogether enviable: certainly its task was far from easy. It was not popular with other European traders who accused it of establishing a monopoly, and it was hated by natives who saw their trading functions threatened. The men of Brass, who were east of Nun and therefore outside the company's boundaries and cut off from their natural markets, grumbled for nine years, and then attacked the company's trading headquarters at Akassa in 1895, burnt it, and ate most of their prisoners. Undeterred by such setbacks, Goldie went on with his work of pacifying the country and establishing law and order.

In 1897, at the head of a company force of 800 men, Goldie met and defeated 15,000 men commanded by the Emir of Nupé. For several years the Emir had been a thorn in the side of the company's stations on the Middle Niger, and the evil genius behind an unending series of slave raids against natives living under the company's protection. Another smaller Mohammedan State, west of the Middle Niger, Ilorin, had given similar trouble, and fell to Goldie after two days' fighting a little later. Immediately a company decree was issued which abolished the legal status of slavery through the company's territories.

By 1899, Lord Salisbury, anxious to remove any source of irritation which might imperil the success of the Anglo-French Convention of that year, decided that the administrative functions of the Company must be separated from its commercial activities. In 1900, therefore, the Company surrendered its charter, and some 382,000 square miles of Africa passed under direct British rule. Much still remained to be done, but, assured that the political foundations of Nigeria were securely laid, Goldie severed his connection with West Africa. The Royal Niger Company became The Niger Company and reverted to a purely commercial role. From moderate profits before the war, its earnings rose to gratifying dimensions during the war, when it made an average profit of over a quarter of a million per annum. In 1919 it was still a highly tempting prize.

How the negotiations began is obscure. All that is clear is that on 16th January 1920, while Leverhulme himself was in America, one of the Lever directors, John Inglis, called on Sir Robert Nivison, Lever Brothers' broker, and told him 'that Mr. Knowles had been carrying on negotiations with the Niger Company, that the directors were exceedingly anxious to buy it and that they thought they would have to give £6 a share'. Now the nominal value of the Niger Company's Ordinary Capital was £1¼ million, so that this price would represent an outlay of £7½ million—in cash, not shares. Nivison, not unnaturally, refused to commit himself. Meanwhile the Niger Company's directors put pressure on the prospective purchasers: other buyers were in the field—the Niger's great rival, the African and Eastern, and Elder Dempster's, the shipping firm, were darkly hinted at. Payment by exchange of shares was utterly refused. A decision had to be reached by 21st January. Still Nivison refused to commit himself. Failure to grasp the prize was unthinkable, so, without any concrete proposal for finding the money to pay, the Lever directors accepted on 21st January

1920 an agreement for the purchase of the Niger shares at a price of £6 10s. each. The payment (of rather more than £8 million) was to be made on or before 1st July 1920. Two points about this astonishing transaction should be noticed here: first, that there was no investigation of the accounts of the Niger Company before the agreement was signed; secondly, that the management of that company's affairs was to remain for a further five months in the hands of the Niger Company itself. Consideration of these things—if indeed they were considered at all in the feverish atmosphere of the times—did not deter Leverhulme from sending an approving telegram to Knowles: 'Congratulations. Price high but suicidal if we had let opportunity lapse.' And even the general manager of Lloyds Bank hastened to offer 'every consideration' to the requirements of Lever Brothers' new acquisition.

By the spring of 1920, the frenzy which had overtaken the business world was on the wane. Not since the end of the South Sea Bubble in 1720 had a comparable speculative mania subsided in such spectacular fashion. (As a matter of interest the two phenomena were separated by two hundred years to the month.) The storm broke first in the East: a bubble in silk burst in Japan; famine descended in India and starvation in China was accompanied by rebellion. Swiftly the storm passed to Europe where the swollen stream of purchasing power of 1919 had already dried up. Everywhere consumers were on strike against exorbitant prices, and the replenishment boom was on the wane. Government spending was cut drastically and the banks no less drastically reduced credits—too drastically perhaps. Prices fell rapidly and were to continue to fall for another year until stability was finally reached at a level about fifty per cent above pre-war figures.

Oils and fats were peculiarly sensitive to these disturbances. Even by March 1920 the Lever management was noting with some concern the growing stocks of unsold soap, a marked slackening in trade, and above all the considerable fall in raw material prices. In February 1920, at the peak of the boom, palm kernel oil was fetching £115 a ton; by July it was only worth £55. Palm oil fell in the same period from £98 to £53 a ton. The gravity of such a collapse in prices will be apparent when it is recalled that Lever Brothers and their associated companies were holding raw material stocks which had cost them £18 million. What was even more serious was that the Niger Company—still managed by its old Board and independent of any control by Lever Brothers—was, in this very period, not only holding large stocks but was actually attempting to support prices by buying heavily in the open market.

Not the least serious aspect of the loss of confidence was its effect on the money markets. Some decision about the financing of the Niger purchase could not be much longer delayed but as the clouds of depression continued to gather money became daily more difficult to raise. 'When I returned from New York', wrote Leverhulme, 'I found all my colleagues cheering and hurrahing over the Niger purchase and not one thought being given to what it meant to raise and provide £8 million by July 1st.'

An issue of £4 million by Lever Brothers in March was all absorbed in the main business; though it is a measure of the feverish confusion which prevailed that until June Nivison was under the impression that the issue was intended to provide part of the Niger purchase money. Thus within two months of the day when £8 million must be provided, the directors were still without any clear idea where it was to come from. Blow followed blow, for while Leverhulme was still toying with the idea of yet another £4 million issue to help to bridge the gap, it transpired that the Niger Company was under obligation to its bankers to repay an overdraft of nearly £2 million. In spite of signs that the slump was deepening—departments at Port Sunlight were being closed for a day or a day and a half each week—Leverhulme did not hesitate. To his liability to pay £8 million on July 1st, he now added another responsibility—that of dealing with the Niger Company's overdraft. But as May drew to a close even Leverhulme began to betray signs of anxiety. 'It is becoming dangerously near to the time that we must have our plan cut and dried', he wrote to Knowles, and went on to command him to find ways and means of finding cash to supplement his proposed issue of £4 million shares. For he assumed (as he said) that there would be 'no slip or setback in Sir Robert Nivison's underwriting of Lever Brothers' proposed issue of four million eight per cent Preferred shares. . . .' Once again he was to be disillusioned. On the evening of 26th May, the day after he wrote to Knowles, he visited Nivison at his house. Both men were under great strain and a tense argument ensued. It ended with Nivison's refusing to underwrite an issue on Leverhulme's terms in the existing state of the money market. Thus Leverhulme's worst fear was realized. He was no nearer to raising £8 million—let alone £10 million—than he had been in January. There was only one course open to him; Lever Brothers must float the new issue themselves, unsustained by any underwriter. So the issue was made. What was more it was fully subscribed (except for £450,000 which was taken up by an associated company); and, since Leverhulme was not a man to do things by halves, at the same time the Issued Capital of Lever Brothers Limited was increased from £27·7 million to £46·7 million and completely reorganized. To the proceeds of the June issue were added some leavings from the March issue, and further sums raised by an issue in Holland. One way or another the necessary £8 million was duly scraped together and paid over on the stipulated date. But, as Leverhulme admitted, the transaction had severely strained the credit of the business; and there was another trial to come.

Having paid for his new venture, Leverhulme had to set about discharging its debts. The Niger Company's bankers begged 'formally to call for the repayment not later than 14th August 1920 of all monies due' to them by the Company. Recalling, no doubt, the friendly offers of January, Leverhulme turned to the banks for help. But times, it seemed, had changed. With strikes and dismissals at Port Sunlight, and trade generally in the grip of depression, the bankers were politely discouraging. 'May I say', wrote the first to be consulted, 'that I do not think anybody feels that your great Company is not perfectly good, the assets being what they are, but that a good many of us feel that you have gone ahead too quickly in view of a difficult financial situation. The truth is that there is not enough money to go round, and it has to be strictly rationed as, say, sugar or any other commodity.' Other bankers took up a similar attitude and the only constructive proposal that they could be induced jointly to recommend was that 'it would be in the interests of everybody that Lever Brothers Limited should dispose of the shares in the Niger Company . . . ' a policy which they suggested 'would put the parent company in a very much more healthy financial position. . . . ' Needless to say, the bankers' inspiration did not appeal to Leverhulme. He was never nearer disaster and the sacrifice of all his plans for the future than at this moment. Somehow, nevertheless, he managed to contrive not only to keep the overdraft open but even to reduce it in the months that followed.

The events of the summer of 1920 would have prompted most men to caution. Not so Lord Leverhulme, who, within a month of buying the Niger Company was busily engaged with a project for constructing at great expense facilities on the Mersey to receive ocean-going ships bringing their cargoes of raw materials from West Africa to Port Sunlight.[1] To suggestions that the expansion of his business should now cease he made characteristic reply. 'I know this is the parrot cry', he wrote to a financier, 'but the business can well rest after I have gone to view the daisies from the underside, and perhaps the business will be the better for that rest. . . . Believe me whilst I recognize that expansion may not be so rapid after my death [I also recognize] that consolidation will take its place. . . . The profits are more assured than any other commercial concern I know of.' His confidence undiminished, Leverhulme proceeded to plunge even more deeply into West Africa. Taking advantage perhaps of weakened nerves amongst the directors of the Niger's rival, the African and Eastern Trade Corporation, he signed, in September 1920, an agreement designed to give him control of that company. The African and Eastern had only assumed its latest form in the previous year: but this latest and largest merger, creating a second West African giant, was only the final sequel to a long story of rivalry and amalgamation on the Coast. One of its constituent firms—R. & W. King—dated its origins as far back as 1695. Swanzy's of London and Hatton & Cookson of Liverpool had traded on the Coast since the eighteenth century. Others—Alexander Miller of Glasgow and Thomas Harrison of Liverpool—were nineteenth-century businesses. Until the early years of the twentieth century, there had been a constant tendency towards mergers, from which, however, Miller's stood aloof. The reorganization of 1919 and the period of rapid expansion and acquisition which followed it might well give Leverhulme pause for thought. The attractions of a merger

[1] See also Chapter XV.

were twofold. The African and Eastern—and perhaps they only—had the men who could turn the Niger Company into a going concern. For, in truth, investigation, when it came, showed that not only the finances but the management of the Niger left much to be desired. Secondly, control of the Niger and the African and Eastern Companies would put a large proportion of the African merchanting trade into Lever Brothers' hands. That the proposal was ultimately dropped was due to the appalling chaos revealed by further investigations into the affairs of the Niger Company.

By the end of 1920 the question of the Niger Company's overdraft was once again becoming acute. To meet this, and urgent requirements for working capital, some £2 million was needed. By this time, the banks were thoroughly alarmed by what seemed to them the reckless improvidence of Leverhulme's policy and he himself was not unaware of the fact. There was one man—and perhaps only one man—who could save the situation. From America, where he was busily engaged on further adventures, Leverhulme cabled to his directors: 'Suggest you call in D'Arcy Cooper for assistance if he can help'. Francis D'Arcy Cooper was a member of the family firm of accountants, Cooper Brothers & Company, whose connection with Lever Brothers was as old as the Company itself. For some years before the war he had been closely concerned with their affairs. Army service had interrupted the connection but since the Armistice it had become stronger and more intimate than ever. But even Cooper, whose reputation amongst the bankers was unimpeachable, could not work miracles. His first issue of notes was a failure and the bankers were adamant against any further extension of the overdraft. By Sunday, 6th February 1921, they were willing to delay no longer. Unless they were given satisfaction on their own terms, the Niger Company's bankers threatened to issue a writ. Liquidation would be the inevitable consequence.

From this, as it seemed, well-nigh inescapable fate, the Niger Company was delivered by Cooper. Holding off the creditors with one hand he negotiated with the other terms for a loan from Barclays Bank—terms which, though onerous, were yet to prove the salvation of the Lever group. Financially, they involved the issue by Lever Brothers—clean against Leverhulme's lifelong prejudice—of Debenture Stock, nearly all of which was to be held by the bank as collateral security for their loan.[1] The management of the Niger Company was to be strengthened 'to their satisfaction'. There may have been other terms, dictated partly perhaps by the banks and partly by Cooper himself. Certainly from this time onwards, he acted with an authority which could only have proceeded from the tacit consent of Leverhulme; and for all his respect and even affection for Cooper, Leverhulme was not the man to hand over control of his business to another, however able, except under duress.

On 23rd February 1921, Cooper put the consequences of rejecting the bank's proposals bleakly before Leverhulme. The terms were for acceptance or rejection—not modification—and Leverhulme accepted. Throughout all the anxious negotiations of January and February 1921, he had remained in the background. For the first time, he had surrendered control of the policy of his business to another. But to the outside world, he was still the head—'the Chief'—as he always had been, and his bitterness against those who had, as he saw it, betrayed him, was publicly expressed. The address to the shareholders in April 1921 was made the occasion for a biting attack on the policy of the Niger directors in the period between January and July 1920, which, according to him—and with a certain amount of justice—was the main source of the troubles that had ensued. But more privately and even more pertinently, he wrote to Knowles, the director—next to himself—most responsible for the whole policy: 'What I should like you to do is to write myself . . . what answer I must make . . . when I am challenged by shareholders (and I am almost certain to be) as to why Lever Brothers did not give instructions to the Company's Auditors . . . to make a full investigation of the Niger Company's books before completing the deal'. To that question,

[1] Lever's dislike of Debentures sprang from the fact that Debentures, unlike shares, are legally debts. A Debenture represents a contractual obligation on a company's part to pay, at specified dates, the interest, or principal, or both, whether or not profits are being earned. Any failure by the company to meet these obligations entitles the Debenture holders to certain remedies, usually to appoint a Receiver. Preference or Ordinary shareholders, on the other hand, being proprietors and not creditors, cannot sue at law for their dividends, which are payable only out of such part of the profits earned (if any), as the directors may decide to distribute.

Knowles might fairly have answered that the directors of Lever Brothers were hardly trained to shoulder such responsibilities. It was probably the first occasion in the history of the Company when 'the Chief' had left a major issue of policy in any hands other than his own. In the feverish days of 1920 they were left on their own, and in their anxiety to escape the odium which would certainly have been theirs had they missed the opportunity of the century, they were panicked into a catastrophic imprudence. As Nivison had not failed to point out after his breach with Leverhulme, the whole problem had been immensely complicated by the chairman's own prolonged absences from England during the year. And thereby hung another tale.

The Niger purchase was not the only commitment undertaken at this time. Like Anton Jurgens[1] at the same time, Leverhulme was attracted by the great potentialities of the edible fat market in the States. In November 1919, he had sailed for America to discuss with the American Linseed Company proposals for taking an interest in their new margarine business. By January, a preliminary agreement was signed which foreshadowed heavy capital expenditure. While the lawyers argued over details, Leverhulme's mind turned to the question of raw material supplies—especially coconut oil—for his American ventures, new and old. While in America he had met Mr. Carl W. Hamilton, the President of the Philippine Refining Corporation, an amalgamation of three American-owned companies operating in various parts of the Islands. According to Mr. Hamilton, they would provide 100,000 tons of coconut oil a year. Mr. Hamilton was a man after Leverhulme's own heart. 'I must say', he told his colleagues, 'I admire the nerve and agility with which Mr. Hamilton sets to work. He bought a lot of old tanks when tanks were unprocurable and got them for an old song and had them fixed near San Francisco. He now buys some old machinery and is going to have it fixed in the Philippine Islands. All this shows that Mr. Hamilton is a man of resource.' It only remained to add that he was born the son of a miner, had gone to Yale at his own expense, and even while a student had worked up a business in ironing and pressing clothes which he sold after graduation for $40,000: that he shared Leverhulme's

[1] See Book II, Chapter XI.

love of art, being the possessor of 'an enormously valuable and really wonderful lot of the earliest masters', and that he was earnestly interested in religion and good works, having at one time thought of becoming a missionary. After negotiations only a trifle less perfunctory than the Niger purchase itself, the agreement with Hamilton was signed. In return for an investment of two million dollars, Leverhulme acquired shares which (according to his own view) were 'readily saleable at two hundred per cent premium or three times their face value. . . .' In return, Lever Brothers, Boston, or associated companies were to have first refusal of all oil and products of the Philippine business. 'The whole attraction . . . to myself', Leverhulme wrote, 'was that . . . to have first offer of large quantities of copra oil in the U.S. (which is the basis of the raw material used by the American Linseed Company in margarine) would be a great advantage.' Mr. Hamilton was to have $1,000,000 Common Stock and a ten-year agreement.

Such were the largest commitments which prompted capital increases. The element of risk was present in them all but for all of them it could at least be argued that they bore some organic relationship to Lever Brothers' original line of business: they were all connected with oils and fats. It is less easy to understand some of the other projects of the time. Why, for example, was it considered desirable for Lever Brothers to become part owner of an engineering firm and a paper mill? The engineering firm was J. G. Jackson Limited and the investment cost £50,000. Some months later, Leverhulme was to write: 'I have never myself understood why this business was purchased. I have never seen that it could possibly be of any interest to Lever Brothers or associated companies.' The Thames Paper Company Limited [renamed in 1923 the Thames Board Mills Limited] was certainly a more reasonable proposal, for the object was stated to be 'to secure our supplies' of paper for packing: but it was also a great deal more expensive, costing exactly ten times the Jackson purchase—half a million pounds. Mention should also be made of the purchase of the Sanitas Disinfectant Company,[1] of Trufood (bought to give Lever Brothers patents for their margarine manufacturing), of a Welsh limestone quarry, bought to secure a supply of abrasive materials, of proposals to

[1] Sold again in 1926.

buy a palm oil plantation in Sumatra, a sawmill in Plymouth, and a colliery in the North of England. Some of these can be explained by the notion of a vertical combine, others only by the economic madness which had engulfed even the sanest of business men and sent prudence into temporary exile.

Finally, mention must be made of a group of projects of a quite different kind. They were, in the first instance, purely private ventures of Leverhulme's, having no relation to his main business whatever. Indeed the largest of them—the purchase of the greater part of the Islands of Lewis and Harris in the Outer Hebrides—was in all probability prompted by the desire to own an estate on which he could spend the increased leisure to which he looked forward in 1917. Lewis was bought in 1918, South Harris in May 1919, and North Harris in the following November. The Islands quickly took a hold on his romantic imagination. Philanthropy—for that was what it was in spite of all his denials—the desire 'to organize, organize, organize', and a hankering after feudal grandeur, combined to produce giant schemes for the improvement of the Islands and their people. The story of his plans—to organize and extend the fishing and tweed weaving industries, to build ports, canning factories, roads, gasworks, electric plants, laundries, and other industries — has been told a number of times[1] and need not be repeated. It is enough to recall that in Lewis at any rate, he was defeated by the combined opposition of the crofters and the Board of Agriculture and ultimately departed after explaining his motives to the Islanders in a remarkable speech which ended thus: 'I am like Othello, with my occupation gone and I could only be like the ghost of Hamlet's father, haunting the place as a shadow.'

The immediate importance of the Hebridean exploit was to increase enormously the financial embarrassments in which their author found himself after the Niger fiasco of June 1920. There was a remoter importance, too. In his anxiety to create a reliable marketing organization to handle the products of the Islands' fisheries, he bought a chain of retail fish shops. The first was acquired in February 1919 and by the end of 1921 a chain of three hundred and sixty shops, the Mac Fisheries, had been established. Amongst the subsidiary groups acquired as the

[1] Notably in the *Life* by his son and in *Highland Journey*—Colin Macdonald (Moray Press, Edinburgh & London, 1943).

result of this policy were several which already had their own supply of fisheries, ranging from the Aberdeen Steam Trawling Company in North Scotland to the Helford Oysterage in the Duchy of Cornwall. In the same sortie may be included his purchase of an interest in the fish canning business of Angus Watson & Company of Newcastle. Here again, the origins of the transaction were seemingly personal rather than economic, for Angus Watson was an old employee of Lever Brothers. Later his ascent in the business world had been rapid but the capital shortage had overtaken him as it had many others and at the time of the investment he was only too glad of Leverhulme's assistance.

Thus, from being virtually a retirement hobby, the Islands exploit had become an immense economic venture on its own. Fisheries—fish shops—canning industries; here were the makings of another and quite independent 'vertical' combine. As yet it bore no relation to Lever Brothers' main business financially and virtually none in any other way. As Leverhulme wrote to a friend in 1918: the Island of Lewis and canned fish 'can only be remotely connected with Lever Brothers' business. Still, as you know, there are by-products of fish oil which may be of interest to Lever Brothers.' It was a slender thread. Yet under the stress of circumstances, the whole of this embryonic combine was also to be grafted on to Lever Brothers' business.

By the end of 1920, it was apparent even to Leverhulme that continuing disaster must put an end to his schemes for expansion. After a slight rally in the autumn, the fall in raw material prices had gone on unchecked. Lever Brothers' own losses on raw material stocks were estimated in December at nearly two million pounds. What the losses of the Niger Company were it is difficult to say: certainly they were far larger than Lever Brothers' own. But it was not only the raw material side of the business which was hard hit by the slump. Planter's margarine had been feeling the pinch of fierce competition since rationing had been abolished early in 1919. The first quarter of the year brought heavy losses and for the whole year the loss per ton was calculated at nearly £2. In 1920 things were no better, for Planter's, like the Dutch companies, continued to feel the effects of the disastrous competition of the Maypole Dairy Company.[1]

[1] See Book II, Chapter XV.

To some extent, Planter's difficulties were no doubt due to inexperience of the problems of manufacturing and, especially, of selling margarine. But even more they arose from the removal of the artificial protective screen behind which the company had sheltered during the war. Peace removed the windbreak; the two basic assumptions upon which Planter's had been founded —that there existed in peacetime England a large unexploited market for margarine, and that Lever's could easily invade their rivals' markets—were now for the first time exposed to the test of reality.

Yet, when all was said and done, the main trading activity of Lever Brothers remained the manufacture and sale of soap. And although the slump from April 1920 hit the soap trade hard, it yet remained sufficiently prosperous to counterbalance the fearful losses sustained by other departments of the business. That, at any rate, is the only conclusion that can be drawn from the fact that, somehow or other, Leverhulme managed to pay all his Preference dividends and to declare an Ordinary dividend of twenty per cent for 1920. A fine gesture of defiance; but there must have been others who shared the bewilderment with which this news was received in knowledgeable circles in the City. 'Read in cold print', said the *Investor's Chronicle* of the Chairman's Speech, 'we confess that his remarks leave us with a feeling of emptiness'.

During the following year the pattern of the future, though still blurred, began to emerge. In size, the Lever group had few equals in the world. Its authorized capital stood at £130 million, of which £46·7 million had been issued. There were one hundred and fifty-eight associated companies, and so far as the United Kingdom soap trade was concerned, one director could say that 'the Co-operative Wholesale Society was practically the only outsider'. That was an exaggeration, but it was true that the C.W.S. was the only large competitor left—for the time being. Besides soap, Lever Brothers had also their margarine business, represented primarily by the vast plant built at Bromborough and capable of refining and hardening materials sufficient to sustain a production of margarine at the rate of 2,500–3,000 tons a week. Overseas, there were soap factories and ancillary plants in many European countries and in four Dominions. In America, the stresses of 1921—shortage of money on Lever's side and threats of a lawsuit under the Sherman Act against the American Linseed Company—caused the agreement in respect of that company to be abandoned, though not before Lever Brothers, Boston, had issued $21,000,000 Common Stock in anticipation of the deal. It was too late on the other hand to cancel the purchase of the Philippine Company whose only justifiable purpose was to supply the Linseed Company with its raw materials for margarine, and it was left, for the moment purposeless, on Lever's hands. Another raw material scheme—the proposal to buy the African and Eastern—was jettisoned; but, dominating all else, there remained the Niger Company, loaded with debt, with a heavy burden of stocks grievously depreciated, and with a management whose defects grew every day more apparent.

The underlying assumption governing the entry into the raw material business—whether in the Congo, in West Africa, in the Solomons, or in the Antarctic whaling grounds—was that possession of such resources might give Lever Brothers an advantage and at worst could not bring disadvantage since prices in the oils and fats markets would always be the same for their competitors as for them; to them, in fact, would fall also the profits in times of raw material scarcity. Even in 1920 this might have held, for Lever Brothers' own West African companies had actually sold heavily in the spring of 1920 as soon as the market had begun to slide, avoiding losses and perhaps making some little profit. But tied as they all were to the misguided giant who was their neighbour and ally, the fruits of their prudence were merely cast away. The mistakes of the Niger Company governed the fate of all for its influence extended far beyond its own losses. As Leverhulme pointed out to his colleagues in November 1920, Lever Brothers, the soap makers and margarine makers, were now compelled to specialize in the use of West African oils and fats to the exclusion of other and possibly cheaper materials, in order to support their West African interests. 'My feeling is', he concluded, 'that we are no longer free to buy in the cheapest market during the next six months.' There was, it seemed, a darker side to the whole theory of 'vertical integration'. Instead of bringing independence, security and profit, it could bring bondage, insecurity and loss. The position was best summarized by Leverhulme himself, thus: 'We are tied to the West African market, otherwise our position will be extremely difficult in dealing with our West African interests'. In short, Lever Brothers' costs might well be higher for the time being than those of competitors who were free to buy materials in the cheapest market.

The immediate consequences of the disastrous collapse of the raw material markets were grievous losses for all the raw material companies. Against these losses stood the profits once again being made by the soap trade. True, the export trade was having a difficult time—it had dropped to perhaps less than half its 1920 sales value—but the home and overseas factories were recovering their balance. Indeed, once the stocks of raw materials bought dearly in 1919 and early 1920 had been disposed of, they found themselves able to sell soap at a profit per ton which reached unheard of levels—and this at a time when sales figures were beginning to pick up from the low levels of 1920. Home companies showed a sound profit. Overseas companies made a good contribution—America, Belgium, Holland, and Canada doing especially well. Every penny of these profits, and more, was nevertheless required to pay the dividends on the Preference shares held by soap companies acquired so expensively since 1918. For the time being also, soap profits were having to carry raw material losses. The fact was suspected by the official committee which inquired in 1921 into prices in the soap trade. It was nevertheless unfair to conclude that the whole burden was borne by the consumer. To enable the company to write off certain losses, the chairman, as Ordinary shareholder, made a large private contribution, and other investments were written up to their estimated value; and such was the essential strength of the Lever Business, such was the audacious skill of its chairman—and such, it should be added, were the relatively complaisant terms of the Companies Acts of the day—that a profit of £4 million could be shown, out of which all fixed charges for Debentures and Preference Capital were met, an Ordinary dividend of ten per cent paid and large sums placed to reserve. So that an admiring shareholder, after reflecting on these marvels which had been performed in 'a period of bad trade such as had never been seen by any man or woman present in this room' went on to wish aloud that he had had the good sense to put all his money into Lever Brothers, instead of 'scattering it up and down with the idea of not having too many eggs in one basket'. At the time, such confidence was still premature; twelve months later, it would have been amply justified. Debts and Debentures might remain, but the issue was no longer in doubt: the business had weathered the storm. There remained the indispensable phase of retrenchment and reform. For the Niger purchase had not only changed the structure of the company: by demonstrating beyond any reasonable doubt that the personal autocracy by which the business had been built up was no longer adequate, it was to change the whole *ethos* of the business.

CHAPTER XIX

THE FIRST PHASE OF RECOVERY

1921–5

'. . . we are not entirely our own masters at the present moment and I am not captain of my own ship and shall not be until the Debentures are paid off.'

Lord Leverhulme, 1921

THE years that followed the business crisis of 1920 were troubled ones in Europe generally. In Britain they were a time of deflation. The landslide in prices in that year had dealt a blow to confidence and recovery was slow. An all round contraction in the volume of trade brought in its wake mass unemployment; in May 1921 there were two and a half million men out of work and even by the end of 1923, the figure was still nearly a million and a quarter. In Europe—and especially in Germany—the inflation continued and a price index for Germany based on 1913 figures showed figures for November 1923 that were so high as to be almost meaningless. Only the neutrals—and Britain—managed to keep their currencies relatively 'strong'. The dislocation of currencies only added another argument for higher protective tariffs. Reparations and war debts added to the confusion.

The Threefold Problem

This was the economic background against which Leverhulme had to try to restore the fortunes of his business. The problem he faced—he was now in his early seventies—was threefold. First, he must reduce this vast conglomeration of individual firms to some sort of administrative order. Second, he must pursue efficiency and economy in the factories and offices, cutting away the accretions of a long war. Third, he must face once more the revival of serious competition in the soap trade.

Quite apart from the threatened cataclysm of 1920, the very size of the business would have rendered some degree of administrative reorganization necessary. In 1921, the authorized capital stood at £130 million, issued capital at £47 million.

Nearly three and a quarter millions were required to pay the Preference dividends alone.[1] On top of this had been superimposed Debentures to the tune of nearly £8 million, carrying interest at five to seven per cent, as well as temporary, but heavy, bank loans. Criticism of this financial structure was not lacking. The burden of prior fixed charges, it was said, put Lever Brothers' Preference shares on the same level of risk as Ordinary shares in less overweighted companies. Moreover, under the agreements by which Lever Brothers had acquired certain associated companies those companies had come to hold a considerable proportion of Lever Brothers' Preference capital[2]: but to this had been added Lever shares taken up by associated companies to support the market. By 1922, capital held in this way came to over £7 million. As yet, this vital fact was not revealed by the printed accounts, where the trading and shareholding functions of the parent company were combined—some might have said confused. The profit figure shown on the balance sheet was misleading unless reduced by the amount which was owed in dividends to associated companies. There was criticism, too, of the provision whereby the chairman had the right to call for the issue of certain classes of shares to himself at par so that he in turn could sell them at market prices and retain the profit. Finally, the decision to 'write up' assets in 1920 attracted adverse comment in the City. 'Obviously', remarked the *Investors' Chronicle*, 'if

[1] The relationship between Preference and Ordinary capital was as follows:

£	s.	d.				
23,567,011	0	0	7%	Cumulative	Preference	Shares
15,469,362	0	0	8%	,,	,,	
1,500,000	0	0	20%	,,	Preferred	Ordinary
3,000,000	0	0	20%	,,	,,	A
262,000	0	0	20%	,,	,,	B
903,949	5	0	5%	,,	,,	
2,280,000	0	0		Ordinary Shares		
£46,982,322	5	0				

[2] It happened in this way: after the acquisition by Lever's of the Ordinary capital of certain companies there remained outside investors who held Preference shares in these companies. To ensure payment of their dividends they or their representatives stipulated in the agreements conferring control on Lever's that Lever's should issue to these companies sufficient of Lever Brothers' Preference capital to enable them to pay their Preference dividends, no matter what might happen to their trading operations.

you own all the shares in any Company you can call the value of them what you like. But the prudent man would be slow in valuing his own investments to offset definite loss in one direction by theoretical gains in another.'

Most of these defects to which critics pointed may be traced to one source. The control of this vast business with world-wide ramifications was still a personal autocracy, just as it had been over thirty years before when it consisted of a small factory at Warrington. Its organization and finances reflected faithfully the personality of the author—his conviction that the business was his personal creation, that the risk of loss fell on him and him alone (as sole Ordinary shareholder) and that so long as the consumer got a good article at a fair price, his workpeople a fair deal, and the Preference shareholders their dividends, the rest was for him to decide. In ordinary times all these views might command a good deal of sympathy. Certainly there is no need to challenge the sincerity with which they were held, nor the contention that responsibility must lie where the risk lies. Even the controversial matter of shares issued to Leverhulme at par could be countered by the argument that resulting loss would only fall on the Ordinary shareholder. The trouble was that the times were not normal, and the errors of 1920 had intruded a new element into the financial structure. Along with the entry of the bankers as Debenture holders upon the scene, had come a measure of external control. Hard though the decision was, Leverhulme had had to accept it and it was to prove, in the long run, the salvation of the business. From the early months of 1921, Francis D'Arcy Cooper was consulted on matters of policy as if he had been a director, though in fact he did not join the Board officially until 1923. It is reasonable to infer that his appointment was made with the blessing of the banks, possibly even at their instance. Certainly he held a position quite different from any of the other directors, all of whom were Leverhulme's own nominees. At the same time, Leverhulme had sufficient generosity to see the matter in the best possible light, and he remarked to Angus Watson that Cooper was 'one of the type of men that I consider most resemble a warm fire and people naturally seem to come up to him for warmth'.

It is probably no mere fancy to see the hand of Cooper at work in the administrative reorganization of these years. The

Policy Council, as is the habit of committees, had grown overlarge in its nine years of life: from its original membership of nine, it had become a body of perhaps twenty or more. It was too big to take broad and rapid decisions on high policy. In January 1921, therefore, an 'Inner Cabinet'—the Special Committee—was established. Its original members were the chairman and his son, and two directors, Harold Greenhalgh and John McDowell. But they took power 'to co-opt any professional gentleman not being a director of the Company to assist and advise them'—a formula which spelt Cooper as clearly as the letters of his name. By July, the new Committee was working smoothly and the Policy Council met for the last time.

Below the Special Committee came other more specialized committees—one to control the manufacturing companies, another for finance and yet another to manage the West African interests. The organization was left flexible and in fact was altered to meet changing conditions. Originally, the manufacturing companies were grouped territorially but in 1923 this gave way to grouping by types of product. Each member of the board in charge of such a committee held regular meetings with the chairmen of the companies under his control; the business of the board itself was thus reduced to resolving controversial points of policy where agreement could not be reached in the group itself. For the Finance Committee there was certainly work enough in these years—above all the delicate negotiations with the banks. One result of its operations, however, appeared almost at once to the public eye. The Balance Sheet published in 1922 revealed for the first time the amount of capital held internally—that is to say by associated companies. The amount was then nearly £8 million; by 1925 it dropped to just over £5½ million. For this revelation there was as yet no legal requirement and again it may be concluded that the move originated with D'Arcy Cooper.

Nowhere was reorganization more necessary than in the counsels of the Niger Company. Lord Scarbrough, its chairman, and four of his colleagues retired in 1921, and two of Lever Brothers' own directors joined the Niger Board. But Leverhulme was more concerned with events in Africa than events in London, and in the early summer of the same year his son, Hulme Lever, together with L. H. Moseley, Levers' African expert, two members of the Niger Board, and an accountant left for Nigeria. It did not take the expedition long to diagnose the main cause of the Company's troubles. The administration from London was defective and so was the administration in Africa. London kept Africa in ignorance of what it was doing while the state of the finances in Africa may be judged from a single instance: 'At Kano a native clerk admitted to having put in an imaginary figure to make his books balance but this was left to our accountant to find out, instead of being spotted by the divisional agent.' There was no coherent policy governing the price to be paid to the natives for raw materials and altogether the Company was in no condition to face competition from more highly organized rivals such as the African and Eastern.

The principal reform resulting from the inquiry was the rule that in future directors resident at home should visit Africa—an unprecedented innovation. The accounting system was tightened up, price policy was more closely supervised from London, and the staff was overhauled. For all that, Leverhulme was not satisfied and even in 1924 he felt that 'the position in West Africa', was still 'most serious'. In spite of opposition from Cooper and Hulme Lever, he decided, at the age of seventy-three, to go to Africa himself 'even if the path was lined with machine guns, poison gas and undermined. We are simply fiddling in Western Africa while Rome is burning and something very extreme has got to be done.' Finally, in 1924, two more organs were added to the machinery of central government in the business. Lever Brothers controlled by this time something like ninety per cent of the British export trade in soap, and what with currency difficulties and the universal growth of tariffs, things were far from well with this side of the business. Matters were made worse by the ancient, and by no means extinguished, rivalries between the three companies mainly concerned with the export business—Lever's, Crosfield's, and Gossage's. In the summer of 1924, therefore, Leverhulme appointed a single head of the export business of the three firms. To help him, he had an Export Trade Board whose functions were 'to obviate any undue competition between Companies, to facilitate the working of the Export business, and to increase the Export trade. It will not', Leverhulme continued, 'be only a board of consultation and of conciliation, but a body of creative initiative and of active management as well.' Along with the Export Board, another committee, the Foreign Associated Companies Control Board, was set up to provide an opportunity for 'periodical discussion of the affairs of the various Overseas Companies'. Its chairman was Ernest Walls who had joined Christr. Thomas at Bristol on coming down from Oxford. From Bristol he had been brought to headquarters by Lever who had been much impressed by his driving force and incisive mind. With Ernest Walls was Geoffrey Heyworth, one of three brothers who had gone into Lever's on the overseas side. Since 1913 he had had his training as an accountant under J. E. Ganong in Canada. Service with the Canadian army during the First World War interrupted his career but on demobilization he returned to Canada where he remained until 1924. There he had been made aware of the problems of the North American market and in particular of the strength and ingenuity of United States competition in Canada. Amongst other tasks it had fallen to him to rationalize the price structure of Lever's Canadian business, burdened at that time with an impossibly large number of brands. His attitude to the problems of control was therefore that of a man trained in a hard and practical school, a school moreover where he had learned that it is sometimes necessary to speak unpalatable truths to one's superiors, a procedure that had so far not been encouraged in high places in the Lever business. Both his ability to think on broad, yet practical lines and his capacity for plain speaking recommended him to D'Arcy Cooper, and it was a sign of the times that he not only survived but almost at once began to move rapidly upwards.

One other significant event of 1921 must be recorded. In the early months of that year, Lever Brothers' administrative headquarters was moved from Port Sunlight to De Keyser's Royal Hotel by Blackfriars Bridge, which was renamed Lever House. For some time, Leverhulme had been compelled to spend an increasing amount of his time in London. The move underlined the fact that the business of Lever Brothers Limited was no longer only soap making on Merseyside but the control of a world-wide heterogeneous industrial combine. Port Sunlight was now to take its place among the factories as a *primus inter pares* (though the fact did not take legal form for another sixteen years). The care of Lever's favourite creation was entrusted to

C. W. Barnish. It could not have been in better hands. Barnish, like so many of Lever's closest colleagues, was a Lancashireman, the son of Lever's doctor, born and bred in Wigan. To the direction of Port Sunlight he brought all his superabundant energies, an innate democratic sense and a complete fidelity to the aims and principles of his 'Chief'.

In much of this reorganization—the substitution of measures for men—one may detect the cool and methodical brain of Cooper, who retired from Cooper Brothers and joined the board of Lever's in 1923 and shortly afterwards became Vice-Chairman. The fact itself was not unimportant: perhaps it may be regarded as an indication that Cooper himself was satisfied that the business was by now capable of being placed on a sound basis. Yet the importance of these administrative changes must not be exaggerated; they were significant more for the future than for the immediate present. Circumstances had compelled Leverhulme to bow to the bankers; that did not prevent him from remarking publicly that bankers were 'as timid as rabbits' nor did it prevent him from remaining, within very wide limits, master of his own affairs. In 1921, he was seventy years of age. His training, experience and success had all been gained before 1914, and the architect of one of the biggest combines in the world believed as firmly as he had ever done in the virtues of self-help, free competition, and the prospects of boundless economic expansion. In the world of the twenties, he was perhaps out of place; consolidation rather than expansion became the rule in business, and men began to speak of rationalization as a means of dealing with 'over-production'. With this view he had no patience, and in 1921 he wrote to Caesar Schlesinger in South Africa, who was tainted with the heresy of rationalization, rejecting all proposals for closing down works: his experience in England, South Africa, and America led him to conclude that such a policy had always led to a loss of trade. Within his own business he salved his Victorian economic conscience by the application of competitive principles; all associated companies should 'compete strongly with Lever Brothers in every line . . . but always of course without either frenzied competition in advertising or cut-throat competition in price, competition of efficiency being our aim and desire'. Advertising expenditure and policy were therefore controlled from headquarters by

Ernest Walls from 1923 onwards. On the other hand, the evil effects of too much central control on local initiative were recognized and a too pliable provincial chairman was held up as an example to his fellows: chairmen of associated companies were 'to give us their views at all times frankly, fully and fearlessly', and to defend them to the point of resignation. He had put the same point to the Parliamentary Committee on Prices when they ventured to criticize him for not introducing more extensive measures of rationalization; reasonable competition between associated companies was, he told them, 'the only way the string of the bow was kept tight'. There were plenty of younger men in the business who did not share his views but there is little evidence that their opinions were of much practical importance while Leverhulme was alive.

The administrative problem was rendered even more acute by the acquisition round about 1920 of various businesses whose activities were at best only very loosely connected with soap making.[1] True, in one of these businesses, candle making, an agreement of 1922 seemed on the face of things to spell a measure of rationalization. It provided that Lever Brothers and the Shell Oil Group should form a joint company to which all Lever's candle-making interests were to be sold. In reality, Leverhulme only consented to the arrangement because the alternative was a battle with the oil companies which produced the paraffin wax used in candle making: to have stood out would have entailed a fight not only with British but with American oil companies too, and, as Leverhulme observed, '. . . I have not the slightest doubt in my mind that in a three-cornered fight the Lever Group will get the worst of it'.[2] But if the candle agreement somewhat simplified the business organization, other events complicated it. For as adversity pressed ever more hardly upon him, Leverhulme was compelled to divest himself of his personal extravagances of 1920, and he sold them to the most convenient buyer—his own business of Lever Brothers. Mac Fisheries was the first to go, in March 1922. By this time it was a holding company in itself, with capital invested in retail shops, trawling companies, wholesale fish businesses at Billingsgate, and Wall's sausages. Wall's had been bought originally to

[1] See Chapter XVIII.
[2] These interests were disposed of later. See Epilogue.

provide the sausages which were an indispensable part of a fishmonger's stock-in-trade. But since the war, they had taken to ice-cream manufacture to make good the summer slackness in the sausage trade and with the invention of the 'Stop-me-and-buy-one' tricycle had established a minor national institution. In 1923, Angus Watson's went the same way as Mac Fisheries and Lever Brothers found itself the owner of this business famous for its 'Skippers' and tinned salmon. Other businesses followed the same course, amongst them two more canned goods firms and a chocolate factory at Watford, known after its transfer to Lever's as Planter's Products.

All these transfers were no doubt convenient to Leverhulme but they set the parent company new problems of management in matters of which, to say the least, they had little experience. And even while the process of absorption was still incomplete, Lever's acquired two businesses making toilet preparations—one of them owning a well in the deserts of Algeria, which was said to yield water peculiarly valuable for toilet preparations but was described gloomily by a Lever investigator as 'an incubus to the Company'. What was most serious, however, was that most of these businesses were losing money; their acquisition could therefore only fix the burden of profit-making more firmly than ever on the soap companies. Consolidation or rationalization being out of the question while Leverhulme held sway, the problem was how to make the soap trade more profitable by measures short of radical reorganization. Fortunately there was a good deal of slack which could be pulled in. The first need was for efficient production and lower costs.

Accepting the business structure as it stood, Leverhulme turned his attention to the question of industrial efficiency in the individual factories, bringing to the task a black energy which resembled only in its intensity the driving enthusiasm of his earlier career. Since 1914, the numbers of workers employed at Port Sunlight had risen from 5,748 to a peak of just over 8,000 in 1919 and 1920. The slump had arrived at the same time as the first real wave of labour trouble ever experienced at Port Sunlight. The source lay not in Lever's factory but in a dispute between two unions, and the result was a strike of clerks. By July 1920, the Policy Council had decided that the slump made it imperative to reduce staff by seven hundred men and three hundred girls, but were opposed to any discrimination against those who had been on strike. Leverhulme's reaction had been immediate and violent. 'All a muddle', he had scrawled across a page of the Policy Council minutes, 'by reason of wrong acceptance of strikers ban and not founded on T.U. practise or power—all a myth. Simply the words of timidity—without the courage of rabbits. We do not intend to victimize a single Trade Unionist. . . . I will face anything and everything rather than any injury be suffered by loyal members of staff. . . . An injury to one single Loyal Man or Woman is a tenfold blow at myself.'

As time went on, it nevertheless became clear to him that his factory was overstaffed. The great increase in the working force had not been accompanied by any proportionate increase in output. There were too many passengers to be carried. 'If a man had been with Lever Brothers for twenty years', wrote Leverhulme, 'he leaned upon us and thought his position was one in which he could come-aday, go-aday, God send Sunday, with his eye on the clock and that was quite enough.' There were 'too many inefficient men, too many highly paid men, too many elderly men, and men past their work. . . .' So the dismissals began. The elderly were pensioned; the younger usually given three months' wages to give them time to find another job. By 1921, numbers were down under 6,000 and by 1925 under 5,000. A similar policy was followed in other factories. Cumulatively, throughout the country, such policies added up to the unemployment problem. Harsh the remedy undoubtedly was, but the production figures make it clear that the call for economy and efficiency at Port Sunlight was real enough. In 1927, Port Sunlight was producing the same volume of goods as in 1921 with 4,000 less workers. The explanation lay in increased efficiency. Between 1921 and 1923, the number of man-hours required to produce and pack a ton of soap fell from 115 to 61. The cost per ton fell from £10·01 in 1920 to £3·22 in one week of 1923. The general fall of prices had of course contributed to the fall in costs but even so it is apparent that there had been a startling increase in efficiency.

At the same time wages began to slide downwards. The works manager at Port Sunlight put the case for a local reduction. The cost of living in February 1921, he argued, was one hundred and fifty-one per cent above 1914 rates; wages were up by one hundred and ninty-one per cent. Leverhulme was a little shy of making the move; he did not want the soap industry to be the first to initiate a general reduction of wages. But events moved fast, and by July 1921 reductions were in force generally. Men's wages were cut by four shillings; juveniles' and females' by three shillings. The Unions did not like it, but with unemployment spreading, their bargaining position was far from strong; and even after the reductions, Lever Brothers' rates remained, by deliberate policy, above Union rates. As Leverhulme observed: 'What can Union do to keep back tide—Labour leaders may mimic King Canute but they cannot be more successful than he—let us treat our men justly and sympathetically *under all* circumstances. Soap may have its bad times to face—today soap makers' wages are above (and we rejoice) the average labour of U.K.' Salaries as well as wages came under the axe. In 1922, savings of £5,000 a year in management salaries and of £4,000 a year in clerical salaries were reported from Crosfield's. At Price's, similar cuts saved £11,000 a year.

Yet these years were not marked by unrelieved severity in labour policy. In July 1922, Leverhulme introduced a new benefit scheme for his workpeople, designed, as he claimed, to lay 'three ghosts—Unemployment, Sickness, and Death'. Any employee thrown out of work through causes over which he had no control—such as slackness of trade—was to have half pay for the first four weeks. An employee who fell sick was to have half pay for four weeks, or longer at the Company's option. Thirdly, co-partners were to have free life insurance for varying sums according to their grade. It is easy to see now that Leverhulme's claim to have laid the 'ghosts' is open to challenge. It was not within the power of a single business to achieve even a local solution by its own action. The importance of the new policy—like the importance of the Port Sunlight experiment itself—lay in the humane conception behind it. It was evidence of a more enlightened policy towards labour.

One other project started in these years and designed to reduce costs was the Bromborough Dock. The idea of possessing a dock opening on to the Mersey, capable of taking large ships and close to Port Sunlight, had long been in Leverhulme's mind. But, as the Bromborough margarine plant grew, he became convinced of the necessity of such a dock if he was to compete with the Dutch margarine makers who '... had an advantage in Java copra ... and in being able to buy coconut oil in bulk'. A dock would not only give him a similar advantage but would, he estimated, save him four shillings a ton in transport charges. With the growth of the West African interests, with Dutch competition severe, and with the possibility of having to handle large whale oil cargoes, the dock was indispensable. A Bill was promoted in 1922 and although unpopular with local transport interests it received the Royal Assent in the following year. The remaining history of the dock's construction could hardly have been less fortunate and its completion was to take another eight years.

The third problem—competition in the soap trade—was not new, but it was destined in the twenties to take a new form. It was Leverhulme himself who had scouted suggestions of monopoly before the Government Sub-Committee on soap prices[1] in 1921, by pointing out that even a suspicion of monopoly prices would immediately bring in fresh competition in the shape of new home production and imported soaps. The speed with which the prophecy came true must have surprised even the prophet. One formidable rival he recognized—the C.W.S., whose production was running in the early twenties at a rate about two-thirds of that of Port Sunlight. So much Leverhulme probably reckoned on. He could hardly have been prepared for the invasion of the soap trade by the oil millers which formed a major threat to his recovery from 1922 onwards. The British oil milling industry had undergone a tremendous process of expansion during the war and a large part of it came under the aegis of the group known as the British Oil & Cake Mills. The B.O.C.M. dated from 1899 when a group of twenty-eight mills and twelve oil refineries mainly in Hull, Liverpool, Glasgow and London came together. Amongst them was the firm of Pearson, Beckett & Company of Glasgow which traced its ancestry back to an oil-milling business in Gainsborough, Lincolnshire. When, very early in its career, the B.O.C.M. ran into difficulties, it was a young member of the family—J. W. Pearson—who was selected to reorganize it. By 1910, he had reached the office of chairman, and under his vigorous direction the B.O.C.M. continued to acquire other mills. When the war came, and the British milling

[1] See Chapter XVIII.

industry was compelled to handle a range of raw materials previously left to its German rivals, the necessary reorganization fell to Pearson. Pre-war the British oil-milling industry crushed seed primarily for cattle cake—unlike the continental milling industry which crushed primarily for the production of edible fats. (The difference came out in contemporary terminology: in England you were a 'cake manufacturer' or 'seed-crusher': in Germany and Holland you were an 'oil manufacturer'.) The war upset this old system; the demand for glycerine and edible fats put the emphasis on oils and fats production. The refining side of the industry was enormously expanded and the B.O.C.M. themselves went into margarine production. Then came the slump of 1920; butter again became cheap and plentiful and both the milling and the margarine businesses faced hard times. But J. W. Pearson was a man of resource. In his capacity for handling large issues, his optimism and his gift of pungent expression, he was not unlike Leverhulme. His own organization, with its branches into raw materials, refining and edible fats, already bore some resemblance, though on a smaller scale, to the Lever business and he did not fail to see that in these years of depression Lever Brothers were kept afloat on the profits of soap. In 1921, therefore, the B.O.C.M. put forward another offshoot—the British Soap Company—manufacturing a soap called 'New Pin', very much on the lines of Sunlight itself. The new soap was backed by flamboyant advertising schemes which included gifts for soap coupons on a lavish scale. By 1922, Lever Brothers had seen the red light. 'Do you notice New Pin competition?' Leverhulme asked the chairman of Gossage's in February 1922. 'It is not an effective one but sounds a danger signal to other soap makers in that there are always people attracted to Competition [gift] schemes and if we don't mind, New Pin or others will get them.' (The 'others' referred probably to Bibby's of Liverpool, another large oil-milling business which, like B.O.C.M., went at this time into soap making.)

During the first two years of its existence, New Pin production continued small—three to four thousand tons a year—but by 1923, the advertising had taken effect and sales leapt to over 21,000 tons. By 1925, they were to be nearly 34,000 tons. Not only Port Sunlight but the other members of the family—Watson's and Crosfield's in the North and Christr. Thomas in the West—began to feel the draught. Counter attack in advertising brought results in the West where Thomas's went ahead of New Pin in South Wales, but the cost was heavy. The main disadvantage of the new struggle was that it threatened to revive the whole vexatious policy of gift schemes—dead for more than a decade. In the latter months of 1924 there were long negotiations between Lever Brothers and the British Soap Company for the cessation of prize schemes. Just when agreement seemed to be in sight, the negotiations were abandoned, Leverhulme withdrawing his consent because the proposals envisaged limitation of the output of New Pin which he described as 'wrong and viciously improper'. The deadlock was only temporary and, as was to happen more than once in such negotiations, the failure of the lesser scheme merely led to the acceptance of a greater. The amalgamation of Lever Brothers and the B.O.C.M. did not in fact take final shape until after Leverhulme's death in 1925 (when Lever's took the Ordinary share capital of B.O.C.M. and B.O.C.M. acquired twenty per cent Preference shares in Lever Brothers), but the policy of this acquisition may be fairly regarded as Leverhulme's own. The trade in New Pin came under Lever's control, together with a powerful group of oil mills and refineries possessing a turnover which in 1925 amounted to over £17 million. Not the least important aspect of the transaction was that it brought J. W. Pearson on to the Board of Lever Brothers with the special charge of supervising the oil-milling interests.

While the household soap trade was thus threatened from home, the toilet soap market was invaded from abroad. Leverhulme, as a free trader, often said that he was not afraid of foreigners: that if they thought they could afford to import soap into England and sell it profitably, they were welcome to try. But he had remarked to the Government Sub-Committee on Soap Prices that 'if American soap got here, it would be a quarter of a century before we could get it out again'. It got here about 1923, after some abortive negotiations between Lever's and the Palmolive Company for a union. After the breakdown of talks, Palmolive began in earnest their campaign to put their now familiar green toilet soap on the English market. They made great play with the name and the ingredients and in 1923 Leverhulme was writing angrily of 'the pretentious claims of the Palmolive people to a monopoly of the words "Palm and Olive Oil"'. It took a little time for him to devise counter-measures, but by 1924 he had them: in Britain and America, Lever's put out a green soap of their own—Olva. The resemblance to Palmolive was so marked that the opposition alleged—to Leverhulme's astonishment, he said—that the scheme was 'not entirely ethical'. They need hardly have worried, for Olva's career was not marked by any startling success and two years later it had to be admitted that 'the biggest seller in toilet soap is still Palmolive'. But the real answer—Lux Toilet Soap—was a later story.

In Africa, too, competition in the soap trade was threatening. There is little doubt that the African and Eastern Trade Corporation was better managed than the Niger Company. Anton, head of the Jurgens business in Holland, for example, wrote to his family partners in 1923 that this was so 'for the reason of the people at the head being experienced in the West African trade and confining all their attention to this business, whilst Lord Leverhulme is no expert in this trade and cannot make it a speciality, but has to leave it to a Board of Directors which he has changed three or four times during the last two years'.

Leverhulme himself had no illusions about the Niger management. It was a case, he told Knowles, where 'men inexperienced in leather buy leather and raw hides, men inexperienced in cocoa buy cocoa, and anybody with inferior produce to sell on the Coast could always sell it to the Niger, when no other dealer would buy....' Now the African and Eastern took control, in 1920, of T. H. Harris and Sons Ltd., a London soap-making firm. By 1924, they were reported to have fifty per cent of the soap trade in West Africa. Some of the rest went to Bibby's of Liverpool, and even the possession of a local soap factory at Apapa afforded Lever's very little help. The truth was, as Leverhulme said, that 'Apapa made soap is not equal in quality to imported soap and the natives are very quick to find this out'. In order not to set up what they held to be unfair competition against their British exports, Lever's had made it a rule that their locally made soaps should not be sold more cheaply than their imported soaps. So the only remedy was to reduce the prices of local soaps and let Apapa lose money.

The soap trade was not the only one to feel the edge of keen competition. Besides the African and Eastern, John Holt & Company were a vigorous rival in the Coast trade; and beyond the ranks of the large European companies stood an array of small firms of all nationalities—Papadimitrios, Testaibis, Hassan, and Roloffe—as well as an army of African traders who bought up cottons all over Nigeria and, free of all costs save time and food, undersold the Niger Company on the River Benue. The only remedy to these manifold problems of West Africa was an agreement between the two giants of the trade. As Harold Greenhalgh told D'Arcy Cooper in 1923, if they could even agree on a minimum profit below which they would not trade, the rest would follow. But that was not yet to be.

Finally, there was the margarine trade at home. Here the post-war period saw a price war unequalled in any other branch of the Lever business, for not only was there an excess of producing capacity but a plethora of butter, too. Nor did Leverhulme disguise from himself or others his particular displeasure with the quality of his own product. 'I am very distressed', he told Hansen, 'at our position in margarine; our quality ought to be irreproachable. I know that Van den Bergh's are putting a strong press advertising campaign out on their Blue Band. I wish I had the confidence. . . . to do the same. . . .' Nor was he any more satisfied with Planter's advertising policy. Van den Bergh's had stuck to a consistent policy of selling a good article at a shilling a pound. Planter's had 'wobbled' . . . 'and I must confess', he wrote to his son, 'that I have been as big a wobbler as any'. Underlying the whole problem, he confessed, was 'my own ignorance of the margarine business'. If he had been as ignorant of the soap trade in 1884, he admitted, his firm would still in 1923 have been 'pushing Bar soaps, Blue-mottled Scouring Soaps and so on'. In other words, he had failed in the margarine trade to establish an article recognized by the public for its unique quality.

On top of these deficiencies was the expense of a plant at Bromborough capable of producing five times the demand for Planter's margarine in 1923 and an oil refinery 'rather grotesque in size [compared] to what is really required under present day methods'. The tonnage of margarine sold fell from over 54,000 tons in 1919 to just under 20,000 tons in 1925; the money value of these sales from nearly £5½ million to under £1¼ million.

Leverhulme's impression that his Dutch rivals were, if not prospering, at any rate suffering less than he, was substantially correct. But the price war had rendered some form of co-operation acceptable even to them. An Association (the aims and objects of which are uncertain) met the fate common to such bodies in 1921. In 1922 Anton Jurgens was still pressing for an agreement to fix an absolute minimum price. But Van den Bergh's and Lever's would not commit themselves, and when, in 1923, an attempt was made to increase prices by common action, it was Jurgens who killed the proposal. Although the fate of such attempts did not encourage much hope of co-operation, the tone of the discussions was not unfriendly; it seemed clear that if only their conflicting interests could be reconciled, margarine makers would be relieved to substitute some form of co-operation for a system of unlimited competition that threatened disaster for all.

Development of the Business

Meanwhile, the development of the overseas activities of the Lever companies continued and a comparison of sales tonnage figures of soap for 1925 with those for 1920 gives some impression of the recovery and expansion of the Lever businesses during the period after the slump:

METRIC TONS

	1920	1925		1920	1925
U.K.	190,369	215,589	Denmark	235	238
U.S.A.	21,105	40,573	Finland	—	492
Canada	19,062	23,362	France	12,219	13,040
S. Africa	13,590	15,196	Germany	—	9,037
Australia	4,315	30,108[1]	Holland	3,291	4,615
New Zealand	892	1,146	Italy	580	376
China	9,751	7,273	Norway	859	874
India	—	17,136	Poland	—	47
Austria	—	472	Sweden	397	581
Belgium	9,916	18,785	Switzerland	1,503	2,482

[1] Includes the Kitchen-Burford sales (acquired 1914).

From these figures, certain facts emerge. The first is the recovery of sales in the United Kingdom—still the hub of the business. No less remarkable is the rapid growth of the American business. Thirdly, the solidity of the Dominions' businesses where sales showed satisfactory though not startling increases. Fourthly, the recovery of the established continental businesses, where Belgium in particular was doing well and the German business had once more been brought back into the family. Finally, the beginning of a drive to acquire new markets especially in Northern Europe. Sales, however, were not everything and the true picture can only be obtained by looking at the general condition and especially at the profits of the different trading areas.

The net profits of the Combine in 1925 came to £4¼ million. It was not enough to meet the demands for Debenture interest, and dividends on Preference and Ordinary Capital. The position was far from comfortable, but it was vastly better than in 1920–1 when there was no true profit at all but losses running into millions. The recovery was in large measure due to the revival of the home soap trade. The profits of the home associated companies amounted to £2½ million, and well over a million of this came from two sources—Port Sunlight and Hudson's. Hudson's contribution was interesting; throughout even the worst period of the slump their sales had mounted—evidence of the growing tendency of housewives to use powdered soap in preference to hard soap. Most of the rest of the profit came also from associated soap companies. Nor, apparently, had the consumer any reason to grumble about prices. Between 1921 and 1926 the average price of soap fell from 10d. to 6d. a pound and, as an investigator into prices at the time remarked, 6d. a pound was actually a penny below what the Committee of 1921 would have considered reasonable.[1] To some extent the reduction reflected the all-round deflation of price levels in the early twenties but credit must also be given to the vigorous measures taken by the business itself to cut costs and increase industrial efficiency.

The improvement in the situation of the home companies was satisfactory so far as it went; but it was becoming clear that there were limits to the home soap market and that there was some reason for supposing that those limits were almost reached.

[1] P. Fitzgerald, *Industrial Combination in England*, 1927, p. 65.

Further expansion could only be achieved elsewhere. There were two groups of businesses which by 1925 offered scope for expansion; the home food businesses and the overseas soap businesses. The acquisition of the food businesses—Planter's Margarine, Planter's Products (an outlet for cocoa from the West African Companies), Mac Fisheries, and Angus Watson's—had been a queer mixture of accident and design. In the gloom of the early twenties, Lever's had hung on grimly, largely because Leverhulme was not a man to admit defeat easily. But by 1925 some sort of pattern was beginning to emerge. Except for the chocolate business, the food businesses were making profits—not very big profits as yet but the promise was there. And even as the conception of the 'vertical combine' faded, another was beginning to take its place—the conception of a group of businesses linked 'horizontally'. The three main sections—raw materials, soap, and food—had a common basis; oils and fats figured in all three, but activities were not to be limited to commodities made solely of oils and fats. It was becoming clear that common raw materials were not the only basis for combining businesses; that in some ways, the problems of marketing, say, margarine were more like those of marketing other foods than they were like those of selling soap. The food businesses tended to gravitate together, and new food products were drawn into the orbit of the old. The food group was beginning, in fact, to assume an organic character of its own. That this was hardly even suspected in the hectic days of 1920 when the businesses were purchased did not make the fact any less real.

Amongst the soap companies abroad, the brightest hopes were founded on the progress of the American business. Lever's, Boston, had not looked back since the year in which F. A. Countway assumed command—1912. With the assistance of A. F. Bernhard, his sales manager, Countway had set a pace of expansion scarcely equalled in the records of twentieth-century business. A few figures of sales value and net profits give an idea of the results he achieved:

	Sales	*Net Profits*
	$	$
1913	843,466	733
1920	12,494,313	762,846
1925	18,938,287	1,599,456

Of course, the prosperity of the American business in the twenties was partly a reflection of that seven years' Golden Age which began in 1922. But intelligent management played an equally important role. Countway had recognized two major errors of his predecessors' policies: he gave up the attempt to make Sunlight Soap a leading line in America, and he courted assiduously the wholesale merchants instead of selling direct to the retailers.[1] The sales of Lifebuoy and Welcome soaps were boosted to the accompaniment of every device known to the salesman—gift schemes, special displays, working demonstrations, house-to-house visits by special teams of canvassers, and so on. But it was in Lux soap flakes that Countway's greatest weapon lay. Lux had already been advertised as a product suitable for washing woollen fabrics—blankets, underwear and baby clothes. But a change was taking place in fashions. With a higher standard of living and newer and more delicate fabrics available at low prices, silk or artificial silk lingerie and hosiery were beginning to displace cotton camisoles and stockings. Countway seized on the change as an opportunity for building up a market for a fine soap which would not injure the most delicate fabric, and from 1914 the Lux campaign gathered strength. The big department stores were induced to conduct washing demonstrations; customers were invited to bring garments to the stores to be washed. Sales of Lux, about 3,000 cases in 1913, were a million and a half cases by 1919. Then came Countway's second string—Rinso soap powder. A selling campaign inaugurated in 1919 sold 64,000 cases; by 1923 the sales had risen to 800,000. Meanwhile, Lifebuoy continued to do good business, sales rising from 84,000 cases in 1913 to 550,000 in 1923. The days when Lever decided that the main market for soap in America was the East were long past, and the old division of the market into New England and the 'General Territory' equally outmoded. To handle these expanding sales, Countway in 1919 devised a new organization, dividing the United States up into ten selling divisions each with its own sales office. For a few years, he was content to base his business firmly on the three main brands—Lux, Lifebuoy, and Rinso. But the American market was highly competitive, and Countway was not a man to rest for long. In the early twenties he took over

[1] See Chapter XIII.

the export trade to the West Indies and the Philippines, and then in 1925 launched Lux Toilet Soap on the American market. It was the Sunlight story all over again. Port Sunlight had urged Countway to launch Olva in competition with Palmolive but Countway knew the American market too well. Tests showed that a white soap with the Lux reputation behind it was more likely to be acceptable to the American customer than a palm-and-olive soap; and he was right. In the first year, sales reached a figure of 135,000 cases.

Countway's successes were not achieved without tremendous advertising expenditure. In 1923, his advertising cost nearly six million dollars—almost as much as the whole of the rest of the Lever group at home and abroad—and this at a time when economy had caused Leverhulme to put all advertising expenditure under very close central control. But Leverhulme recognized nevertheless that Countway and his problems were both unique and must be treated accordingly. '. . . Mr. Countway', he observed 'gets results and meets competition without injury to the business, which we must bear in mind.' The truth was that Leverhulme and Countway were made in the same mould; but Countway's tactics raised problems which were analysed by D'Arcy Cooper in a statement which summarized the situation coolly while at the same time conveying vividly the restless energy of Countway's methods; '. . . the difficulties in Boston's position—were that though they had a wonderful business in Lux they had not been content to use its surplus profits on building up Lifebuoy but had put on Rinso before Lifebuoy had become a paying proposition, and so added to the burden of Lux. They had not stopped there but had put on Lux Toilet Soap and were now proposing to put on Olva and shaving cream; the cost of all these ate up the profits of their outstanding line.' Time was to show that Countway had his answer to that argument too. For the moment, it was enough that Boston in 1925 contributed a quarter of a million to Lever Brothers' profits.

Over the border, although sales were maintained, American competition was troublesome and there had been no expansion of the Canadian business to speak of since 1913. Three of the companies showed losses in 1925, and the Chairman was perturbed by 'the very serious decrease in profits in that Dominion', hinting at radical change in the business. In South Africa, too, 'radical change' seemed to be foreshadowed. Profits there were still large—more than £100,000 in 1925—but evidently that was not considered good enough. There was talk of 'excessive competition' especially from 'numerous Russian Jews' who had come into the Union after the Revolution. Only Leverhulme's obstinate opposition to rationalization postponed the closing of factories; immediately after his death in 1925, one of the four on the Rand was shut down. In Australia, on the other hand, business was at last doing well and Australia contributed nearly £300,000 to the parent's profit and loss account.

In Europe the aftermath of the war was prolonged and severe, and on balance the European companies were still losing money in 1925. Belgium and Switzerland were the brightest spots in a somewhat sombre picture. For once, France was doing pretty well and, for once, Holland doing badly. The German connection had been re-established—after a struggle—but native interests had now come into the business and Lever's could hardly claim to be masters of their own house. It was not surprising that the German business made a loss of £137,000 in 1925, for the repercussions of the trouble in the Ruhr and the inflation were still being felt, and the Dawes Plan was still on paper.

Several factories in North Europe made their first appearance on the profit and loss account in the early twenties, and the results in 1925 were still all in red figures. In Norway, Sweden, Denmark, and Finland, the effort as yet was on a small scale but the acquisition of factories in all these countries within a space of a few years gives all the appearance of a deliberate drive into Scandinavia. The movement started, in part, from the expansionist ideas of 1919 when H. G. Hart, the director charged by Leverhulme with the responsibility for Scandinavian affairs, was exploring various schemes for developing the existing interest in the Norwegian hardening plant De-No-Fa. The frenzied search for new fields to conquer is perhaps in itself sufficient answer to the query—why Scandinavia? But there were additional and more rational reasons. The industrial revolution was late in Northern Europe but in the early years of the twentieth century Scandinavia experienced a process of industrialization—especially rapid in Sweden. There was a natural tendency for living standards to rise and neutrality in the war gave an additional fillip to the Scandinavian economies. Such was the background to Lever's activities in the early twenties. Nothing came of the proposals in 1919 to establish a factory at Nodinge (on the west coast of Sweden) and to buy up the chemical and soap business of Barnangens in Stockholm. But in 1923 an empty factory was acquired at Nyköping about seventy kilometres south-west of Stockholm. In the same year, a small soap factory was acquired at Glostrup near Copenhagen and opened with a characteristic flourish by Leverhulme himself. Two years later, the Abo soap factory was bought in Finland. All this followed the familiar pattern, for the factories all replaced a former trade in Lever's imported soaps. So far everything was on a tiny scale and the result was financial loss but the ambition behind it was enough to cause some anxiety in local business circles. In 1924 in the course of an attack on the Lever penetration into Norway, where Leverhulme had just founded a small company, a Norwegian critic referred to Leverhulme as 'a powerful and dangerous man'. 'It is consequently exceedingly probable,' he went on, 'that if he secures a firm footing on Norwegian ground he will be able to crush the Norwegian soap industry.' It was perhaps the first hint that Scandinavia was not going to be an easy market.

The raw material businesses produced varying results. The most cheering news came from the Belgian Congo. The Huileries du Congo Belge had taken a long time to get into its stride, but in 1923 one of its directors was bold enough to claim that it had 'at last reached a period of constant prosperity'. Prices of course had fallen from their post-war peak, but under Edkins' vigorous management production had just about doubled in the period 1920–5. When Lord Leverhulme visited the Congo in 1925 his comments were not quite so unreservedly enthusiastic as those of his colleague in 1923. Of one plantation he said that the palmery sites were 'squandered and mainly limited in area'; of another that there 'were crowds of managers and the place badly managed'. But his natural optimism was sustained by the general evidence of progress; he planned new developments with energy apparently undiminished by age or tropic heat and wrote home: 'Although we were all greatly impressed with what had been done, we have really only begun to scratch the soil . . . we are all full of enthusiasm and confidence in the future of our Belgian Concessions.'

The Pacific plantations were doing well. Profits and production had risen steadily since 1920. The Southern Whaling and Sealing Company had a good year in 1925, contributing profits of nearly a quarter of a million pounds. Against these profits had to be put the losses of the Philippine Refining Corporation; in trouble ever since its acquisition, its affairs had been the subject of various inquiries, and in the end the ebullient Mr. Hamilton had to be removed from office. Nor were the affairs of the Niger Company yet in equilibrium. The best that could be said of it was that its losses were very much smaller than in 1921, that the reforms in its management were beginning to take effect but that it was still loaded with debts and losses. One of Leverhulme's last acts was to announce a bold stroke of financial surgery which it was hoped would help to cure its sickness—the exchange of eight per cent Preference shares for seven per cent Debentures and the surrender of all claims to arrears of dividend.

William Lever—A Summing Up

Leverhulme arrived back in England from a journey to the Congo on the 19th of March 1925. He died seven weeks later from a chill contracted, perhaps, as a result of too sudden a change of climate. A fortnight before he died he presided over the Annual Meeting of Lever Brothers and delivered a trenchant and characteristic account of his stewardship. His shareholders, he pointed out, numbered 187,000; the profits which went partially to pay their dividends were the work of 60,000 white people 'living and working in almost every country in the world' and of 25,000 native Africans working in Central Africa. There were, besides, over 1,000 directors of associated companies with their managers and foremen. Co-partners numbered 18,000; they, and he as Ordinary shareholder, had 'to make twenty shillings for others, to receive sevenpence-ha'penny for themselves'.

No one who has examined the progress of his firm can fail to comprehend the influence which Leverhulme's driving personality exercised over its growth. By unremitting effort, boundless ambition and powerful imagination he built up this business: with its issued capital in 1925 standing at nearly £57 million it was one of the largest commercial undertakings of its kind in the world. There is a view of economic history which regards the capitalist as only a cork bobbing on the economic tide. To regard a phenomenon such as the Lever business merely as an inevitable result of the tendency towards large-scale organization and the destruction of competition would be to court ridicule. Without Lever there would have been no Lever Brothers, and the whole structure of a national industry and a by no means negligible section of British world economic interests might have borne a very different aspect. In shaping the process of growth many factors, personal and social, had played a part. Some of the social factors—notably the rising standard of living and the urge towards urban and industrial growth—have been examined. It remains to say a word of the personal factors.

Leverhulme's personality was complex; it was not perhaps more contradictory than most but the scale on which he worked emphasized the strange paradoxes of his make-up. A liberal by upbringing and conviction, he was yet capable of tyranny. A free trader and a firm believer in *laissez-faire*, he built up one of the biggest combines in history. In many ways a ruthless man, he was sensitive to criticism and anxious to be thought well of. Never tired of emphasizing that he acted largely for motives of business, he was at heart a sentimentalist. A rich and acquisitive man, he was probably speaking the truth when he said that money as money had little attraction for him. A man of iron courage, he was yet essentially a shy man, often intensely troubled by his own fears. It is in this last paradox that one may find one of the keys to his character and his restless urge to work. He wrote to a colleague in 1923:

> I ask myself what has caused me to begin work at 4.30 in the morning during the last two or three years, and to work laborious hours, and to have only one absorbing thought, namely my own efficiency and the maintenance of my own health for the task I had to perform; and I am bound to confess that it has not been the attraction of the dividends but 'fear'—merely 'cowardly fear'. I could call it by lots of high sounding names, but if I must be perfectly candid with myself I am convinced that it has been the gnawing fear in my heart that Lever Brothers would have to

> pass their dividends. I had placed myself in this position by accepting money from all classes of investors, including widows, spinsters, clergymen, and others—all subscribers for Lever Brothers' shares from the confidence they had in the business and myself and that these might possibly have to forego their dividends which would mean probably curtailment of what they depended upon for their day-to-day food, clothing, rent, etc. Candidly, this has been my great 'fear', and this is what has caused me to get up at 4.30 in the morning.
>
> If it had been said to me three years ago 'I will increase your dividend if you will get up at 4.30' I am certain it would have been quite ineffective, but when I saw clearly staring me in the face, as I did three years ago, a situation which if not dealt with would have resulted in the ruin of Lever Brothers and of many others besides myself, then that supreme 'fear' has caused me to work as I have done.

Work and success had brought him what he at once desired and feared—power. It may be that he wielded more power than any one man should, but it must be said that though his faults were obvious, lack of a sense of responsibility was not amongst them. He never lost touch with the things he sold nor with the people who made them and bought them. To the last, the quality of the products of his factories and the well-being of his employees remained an obsession with him.

With the collapse of the big negotiations in America and England, Lord Leverhulme's boom-time exaltation passed away, to be succeeded by black anxiety and a ruthless, fear-driven pursuit of 'efficiency'. In 1923 he described in a private letter the mood induced by the shocks of 1920, and its effect upon his management of the business:

> Now what has produced the efficiency since 1921? Not the fact of any increased bonus, but the fact that we had begun to comb out inefficient men. We have been combing out inefficient men, and too highly paid men, elderly men, and men past their work steadily for the last three years, and I am confident that this has produced a state of 'fear' in the minds of the remainder that if they were not efficient their turn would come next, and it is this, in my opinion, which has been the cause of the improved efficiency results achieved today.

This is a grim picture: it contrasts sharply with the exuberant self-confidence of Leverhulme's early career, and it accords well with the impression gained of him by many who knew him in his later years: the impression of a driving tyrant, prone to find fault with his subordinates, yet possessed still of a fighting spirit which compelled their profound admiration.

Finally, a word about his economic ideas. In the course of more than half a century's experience of business, he built up an economic philosophy which was not more inconsistent than most abstract systems of political economy, and a good deal more consistent than the patchwork of unrelated economic ideas which is sometimes enough to satisfy the purely practical mind. In his retentive memory he stored the impressions of a lifetime of reading as well as the observations of journeys to America, the Pacific, the Dominions, and tropical Africa. The core of his ideas is to be found in the papers he delivered throughout the first twenty years of the twentieth century to audiences as various as Sheffield University, the Liverpool Trades and Labour Council, his own Port Sunlight staff, and the P.S.A. Brotherhood of a Congregational Church at Bolton. He usually spoke with only a few notes and delivered his address in a strong vigorous voice, his normal Lancashire accent broadening into full dialect as he pointed his economic discourse with one of his favourite Lancashire stories.[1]

The basis of his philosophy was his outright rejection of the labour theory of value. '. . . there is a theory, and you know the theory as well as I,' he told a meeting of Liverpool Trade Unionists, 'that labour produces all wealth. It was started by Adam Smith, and is worshipped by many today. . . . Don't you think', he continued, 'it was just as sensible of the old man who blew the organ to say that he produces the music as to say that it is labour that is the source of all wealth? I like this illustration because it is quite obvious that if the man ceases blowing the organ there will be no music; but it is equally true that he may blow the organ as much and as laboriously as he likes, and that unless there is someone there to play and touch the notes with discrimination and skill there would be no music.' No, the source of wealth was not merely labour, not merely capital and labour; it was 'a three-legged stool'—Capital, Labour, and Management,

[1] A collection of his papers setting out his economic philosophy *in extenso* was published under the title of: *The Six-Hour Day and Other Industrial Questions*, Allen & Unwin, 1918.

this latter 'sometimes part of the activities of Capital and at other times must be included with Labour'. Capital accumulation resulted from the joint activities of Management and Labour for 'good Management always accumulates Capital'. Good Management it was which provided the guidance without which both Capital and Labour must be sterile—the 'someone to play and touch the notes'. The production of wealth was thus a partnership: the object of that partnership—more and more production, for '. . . there can be no other way in which we can get greater comfort and happiness for each of us than producing more goods'.

So far the acquisition of capital had presented no difficulties but the faulty distribution of capital was 'the root and cause of all the antagonism of Capital and Labour'. This antagonism threatened the partnership and imperilled its object. It had to be recognized that Labour was dissatisfied—and rightly so—with its share of the bargain, for the wages system, though indispensable as *part* of the economic mechanism '. . . had broken down as a sole and only solution'. A good deal of the blame for this Lever ascribed to his fellow business men. 'The so-called practical business man, ostrich-like, buries his head in his ledger and ignores the writing on the wall.' On the other hand, the solution of too many Trade Unionists—'ca' canny' and restrictive practices—was grievously mistaken. Ca' canny could only increase the cost of living; it was 'a robber of wealth and of fellow workmen and reduces and lowers the level of every workman'. It was therefore essential for both employers and employees to rid themselves of false prejudices: 'All employers must abandon their idea that low wages mean cheap production and high profits, and I think the workman must equally abandon his idea that limited production means more labour employed and at higher wages. They are both wrong and two wrongs do not make one right.'

Where, then, did the solution lie? First of all, in the recognition of the target and the means to achieve it. 'We want more capital invested in labour-saving machinery to give us increased output, higher wages, shorter hours, reduced cost of production, and we want to eliminate the element of fatigue by the reduced hours as well.' Even these things by themselves, however, were not enough. Labour had ambitions as well as economic interests that needed satisfying: 'If high wages, short hours, good housing meant finality to Labour Unrest, then Labour would not be a man but a vegetable.' Leverhulme, himself a self-made man, rejoiced at the ambition of the workers to control the industries in which they participated. To him it was one of the healthy signs of the day. But 'merely a desire to sit on a Board of Directors, without a knowledge of all that that position means' could only lead to disaster. It was the object of a shorter working day to allow leisure for education, and education was 'the crown of all, the keynote of the situation'. Behind the employer stood the consumers, themselves workers: only when consumers, workers, and masters were elevated and raised by education would conditions in industry likewise be raised. There must be a ladder from the lowest positions in industry to the seat on the Board for the man who fitted himself to take it. Meanwhile, the gap between Capital and Labour which had widened with the growth of large-scale industry must be closed by dividing the profits of their joint labour fairly and squarely between them. Wages were not enough: Labour must be given an interest in the profits—and the losses—of the joint business. This was where the co-partnership system came in: deserving employees were to have certificates of nominal value, allotted in proportion to their wages, on which they would receive dividends, varying, as Ordinary dividends do, according to the state of profits. Co-partners must be partners in fact as well as name. Capital was not to expect that Labour, after co-partnership, would cease to demand higher wages, or relinquish its Trade Union rights: equally Labour must not expect that Capital and Management would relinquish their functions of control and discipline. The essence of the partnership was that Labour and Capital would both stand to share in the prosperity of the business and both stand to lose from loss and inefficiency.

These, in inadequate outline, were the ideas which Leverhulme sought continually to impress on his audiences. No abstract can give any impression of the vigour and colour which he managed to infuse into his surveys and proposals. They were not entirely consistent theoretically. They contained innumerable practical difficulties—the position of the Trade Unions, the inadequacy of the co-partner's dividend at the lower levels of the wage scale, the fact that such schemes were infinitely more difficult for the basic industries than they were for the soap industry—and so on. They were not a panacea for all industrial ills. They took too little account of unreasoning prejudice and of the genuine risks of monopoly capitalism. There were many who could not share his optimistic view that the 'bad' combines which aimed merely at high profits, restricted output, and the suppression of competition would surely go 'down, down, down, until they disappear'. Yet, in spite of these shortcomings, his analysis and his proposals represented an enlightened attempt to tackle the obvious weaknesses of the existing industrial organization. His own business had shown what could be achieved under the system he advocated. He exemplified to the full his views on the importance of the all-pervading functions of management. In his own theory and his own practice he sought for a solution of economic and social difficulties through enlightened management. That was perhaps his most important contribution to industrial progress, and there was much to be said for his view that the major problems of modern industry were problems arising from the size rather than from the nature of the ownership of industry. To replace private by State ownership would not, in his view, in any way solve the problems of industrial and social relations. Subjective though his views were in some ways, they were ahead of his day. They are primarily a part of the history of his own business, but so long as the economic basis of our society continues to be private enterprise they will not cease to be relevant to the enduring problems of industry, and many of them have passed into common currency even amongst his opponents and critics.

CHAPTER XX

THE SECOND PHASE OF RECOVERY: CONSOLIDATION, 1925–9

'A period of wise consolidation and prudent finance.'
The Second Lord Leverhulme at the Annual Meeting, 1930

THE process of recovery from the adventures and misadventures of the early twenties was far from complete when Lord Leverhulme died in 1925. The most urgent problem was the appointment of a successor. There is no doubt that Leverhulme had cherished hopes of a dynastic succession. His son had been trained in the ways of the business, and indeed had already played a not inconsiderable part in its counsels. He was naturally shrewd and wise. A kindly and unaffected manner made him popular with colleagues and staff. Yet the times called for qualities which he was the first to admit he did not possess, and, with a characteristic sense of reality, he stepped aside and accepted the position of Governor, in which he was able to find full scope for his special knowledge of the business and for his particular interest in questions of industrial relations. For the Chair of Lever Brothers there was really only one candidate: Francis D'Arcy Cooper. Joint Vice-Chairman and a member of the Special Committee since 1923, Cooper's special function had been to keep a firm hand on finance. But time had shown that his abilities were not limited to finance. He was possessed of a natural habit of command and a judgement of men surpassing that of his predecessor. And although blunt, energetic, and emotional—he was quickly angered by anything savouring of dishonesty—he brought to the problems of the business a new quality of thoughtful analysis of long-term issues quite unlike anything it had seen before. He had moreover a gift for developing a sense of responsibility in subordinates, a quality none too plentiful in a business which for thirty years had been run as a dictatorship. Instinctively the board turned to Cooper as the man capable of restoring and inspiring confidence. Within a week of Leverhulme's death, Cooper was appointed to succeed him.

His first care was necessarily the finances of the firm. His actions had already given due warning of his views, but for any who had not heeded them, a private speech to overseas managers made his principles clear. 'We are Trustees', he told his audience, 'for some 200,000 shareholders, and we have no right to spend one penny unless we are absolutely certain we are going to get an adequate return.' Then he went on to outline the problems he faced and the policies he proposed. With Preference dividends demanding nearly £5 million, and heavy demands for advertising and capital expenditure, the business still faced an ugly gap in its finances. This was the short-term problem which called for immediate remedies, as well as for long-term policies which would prevent its recurrence. The treatment was certainly severe. No Ordinary dividend was paid for 1925 or 1926. A less prudent man might well have done so but Cooper's decision to show no profits that allowed of any doubts and to place indisputable profits to reserve was a measure of his determination to put the business on a sure and lasting foundation. His second measure was to sell any assets which could be realized without damage to the essential requirements of the Company. Odd pieces of land—in Japan, Shanghai, New York, and Plymouth—with no particular future, were sold, and when Harold Greenhalgh left for the East, Cooper remarked that he was not returning until he had disposed of 'every surplus property in China, India, and Canada'. Likewise, though rather more selectively, shareholdings in less successful businesses were sold, though only one business actually founded by Lever Brothers—in Japan—was disposed of. The criterion was largely that of profitability, not yet of rationalization. Businesses which showed no profit and no prospect of profit went. Within a year of Cooper's appointment this process of trimming had brought in about a million and a quarter; the gap was not yet closed but it was narrowing. To eliminate it completely would require something more than financial first-aid, and so there emerged gradually a policy of reorganization which, if incomplete by later standards, went far further than any previous attempt to equip the business to meet altered conditions.

That conditions were altering admitted of no doubt. First, there was a change in the nature of the market which Lever's served. Since the early years of the century the total consumption of soap in the United Kingdom had expanded but slowly, *per capita* consumption rising only from 17·3 to 18·2 pounds between 1901 and 1921. Within this market Lever Brothers' home sales were only barely holding firm. The new chairman had hopes that skilful advertising might start the total consumption in the country moving upwards again, though by 1929 these hopes had reluctantly yielded to a fear that the soap trade had reached 'a fixed state'. Again, within this stationary market another important change was taking place. For twenty years before 1925 the use of soap flakes and powders had been growing, partially at the expense of the trade in hard soap of the Sunlight type. The war had hastened the process, laundry consumption of hard soap falling by as much as a third. By the late twenties, the home sales of flakes and powders represented more than a quarter (by volume) of total home sales. When the Lever management surveyed the home trade in the years between 1925 and 1929 they had two main problems in mind. One was the adaptation of the combine's policy to this changed demand; the other was consideration of the measures to be taken against outside competition.

Cooper's first action was to overhaul the machinery for the control of policy and finance. The Special Committee remained intact. Almost at once the Managing Directors' Conference began its weekly meetings. Really a reincarnation of the old Policy Council, it was a Committee of the whole board, which met after the weekly board meeting. Detailed minutes of its proceedings were taken, and its Secretary was L. V. Fildes, a barrister whose lucid mind and sound judgement had made him a force at Port Sunlight and no less clearly marked him out for a wider sphere. Since 1919 he had been Secretary of the Company, but so long as he remained at Port Sunlight his office was necessarily limited in scope. Summoned to London within a few days of Cooper's assumption of office, Fildes proceeded to transform the Secretaryship into an active part of the mechanism of central control. Under the general direction of the Conference a number of committees was set up to deal with specialized aspects of the business. A number of functions and functionaries was transferred to London. Port Sunlight became more than ever a local, self-contained unit while London became yet more conspicuously the centre of affairs. Meanwhile two 'Investigating

Committees' appointed by the board set to work. One advised that all existing technical controls should be concentrated under one central department (an idea behind the Trust of 1906 but still unachieved). The outcome was a Technical Committee which lasted for about two years. It was to determine the duties of each technical department within the concern, to lay down a programme of research 'directed to commercially profitable results' and to ensure co-operation between the technical experts of the associated companies. It was to communicate with the board through its chairman who, D'Arcy Cooper decided, needed no technical experience; there would, in fact, be 'an advantage in his not having it'. The appointment went to L. V. Fildes, the Secretary of the Company. The second committee under J. McDowell inquired into advertising policy—a matter of the first importance in the soap trade where advertising expenditure was liable to consume a high proportion of the profits: important too because it touched on the fundamental relationships between the various firms in the Combine. The old policy had been to achieve efficiency by full competition within the combine. As in technical matters, so also in advertising, the new trend towards centralized control and restricted competition between members of the family became clear. McDowell's committee recommended that advertising allocations should be determined by the central Board. Centralized buying of advertising space was to continue, and it was to be 'the duty of each Control director to avoid clashing of advertisements in his section'.

No one, least of all Cooper, supposed that the creation of central committees of control would at once reconcile the desires and interests of the large number of businesses which now constituted the combine. Two years later J. W. Pearson was still uneasy about competitive advertising within the family. He thought there was 'an impression amongst the public that there was a certain wastefulness in our methods because of the number of lines that different associated companies advertise against each other'. Cooper was inclined to think differently: 'There was not as much advertising competition within the family as was thought. . . . ' It is difficult to say where the truth lay. Certainly there was still considerable rivalry in advertising, though it may be that it was already on the decline. Persil, made by Crosfield's, competed with Rinso, made by Hudson's. The growing popularity of Lux soap flakes also raised difficulties. Soap flakes owed their success in large part to heavy advertising outlay on Lux. The question was—were associated companies now to be allowed to share that goodwill by manufacturing and selling flakes of comparable quality? The Board had doubts, but the pressure from the companies was too strong to be resisted. By the end of 1926, the rival flakes of associated companies were on sale, the Board bowed the knee to the inevitable, and reduced the price of Lux flakes to compete. A similar problem arose from the introduction of Lux Toilet Soap to the home market in 1928. The home market was under attack from an imported soap from America—Palmolive. The success of Lux Toilet Soap in America had been so startling that it seemed the obvious reply to Palmolive in the United Kingdom. As Cooper said, however, 'the Board had to realize that its introduction might swamp toilet soap sold by associated companies'. Would increased profits justify the move? Against some opposition it was decided to try, and in the event the result was a net gain.

Viewed from any general standpoint, these incidents showed that in spite of the apparent consolidation there was still sufficient competitive life in the combine to allow it to respond to normal business pressures. The same point emerged over price policy, for soap prices in general seem to have fallen by the late twenties to levels which were certainly no higher than the average of general retail prices and, in this respect, the combine appears to have passed on to the consumer the advantages of the fall in raw material prices which took place from the middle twenties. On the other hand, the decisions illustrate the difficulties of reorganization presented by the character of the combine, with its large number of potentially competitive manufacturing units. The natural result of Leverhulme's wholesale buying of companies was that the combine seemed to be dissipating its energies in the manufacture of many brands in differing quantities (some very small) instead of making large quantities of a few successful brands. The virtues of the latter policy were apparent in the United States where Countway had concentrated his energies on a few brands. As a result, mass production on mechanized lines was possible and manual labour was virtually eliminated from large sections of the production processes. Cooper himself shared the view that the United Kingdom companies should follow suit. There were 'far too many packs'; everybody knew, he said in 1927, that 'the ideal position would be to concentrate our energies on about five soaps and four powders'. Yet to achieve this, rationalization with all its consequences—the closing down of small factories, the dismissal of staff, and possibly initial capital losses—would be necessary. There were those on the Board who would have had no hesitation in accepting such consequences: 'If . . . the manufacture of all articles were pooled and carried on at three or four centres, as was the case in the Tobacco industry, saving of £2 per ton would be made on distribution costs alone'. But the late chairman's ghost still walked, for his successor replied: 'The great objection to the wholesale closing down of the smaller factories was the fear that the goodwill of the products of the associated companies would be lost if the companies did not manufacture them themselves and that the goodwill would not be recovered by the remaining companies. The smaller companies also served to protect the larger ones by keeping others out.' It was impressive evidence that Leverhulme's objections to the neat formula of rationalization were not merely outmoded Victorian prejudices. In an irrational world it behoved the rationalizer to go slowly. Customers had some queer and obstinate tastes.

It would be inaccurate to say that no rationalization took place in this period. On 27th May 1925, to the 'enormous surprise' of the trade and the City (according to Anton Jurgens) Lever Brothers became effectively the owners of a controlling interest in the British Oil and Cake Mills, including its subsidiary, the British Soap Company, whose New Pin had given such trouble to Lever's.[1] One object of the purchase was to kill the gift schemes by which the sales of New Pin had been built up. Immediately after the acquisition, the gift schemes ceased. Sales of New Pin fell from nearly 34,000 tons in 1925 to 6,000 in 1928: the British Soap Company was slowly allowed to die. Elsewhere, the Chairman declared himself 'ready to close down a factory, on favourable terms, which was not wanted'. Four small companies—Cook's, Wilkie & Soames', T. B. Rowe (all old London firms) and Doudney's factory at Portsmouth—came under the

[1] See also Chapter XIX.

rubric, but even on this minor scale rationalization was a slow process, and it was not until the thirties that the factories were finally closed and their production transferred to bigger factories.

Thus, to a large extent for internal and organic reasons, the structure of the business was gradually simplified, centralized and—to a small extent—rationalized. But these measures were only the minimum necessary to equip the business to meet an external situation which demanded that there should be no relaxation of vigilance. In general the economic situation between 1925 and 1929 was not unfavourable, though industrial disputes which followed the return to the Gold Standard were blamed for some falling off in the soap trade in the coal, iron, and steel areas. In general, however, the consumption of soap remained fairly stable. What chiefly worried the Board was the renewed growth of competition. The toilet soap market was already under invasion from America, but the chief rival was the C.W.S. whose sales, after being fairly steady up to 1925, rose by about twenty-five per cent, while those of the Scottish C.W.S. rose by fifty per cent between 1926 and 1929.

New conditions called for new measures. Cooper therefore decided to withdraw from the United Kingdom Soap Makers' Association, which was by this time virtually moribund. The real need of the day—the co-ordination of sales policy—could best be furthered by a new body within the Lever organization—the Sales Executive Committee. The Executive was the normal complement of the policy of reducing competition within the family; its duties—'to be responsible to the Board for the sales policy of the soap Companies in the Family . . . ' so that companies could ' . . . concentrate as little as possible on fighting each other and as much as possible on fighting outsiders'. Similar considerations underlay the formation of United Exporters Limited in August 1928. The export trade was a particularly difficult one to manage, not least because the traditional rivalry between the three biggest exporters in the family—Lever's, Crosfield's, and Gossage's—died hard. Even more than in the home market, it was clear to the Board that 'there had been an unnecessary amount of fighting between the various associated companies, and the position had to be tackled'. Here again there was a limited measure of rationalization. About one hundred and fifty clerks had to be dismissed (with gratuities 'on a generous scale'). No married men were dismissed, and the older men were pensioned. United Exporters Limited was managed from Lever House and manufacturing was to be done by Port Sunlight, Crosfield's or Gossage's as circumstances might require. The aim: to 'get rid of friction', to give Lever Brothers effective control over 'inter-family competition in the Export Trade' and provide £100,000 more profit within two years. It was one more example of the new policy of centralized control.

The contemporary trend towards the establishment of various forms of mergers and pools, noted by both the Balfour Committee on Trade and Industry (1924–7) and later by the MacMillan Committee on Finance and Industry (1931) as characteristic of these years, was not lost on the Board. The developing situation was described by J. W. Pearson late in 1926: he referred 'to the growing tendency to establish pools, cartels, etc., for many commodities, the movement being chiefly noticeable in the case of manufactured articles intended for re-manufacture. He gave as instances the margarine, seed crushers, soya oil, whale oil pools in which we were ourselves interested, and he asked what was to be our policy towards this movement in view of the possibility that this tendency would be to stiffen prices against soap manufacturers.' The discussion which followed made it clear that the general feeling was that in so far as the movement tended to steady prices of raw materials and avoid disastrous fluctuations such as those of 1920 and 1921, it would be generally beneficial to Lever Brothers. Certainly the Soya Bean Oil Pool in which Lever's and the B.O.C.M. were associated primarily with the continental margarine makers achieved 'an extraordinary success' in keeping down prices.

Elsewhere in the raw material world, Lever Brothers' interests were rather different. By the end of 1926, the Niger Company, under which most of their West African interests by now had come to be grouped, was at last showing a profit. Its great rival, the African and Eastern Trade Corporation, had, on the other hand, run into difficulties, and in 1928 Cooper told his colleagues that he understood they were heavily overbought. The situation was not as satisfactory as might have been expected, for the African and Eastern had cabled to the Coast to sacrifice their stocks, and it seemed that the Niger Company might have to follow suit to avoid being undersold by their rival. Sir Robert Waley Cohen, who became Chairman of the African and Eastern in December 1928, was a formidable strategist who was not likely to overlook the strength of his bargaining position. Some sort of price agreement between the two companies was essential if there was to be any profit in the African trade. Negotiations began in January 1929, but the protagonists were 'poles apart' and it took six weeks of bitterly fought bargaining before an agreement was signed on March 14th. Out of the stormy diplomacy there emerged the United Africa Company, a giant concern with a capital of £13,000,000 held in equal amounts by the Niger Company and the African and Eastern, and controlling by far the biggest proportion of the West African trade. In its broadest context, the African situation illustrated the plight of the primary producing areas which was to evoke special comment from the MacMillan Committee in 1931. The high prices during and after the war had stimulated production and investment to a point where over-production itself produced lower prices. This price fall, noticeable after 1926, was exaggerated by the competition of other types of raw materials which could often be substituted for African materials in the edible and non-edible oils and fats industries. That dominance in the Coast trade which Leverhulme had long striven to achieve was an accomplished fact by 1929, but the victory seemed a barren one. Yet, from the point of view of the combine as a whole, it remained true that there was much to be gained from stable price levels. The formation of the United Africa Company may not have seemed to do more for the moment than avoid positive loss but in so far as it helped to achieve economic stability it made a contribution to the health of the business.

The trade in edible fats was likewise in a state of war. Alliances and counter-alliances were the order of the day and though for the moment Lever Brothers were able to preserve a sort of isolation, it was evident that sooner or later they would be drawn in. It was, as we have seen, Cooper's view that the Lever soap trade had reached a 'fixed state' that gave particular importance to his further remark that 'our unknown possibilities lie in the edible trade'. He based the first part of his remark, doubtless, on his experience of the previous four or five years when Lever's had been hard pressed by competition in a soap market which seemed very difficult to expand. It is harder to understand whence he derived his optimism about the edible fats trade. Planter's margarine sales, which had fallen from 54,500 tons in 1919 to just under 20,000 in 1925, dwindled further in the later twenties and for 1929 they were 13,849 tons. In these figures there would seem to have been little cause for hope, and there is no evidence that the sales of any other edible fat product were more encouraging. None the less, the importance which D'Arcy Cooper attached to the development of Lever Brothers' business in edible fats is obvious.

Although Planter's sales were falling, Lever's were in these years bringing to commercial possibility their most important contribution to the technique of the industry: the addition of vitamins to margarine. Research by Lever Brothers on the problem began soon after their entry into the margarine industry in 1914 and went on, at Cambridge University and elsewhere,[1] until by the beginning of 1927 a margarine was ready for the market which contained 'substantially tasteless vitamin concentrate', prepared from liver oils. The vitamins concerned—A and D—were those in which margarine had formerly been deficient as compared with butter, and the advantage of the new process, when perfected, was that by the addition of the concentrates in suitable quantities the vitamin content of margarine could be held constant, whereas that of butter varies with the seasons. The chairman's reception of the scientists' triumph was tepid: 'He had tried', he said, 'a sample of margarine containing the new Vitamins Concentrate which Planter's had sent him. He did not find it palatable, but he did not like ordinary margarine any better.'

The first sales of the new margarine, under the brand 'Viking', were reported at the end of January 1927. It was put out purposely as 'an expensive article with special claims', but at 1s. 2d. a pound its price was uncomfortably close to that of butter, at that time between 1s. 4d. and 1s. 6d., and C. W. Barnish, reporting to the board, suggested in March that the

[1] In 1916, the journal of *Physiology* published the results of feeding tests on animals carried out under the direction of J. L. Buchanan, Lever Brothers' technical director, and A. Andersen, Planter's technical expert. From 1917, Buchanan and Andersen were in constant touch with Gowland Hopkins at Cambridge over the development and practical application of the new discoveries.

advertising ought to be heavier. The board agreed, but, in the autumn, sales were still in the doldrums and Barnish 'had to confess that he was not elated by the prospects of this line'.

While Planter's struggled to convince the consumer of the merits of their invention, Van den Bergh's and Jurgens' entered the last phase of their existence as separate companies. Since 1925, the operations of most of the firms in the margarine trade had been regulated by a pool agreement, to which Van den Bergh's and Jurgens', as well as Planter's, had been parties. At the beginning of 1927, Hartog's, one of the pool companies, dropped their price for margarine from 8d. to 6d. a pound: the arrangement broke down, and an effort to reconstitute it failed because Lever's refused to have the basic price reduced from 58s. to 48s. per cwt., notwithstanding the fact that D'Arcy Cooper estimated Planter's loss through the break-up of the pool at £70,000.

Freed thus from their engagements, Van den Bergh's and Jurgens' began cutting prices. Lever's were uncertain of their motives. 'Planter's', said Barnish, 'would be helped in deciding what policy to adopt if they knew whether the present price war was directed against them or whether the struggle was between the larger makers.' It soon became apparent that the main seat of war was on the Continent, where in June, according to Harold Greenhalgh, 'Van den Bergh's and Jurgens' were having a stiff fight over prices'.[1] The answer to Barnish's query was evidently that the struggle was between the larger makers, and Lever's took up the role of spectators, remarking in July that 'in view of the disturbed state of the margarine trade . . . the policy of the Company was to improve the quality of its products rather than to cut prices'. Reports of peace negotiations were made only to be discredited immediately. Margarine prices in Holland were reported to have touched 2½d. a pound, and 'the Chairman's comment was that the keener the fight the sooner the peace'. Lever's, in the person of Greenhalgh, hoped that the fight would so weaken the two chief protagonists that 'the trade might look forward to a reasonably quiet time in England', but in the meantime the struggle had unfortunate repercussions on Planter's profits. In the June quarter of 1927 they lost between £12,000 and £15,000 on trading, after meeting their overhead charges.

[1] See Book II, Chapter XV.

The end, so far as Lever's could see, came quite suddenly. At the beginning of September, Barnish reported that there was no improvement in the position and that 'the end of the price war on the Continent was apparently nothing more than a rumour'. At the end of the month 'Mr. McDowell referred to the merger of Jurgens' and Van den Bergh's'. Thus Lever's were confronted with a coalition between the two companies which, besides themselves, were the greatest powers in the European oils and fats industry. Over the eighteen months which followed the foundation of Margarine Union, as the new partnership was called, it became apparent that a grand alliance was being built up, for in January 1929 Hartog's, another substantial Dutch manufacturer, joined the Union and in April of that year the great Central European concern of Schicht followed their example. The nature of the raw materials which all these manufacturers would require made it certain that their joint power would be felt on Lever's business not only in margarine but in soap.

Finally there remained the problem of controlling the destinies of the Lever overseas companies, spread over a diversity of continents. In April, 1926, Cooper had called a conference of the principals of these companies in London. Its prime purpose was to explain the financial policy of the new management and to bring home the need for economy. 'When you find the London Board rather sticky on the question of capital expenditure and development', he told his listeners, 'you will appreciate it is not because we do not want to develop our businesses—we all do—but simply that we have to be cautious.' But beyond this immediate aim, the conference had another and less easily definable one—the task of giving the overseas managements some idea that they belonged to a corporate body, that the success or failure of one was in a measure the success or failure of all. It was in particular important to enable different companies to exchange ideas and discuss common problems. Without some such sense of identity of interests and understanding of the major issues, the new policy of centralization must necessarily fail. The fact that the 1926 Conference was not repeated, as was originally planned, is no evidence that it was not successful. It was merely that less formal methods were ultimately devised to achieve its objects. But its main interest lies in the conscious attempt to tackle the problems of administering a world-wide business as an organic whole.

In general, economic conditions were by no means unfavourable to progress overseas. Everywhere, but especially in Europe and America, the years from 1925 to the onset of the depression of 1929 saw an increase in the growth of population and in the volume of industrial production. These facts were reflected in the progress of the companies in Europe and the United States. By 1929, all the older Continental companies were making profits and such red figures as showed up came from the new ventures—Austria, Italy, Poland, Scandinavia, and the Balkans—which were still in the early stages of development. Behind the scenes, it is true, anxieties were not lacking. Chief amongst them were the activities of Henkel, the German manufacturer of Persil. In 1926, H. G. Hart, the director principally responsible for the European countries, said that the position of Rinso, Lever's competing product, was seriously threatened by Persil: for except in France and the United Kingdom, the European manufacturing rights for Persil were held by Henkel. Henkel's competition was especially severe in Scandinavia and Switzerland; in the latter country Lever's adopted a policy of improving Rinso's power to compete. In Germany ('an almost untapped country considering its size and the smallness of our share of the trade at present') Rinso was not manufactured, so that Persil competed with Lever's hard soap trade; but so successful was Henkel in converting the public to the use of powders that it was felt an attempt must be made to fight him on his own ground. The result was a powder 'Suma' which the technical experts reported had a 'theoretical advantage' over Persil. Theoretical or not, Suma was not a success, and by 1929 the policy had been replaced by one of attacking the market with hard soaps or flakes.

The outstandingly successful overseas business continued in the late twenties to be North America, where Countway continued to make spectacular progress. His latest success was Lux Toilet Soap, sales of which 'had exceeded all expectations' by 1928. Between 1925 and 1929, the total volume of soap sales rose from 40,000 tons to 91,000 tons; profits from a million and a half dollars to over three million. By the latter year, prospects were so good that Countway proposed to build a second factory at Hammond, Indiana, to serve the Middle Western and Western markets. It was eloquent comment on the condition of the American business that he proposed to finance the project largely by retaining Boston's profits in the United States.

The story in the British Dominions was not quite so satisfactory, and the South African market in particular called for a change of policy. Here, where Lever's had about sixty per cent of the trade, a policy of high prices in the early twenties had resulted in a loss of trade to other makers estimated at about 2,000 tons a year (or about ten per cent of the market). When Cooper visited the country in 1926, therefore, he ordered a reversal of policy. Cheap soaps were to be sold at prices unprofitable to rivals, proprietary soaps, flakes and powders were to be pushed. Three factories were to be closed and their production transferred elsewhere. The Premier Whaling Company (the property of the New Transvaal Chemical Company) was to be sold. Neither Canada nor Australia could be said to be really healthy, though here the need was for new blood in the management, and with P. P. Tyler established in Canada and J. L. Heyworth[1] in Australia the Board hoped for better things.

The organization of the business had altered very considerably since the death of the founder. In one way it had become more liberal, in that it was no longer a one-man business: in another, less so, in that the activities of the companies were more highly co-ordinated from the centre. A desire for rationalization had been expressed, though not yet very drastically put into effect, and a tendency was noticeable to transfer certain functions away from the manufacturing companies to other companies especially founded for their performance. So far, export had been concentrated in the hands of United Exporters Ltd., and sales of glycerine in those of Glycerine Limited founded early in January 1929. This plan of divorcing selling from manufacturing was to expand later into the creation of marketing companies such as Lever Sales Limited, Hudson & Knight, and Crosfield, Watson & Gossage. Thus the administrative policy of the concern, under its new management, was evidently to organize specialist companies for the performance of duties in the interests of the business as a whole rather than for the benefit of its component parts.

[1] The eldest of the three brothers in the business (see Chapter XIX).

The financial recovery of the company since 1925–6 had been impressive, and the accounts for 1929 provided a remarkable contrast. The total profits of the group were £5,594,389 and not one of the main geographical sub-divisions showed a loss. The United Kingdom, as always, returned considerably the largest portion of the profits—£3,013,648. Of that sum, the bulk was contributed by the soap companies, although among the individual companies two of the biggest earners were Mac Fisheries (£237,896) and Southern Whaling (£199,105); Planter's Foods showed a loss of £50,943, reflecting the overcrowded condition of the margarine industry. Overseas, such losses as there were came mainly from the newer soap ventures in Europe, so that 'Continental Subsidiaries', in spite of a profit of over £177,000 from Belgium, returned a net profit of £166,199. From other parts of the world (except West Africa) the net profit was £1,560,805 and the only losses of any moment were among the associated companies in South Africa, and the profits of Lever Brothers, South Africa, itself were sufficient to offset them. Considerably the best earner was Lever Brothers Company, Boston, with over £620,000, but among the remainder, the Philippine Refining Corporation, Manilla, returned £152,000 profit, which in itself was an index of the improvement in Lever Brothers' affairs since 1925. Another was the contribution of £106,966 profit from the Niger Company.

The published balance sheet for the year 1929 still disclosed Debenture stock to a total of more than £7,000,000, but most of the other disturbing features of the balance sheets of 1920 and 1925 had disappeared or very much diminished. 'Creditors', for example, were owed under a million, against eight million in 1920 (the Debenture issue, of course, accounted for much of this decrease). The financial structure was, nevertheless, still open to one serious criticism: enormous increases in capital had taken the form almost exclusively of additions to Preference shares carrying fixed interest. The Ordinary share capital remained a very small proportion of the whole. In his anxiety to reserve the Ordinary shares to himself Lever had inevitably limited the amount of risk-bearing capital to the amount he could purchase from his own pocket. At the end of 1929, therefore, the capital was divided as to fifty-four and a quarter million Preference and two and a half million Ordinary shares. It was a big burden for any business to carry.

This, then, was Lever Brothers Limited on the eve of the merger with the Margarine Union. Its size and strength, to the outside eye, were impressive, with its Issued Capital of over £56 million (out of £130 million authorized). The façade had sometimes in the recent past been deceptive, but by 1929 it was no longer so. The costs of production, advertising, and selling had all been reduced, while tighter control from the centre had done much to eliminate waste and duplication. The Second Lord Leverhulme, at the Annual General Meeting of 1930, spoke of the previous five years as 'a period of wise consolidation and prudent finance', and of 'the quality of the broad foundations upon which the Company had been built up'. Making all due allowance for the nature of the occasion and the purpose of the speech—which was to second the resolution adopting the Report and Accounts—it is still possible to accept his picture of broad-based strength as a true description of Lever Brothers Limited in 1929. In an era of mergers and rumours of mergers, the Company's bargaining power was formidable.

APPENDIXES

APPENDIX I

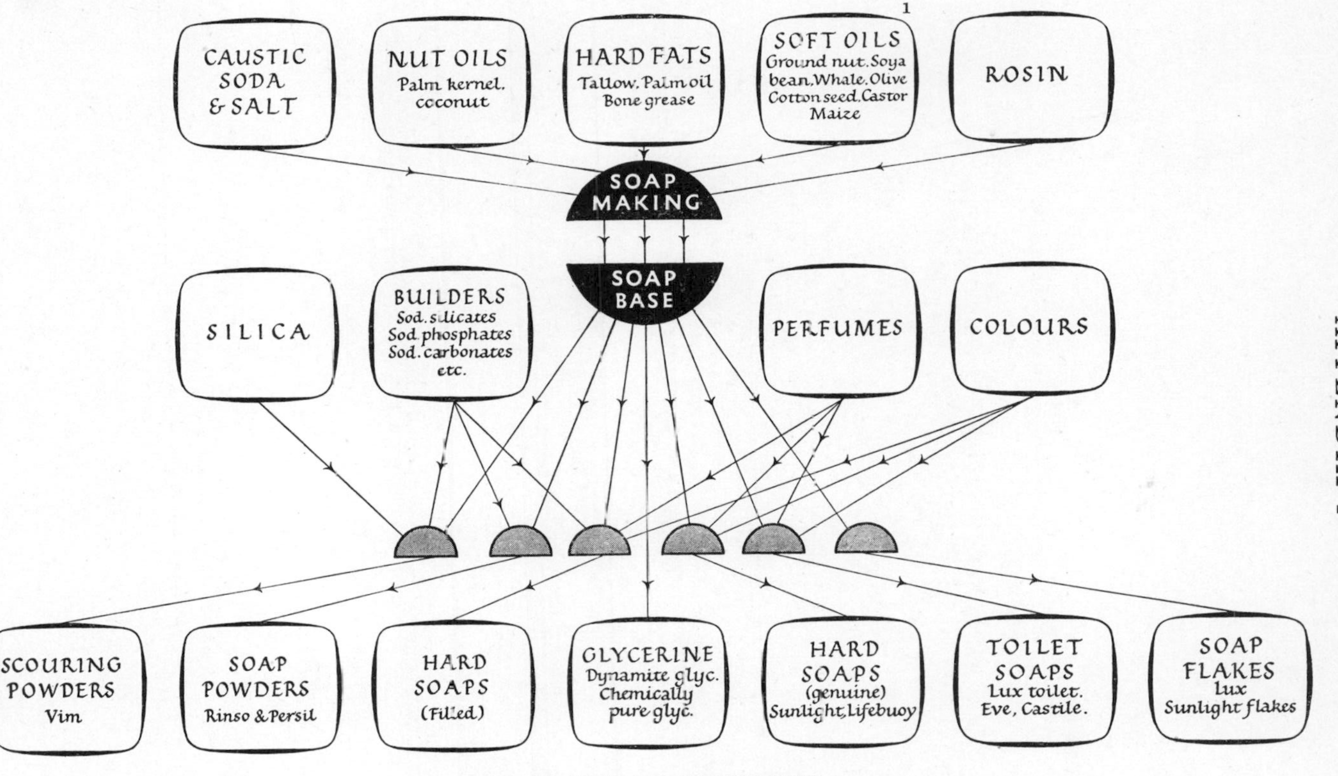

THE SOAP-MAKING PROCESS

[1] Soft oils were increasingly used as hardened fats after the invention of hardening.

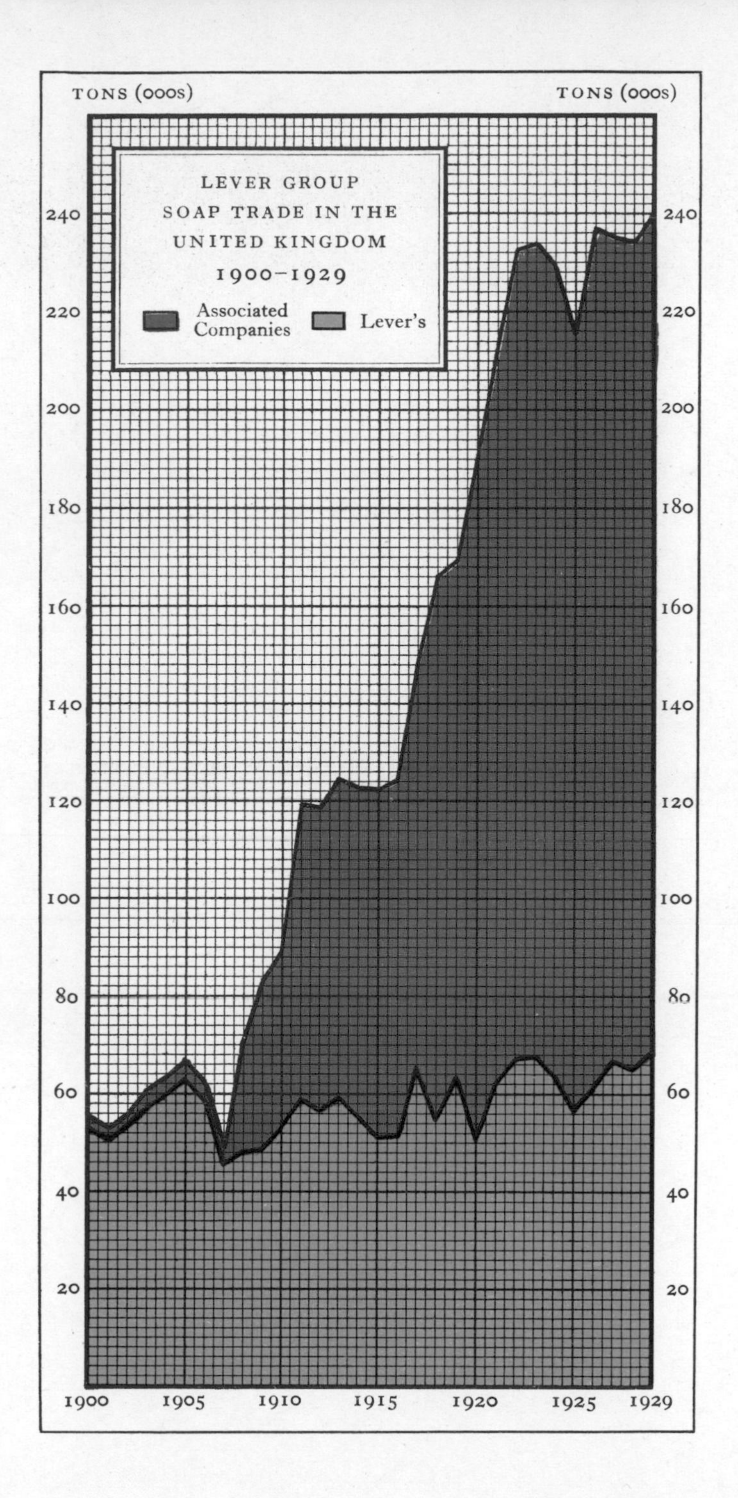
TONS (000s)
TONS (000s)
LEVER GROUP
SOAP TRADE IN THE
UNITED KINGDOM
1900–1929
Associated Companies
Lever's
240
220
200
180
160
140
120
100
80
60
40
20
1900
1905
1910
1915
1920
1925
1929

APPENDIX 2

APPENDIX 3

LEVER BROTHERS LIMITED

CAPITAL EMPLOYED (IN STERLING) 1894–1929					
Year	Preference Capital	Ordinary Shareholders' Funds		Loan Capital	Total Capital Employed
		Capital	Reserves		
1894	750,000	750,000	38,910	—	1,538,910
1895	750,000	750,000	82,985	—	1,582,985
1896	1,000,000	775,000	154,269	—	1,929,269
1897	1,000,000	800,000	178,029	—	1,978,029
1898	1,250,000	844,667	268,567	—	2,363,234
1899	1,500,000	987,534	303,503	—	2,791,037
1900	1,879,886	1,190,602	321,562	—	3,392,050
1901	1,999,997	1,195,000	321,958	—	3,516,955
1902	2,000,000	1,195,000	322,032	—	3,517,032
1903	2,000,000	1,300,000	323,129	—	3,623,129
1904	2,000,000	1,400,000	313,486	—	3,713,486
1905	2,000,000	1,850,000	315,757	—	4,165,757
1906	2,540,000	1,850,000	317,152	—	4,707,152
1907	2,915,000	1,850,000	321,706	—	5,086,706
1908	3,250,000	1,850,000	324,642	—	5,424,642
1909	3,250,000	*1,850,000	329,004	—	5,429,004
1910	5,220,458	*1,000,000	378,767	—	6,599,225
1911	6,592,500	1,000,000	434,111	—	8,026,611
1912	7,600,000	1,000,000	438,604	—	9,038,604
1913	9,713,424	2,000,000	452,463	—	12,165,887
1914	11,247,598	2,000,000	468,058	—	13,715,656
1915	12,001,838	2,000,000	480,910	—	14,482,748
1916	12,023,518	2,000,000	485,222	—	14,508,740
1917	13,202,799	2,000,000	490,802	—	15,693,601
1918	15,065,340	2,000,000	496,755	—	17,562,095
1919	23,427,312	2,280,000	500,792	—	26,208,104
1920	44,489,079	2,280,000	505,727	—	47,274,806
1921	44,702,322	2,280,000	809,855	4,000,000	51,792,177
1922	45,877,208	2,400,000	1,061,099	8,000,000	57,338,307
1923	49,075,363	2,400,000	836,741	8,000,000	60,312,104
1924	54,227,546	2,400,000	476,754	7,967,400	65,071,700
1925	54,227,546	2,400,000	22,600	7,815,166	64,465,312
1926	54,227,546	2,400,000	27,038	7,652,087	64,306,671
1927	54,227,546	2,400,000	401,795	7,461,577	64,490,918
1928	54,227,546	2,400,000	660,337	7,331,562	64,619,445
1929	54,227,546	2,400,000	1,119,192	7,188,062	64,934,800

* In 1910 £850,000 of the Ordinary shares were converted into 15% Preferred Ordinary shares.

APPENDIX 4

LEVER BROTHERS LIMITED

Directors

1894–1929

	From		*To*
William Hesketh Lever	1894	Chairman 1894	1925
James Lever	1894		1897
James Darcy Lever	1894		1897
Percy James Winser	1894	Vice-Chairman 1897	1901
John Smith Ferguson	1895		1897
Martin Harvey	1896	Vice-Chairman 1899	1902
William Owen	1897		1900
Alfred John Wolfendale	1897		1899
William Young Robinson	1897		1899
Robert Barrie	1897		1909
Sidney Gross	1898		1911
Charles A. Kirkby	1898		1901
Joseph Meek	1898		1901
John Lever Tillotson	1899		1915
John Gray	1907	Vice-Chairman 1917	1920
James Lever Ferguson	1907		
Edmund Vannutelli Salaman	1910		1922
William Hulme Lever	1910	Vice-Chairman 1914 Act. Chairman 1917 Governor 1925	
James Darcy Lever, Jr.	1910		1914
Clarence Charles Knowles	1910		1921
John Loudon Buchanan	1911		1922
John Kevan Greenhalgh	1911		1912
Harold Robert Greenhalgh	1915	Vice-Chairman 1921	
John McDowell	1915	Vice-Chairman 1925	
William Keay Findlay	1915		1921
Charles Edmund Tatlow	1915		
Gilbert Wheaton Fox	1916		1920
Major Gen. S. S. Long	1917		
John Inglis	1917		1923
James Lomax Simpson	1917		
Harry Goodwin Hart	1918		
Edward Leonard Cook	1919		1925
Ernest Walls	1919		1927
Charles Rowarth Baker	1919		
Lichfield H. Moseley	1921		1925
Croudson William Barnish	1921		
The Marquess of Carisbrooke	1922		

	From		To
John Cheshire	1922		
Francis D'Arcy Cooper	1923	Vice-Chairman 1923 Chairman 1925	
L. H. Hartland-Swann	1923		
William Livesey Helm	1924		
Sir Herbert E. Morgan	1925		1926
John Westall Pearson	1925		
Horatio Ballantyne	1928		
Deputy Directors			
John Smith Ferguson	1902		1905
James Lever Tillotson	1902		1905
Alexander Whyte	1905		1906
John Gray	1905		1907
James Lever Ferguson	1905		1907
Robert Atkinson McQuitty	1906		1907
William Hulme Lever	1909		1910
James Darcy Lever, Jr.	1909		1910
John Kevan Greenhalgh	1910		1915
John Loudon Buchanan	1910		1911
Harold Robert Greenhalgh	1912		1915
Harry Goodwin Hart	1915		1917
Ernest Lawrence Peck	1917		1921
William Easterbrook	1917		1925
Croudson William Barnish	1917		1921
Lichfield Henry Moseley	1918		1921
Charles Frederick Rutty Knowles	1918		1921
Herbert George Rushton	1919		1921
John Cheshire	1919		1922
John Glen Tyrell	1919		1921
Arthur Paul Miller	1919		1921
Secretaries			
J. S. Ferguson	1894		1895
J. McGowan	1895	Pro tem.	
G. A. Kirkby	1896		1898
J. Oliphant	1898		1900
A. Whyte	1900		1905
J. McDowell	1905		1915
J. W. Millen	1915		1917
L. V. Fildes	1919		
Chief Accountants			
J. K. Greenhalgh			1910
John Inglis	1911		1917
R. N. Barber	1917		1921
N. Locking	1921		

NOTE ON THE STATISTICAL MATERIAL USED IN THE APPENDIXES TO VOL. I

Appendix 2. Based on a Statement of Sales (in tons) by Lever Companies in the United Kingdom (including Eire).

Appendix 3. Based on the Annual Reports and Accounts of Lever Brothers Limited.

INDEX

INDEX